Atlas Rive-Sud et Montérégie & South Shore Atlas

D1320661

Table des matières ❦		❦ Table of Contents

CARTOTEK GEO

Publié par - Published by
Cartotek Geo inc.
1280 Bégin, St-Laurent (Qc) H4R 1X1
Tél.: (514) 336-0031, (fax) 336-0034
1-800-563-0031
4e édition / 4th edition

Cartographic Design • *Conception cartographique*
Luc Fournier

Cartography • *Cartographie*
L. Bernard • L. Deschênes-Damian • L. Jones • L. St-Jean • S. Wait

Production Team • *Équipe de production*
I. Gilles • A. Lachance

© **Copyright 1999**
Imprimé au Québec • Printed in Québec

Published by – Publié par
Cartotek Geo inc.
1280 Bégin, St-Laurent (Qc) H4R 1X1
Tél : (514) 336-0031, Fax : (514) 336-0034
www.cartotekgeo.com

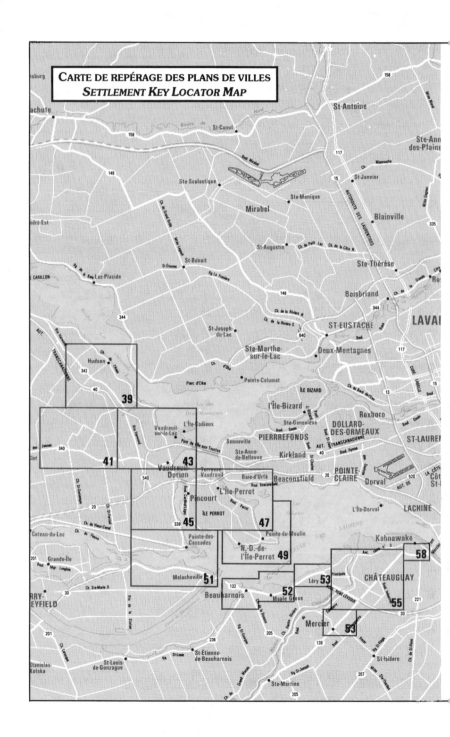

CARTE DE REPÉRAGE DES PLANS DE VILLES
SETTLEMENT KEY LOCATOR MAP

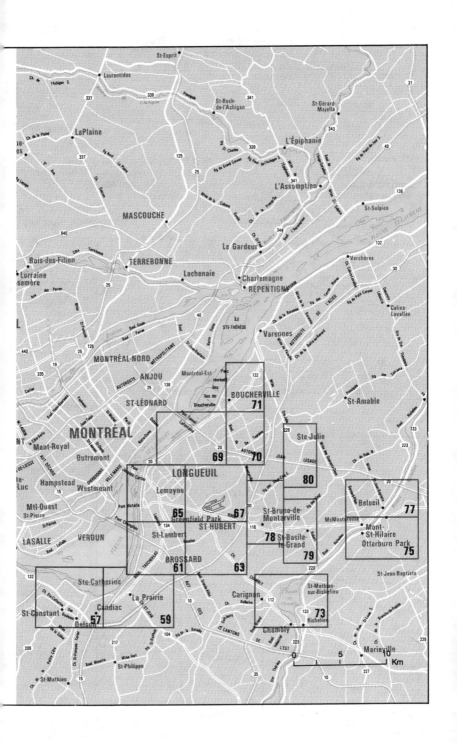

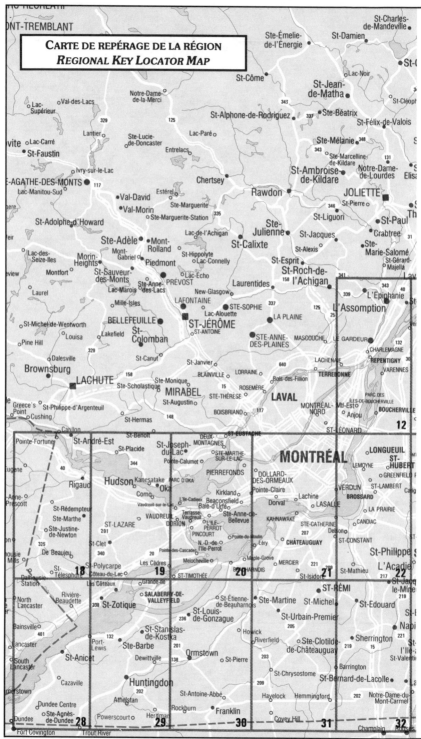

CARTE DE REPÉRAGE DE LA RÉGION
REGIONAL KEY LOCATOR MAP

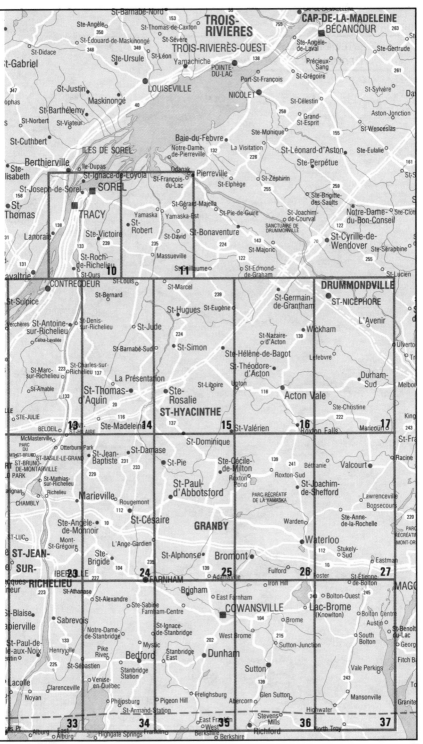

7

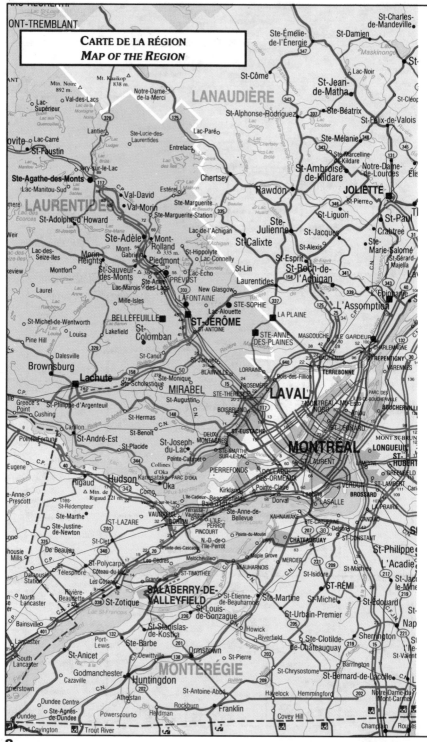

CARTE DE LA RÉGION
MAP OF THE REGION

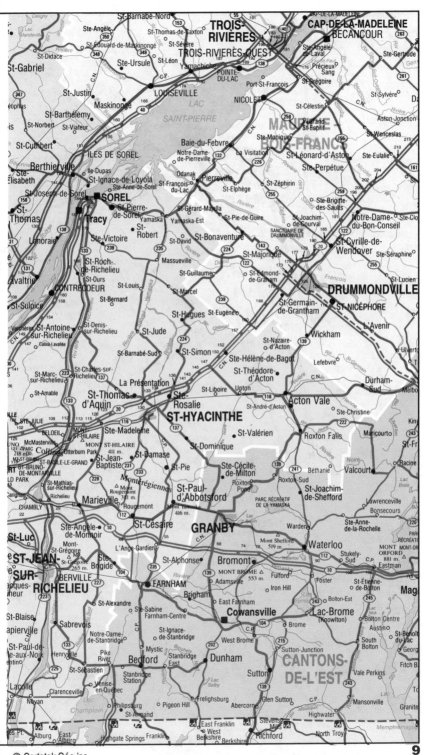

© Cartotek Géo inc.

9

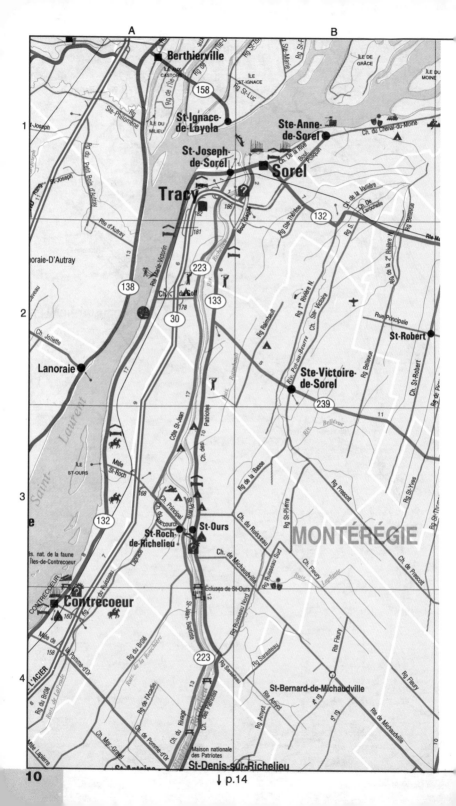

A   B

Berthierville

ÎLE AUX CASTORS

ÎLE DE GRÂCE

ÎLE DU MOINE

ÎLE ST-IGNACE

Rg Ste-Marie

Rg de l'Île

158

St-Ignace-de-Loyola

ÎLE DU MILIEU

Rg St-Luc

Ste-Anne-de-Sorel

Ch. du Chenal-du-Moine

1

St-Joseph

Ste-Philomène

St-Joseph-de-Sorel

Ch. De la Rive

Boul. Poliquin

Sorel

Ch. de la Vallibre

Ch. De Larochelle

Rg Bellevue

Rte Ma

Rg du Petit Bois d'Autray

Tracy

82

186

Boul. Gagné

7

132

Rg S

Ch. St-Joseph

Rte d'Autray

181

Riv. Richelieu

Ste-Thérèse

Rg de la 2e Rivière N.

-oraie-D'Autray

223

Rg 1re Rivière N.

138

Ch. du Golf

133

Rg Raimbault

Ch. Ste-Victoire

Rue Principale

2

30

178

5

St-Robert

Ch. Joliette

Riv. Pot-au-Beurre

Ste-Victoire-de-Sorel

Rg Bellevue

Ch. St-Robert

Lanoraie

17

239

11

Rg de Pi

Riv. Ruisseault

Rg Bellevue

9

17

Riv. Bellevue

Côte St-Jean

Ch. des Patriotes

Rg de la Basse

Rg St-Yves

St-

Laurent

ÎLE ST-OURS

Mtée St-Roch

168

Ch. Principal

St-Pierre

Rg St-Pierre

Rg Prescott

Rg St-Thom

3

Ch. Oldecourcet

St-Ours

Ch. du Ruisseau

MONTÉRÉGIE

132

St-Roch-de-Richelieu

Ch. de Michaudville

Ch. Fleury Laplante

Ch. de Prescott

Ruis. Fleury

Rg Ruisseau Sud

és. nat. de la faune Îles-de-Contrecoeur

Lapraye

7

Écluses de St-Ours

Rg Ruisseau Nord

CONTRECOEUR

160

Contrecoeur

Ruis. de l'Acadie

12

Rte Fleury

Mtée de A

Rg du Brûlé

158

Rg du Brûlé

Ruis. de la Bouchière

Rg Sarasteau

L'ACIER

223

Rte Fleury

St-Jean-Baptiste

Rg Amyot

St-Bernard-de-Michaudville

4 rg

Rte de Michaudville

6

Rg du Rivage

Ch. de Pomme-d'Or

13

Ch. du Rivage

Rg de l'Acadie

Ch. des Patriotes

Rg Sarasteau

5 rg

Mtée Lapierre

Ch. Mgr-Graver

Mtée de Pomme-d'Or

Maison nationale des Patriotes

St-Antoine

St-Denis-sur-Richelieu

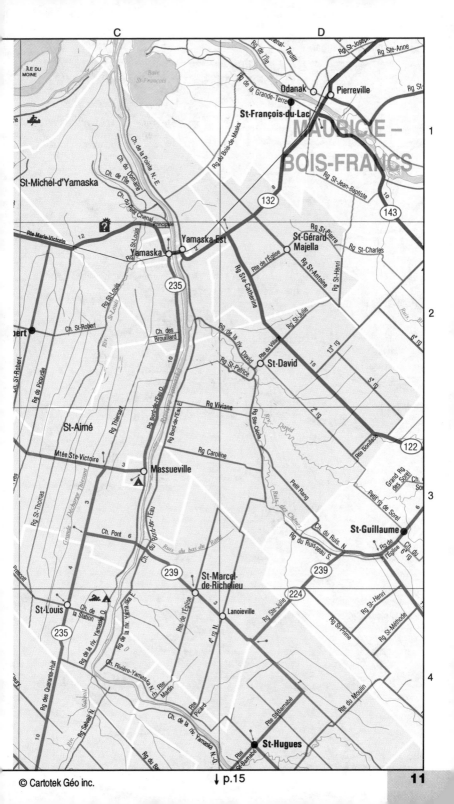

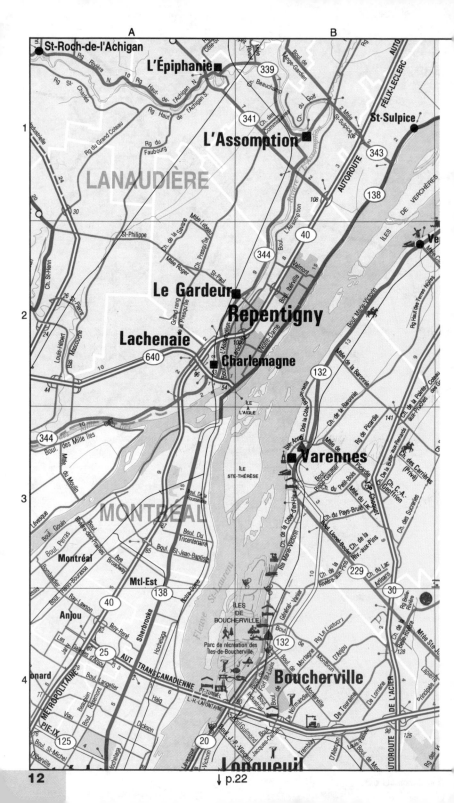

↓ p.22

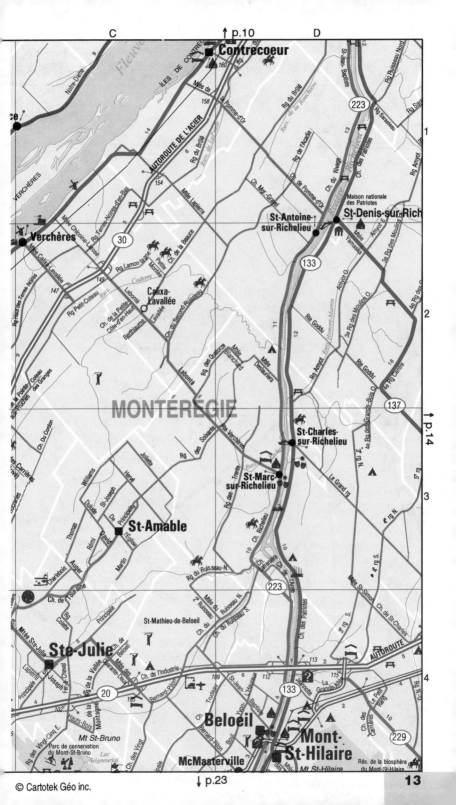

Contrecoeur

Fleuve

ÎLES DE CONTRECOEUR

Notre-Dame

160

158

AUTOROUTE DE L'ACIER

Mtée de la Pomme-d'Or

Rg du Brûlé

St-Jean-Baptiste

Rg du Rivage

Rg du Ruisseau Nord

Rg Surestau

223

Rg Amyot

Rg Sar

1

154

Mtée Lapierre

Rg du Brûlé

Rg de l'Acadie

13

Ruis. de la Ronchère

Ch. Marc-Gravel

Ch. de Pomme-d'Or

Ch. du Rivage

Rg des Patriotes

Maison nationale des Patriotes

St-Antoine-sur-Richelieu

St-Denis-sur-Rich

VERCHÈRES

Mtée Chicoine-Larose

Rg Terres-Noires-d'en-Bas

Rg Haut-des-Terres-Noires

Mtée Calix-Lavallée

30

Rg Lamontagne

Petite Montée

Ch. de la Beauce

133

Amyot E.

3e Rg des Moulins O.

Mtée Yamaska

Verchères

149

147

Rg Petit-Coteau

Coderre

Ruis.

Calixa-Lavallée

Lavallée

Ch. de la Petite Côte-d'en-Haut

Berthiaume

Ch. du Second Ruisseau

Rg des Quarante

Mtée Blanchard

Mtée Desfauriers

Rg Amyot

Rg Honoré-Martin

3e Rg des Moulins O.

Rte Godbi

2

11

12

Rte Godbi

4e Rg Centre

1a

4e Rg Centre

Laborté

MONTÉRÉGIE

Ch. Du Cordon

es Carrières

Rg des Pointes-Coteau des Granges

arc-Prichées

Rg Sabrevois

Mtée Verchères

Rg

Joliette

137

↑ p.14

4e Rg des Grands-Bois O.

St-Charles-sur-Richelieu

Le Grand rg

Rg S.

4e rg N.

3

Williams

Hervé

St-Joseph

Dulude

De

Principale

St-Amable

Rg des Trente

St-Marc-sur-Richelieu

Ruiss. Richelieu

Thomas

Rémi

David

Martin

Ch. de l'Église

Ch. Richelieu

10

Ch. Richelieu

3e rg S.

Res S.

4e rg N.

Charlebois

Auger

Touraine

Rg du Ruisseau-N.

2e Mtée du Ruisseau N.

Ch. Larivière

Ch. de Trans

Mtée St-Simon

Ch. de St-Charles

Ch. de

Colette

Rg

Principale

St-Mathieu-de-Beloeil

Ch. du Ruisseau S.

223

3e rg S.

Mtée Ste-Julie

Lapierre

St-Joseph

Ch. de la Vallée

Mtée de Beloeil

Charette-Dutil

Ch. de l'Industrie

Ste-Julie

20

Rg Fer-à-Cheval

Principale

Rg de la Montagne

Bernard-Pilon

Trudeau

109

St-Jean-Baptiste

113

112

115

Jeannotte

La Grande-Allée

Ch. des Patriotes

Rg S.

133

3e rg S.

Ch. des Carrières

Le Petit Rang

Rg N-U.

4

AUTOROUTE

229

Hauts-Bois

102

Mt St-Bruno

Parc de conservation du Mont-St-Bruno

Rg des Vingt-Cinq E.

Lac Seigneurial

Ch. des Vingt

Beloeil

McMasterville

Bernard-Pilon

Mont-St-Hilaire

Mtée St-Hilaire

Rés. de la biosphère du Mont-St-Hilaire

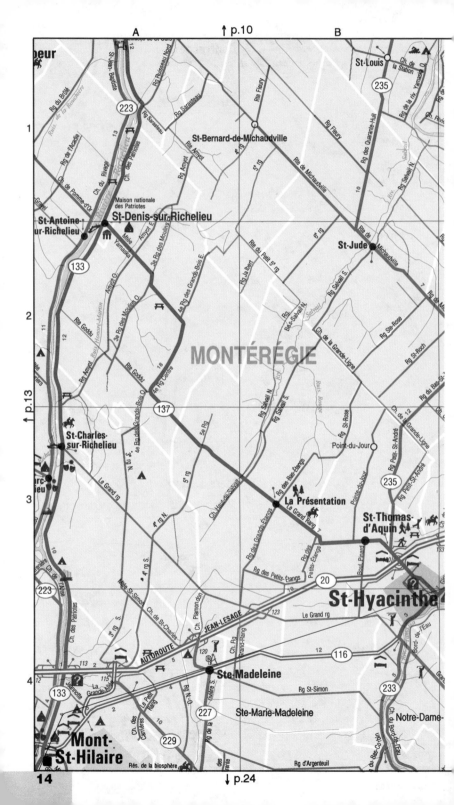

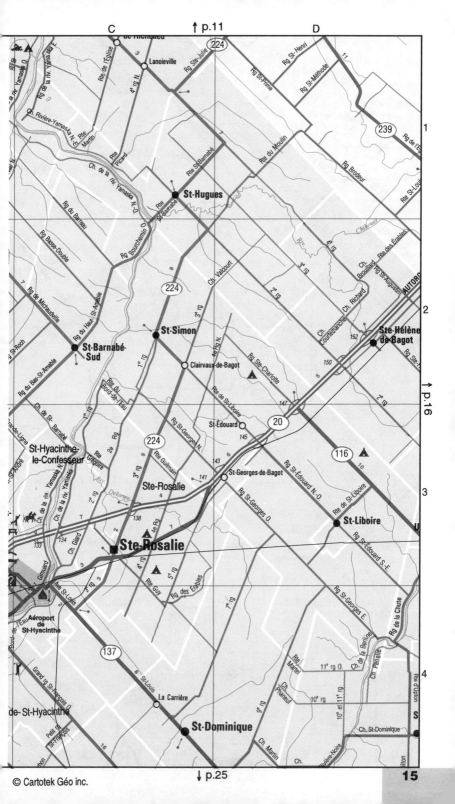

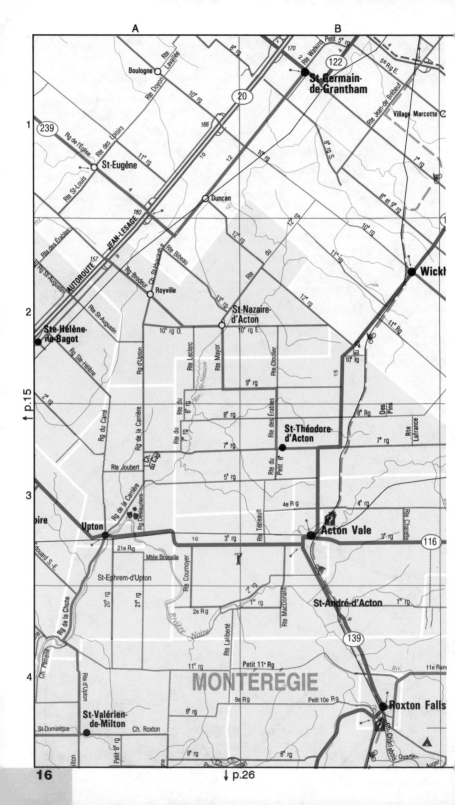

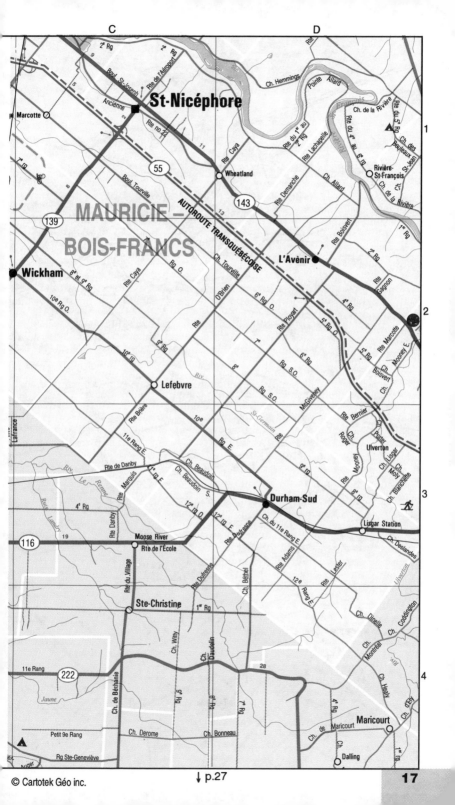

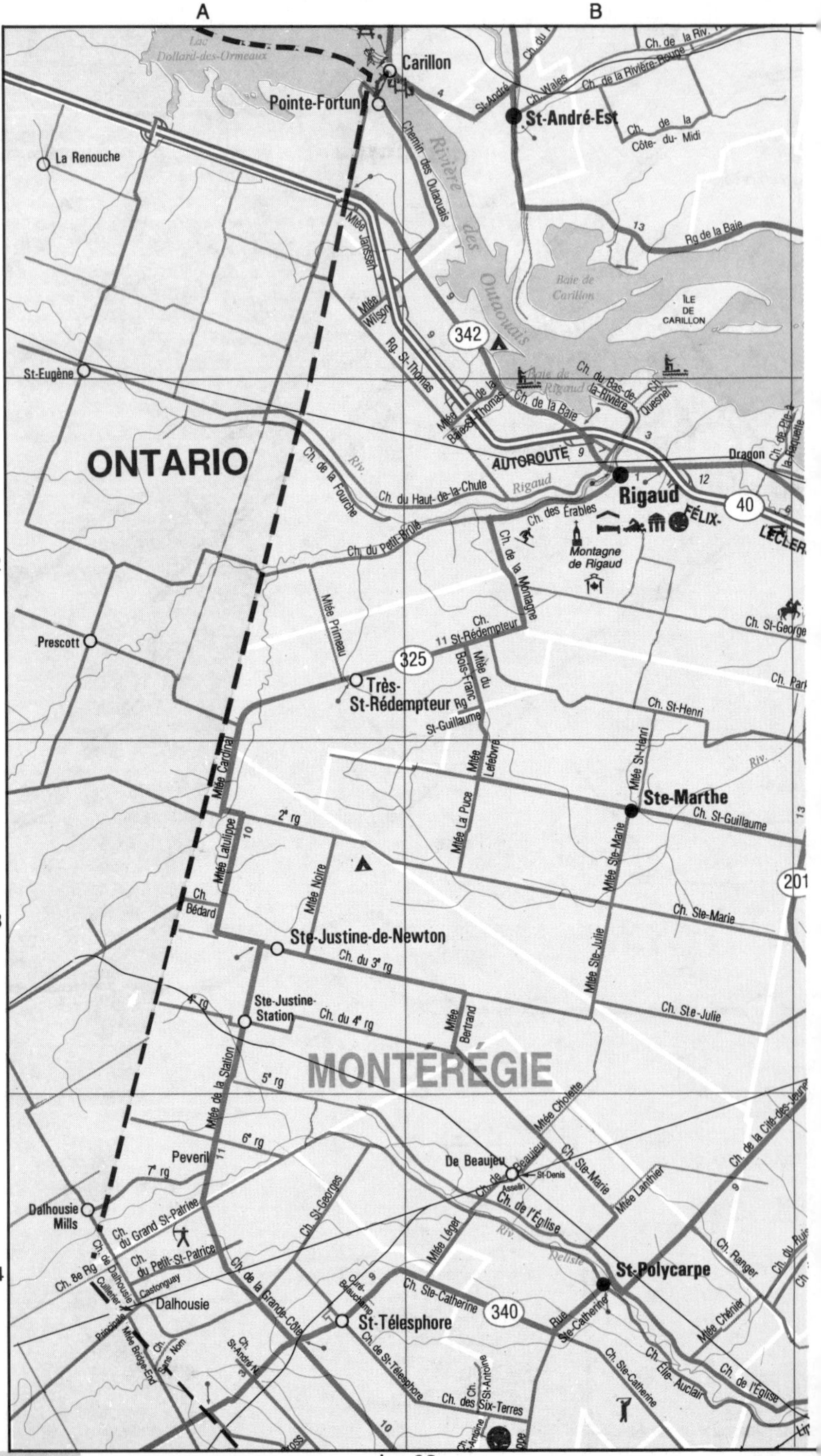

A
B
1
2
3
4
Lac Dollard-des-Ormeaux
Carillon
Pointe-Fortune
St-André-Est
La Renouche
Ch. de la Riv.
Ch. de la Rivière-Rouge
Ch. Wales
Ch. de la Côte- du- Midi
Chemin des Outaouais
Rivière des Outaouais
Rg de la Baie
Baie de Carillon
ÎLE DE CARILLON
Mtée Janssen
Mtée Wilson
Rg. St-Thomas
342
St-Eugène
Baie de Rigaud
Ch. du Bas-de-la-Rivière
Ch. Quesnel
Ch. de la Baie
Mtée de la Baie-St-Thomas
ONTARIO
AUTOROUTE
Dragon
Ch. de Pte-à-la-Raquette
Ch. de la Fourche
Ch. du Haut-de-la-Chute
Rigaud
Rigaud
40
FÉLIX-LECLERC
Ch. des Érables
Ch. du Petit-Brûlé
Ch. de la Montagne
Montagne de Rigaud
Mtée Primeau
Ch. St-Rédempteur
Prescott
325
Très-St-Rédempteur
Mtée du Bois-Franc
Rg St-Guillaume
Ch. St-Georges
Ch. Park
Ch. St-Henri
Mtée Cardinal
Mtée Lefebvre
Mtée La Puce
Mtée St-Henri
Ste-Marthe
2e rg
Ch. St-Guillaume
Mtée Latulippe
Mtée Noire
Mtée Ste-Marie
201
Ch. Bédard
Ch. Ste-Marie
Ste-Justine-de-Newton
Ch. du 3e rg
Mtée Ste-Julie
4e rg
Ste-Justine-Station
Ch. du 4e rg
Mtée Bertrand
Ch. Ste-Julie
MONTÉRÉGIE
Mtée de la Station
5e rg
Mtée Cholette
Ch. de la Cité-des-Jeunes
6e rg
Peveril
De Beaujeu
Ch. Ste-Marie
7e rg
Ch. de Beaujeu
St-Denis
Ch. Asselin
Mtée Lanthier
Dalhousie Mills
Ch. du Grand St-Patrice
Ch. St-Georges
Ch. de l'Église
Riv. Delisle
Mtée Léger
Ch. Ranger
Ch. du Ruisseau
Ch. 8e Rg
Ch. de Dalhousie
Ch. du Petit-St-Patrice
Castonguay
Ch. de la Grande-Côte
St-Polycarpe
Cuillerier
Dalhousie
Curé-Beauchamp
Ch. Ste-Catherine
340
Mtée Chénier
Principale
Mtée Bridge-End
Ch. Sans Nom
St-Télesphore
Rue Ste-Catherine
Ch. St-André N.
Ch. de St-Télesphore
Ch. Ste-Catherine
Ch. Élie-Auclair
Ch. de l'Église
Ch. St-Antoine
Ch. des Six-Terres
Ch. Antoine

↓ p.28

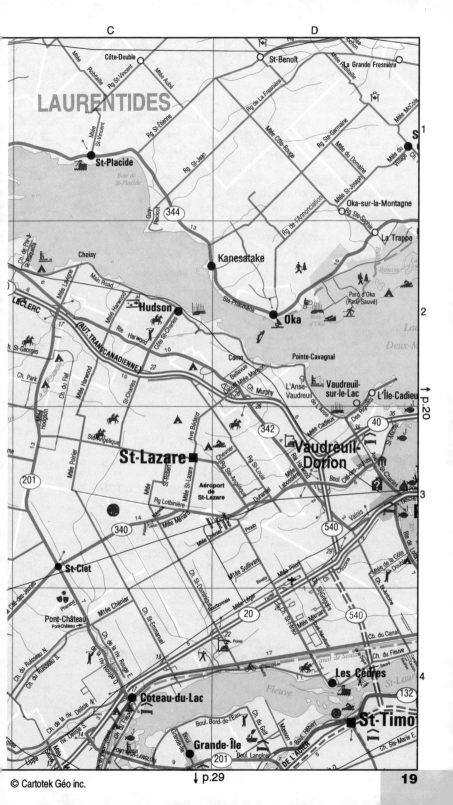

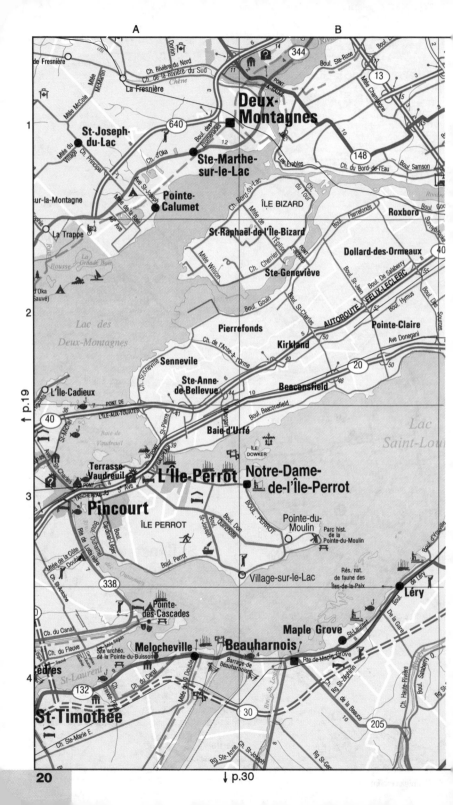

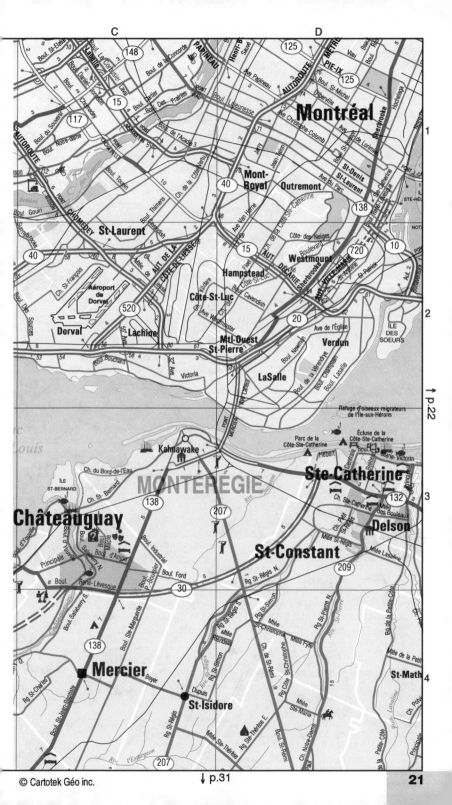

↓ p.31

→ p.22

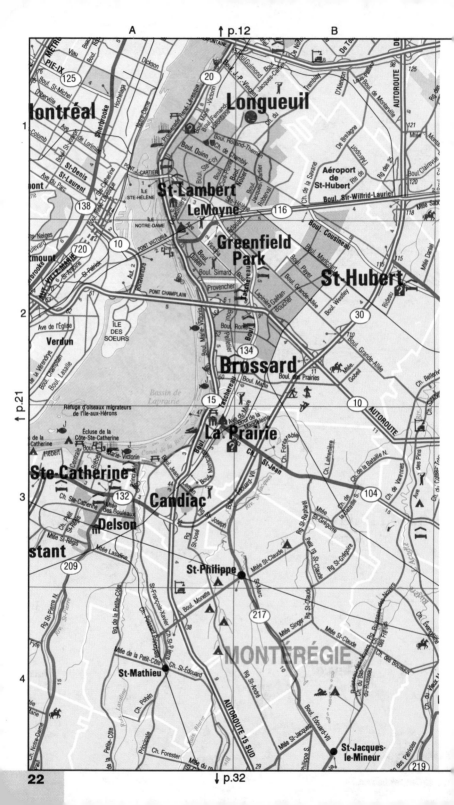

↑ p.21

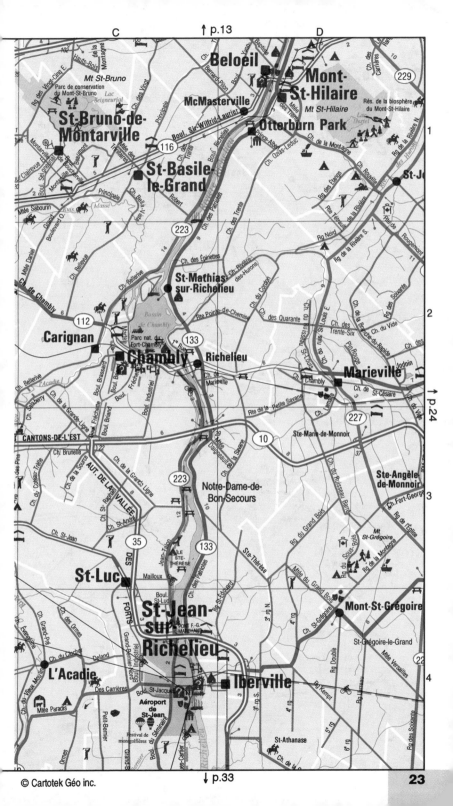

↑ p.13

→ p.24

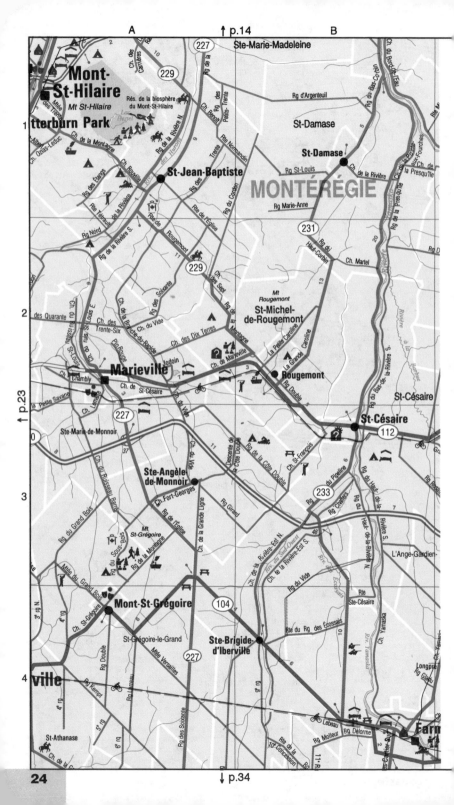

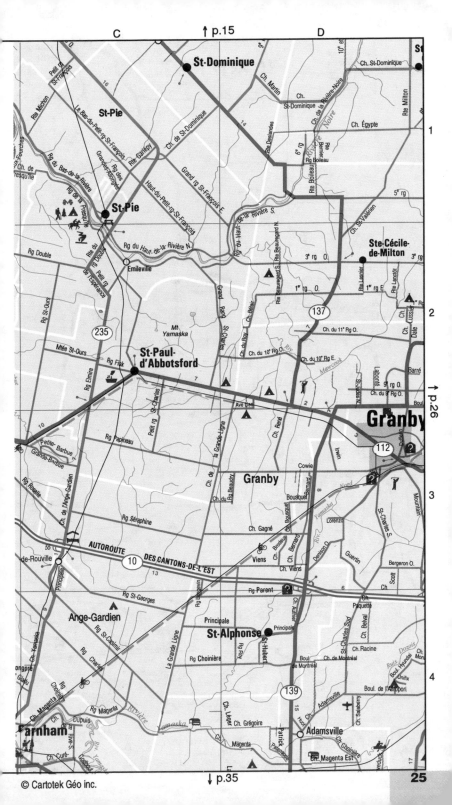

St-Dominique

St-Pie

St-Pie

Ste-Cécile-de-Milton

Emileville

235

Mt. Yamaska

St-Paul-d'Abbotsford

137

Ave Lied

Granby

112

Granby

AUTOROUTE 10 DES CANTONS-DE-L'EST

de-Rouville

Viens

Ange-Gardien

St-Alphonse

139

Farnham

Adamsville

→ p.26

© Cartotek Géo inc.

25

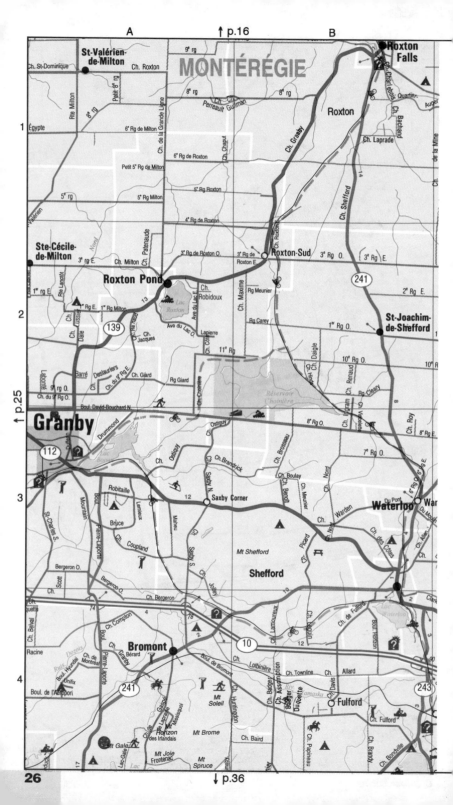

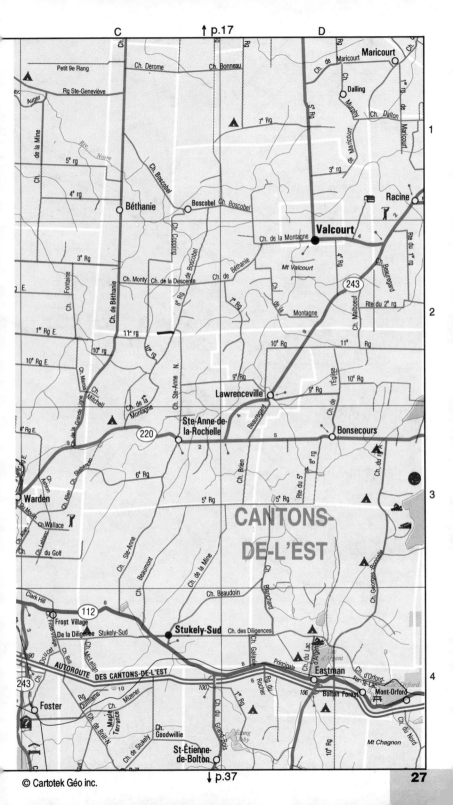

C
D

Maricourt

Petit 9e Rang

Rg Ste-Geneviève

Dalling

Ch. Derome

Ch. Bonneau

Ch. Dalton

▲

Ch. de la Mine

5e rg

7e Rg

3e rg

1

Riv. Noire

4e rg

Béthanie

Boscobel

Ch. Boscobel

Racine

Valcourt

Ch. de la Montagne

4

3e Rg

Mt Valcourt

243

Ch. Fontaine

Ch. Monty

Ch. de la Descente

Ch. de Béthanie

Ch. de Bethanie

Rte du 2e rg

2

1er Rg E.

11e rg

7e Rg

Montagne

10e Rg

11e Rg

10e rg

9e Rg

10e Rg

10e Rg E.

Ch. Marcel Mitchell

Ch. Ste-Anne N.

Lawrenceville

9e Rg

Ch. de l'Église

Ch. de la Montagne

Ste-Anne-de-la-Rochelle

Beauregard

Bonsecours

8e Rg E.

220

▲

6e Rg

Ch. Brien

Rte du 5e

8e rg

Warden

5e Rg

5e Rg

CANTONS-

Ch. Wallace

DE-L'EST

3

Ch. du Golf

Ch. Ste-Anne

Ch. Beaumont

Ch. de la Mine

Ch. Blanchard

Ch. Georges-Bonalla

Clark Hill

112

Ch. Beaudoin

Frost Village

De la Diligence

Stukely-Sud

Stukely-Sud

Ch. des Diligences

▲

Ch. du Lac

Ch. d'Argent

AUTOROUTE DES CANTONS-DE-L'EST

Principale

Eastman

4

243

Foster

Ch. Galaxie

Bolton Forest

Mont-Orford

?

Ch. Goodwillie

Ch. du Grand-Bois

Étang Libby

Mt Chagnon

10e Rg

St-Étienne-de-Bolton

© Cartotek Géo inc.

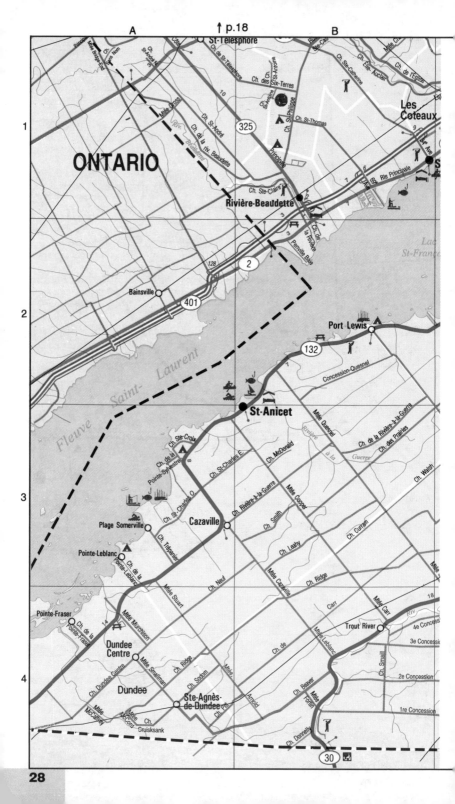

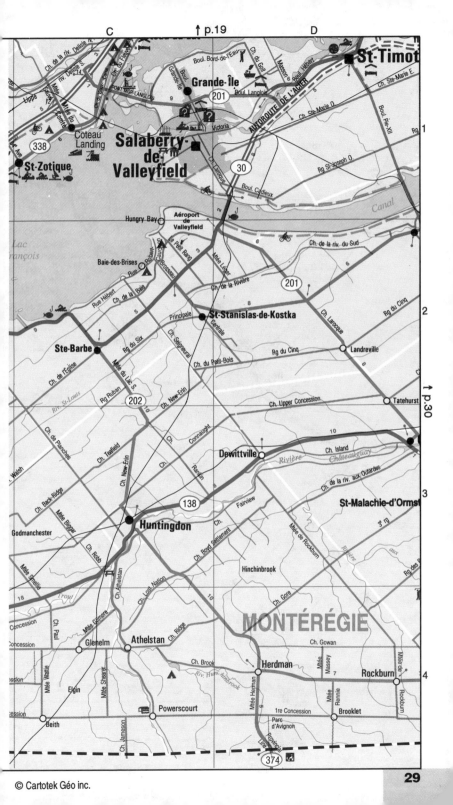

↑ p.30

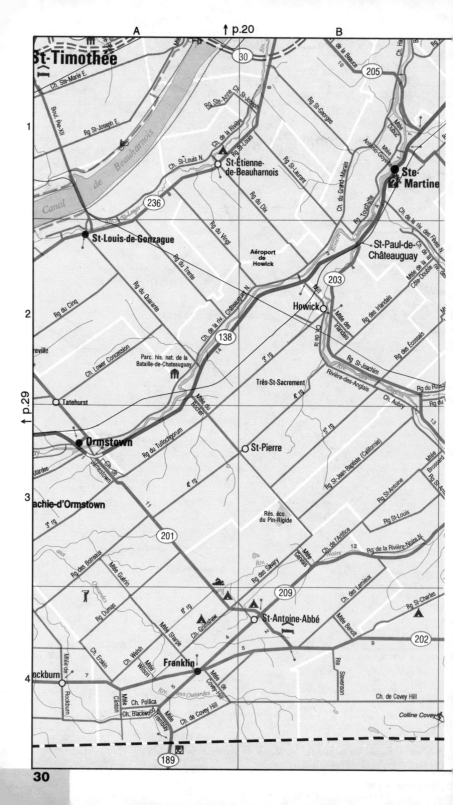

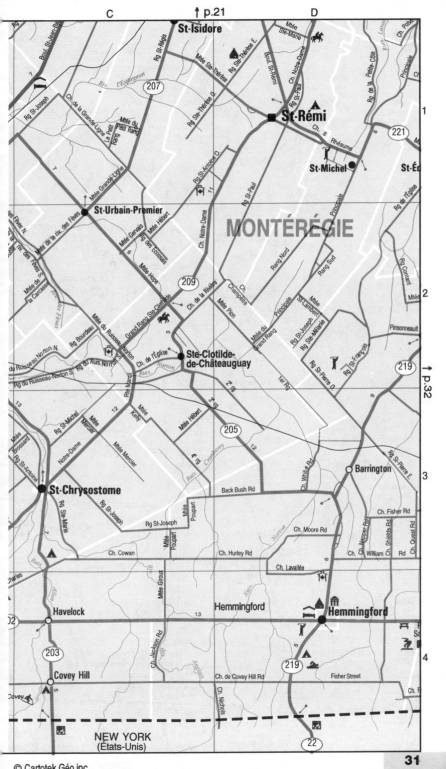

↑ p.21

→ p.32

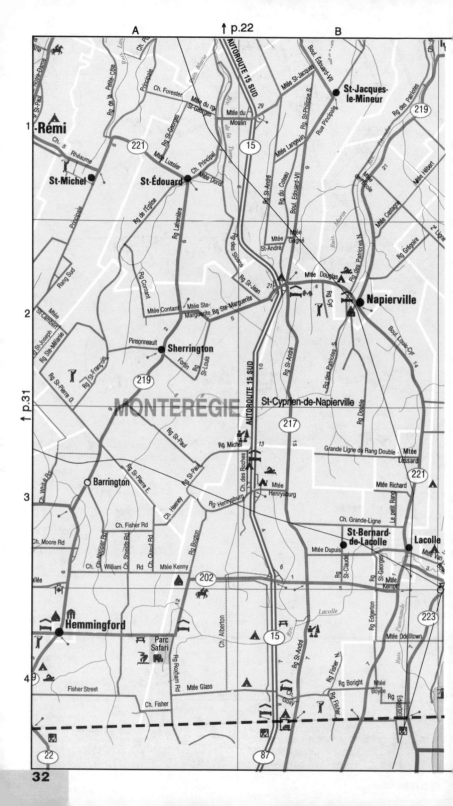

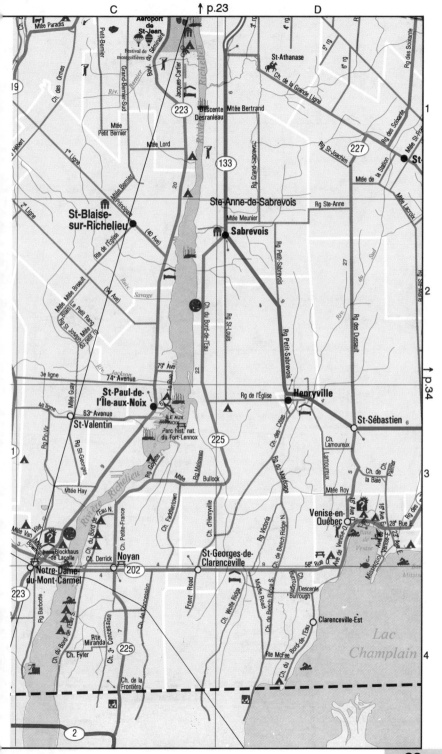

Mtée Paradis
Ch. des Ormes
Petit-Bernier
Aéroport de St-Jean
Festival de montgolfières
19
Grand-Bernier-Sud
Riv. Bernier
Boul. du Séminaire
Jacques-Cartier
St-Athanase
Ch. de la Grande Ligne
Rg des Soixante
Rg des Soixante
Mtée St-Fra...
Descente Desranleau
Mtée Bertrand
Mtée Lord
223
Mtée Petit Bernier
1re Ligne
20
Minnegan
133
Rg Grand-Sabrevois
Rg St-Joachim
227
St-...
Mtée de la Station
1
St-Blaise-sur-Richelieu
Rte de l'Église
(40 Ave)
2e Ligne
Ste-Anne-de-Sabrevois
Mtée Meunier
Sabrevois
Rg Ste-Anne
Rg des Dussault
Mtée Lacroix
Mtée Breault
Mtée St-Blaise
Le Petit Rang
Rg St-Joseph
Mtée petit Ti...
(34 Ave)
Ruis. Savage
Ch. du Bord-de-l'Eau
Rg St-Louis
Rg Petit-Sabrevois
Rg Petit-Sabrevois
27
Riv. du Sud
2
3e ligne
74e Avenue
79e Ave
22
St-Paul-de-l'Île-aux-Noix
4e ligne
Mtée Guay
63e Avenue
St-Valentin
Rg de l'Église
Henryville
Rg des Côtes
St-Sébastien
6
1
Rg Pie-Vir
Rg St-Georges
9
ÎLE AUX NOIX
Parc hist. nat. du Fort-Lennox
225
Ch. des Côtes
Ch. Lamoureux
Lamoureux
Ch. de la Baie
Ch. Palmer
3
Mtée Hay
Rivière Richelieu
Rg St-Georges
Rg Gagetin
Mtée
Bullock
Ch. Faddiettown
Ch. d'Henryville
Rg du Margaga
Rg Victoria
Mtée Roy
Venise-en-Québec
16e Ave
16e Ave
28e Rue E.
Rg des...
Mtée Van Vliet
Mtée Bowham
Ch. du Bord-de-l'Eau N.
Blockhaus de Lacolle
Ch. Derrick
Ch. Petite-France
Noyan
202
4
Rg Mélissa
Front Road
Ch. de Concession
St-Georges-de-Clarenceville
Ch. de Beech Ridge N.
Ave de Venise
Ave de Venise O.
58e Rue O.
Baie de Venise
Missisquoi
3
Notre-Dame-du-Mont-Carmel
223
Rg Barbotte
Ch. du Bord-de-l'Eau S.
Rte Miranda
Ch. Fyler
Ch. 3e Concession
225
Rte McFee
Ch. de la Frontière
Ch. Wolfe Ridge
Ch. de Beech Ridge S.
Ch. Burrough
Descente Burrough
Clarenceville-Est
Ch. du Bord-de-l'Eau
Lac Champlain
4
2

→ p.34

33

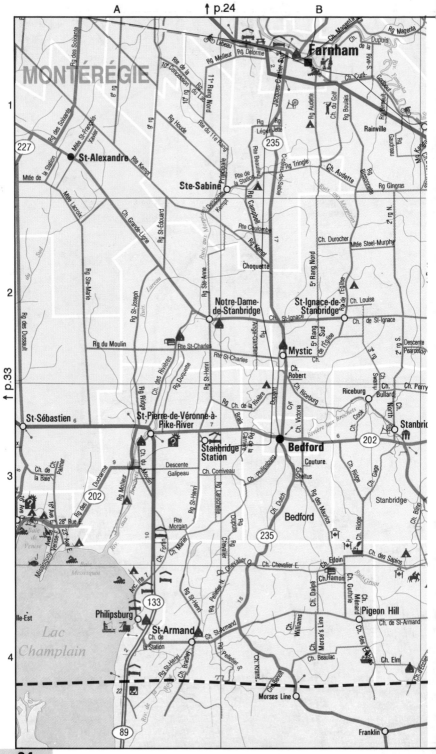

MONTÉRÉGIE

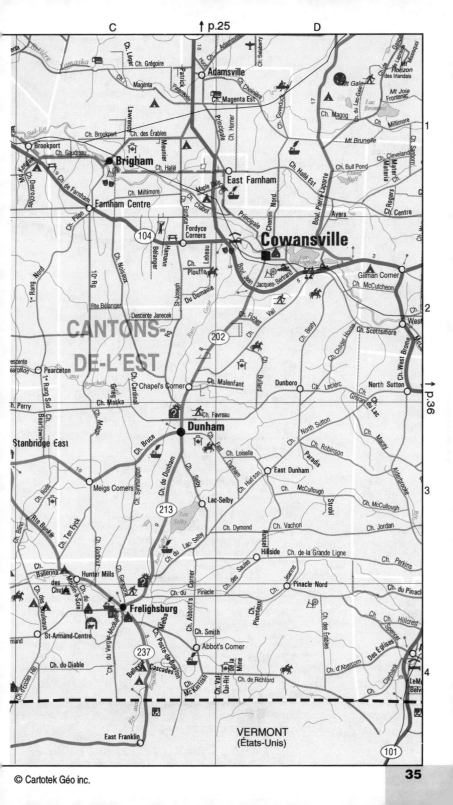

Rivière Yamaska

Ch. Léger
Ch. Grégoire
Patrick Patenaude
Adamsville
Ch. Choinière
Ch. Salsbury
Mt Gale
Mt Horizon des Irlandais
Gascon
Lagrave
Masson
Mascouci
Magenta
Ch. Magenta Est
Pléiade
Ch. Horner
Ch. Covedick
Lac-Gale
Lac Bromont
Mt Joie Frontenac
Ch. Magog
Ch. Miltimore

15

17

Sud-Est
Ch. Brookport
Ch. des Érables
Meunier
Ch. Hallé Est
Mt Brunelle
Cleveland
Ch. Maleri
Étang Bull
Ch. Bull Pond

1

Brookport
Ch. Gaudreau
Brigham
Ch. de Farnham
Ch. Hallé
East Farnham
Boul. Pierr-Laporte
Ch. Sanborn
Rogers
Ch. Materia

Mt Keegan
Ch. Desrochers
Ch. Miltimore
Maple Dale
Ch. Centre

Farnham Centre
Ch. Pilen
Ch. Chabot
Principale
Ch. Nord
Ayers

104
Fordyce Corners
Lebeau
Cowansville
Ch. Plouffe
Boul. Jean Jacques-Bertrand
Gilman Corner
Ch. McCutcheon

1er Rang Nord
10e Rg
Hamann Bélanger
St-Joseph
Du Domaine
Lac Avignon
5
3

CANTONS-
Descente Janecek
Rte Bélanger
Ruiss. Crosr
Ch. Fichett
Vail
Ch. Beaty
Ch. Scottsmore
West

2

DE-L'EST
202
Ch. Chilcot House
Ch. West Brome

escente earcelon
Pearceton
Ch. Griep
Ruiss. aux Brochets
Ch. Cardinal
Chapel's Corner
Ch. Malenfant
Bullard
Dunboro
Ch. Leclerc
North Sutton
Ch. Ghirard du Lac

1er Rang Sud
Beartown
Ch. Maska
Ch. Favreau
North Sutton
Ch.
Ch. Macey
p.36

Ch. Perry
Ch. Meigs
Dunham
Ch. Est
Ch. Loiselle
Ch. Robinson
Paradis
Aldenbrooke

Stanbridge East
Ch. Bruce
Ch. de Dunham
Ch. Dunham
Ch. Hudson
East Dunham
McCullough
Strobl

10
Ch. Ross
Ch. Symington
Ch. Selby
Lac-Selby
Strobl
Ch. McCullough
Ch. Jordan

3

Rte Bunker
Ch. Ten Eryck
Ch. Godbout
213
Lac Selby
Ch. Dymond
Ch. Vachon

Ch. Blinn
Ch. Garagona
Ruiss. du Lac-Selby
Ruiss. Russell
Riv.

Ch. Ballerina
des Chut
Hunter Mills
Corner
Hillside
Ch. de la Grande Ligne
Ch. Perkins

Ch. du Moulin-à-Scie
Ch. du
Pinacle
Ch. des Saules
Jeanne
Pinacle Nord
Ch. du Pinacl

St-Armand-Centre
Ch. du Verger-Modèle
Frelighsburg
Melba
Ch. Plomteux
Ch. des Érables
Ch. Hillcrest

mand
237
Ch. Abbot's
Ch. Smith
Abbot's Corner
Ch. d'Abercorn
Ch. Spencer
Des Églises

Ch. du Diable
Bellevue
Cascades
Ch. McKintosh
Ch. Val-Our-Rit
Ch. de la Mine
Ch. de Richford
Ch.
Carbank
LeMe
Belv

4

Ch. des Écluses
Ruiss. aux Brochets
101

East Franklin
VERMONT
(États-Unis)

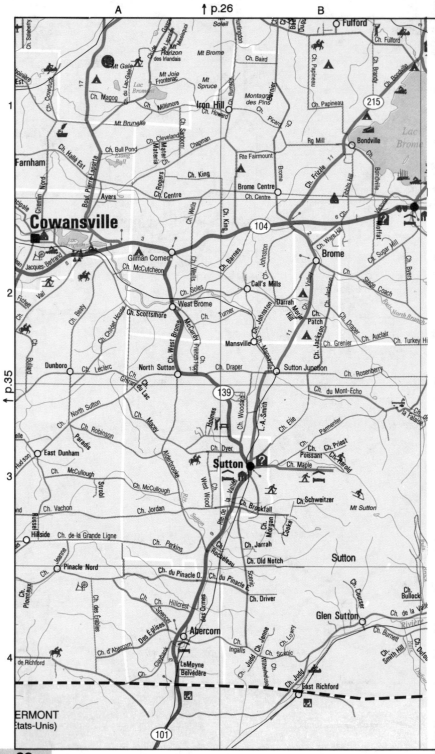

↑ p.26

↑ p.35

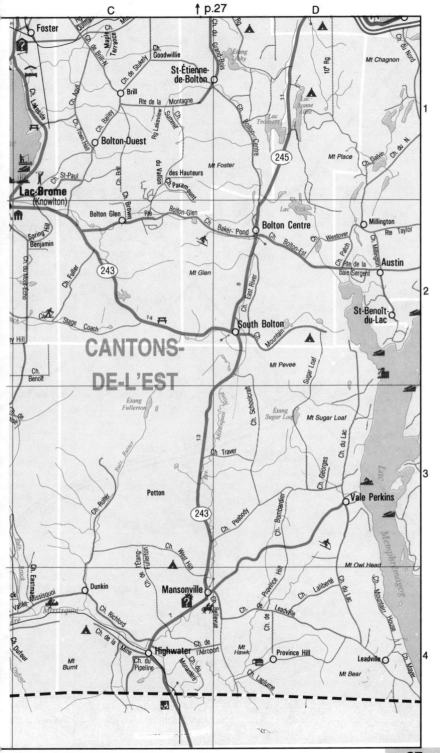

C   D

Foster

Ch. du Nord

Mt Chagnon

Ch. Goodwillie

St-Étienne-de-Bolton

Étang Libby

10e Rg

Ch. de Boll-N.

Maple Terrace

Ch. Quilman

Ch. de Stukely

Ch. Aguil

Brill

Rte de la Montagne

Rg Lakeview

Ch. Bailey

Ch. Town Hall

Ch. Summit

Lac Bonne Idee

Lac Trousers

1

Bolton-Ouest

Ch. Brill

Ch. Summit

Mt Foster

245

Mt Place

Ch. Galvin

Ch. du N.

Ch. St-Paul

des Hauteurs

du Vallon

Patamount

Lac-Brome (Knowlton)

Spring Benjamin

Ch. Brown

Bolton Glen

Rte Bolton-Glen

Ch. Baker-Pond

Bolton Centre

Lac Nick

Ch. Bolton-Est

Ch. Westover

Millington

Rte Taylor

Ch. du Mont-Écho

Ch. Fuller

243

Ch. Patch

Rte de la baie Sergent

Austin

2

Ch. Stage Coach

Mt Glen

Ch. East River

14

South Bolton

Ch. Mountain

St-Benoît-du-Lac

ey Hill

Ch. Benoît

CANTONS-DE-L'EST

Mt Pevee

Sugar Loaf

Étang Fullerton

Ruis. Rutter

Ch. Ruiter

Missisquoi Nord

Ch. Schoolcraft

Étang Sugar Loaf

Mt Sugar Loaf

Ch. du Lac

3

13

Ch. Traver

Potton

243

Ch. Peabody

Ch. Bombardier

Ch. Georges

Vale Perkins

Lac Memphrémagog

Ch. Ruiter

Ruis. Missisquoi

Ch. Eastman

Vallée Missisquoi

Dunkin

Ch. West Hill

Ch. de l'Étang-Fullerton

Mansonville

Ch. Bellevue

Province Hill

Ch. Laliberté

Mt Owl Head

Ch. du Lac

Ch. Mountain House

Ch. Mayer

Ch. Richford

Ch. de la Mine

7

Ch. de Leadville

Ch. de l'Aéroport

Mt Hawk

Province Hill

Leadville

4

Mt Burnt

Highwater

Ch. du Pipeline

Ch. du Monastère

Ch. Laplume

Mt Bear

Dufour

Ch. Dufour

© Cartotek Géo inc.

H

I

J

K

St-Lazare

Rivière

Viviry

Saddlebrook

↓ p.40   ↓ p.41

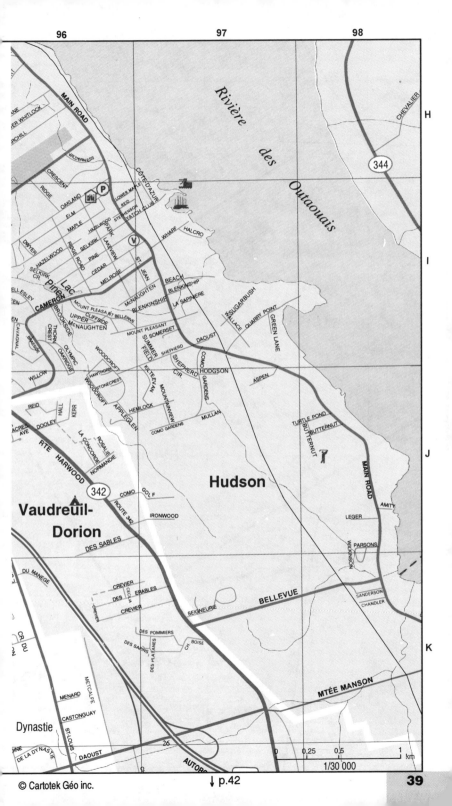

↓ p.42

© Cartotek Géo inc.

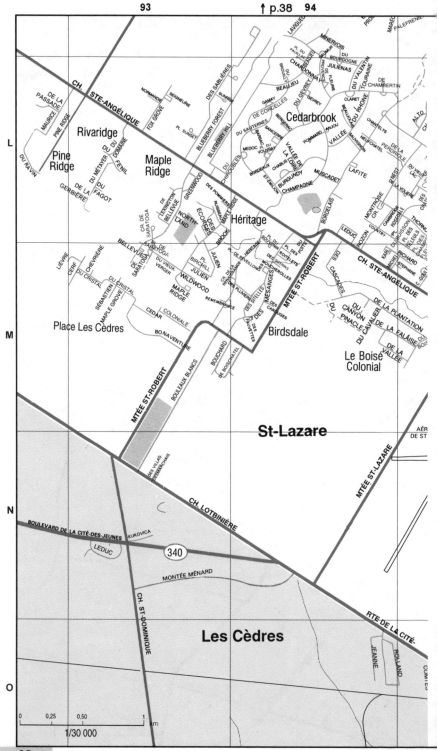

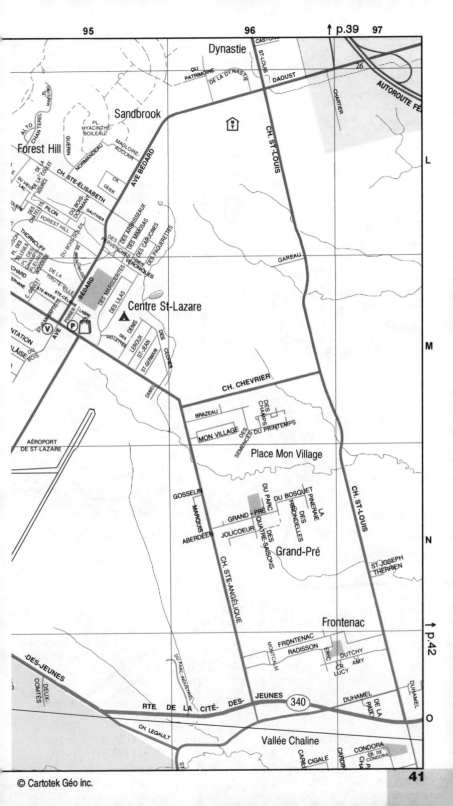

↑ p.39
↑ p.42

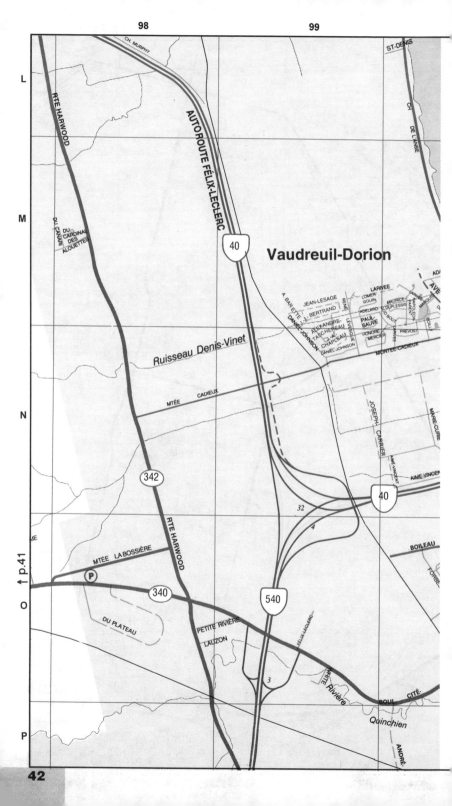

CH. MURPHY

ST-DENIS

L

RTE HARWOOD

AUTOROUTE FÉLIX-LECLERC

CH. DE L'ANSE

M

DU CANARD

DU CARDINAL DES ALOUETTES

40

Vaudreuil-Dorion

ADA

AVE

LARIVÉE

A. BARETTE

JEAN-LESAGE

J. BERTRAND

DANIEL-JOHNSON

RENÉ

L'OMER GOUIN

MAURICE DUPLESSIS

NAPOLEON PARENT

MARCUS

BOLY

ADÉLARD

ALEXANDRE-TASCHEREAU

A. CHAPLEAU

LÉVESQUE

PAUL-SAUVÉ

PRÉVOST

HONORÉ

MERCIER

RIVIERE

DANIEL-JOHNSON

MONTÉE CADIEUX

Ruisseau Denis-Vinet

MTÉE CADIEUX

N

JOSEPH CARRIER

MARIE-CURIE

342

AIME-VINCENT

AIME-VINCENT

40

32

4

BOILEAU

FORBE

↑ p.41

MTÉE LA BOSSIÈRE

RTE HARWOOD

P

340

540

O

DU PLATEAU

PETITE RIVIÈRE

LAUZON

FÉLIX-LECLERC

3

PETITE RIVIÈRE

CITÉ

BOUL

P

Quinchien

ANDRÉ

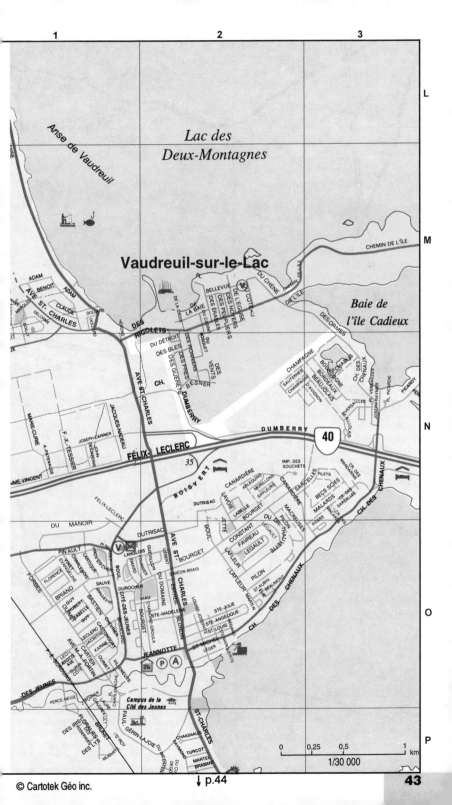

Lac des Deux-Montagnes

Anse de Vaudreuil

CHEMIN DE L'ÎLE

Vaudreuil-sur-le-Lac

Baie de l'île Cadieux

40

0   0,25   0,5   1 km

1/30 000

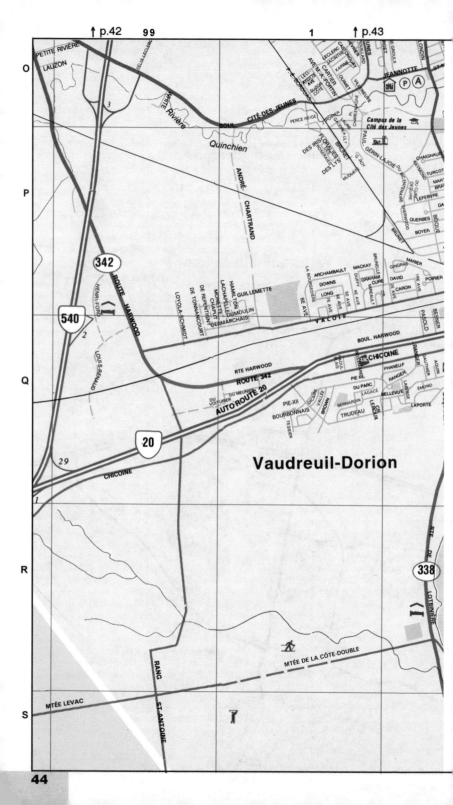

Vaudreuil-Dorion

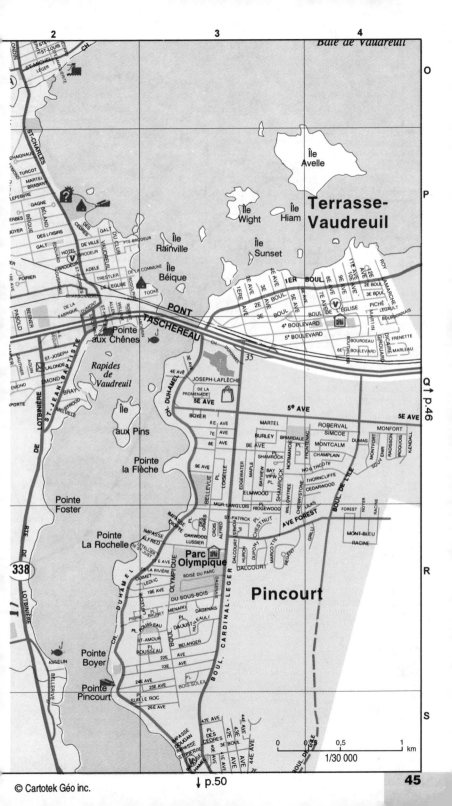

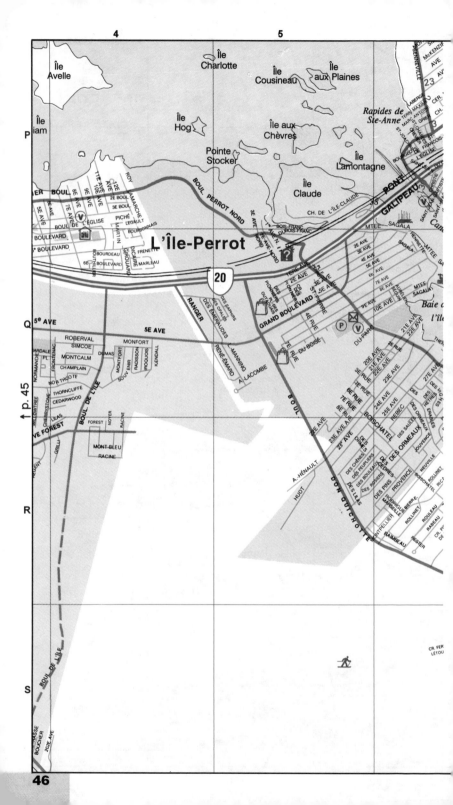

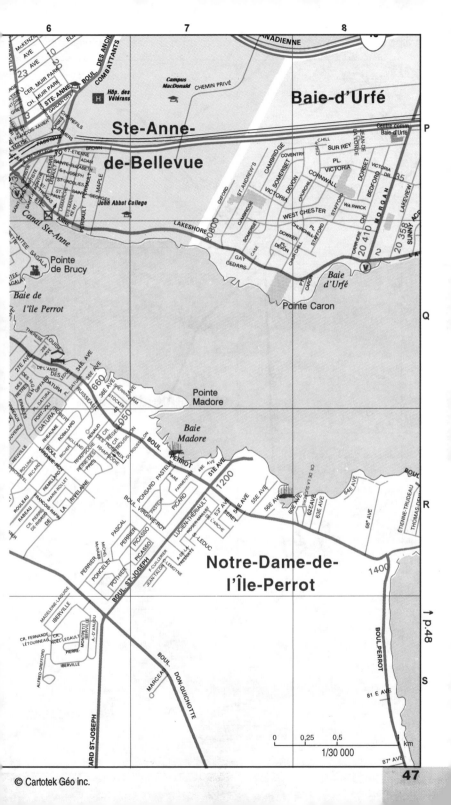

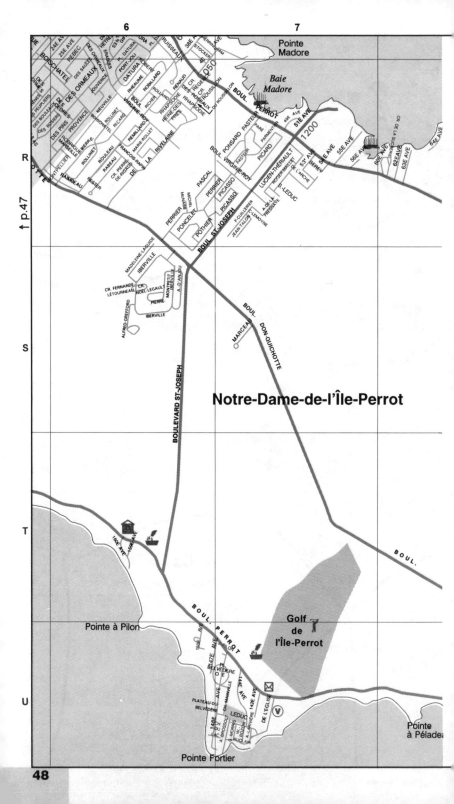

Notre-Dame-de-l'Île-Perrot

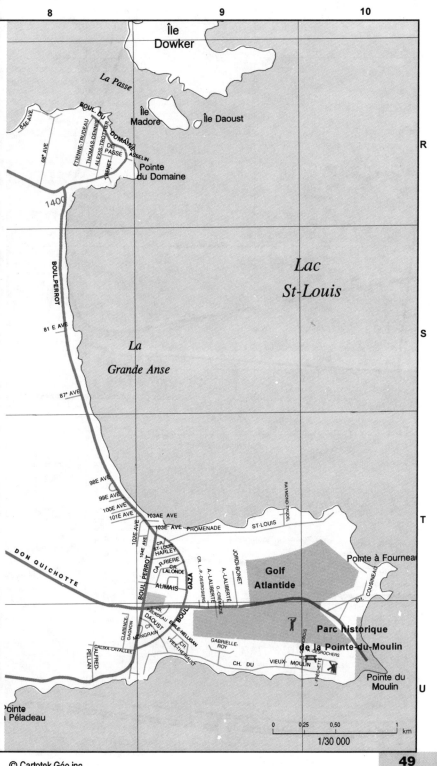

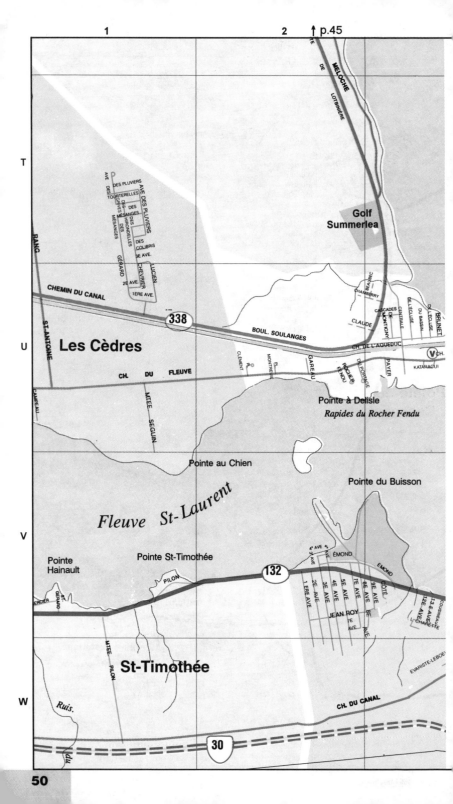

T

Golf
Summerlea

CHEMIN DU CANAL

338

BOUL. SOULANGES

Les Cèdres

CH. DE L'AQUEDUC

U

CH. DU FLEUVE

MTÉE. SEGUIN

KATARAGUI

Pointe à Delisle
Rapides du Rocher Fendu

Pointe au Chien

Pointe du Buisson

Fleuve St-Laurent

V

Pointe
Hainault

Pointe St-Timothée

PILON

132

ÉMOND

ÉMOND

JEAN ROY

St-Timothée

MTÉE. PILON

Ruis.

CH. DU CANAL

W

30

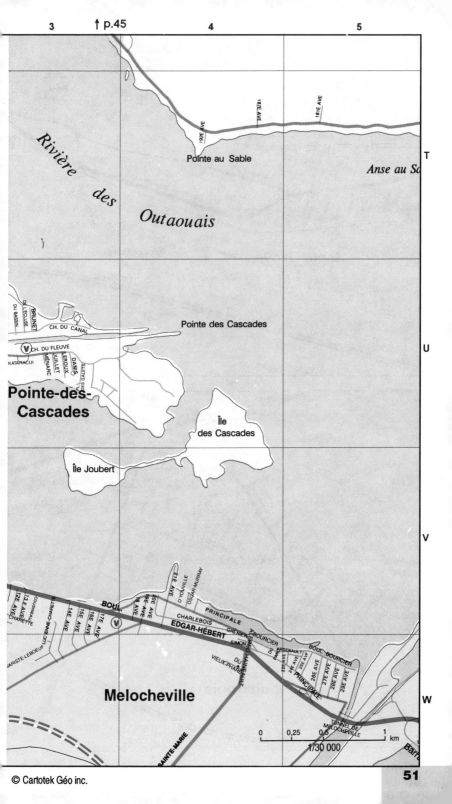

Rivière

des

Outaouais

Pointe au Sable

Anse au S...

T

Pointe des Cascades

DU BASSIN
DE L'ÉCLUSE
BRUNET
CH. DU CANAL
V CH. DU FLEUVE
KATARACUI
MÉNARC
LEROUX
JUILLET
DANIS
DES ÎLETS

Pointe-des-Cascades

U

Île
des Cascades

Île Joubert

V

21E AVE
IOUVILLE
OSCAR-MURRAY
20E AVE
19E AVE
18E AVE
PRINCIPALE
CHARLEBOIS
EDGAR-HÉBERT
GHÉNIER
P. BOURCIER
SIMON
DU PARC
ARSENAULT
P. FRIGON HAMMANT
22E AVE
24E AVE
25E AVE
26E AVE
27E AVE
28E AVE
29E AVE
BOUL. BOURCIER
VIEUX-PHARMANT
DU
PRINCIPALE
BOUL...
12E AVE
13E AVE
14E AVE
15E AVE
16E AVE
17E AVE
COUSINEAUE
LUCIENNE-CHAREL
BL
CHARETTE
ARISTE-LEBOEUF
V

Melocheville

W

SAINTE-MARIE

TUNNEL DE
MELOCHEVILLE

0   0,25   0,5   1   km

1/30 000

Barr...

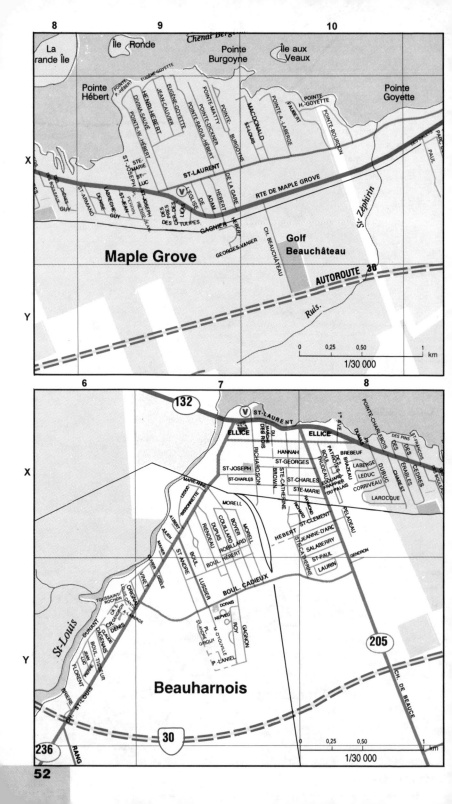

Maple Grove

Beauharnois

1/30 000

52

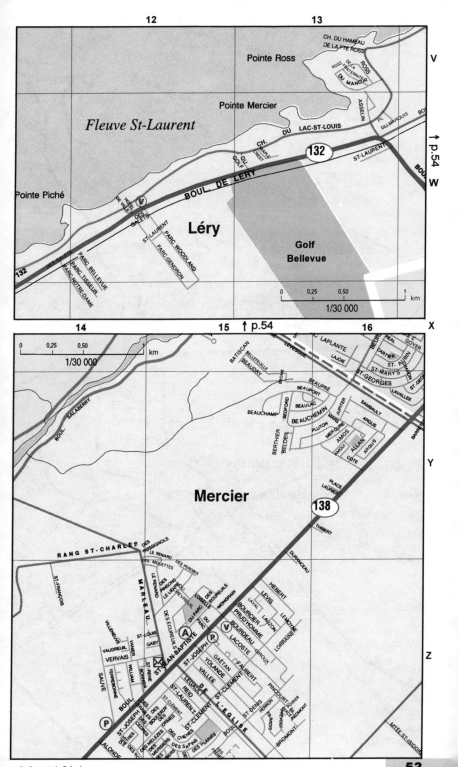

Fleuve St-Laurent

Pointe Ross

Pointe Mercier

CH. DU HAMEAU
DE LA PTE ROSS

ROSS DE LA FRATERNITÉ
ROSS
DU MANOIR

ASSELIN

PL. GILLMARQUIS

LAC-ST-LOUIS

DU

CH. MAPLE CREST

132

ST-LAURENT

BOUL. DE LÉRY

Léry

Pointe Piché

HOTEL DE VILLE

DES GALETS

ST-LAURENT

PARC WOODLAND

PARC-GENDRON

DES GRÈVES

PARC BELLEVUE

PARC-TISSEUR

PARC-NOTRE-DAME

132

**Golf
Bellevue**

0   0,25   0,50   1 km

1/30 000

→ p.54

W

V

↑ p.54

0   0,25   0,50   km

1/30 000

C. LAPLANTE

BATISCAN

BELLEFEUILLE

BEAUDRY

BROME

LÉVESQUE

LAJOIE

ST-GEORGES

ST- MARY'S

BEAUPRÉ

BEAUPORT

BEAULAC

BEAUCHEMIN

SAMBAULT

ST-AUBIN

PARTIER

BÉRUBÉ

RÉAL

GOYER

LAVALLÉE

BEDFORD

JUPITER

ARGUS

BEAUCHAMP

BERTHIER

BELOEIL

PLUTON

MERCURE

MARS

AMOS

ARGUS

AMOUR

ALLAN

CÔTE

BOUL. SALABERRY

Mercier

PLACE
LAURIER

138

THIBERT

DURANCEAU

BARRÉ

RANG ST-CHARLES

DES ROSSIGNOLS

LE RENARD

DES MOUETTES

DES PERDRIX

ST-FRANÇOIS

MARLEAU

LE RENARD

DES PINSONS

LE LIÈVRE

DU PARC

DES ÉCUREUILS

MONGRAIN

HÉBERT

LÉVIS

LAVAL

LAIZON

LEMOYNE

LORRAINE

BOURDEAU

PRUDHOMME

BOURGOIN

GIROUX

VALDREUIL

ST-LOUIS

GABY

ST-JEAN-BAPTISTE

ST-JOSEPH

LACOSTE

A

P

V

BOURDEAU

VAUDREUIL

VINIER

ST-RENÉ

BONNIER

WILLIAM

GAÉTAN

YOLANDE

VALLÉE

ST-CLÉMENT

FAUBERT

PINCOURT

VERVAIS

SAUVÉ

TERREBONNE

LÉGAULT

REID

DE L'ÉGLISE

ST-DENIS

PERRON

PLAMONDON

POIRIER

PIEDMONT

BROMONT

BOUL. ST-JOSEPH

LES TILLEULS

LES ÉRABLES

ST-CLÉMENT

BOUDREAU

DES ORMES

ST-LAURENT

DES CYPRÈS

ST-CLÉMENT

DES MERISIERS

DES SAPINS

DES PLANES

P

ALONDE

DES NOYERS

DES MÉLÈZES

BOUL. DE L'ÉGLISE

MTÉE ST-ISIDORE

X

Y

Z

14   15   16

12   13

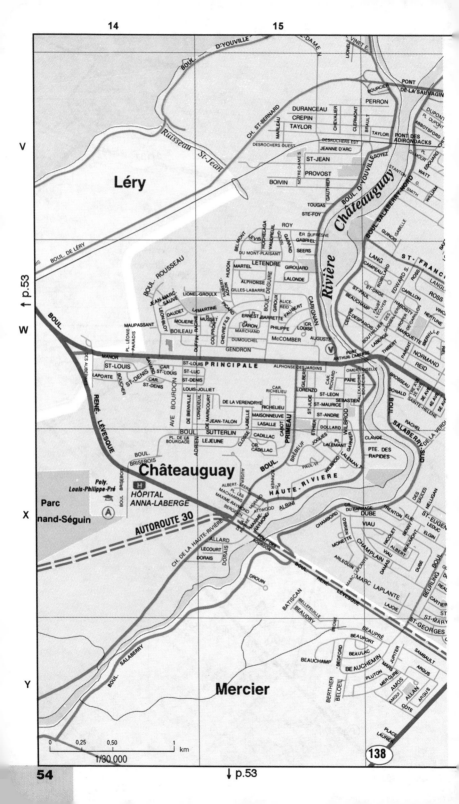

↑ p.53

↓ p.53

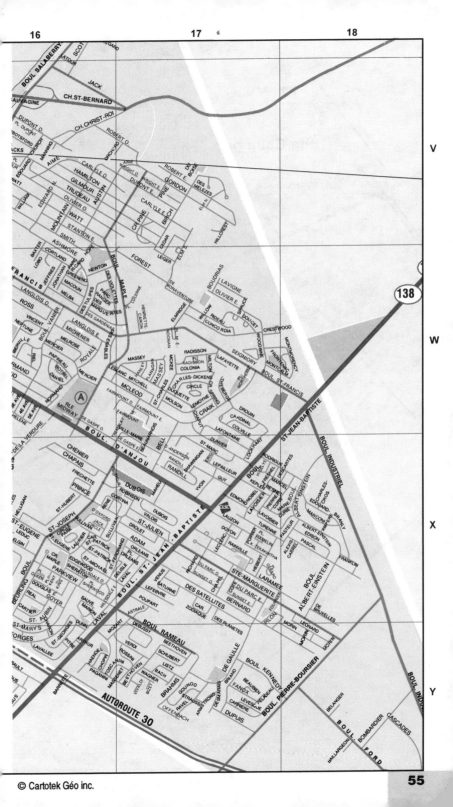

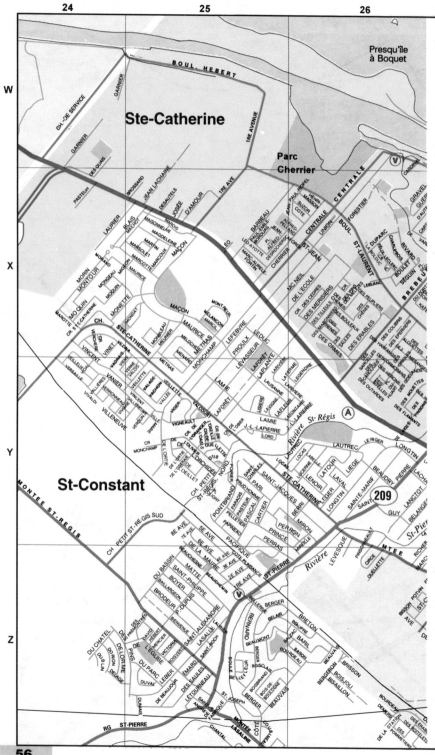

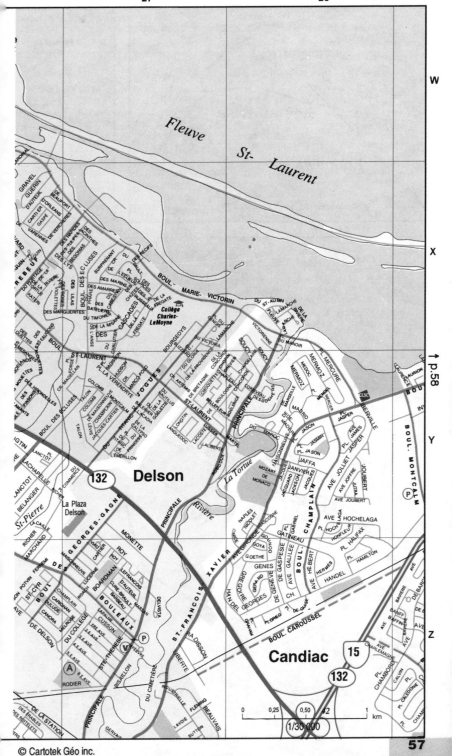

Fleuve St- Laurent

Collège Charles-LeMoyne

BOUL- MARIE- VICTORIN

Delson

132

La Plaza Delson

St-Pierre

La Tortue

MOZART DE MONACO

Riviere

Candiac

15

132

↑ p.58

BOUL. CAROUSSEL

0   0,25   0,50   0,2   1 km

1/30 000

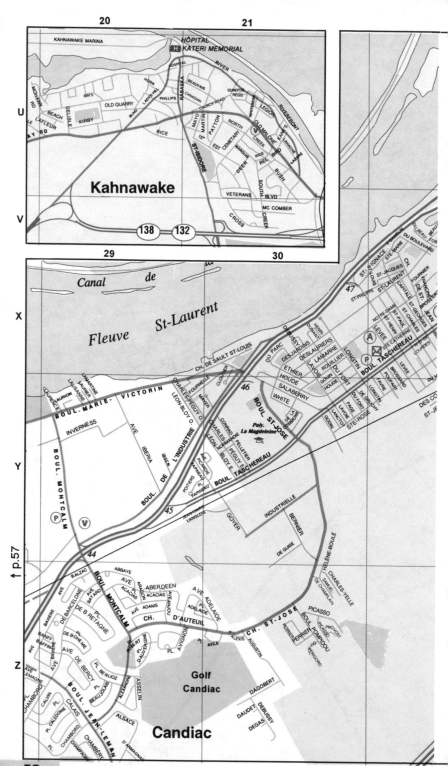

Kahnawake

Candiac

Canal de St-Laurent

Fleuve St-Laurent

Golf Candiac

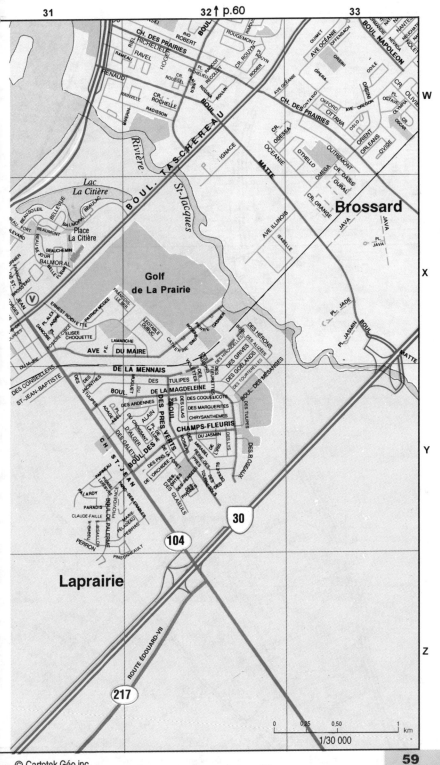

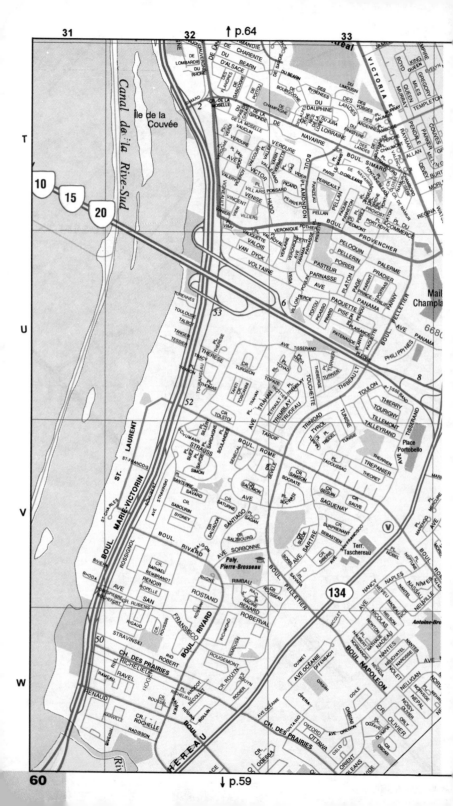

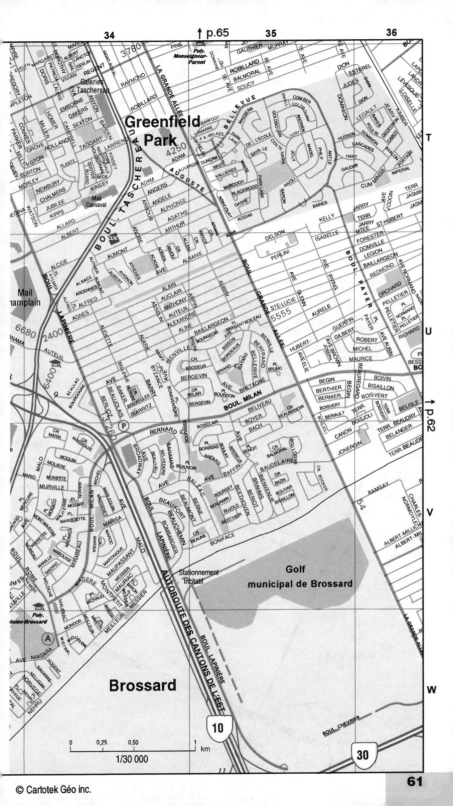

→ p.62

Greenfield Park

Brossard

Golf municipal de Brossard

Stationnement Incitatif

Mail Champlain

Mail Carnaval

Galeries Taschereau

0   0,25   0,50   1 km
1/30 000

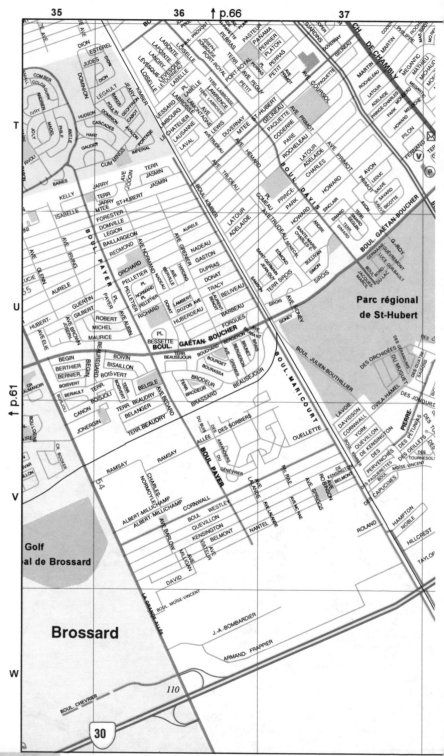

↑ p.61

Parc régional
de St-Hubert

Golf
al de Brossard

Brossard

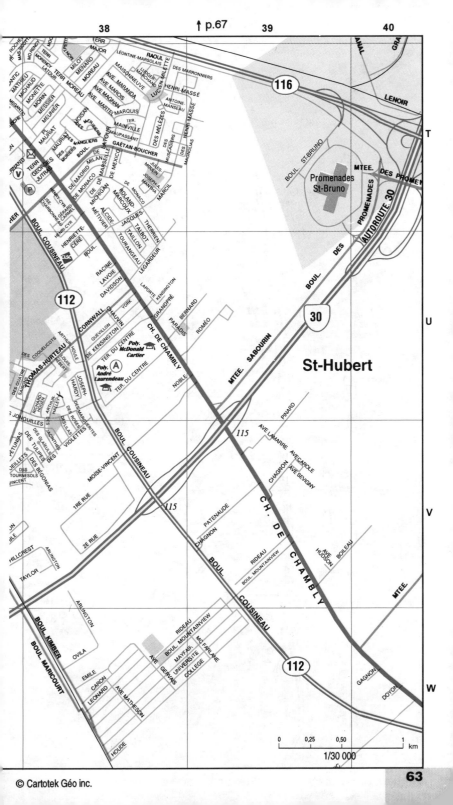

38 39 40

116

LENOIR

T

Promenades
St-Bruno

St-Hubert

112

30

U

115

115

V

W

© Cartotek Géo inc.

0   0,25   0,50   1
km
1/30 000

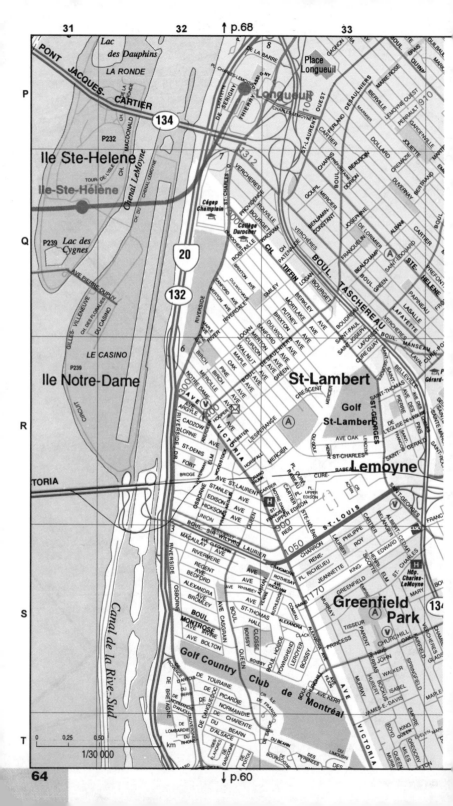

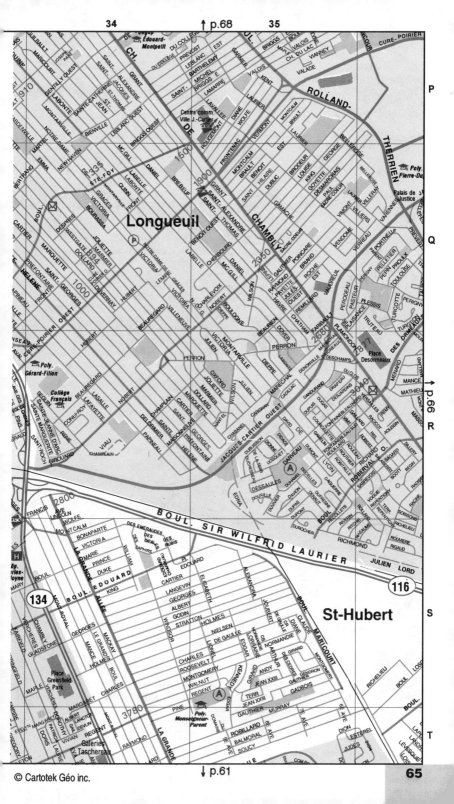

Longueuil

St-Hubert

ROLLAND-THERRIEN

CHAMBLY

BOUL. SIR WILFRID LAURIER

BOUL. MARICOURT

LA GRANDE ALLÉE

BOUL. ÉDOUARD

134

116

P

Q

R

S

T

→ p.66

Poly. Pierre-Du

Palais de Justice

Poly. Gérard-Filion

Collège Français

Centre comm. Ville J.-Cartier

Cégep Édouard-Montpetit

Place Desormeaux

Poly. Monseigneur-Parent

Place Greenfield Park

Galeries Taschereau

Hôp. Charles-Lemoyne

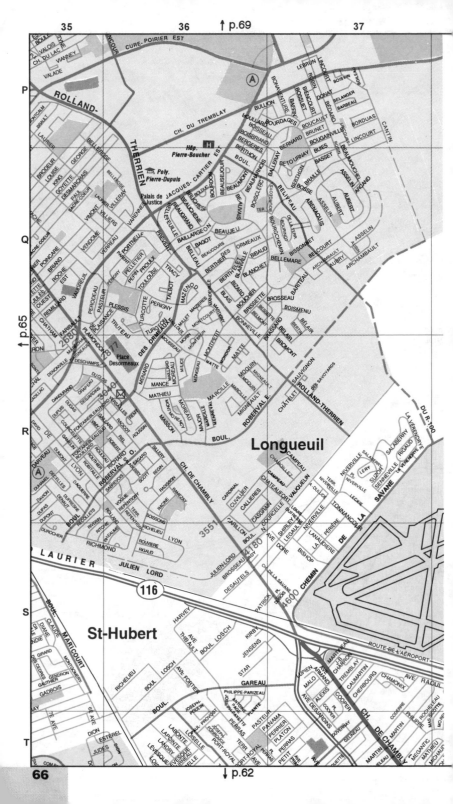

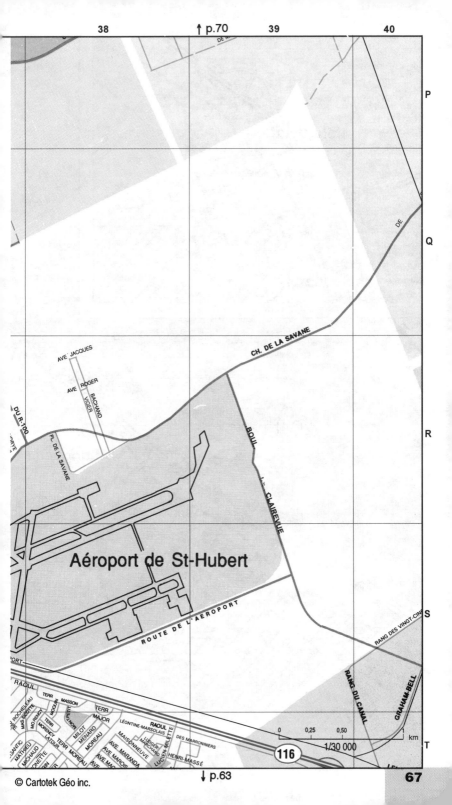

P

Q

AVE JACQUES

AVE ROGER

BACHAND

VIGER

CH. DE LA SAVANE

DU R-100

PL. DE LA SAVANE

BOUL.

CLAIREVUE

R

Aéroport de St-Hubert

ROUTE DE L'AÉROPORT

S

RANG DES VINGT-CINQ

RAOUL

TERR

MASSON

TERR

MAJOR

LÉONTINE-MARSOLAIS

RAOUL

DES MARRONNIERS

RANG DU CANAL

GRAHAM-BELL

TERR

MENARD

MILOT

MOREAU

AVE MARANDA

MAISONNEUVE

LUCIEN-MILETTE

HENRI-MASSÉ

116

0   0,25   0,50

1/30 000

km

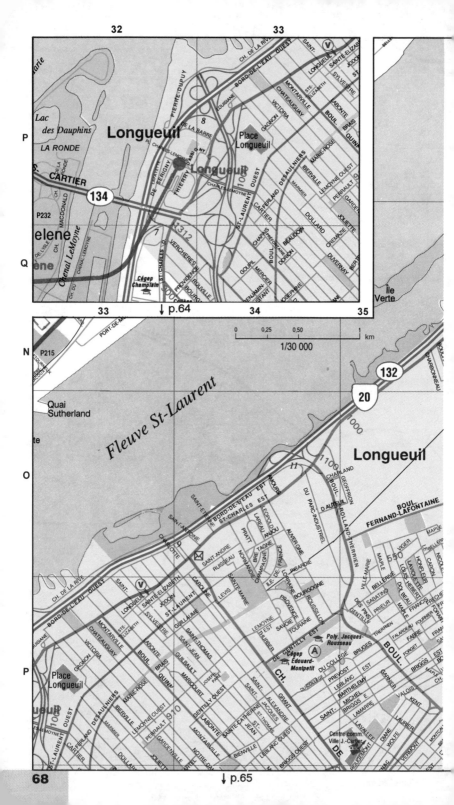

↓ p.64

↓ p.65

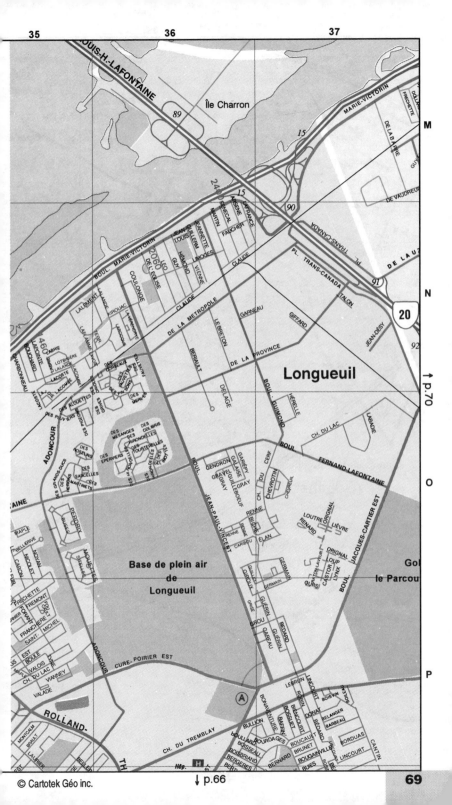

Île Charron

LOUIS-H.-LAFONTAINE

MARIE-VICTORIN

89

15

M

240

15

90

PL. TRANS-CANADA

DE LAUZ

91

92

DE VAUDREU

N

20

BOUL. MARIE-VICTORIN

2060

DE L'ÉGLISE

460

JEAN-P
LOUIS

GUILLERM

JEANNETTE

MARTIN

SÉNÉCAL

ARSÈNE

FAUCHER

LAFRANCE

LIMOGES

VIENNE

GUY

RÉMOND

LÉO

COULONGE

LALEMANT

LALANDE

KIROUAC

LAVÉRENDRYE

LAROCQUE

CLAUDE

CLAUDE

DE LA MÉTROPOLE

GARNEAU

GIFFARD

TALON

JEAN-DÉSY

Longueuil

LEBRETON

DE LA PROVINCE

BÉRAULT

BOUL. GUIMOND

HÉRELLE

LABADIE

CH. DU LAC

DÉLAGE

BOUL.

BOUL.

FERNAND-LAFONTAINE

ABBIE

LOTBINIÈRE

LALANDE

LACOSTE

LACOSTE

LACOMBE

LAFLAMME

PAORI

LAROCQUE

DES PLUVIERS

CORBEUIL

DES ALOUETTES

DES

DES MERLES

ADONCOUR

CHARBONNEAU

BOUCHARD

LACROIX

ROBICHARD

BERD

DES ROSELINS

DES GRANDS-DUCS

HÉRONS

DES SARCELLES

DES MARTINETS

DES MÉSANGES

DES ÉPERVIERS

DES HIRONDELLES

DES COLIBRIS

DES TOURTERELLES

DES GEL

GENDRON

GRAVEL

GAGRAY

GARNEAU

GALAISE

GUILLEBOEUF

GRAY

CH. DU CERF

CHEVROTIN

CHEVROTIN

CHEVREUIL

BOUL.

RENNE

RENNE

BICHE

CARIBOU

JEAN-PAUL-VINCENT

ÉLAN

LOUTRE

RENARD

ORIGNAL

LIÈVRE

ORIGNAL

LOUP

CASTOR

LYNX

OURS

GERMAIN

GERMAIN

LAVEUR

Gol

le Parcou

FONTAINE

MAPLE

BELLERIVE

NOLAN

NICOLET

CARON

PERDRIX

MUSÉE

ALOUETTES

STÉRÊLÉE

Base de plein air
de
Longueuil

GUILLA

GIROUX

GUÉRIN

GRISÉ

BROU

GUÉRIN

GUÉRIN

BÉDARD

GAREAU

FRÉCHETTE

TREMONT

FORANT

FRANCHÈRE

SAINT-MICHEL

EST

BOLLE

VALOIS PL

CH. DU LAC PL

VIANNEY

VALADE

ADONCOUR

CURÉ-POIRIER EST

LEBRUN

LINCOURT

ROBIN

BOISVIN

P

ROLLAND-

MONTCALM

BENAULT

LAURIER

BELLE

CH. DU TREMBLAY

TH

Hôp. **H**

(A)

BULLION

BOUL.LAB

BOURDAGES

BOISSEAU

BERGERES

BOISBRIAND

BERT

BERNARD

BONNAVENTURE

BUES

BOUGAINVILLE

BRUNET

BOUCAULT

BAFFIN

BLISHCOURT

BOSSUET

DONAT

BÉLANGER

BÉDARD

BARBEAU

BORDUAS

LINCOURT

CANTIN

→ p.70

O

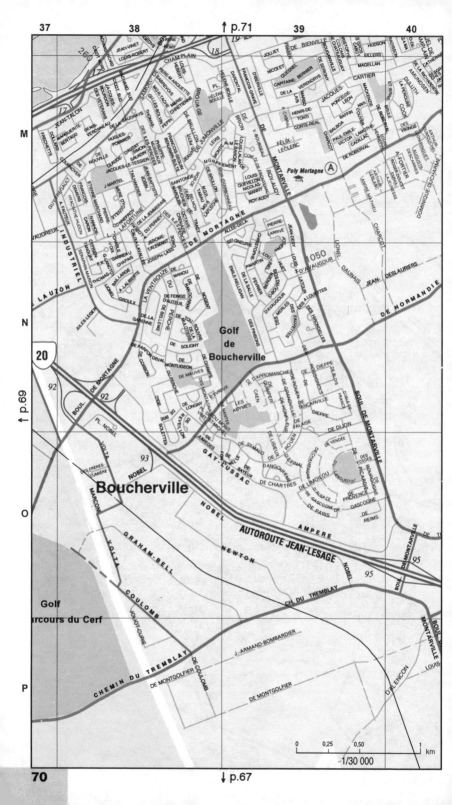

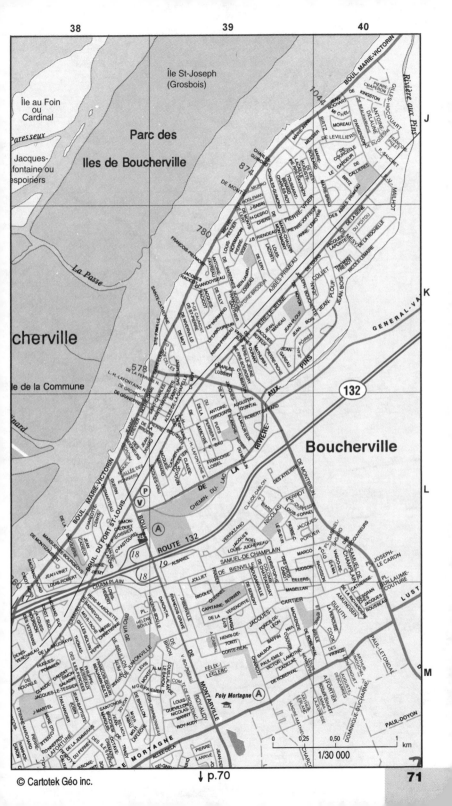

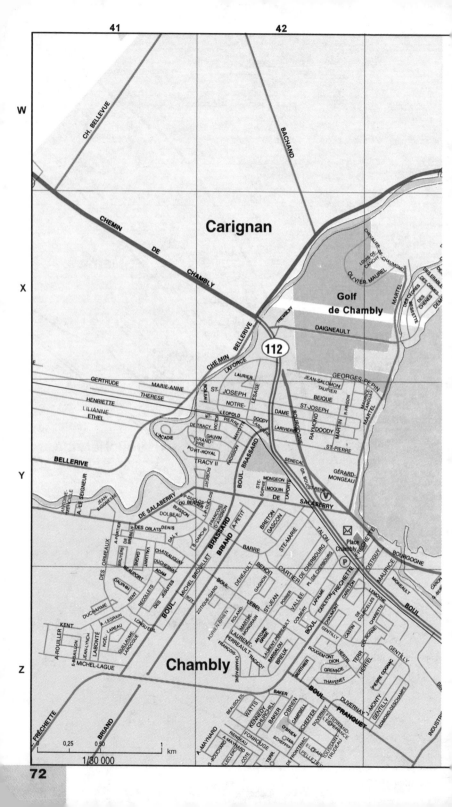

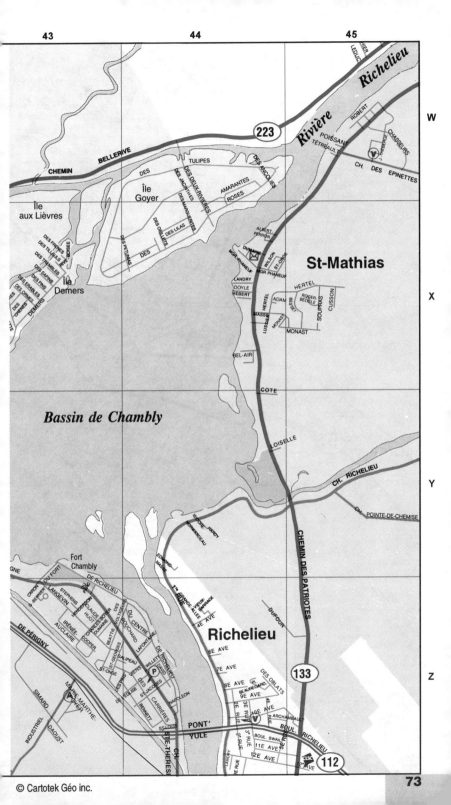

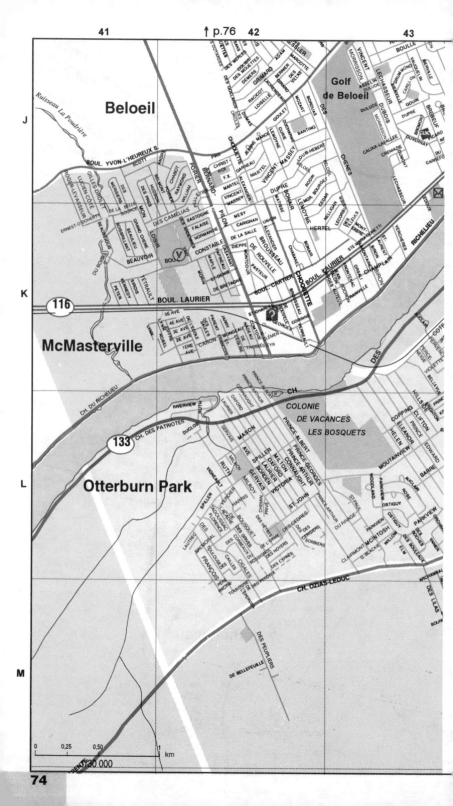

Beloeil

Golf de Beloeil

Ruisseau La Poudrière

J

BOUL. YVON-L'HEUREUX S.

K

116

BOUL. LAURIER

McMasterville

COLONIE DE VACANCES LES BOSQUETS

133 CH. DES PATRIOTES

L

Otterburn Park

CH. OZIAS-LEDUC

M

0 0,25 0,50 1
km

1/30 000

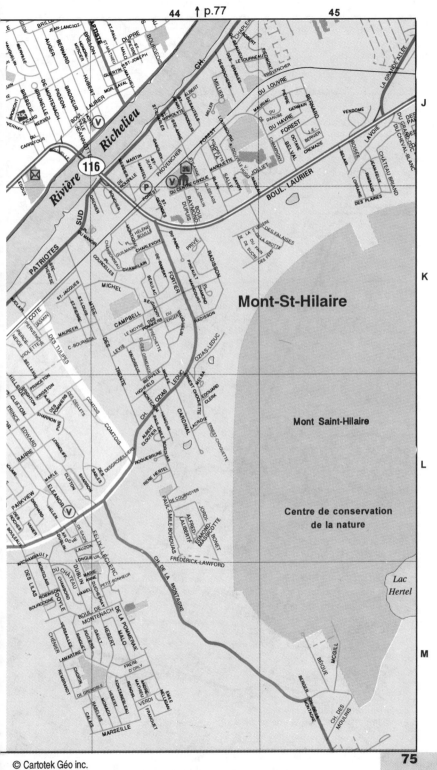

Mont-St-Hilaire

Mont Saint-Hilaire

Centre de conservation
de la nature

Lac
Hertel

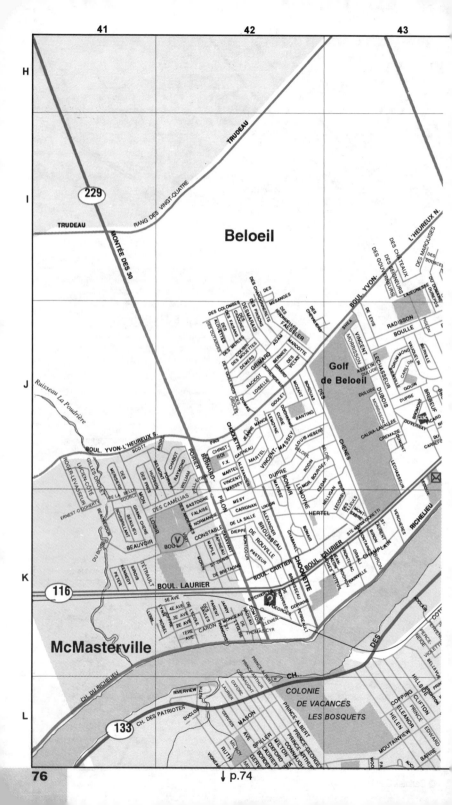

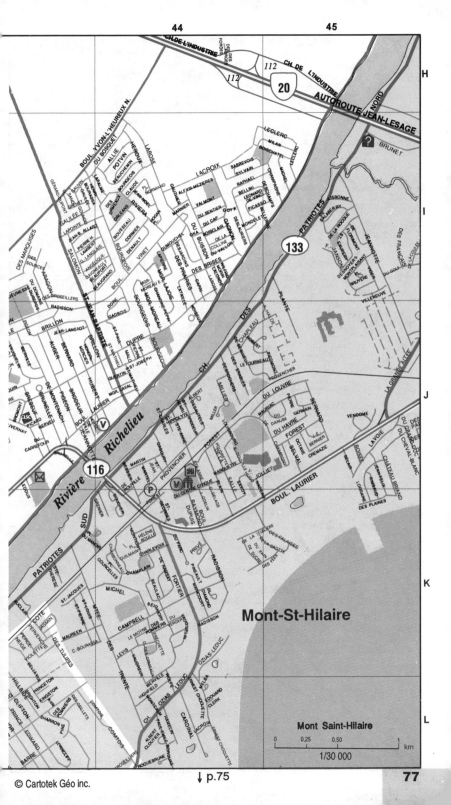

© Cartotek Géo inc.

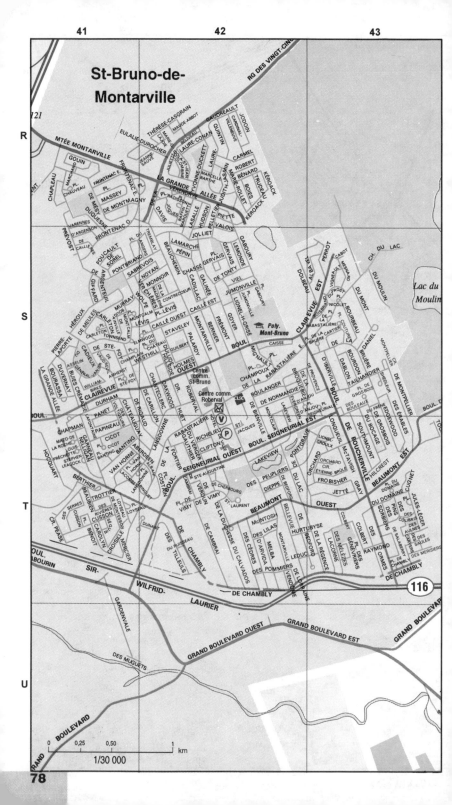

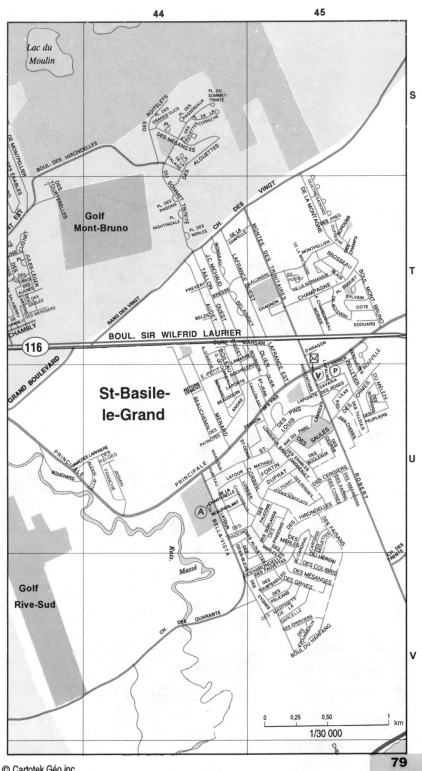

St-Basile-le-Grand

© Cartotek Géo inc.

79

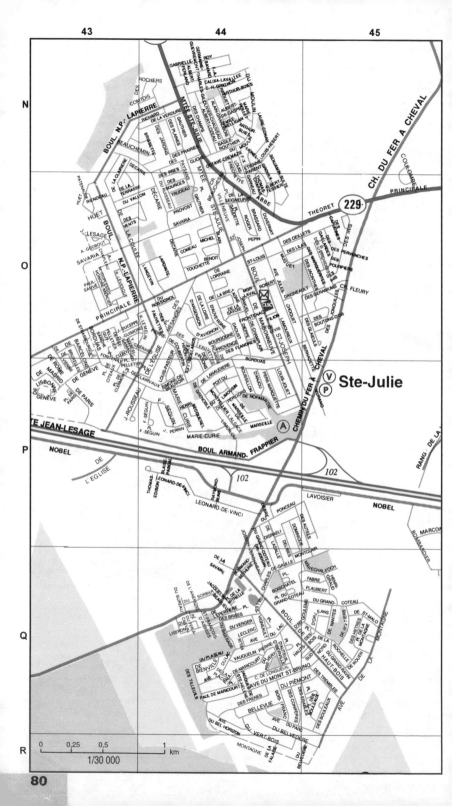

Ste-Julie

80

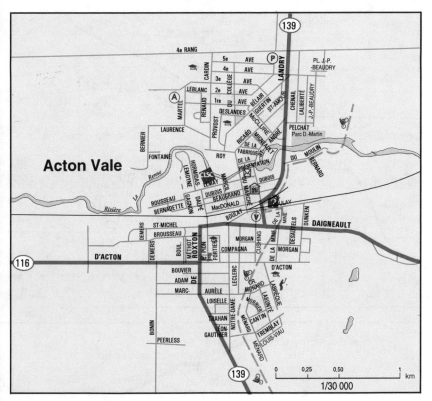

Acton Vale

4e RANG
139
5e AVE
4e AVE
3e AVE
2e AVE
1re AVE
DU COLLÈGE
CARDIN
LEBLANC
MARTEL
RENAUD
PROVOST
DESLANDES
BÉLAIR
GUÉTIN
ST-AMOUR
McCLURE
RICARD
MIGNAULT
ST-ANDRÉ
DE LA FABRIQUE
DE LA PRÉSENTATION
CHENAIL
LAUBERTÉ
J.-P.-BEAUDRY
PL. J.-P.-BEAUDRY
LANDRY
PELCHAT
Parc D.-Martin
BERNIER
LAURENCE
FONTAINE
ROY
HORMIDAS
LEMOYNE
S.-DALPÉ
GAGNON
LEMAY
MADORE
RONDEAU
DUBOIS
DU MOULIN
BERNARD
Renne
Le
Rivière
ROUSSEAU
BERNADETTE
DUBOIS
BEAUGRAND
MacDONALD
GAGNON
PICHÉ
BOULAY
BOULAY
DAIGNEAULT
DE LA MINE
DUNKEN
DEMERS
ST-MICHEL
BROUSSEAU
DEMERS
BOUL.
MÉTHOT
ROXTON
ST PION
FORTIER
MORGAN
COMPAGNA
CUSHING
DE LA MINE
DÉSAUTELS
MORGAN
D'ACTON
116
D'ACTON
BOUVIER
ADAM
MARC-
DE
LECLERC
AURÈLE
LOISELLE
NOTRE-DAME
CR. MÉNARD
MORABER
LABRÈCQUE
LABINTÉ
CANTIN
TREMBLAY
LOUIS-VIAU
MÉNARD
MÉNARD
BONIN
TRAHAN
LÉON-GAUTHIER
PEERLESS
139

0   0,25   0,50   1
km
1/30 000

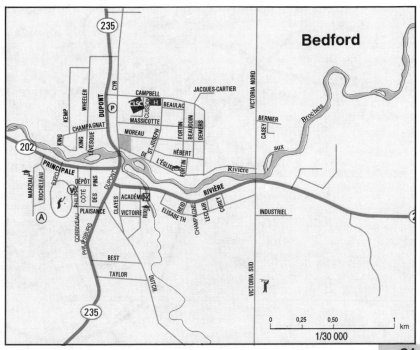

235

Bedford

CYR
DUPONT
CAMPBELL
JACQUES-CARTIER
VICTORIA NORD
WHEELER
KEMP
CUSSON
H
BEAULAC
MASSICOTTE
BERNIER
CASEY
Broches
CHAMPAGNAT
MOREAU
FORTIN
BEAUDOIN
DEMERS
202
KING
KING
LÉVESQUE
DE ST-JOSEPH
HÉBERT
aux
ÉPEL
PRINCIPALE
ROCHELEAU
DÉPÔT
PHILLIPS
CÔTE
DES PINS
DUPONT
L'ÉGLISE
FORTIN
RIVIÈRE
Rivière
MARZIAL
CORRIVEAU
PHILLSBURG
PLAISANCE
CLAYES
ACADÉMIE
VICTOIRE
ROY
REED
CHAMPAGNE
LECLAR
CAREY
INDUSTRIEL
ÉLISABETH
VICTORIA SUD
BEST
TAYLOR
DUTIN
235

0   0,25   0,50   1
km
1/30 000

81

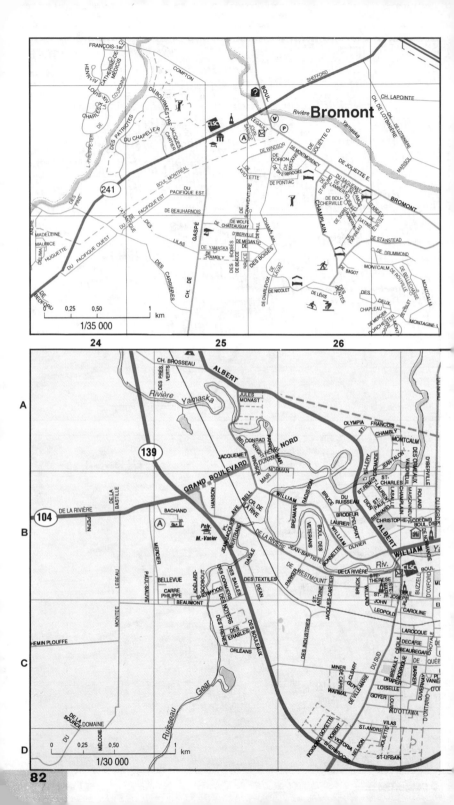

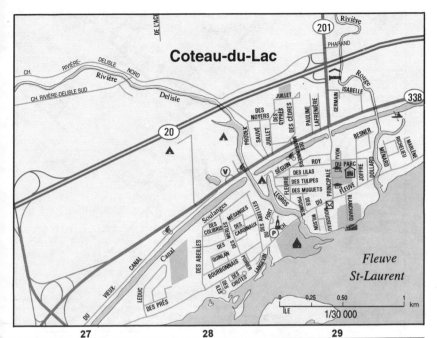

Coteau-du-Lac

Fleuve St-Laurent

ÎLE
1/30 000

27　　　　28　　　　29

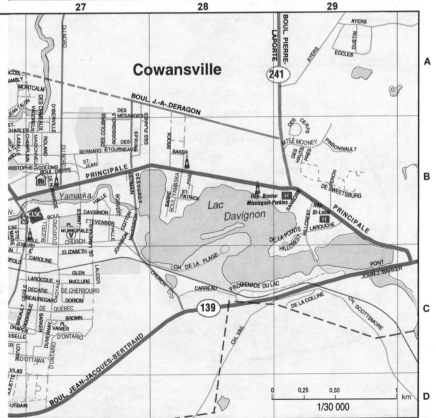

Cowansville

Lac Davignon

1/30 000

A
B
C
D

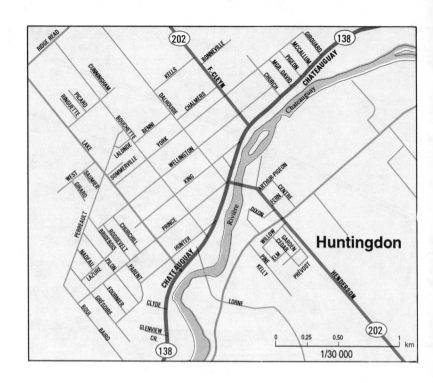

Huntingdon

202 · 138 · CHATEAUGUAY

RIDGE ROAD · CUNNINGHAM · KELLS · BONNEVILLE · F. CLEYN · GIROUARD · McCALLUM · PIGEON · MGR-DAVID · CHURCH · PICARD · RINGUETTE · DALHOUSE · CHALMERS · BOUCHETTE · BENNI · YORK · WELLINGTON · LAKE · LALONDE · SOMMERVILLE · KING · Chateauguay · WEST · SAUMIER · GIRARD · ARTHUR PIGEON · FERN · CENTRE · PERREAULT · CHURCHILL · ROOSEVELT · PRINCE · HUNTER · DIXON · Rivière · BRISEBOIS · PARENT · WILLOW · CEDAR · GARDEN · NADEAU · PILON · ELM · PINE · LAZURE · FOURNIER · KELLY · PRÉVOST · GRÉGOIRE · CHATEAUGUAY · HENDERSON · BOUL · BAIRD · CLYDE · LORNE · GLENVIEW CR. · 138 · 202

0   0,25   0,50   km
1/30 000

---

11   12   13

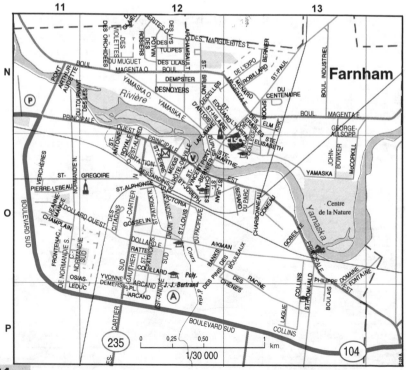

Farnham

N   O   P

235 · 104

0   0,25   0,50   km
1/30 000

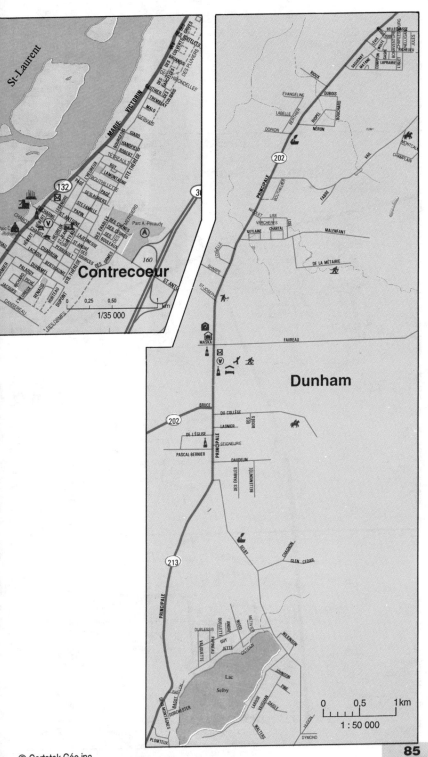

St-Laurent

Contrecoeur

0   0,25   0,50
km
1/35 000

132
30
160

202

Dunham

202
213

Lac
Selby

0   0,5   1 km
1 : 50 000

© Cartotek Géo inc.

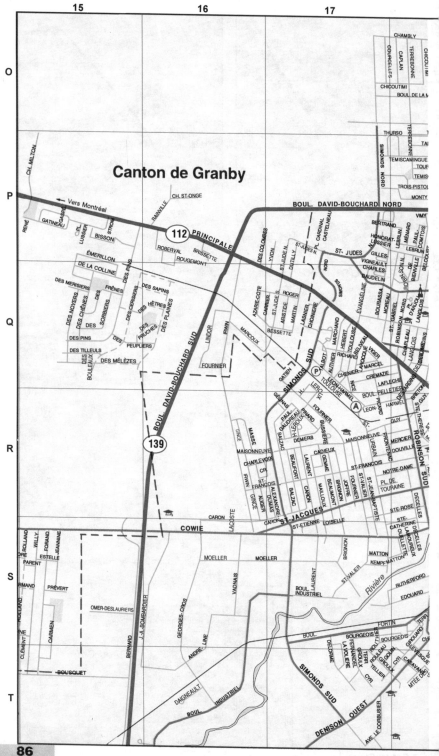

Canton de Granby

← Vers Montréal

112 PRINCIPALE

139

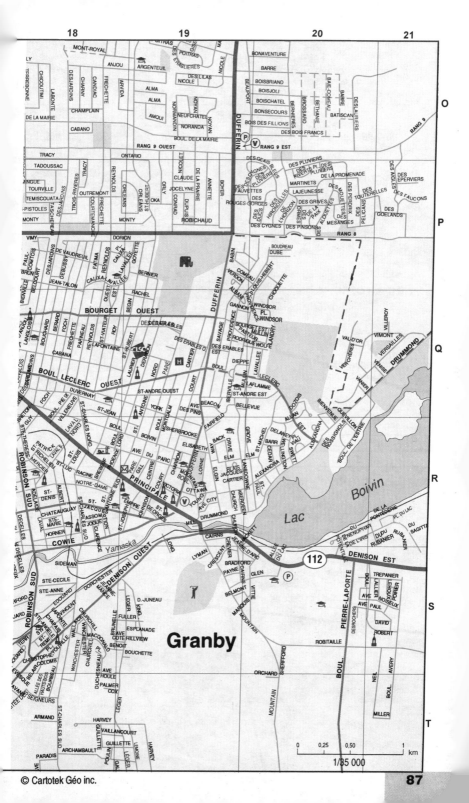

Granby

112

© Cartotek Géo inc.

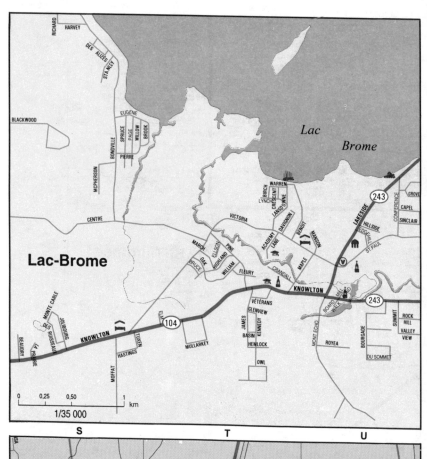

Lac
Brome

Lac-Brome

KNOWLTON

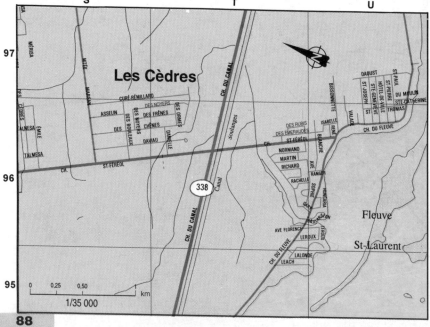

Les Cèdres

Fleuve
St-Laurent

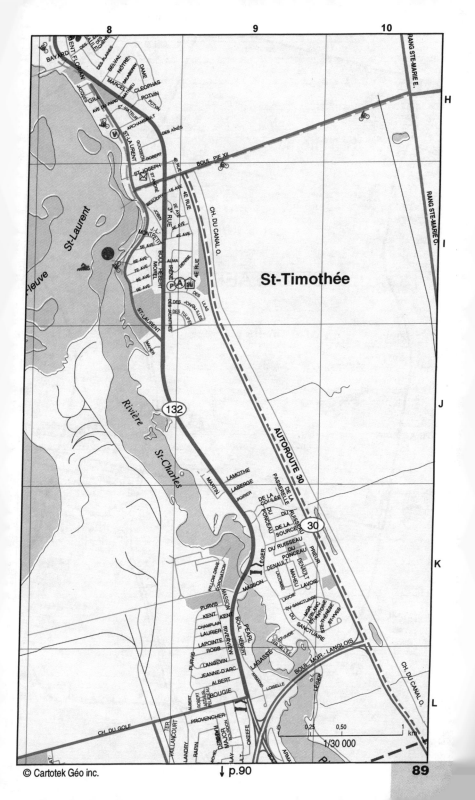

St-Timothée

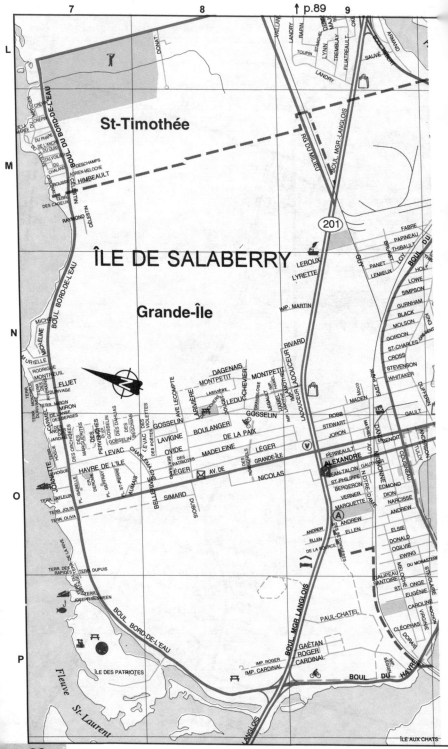

L

M

St-Timothée

ÎLE DE SALABERRY

Grande-Île

N

201

LEROUX
LYRETTE

IMP. MARTIN

FABRE
PAPINEAU
THIBAULT
BRUNET
PANET
LEMIEUX
HOLT
LOWE
SIMPSON
GURNHAM
BLACK
MOLSON
GORDON
ST-CHARLES
CROSS
STEVENSON
WHITAKER

RIVARD

DAGENAIS
MONTPETIT　MONTPETIT
LARIVIÈRE
LEDUC
LECHEVIER
GOSSELIN

GOSSELIN
LAVIGNE　BOULANGER
LEVAC　OVIDE　DE LA PAIX
CHARLES　MADELEINE　LÉGER
LÉGER　GRANDE-ÎLE
AV. DE　NICOLAS

ROBB
STEWART
JORON

PERREAULT
ALEXANDRE
JEAN-TALON　GAUTHIER
ST-PHILIPPE
BERGERON　NOTRE-DAME
VERNER　DION
MARQUETTE　NARCISSE
ANDREW

MADEN

GAULT

BENOIT

COUSINEAU
EDMOND

O

HAVRE DE L'ÎLE

SIMARD

ANDREW
ELLEN
DE LA SOURCE

ANDREW
ELLEN

ELSIE
DONALD
OGILVIE
EWING
DU MONASTÈRE
STE-CLAIRE
SALIPEAU　ST. ONGE
SANTOIRE
EUGÉNIE
CAROLINE
VIRGINIE
CLÉOPHAS
DORAIS

P

ÎLE DES PATRIOTES

Fleuve
St-Laurent

BOUL BORD-DE-L'EAU

BOUL MGR LANGLOIS

GAÉTAN
ROGER
CARDINAL

IMP. ROGER
IMP. CARDINAL

PAUL-CHATEL

BOUL　DU HAVRE

ÎLE AUX CHATS

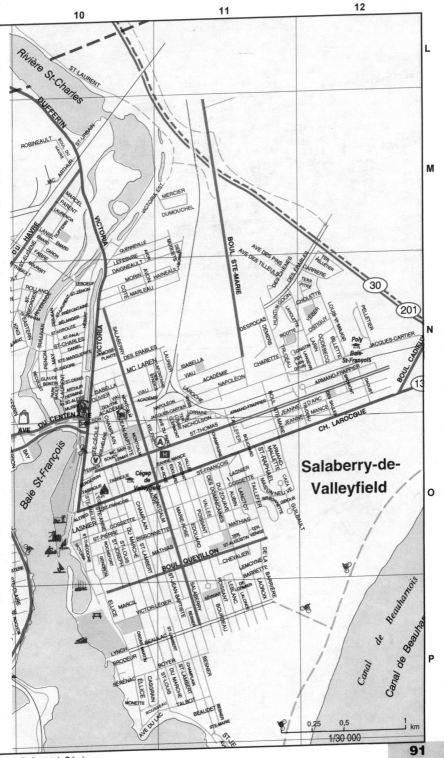

Salaberry-de-Valleyfield

© Cartotek Géo inc.

91

1/30 000

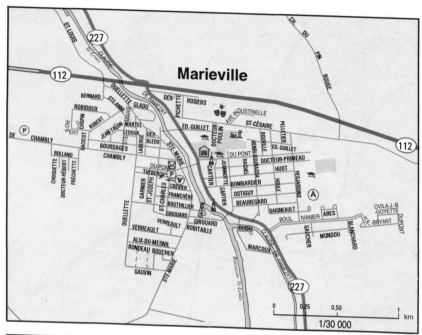

Marieville

1/30 000

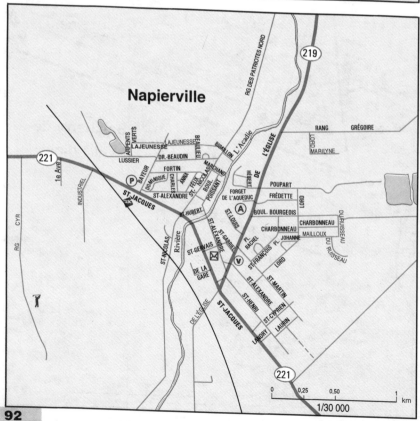

Napierville

1/30 000

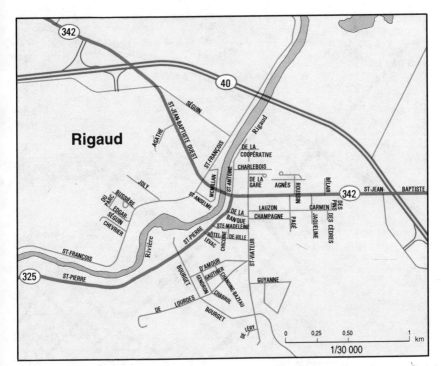

Rigaud

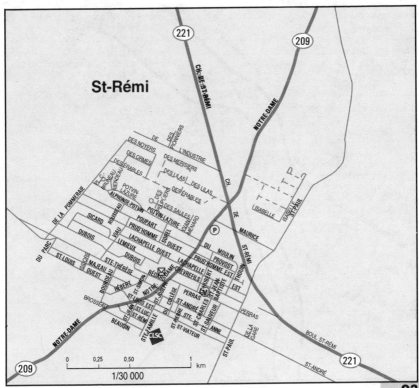

St-Rémi

© Cartotek Géo inc.

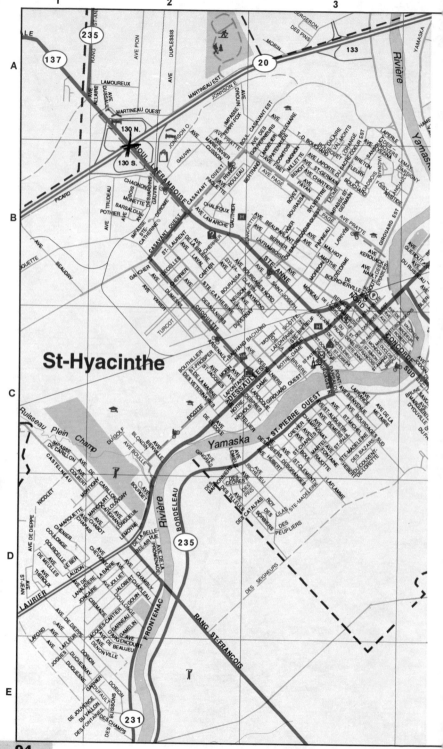

St-Hyacinthe

94

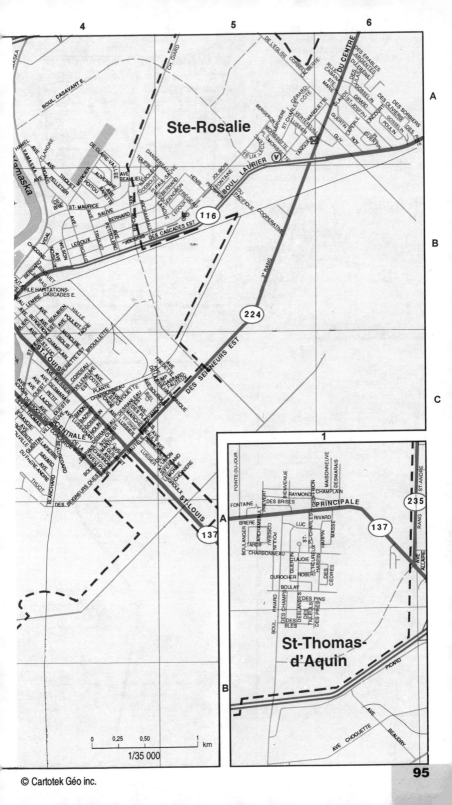

Ste-Rosalie

St-Thomas-d'Aquin

0   0,25   0,50   km
1/35 000

© Cartotek Géo inc.

95

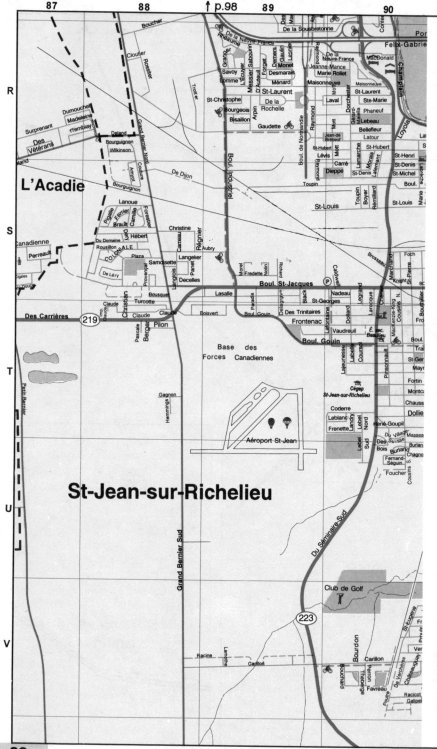

Boucher

De la Neuve-France

De la Sousbretonne

Port

Félix-Gabriel

R

Cloutier   Rossiter

Granger   Rhéaume

Savoy   D'Auteuil   Forget   Demers
Lomme   Monet   Gaulin   Lernier
Ménard   Desmarais

De la Neuve-France

MacDonald

Jeanne-Mance   Marie Rollet

Maisonneuve

Maisonneuve

Trotter

St-Christophe

St-Laurent

Laval

St-Laurent   Ste-Marie

Surprenant

Dumouchel

Madeleine

Tremblay

De la Rochelle

Dorchester
Gérard-Amélia   Phaneuf

Lebeau

Bourgeois   Bisaillon

Arpin   Alpin

Raymond

Bellefleur

Gaudette

Latour

Deland
Bourguignon
Wilkinson

Jean-de-Brébeuf

St-Hubert

St-Hubert

La

Amyot
Coulure

Grand Bernier Nord

De Dijon

Lévis

Mott

Carré
Dieppe

Lamarche   Morais
Lafément

St-Denis

St-Henri

St-Denis   St-Michel

L'Acadie

Bourguignon

Boul. Industriel

Toupin

Boul. de Normandie

Raymond

Boul.

Lanoue

St-Louis

Toupin
Boyer
Rémillard

St-Louis

Marie

Pigale
Ferrier

Camille
Forestier

Canadienne

Du Quai
Hébert

Christine

Brault

COLONIALE
Rousillon

Carreau
Régnier

Brosseau

Foch

S

Perreault

De Léry

Plaza

Samoisette

Langelier

Aubry

Morel   Fredette   Nolin

Richard

Caldwell

St-Pierre

Knight

Panet

Decelles

Boul. St-Jacques

P

Lasalle

Claude
Turcotte

Bousque

Boisvert

Paradis

Delagrave

Black

Nadeau
St-Georges

Legrand

Larocque

Chénier

Boul.

Des Carrières

(219)

Temp.
Gauthier

Pascale
Berger

Claude   Claude
Pilon

Boul. Gouin

Des Trinitaires

Frontenac

Lafontaine

Dollard

Tra

St-Ger

Christian

Vaudreuil

Boul. Gouin

É. sec.
Beaulieu

Mayr

Base   des
Forces   Canadiennes

Lajeunesse

Labelle
Coursol

Pinsonnault

Fortin

Fro

Montca

Petit-Bernier

Gagnon

Hemmings

Cégep
St-Jean-sur-Richelieu

Coderre

Leblanc
Frenette

Landry

Lebel Nord

René-Goupil

Chauss

Dollie

T

Aéroport St-Jean

Du Village
Des
Bois

Lebel Sud

Burland
Burland

Massea

Suisse

Chagno

Fernand-
Séguin

Foucher

Cousins S.

U

St-Jean-sur-Richelieu

Grand Bernier Sud

Du Séminaire Sud

Club de Golf

(223)

Bourdon

St-Eugène

V

Racine

Lamothe

Carillon

Carillon

Bouchard
Thibodge

Peron

Favreau

De Verchères

Châteauguay

Ver

Poire

Racicot
Galipe

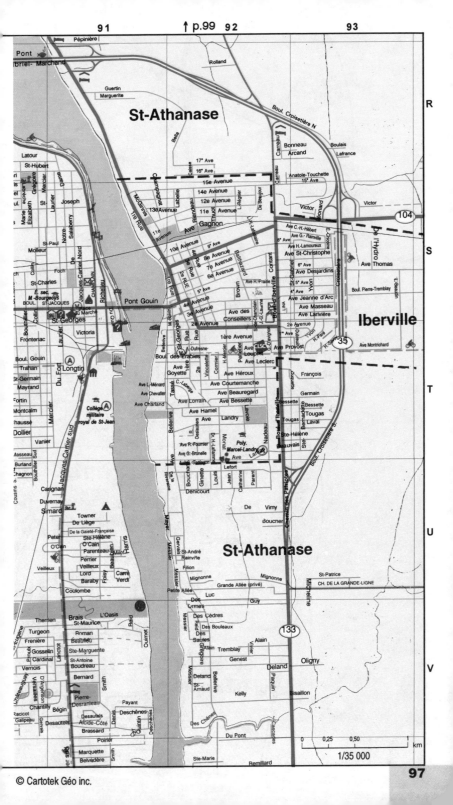

St-Athanase

Iberville

St-Athanase

1/35 000

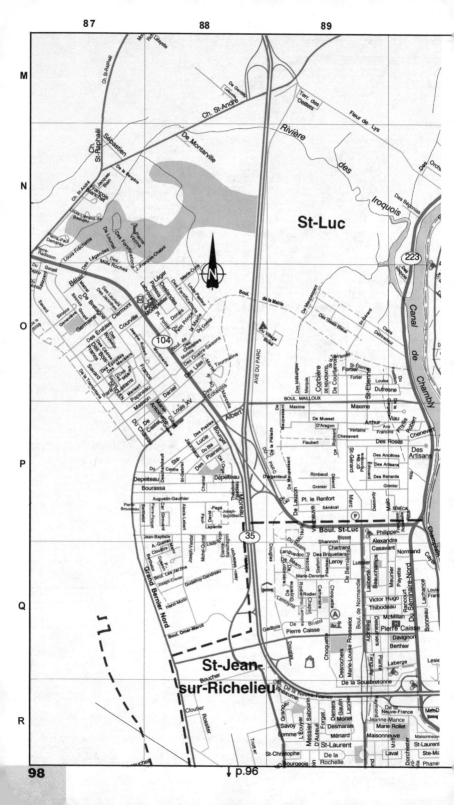

↓ p.96

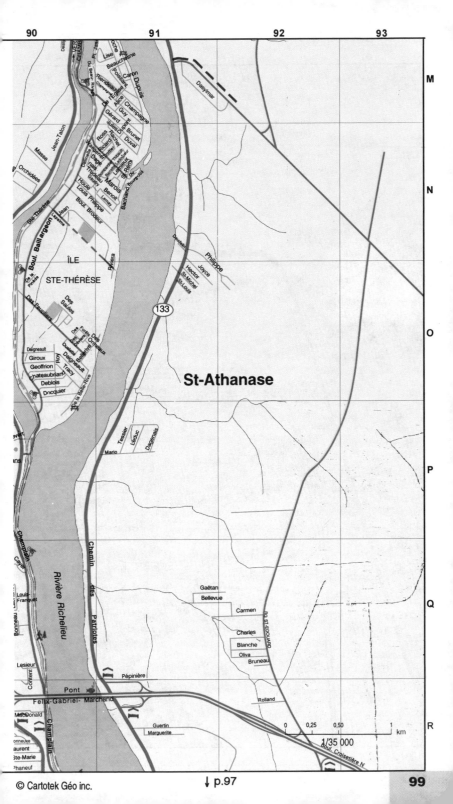

St-Athanase

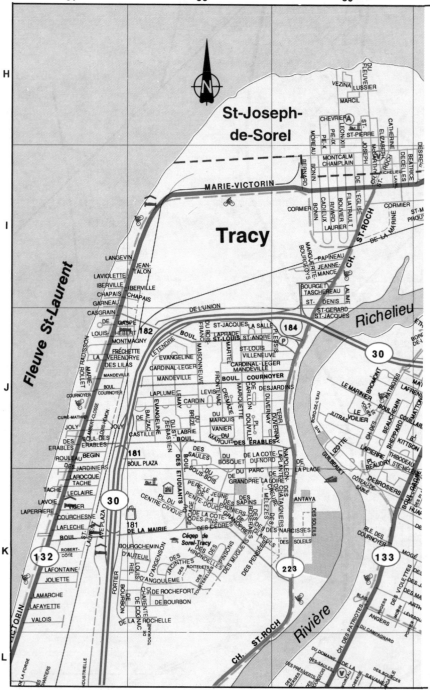

St-Joseph-
de-Sorel

Tracy

Fleuve St-Laurent

Richelieu

Rivière

MARIE-VICTORIN

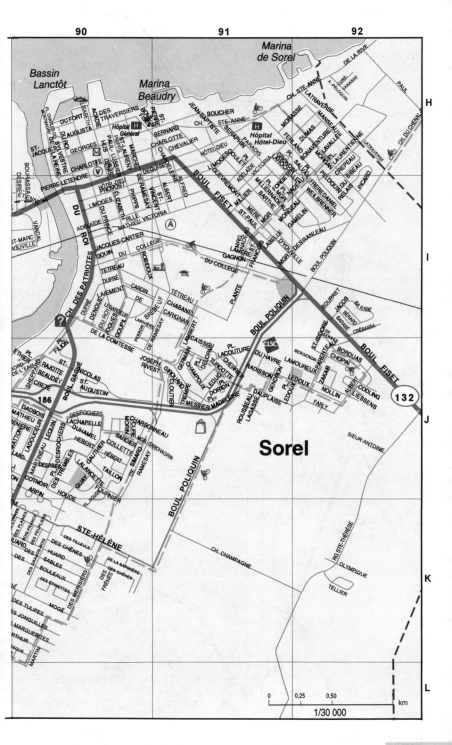

Sorel

1/30 000

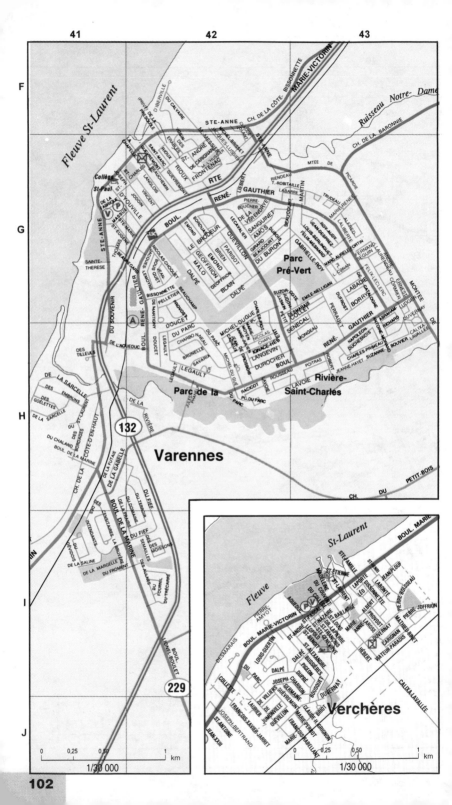

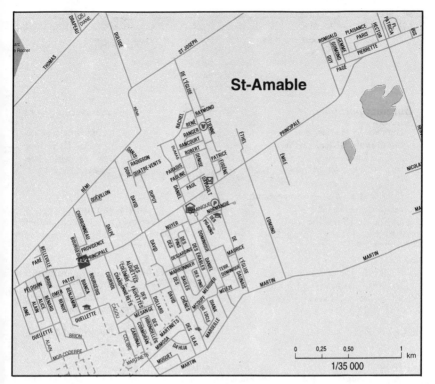

St-Amable

1/35 000

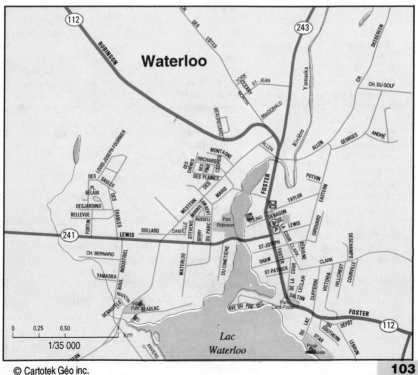

Waterloo

Lac Waterloo

1/35 000

© Cartotek Géo inc.

Tourisme Montérégie
11, Chemin Marieville, Rougemont, Qc, J0L 1M0
(450) 674-5555, 1-800-363-7777
(Internet) : **www.tourisme-monteregie.qc.ca**

Bureaux permanents :

Bureau de tourisme et des congrès de St-Hyacinthe
2090, rue Cherrier, St-Hyacinthe
(450) 774-7276, 1-800-849-7276

Corporation de développement touristique de la Vallée-du-Richelieu
1080, ch. des Patriotes Nord, Mont-St-Hilaire
(450) 536-0395, 1-888-736-0395

Office de tourisme de la Rive-Sud de Montréal
205, ch. Chambly, Longueuil
(450) 670-7293

Permanent Offices

Office de tourisme du Bas-Richelieu
92, ch. des Patriotes, Sorel
(450) 746-9441, 1-800-474-9441

Office de tourisme et des congrès du Haut-Richelieu
31, rue Frontenac, St-Jean-sur-Richelieu
(450) 542-9090

Office de tourisme du Suroît
30, avenue du Centenaire, bur.126
Salaberry-de-Valleyfield
(450) 377-7676, 1-800-378-7648

Bureaux saisonniers : / *Seasonal Offices*

Acton Vale
960, rue Boulay
(450) 546-7642

Beloeil
35, boul. Laurier
(450) 536-2921

Chambly
1900, avenue Bourgogne
(450) 658-0321

Châteauguay
54, rue Salaberry Sud
(450) 698-3193

Île-Perrot
190, boul. Métropolitain
(514) 453-0855

La Prairie
1202, ch. de St-Jean
(450) 444-6720

Roxton Falls
240, rue Notre-Dame
(450) 548-5775

St-Césaire
172, route 112
(450) 469-1188

St-Hubert
5300, ch. de Chambly
(450) 445-8426

St-Jean-sur-Richelieu
Place du Quai, coin rue St-Georges
(450) 358-5984

Ste-Martine
58, rue St-Joseph
(450) 427-2068

St-Ours
2930, ch. des Patriotes
(450) 785-2212

St-Paul de-l'Île-aux-Noix
Route 223 (inter. 202)
(450) 246-3227

Salaberry-de-Valleyfield
980, boul. Monseigneur Langlois
(450) 377-7676

Vaudreuil-Dorion
331, rue St-Charles (Maison Valois)
(450) 424-8620

Venise-en-Québec
250, avenue Venise Ouest
(450) 244-5400

Yamaska
238, Marie-Victorin
(450) 789-0092

Bac St-Denis / St-Antoine
(450) 787-2759

**Bac St-Marc-sur-Richelieu /
St-Charles-sur Richelieu**
(450) 584-2813

**Bac St-Roch-de-Richelieu /
St-Ours**
(450) 785-2161

**Bateau-passeur
Longueuil / Île-Charron**
(450) 442-9575

**Bateau-passeur
Parc des Îles-de-Boucherville**
(450) 928-5088

**Navette fluviale Longueuil /
Montréal**
(514) 281-8000

Traverse Oka inc. Hudson / Oka
(450) 458-4732

**Traversier Le Passeur
Pointe-Fortune / Carillon
(ouvert à l'année)**
(450) 537-3412

**Traversier Parc Bellerive /
Parc des Îles-de Boucherville**
(450) 928-5088

**Traversier Sorel / St-Ignace-de-
Loyola (ouvert à l'année)**
(450) 743-3258 ou (450) 836-4600

**Traversier St-Paul-de-l'île-
aux-Noix / Île-aux-Noix**
(450) 291-5700

Hôtellerie
Auberge Handfield**
555, boul.Richelieu
St-Marc-sur-Richelieu
(450) 584-2226

Auberge Harris***
576, Champlain
St-Jean-sur-Richelieu
(450) 348-3821

Auberge Le St-Ignace
344, ch. du fleuve
Coteau-du-Lac
(450) 763-1251

Auberge Montagnard***
439, boul. Laurier
Mont-St-Hilaire
(450) 467-0201

Hostelry
Comfort Inn ***
96, boul. De Mortage, Boucherville
(450) 641-2880

Hôtel Le Dauphin***
1250, Daniel-Johnson, St-Hyacinthe Ouest
(450) 774-4418

Les villas du fleuve**
1679, route Marie-Victorin
(450) 561-1954

Motel Biscayne **
8900, boul. Taschereau, Brossard
(450) 466-2149

Motel Douglas**
3, route 217, St-Cyprien-de-Napierville
(450) 245-3363

Campings

Canne de Bois de Hemmingford inc.
306, route 219 Sud, Hemmingford
(450) 247-2031

Chenal-du-Moine
1686, Chenal-du-Moine
Ste-Anne-de-Sorel
(450) 742-3113

Choisy
209, route 201, Hudson
(450) 458-4900

Daoust
3844, route Harwood, Hudson
(450) 458-7301

Domaine des Arpents Verts
12, Lussier, Napierville
(450) 245-3638

Domaine des Érables
500, St-Pierre
St-Roch-de-Richelieu
(450) 785-2805

Domaine Florent
272, 23° avenue Est
Venise-en-Québec
(450) 244-5607

Domaine Frontière Enchantée 1987 inc.
474, Covey Hill, Havelock
(450) 826-4490

Grégoire
347, route 221, Lacolle
(450) 246-3385

Campings

Lac des Pins inc.
3625, route 201, St-Antoine-Abbé
(450) 827-2353

Lac Mineur Ltée
397, ch. du Ruisseau, St-Jacques-le-Mineur
(450) 346-2518

Laurier
745, boul. Laurier, Mont-St-Hilaire
(450) 467-2518

Les Cèdres
658, route 219, L'Acadie
(450) 346-9276

Plage La Liberté
129, rang Charlotte, St-Liboire
(450) 793-2716

Sainte-Madeleine
10, St-Simon, Ste-Madeleine
(450) 795-3888

Saint-Polycarpe (1993) inc.
1400, ch.St-Philippe
(450) 265-3815

Tepee
250, Principale, St-Zotique
(450) 267-9843

Trans-Canadien
960, ch. de la Baie, Rigaud
(450) 451-4515

Wigwam inc.
425, Principale, Upton
(450) 549-4513

Culture et Patrimoine   Culture & History

Blockhaus de la Rivière Lacolle
1, Principale, St-Paul-de-L'Île-aux-Noix
(450) 246-3227

Canal historique de Chambly
1840, Bourgogne, Chambly
(450) 447-4805

Canal historique de St-Ours
2930, ch des Patriotes, St-Ours
(450) 785-2216

Centrale hydroélectrique de Beauharnois à Melocheville
80, boul. Hébert, Melocheville
1-800-365-5229

Centre d'art Ozias-Leduc
1090, Ch. de la montagne
Mont-St-Hilaire
(450) 536-3033

**Centre d'interprétation de
la pomme du Québec**
11, ch. Marieville, Rougemont

**Centre d'Interprétation
du patrimoine de Sorel**
6, St-Pierre, Sorel
(450) 780-5740

**Centre interprétation il était
une fois...une petite colonie**
2500, route 219, L'Acadie
(450) 347-9756

Électrium
Autoroute 30, Ste-Julie
(450) 652-8977

Fondation de la Maison Trestler
85, ch. de la Commune, Vaudreuil-Dorion
(450) 455-6290

**Lieu historique National
de Coteau-du-Lac**
308-A, ch.du Fleuve
(450) 763-5631

**Lieu historique National de la
bataille-de-la-Châteauguay**
2371, Rivière Châteauguay Nord, Howick
(450) 829-2003

**Lieu historique National
du Fort Lennox**
1, 61ᵉ Avenue, St-Paul-de-L'Île-aux-Noix
(450) 291-5700

**Lieu historique National
du Fort-Chambly**
2, Richelieu, Chambly
(450) 658-1585

**Maison dite
Louis-Hippolyte-Lafontaine**
314, boul. Marie-Victorin, Boucherville
(450) 449-8347

Maison Lenoblet-du-Plessis
4752, boul. Marie-Victorin, Contrecoeur
(450) 587-5750

**Maison nationale
des Patriotes**
610, ch. des Patriotes, St-Denis-sur-Richelieu
(450) 787-3623

Maison Valois
331, avenue St-Charles
Vaudreuil-Dorion
(450) 455-3365

Musée d'art de Mont-St-Hilaire
150, du Centre Civique
Mont-St-Hilaire
(450) 536-3033

Musée du vieux-Marché
249, Ste-Marie, La Prairie
(450) 659-1393

**Musée québecois
de la céramique**
182, Jacques Cartier Nord
St-Jean-sur-Richelieu
(450) 347-0649

**Musée régional de
Vaudreuil-Soulanges**
431, avenue St-Charles
(450) 455-2092

Muséobus
760, ch des Patriotes
Otterburn Park
(450) 464-0201

**Parc archéologique de la
Pointe-du-Buisson**
333, Émond, Melocheville
(450) 429-7857

**Parc historique de
La Pointe-du-Moulin**
2500, boul.Don Quichotte
Notre-Dame de l'île-Perrot
(514) 453-5936

Parc historique des Ancres
76 rue du Canal
Pointe-des-Cascades
(450) 455-3414

Pont couvert à Powerscourt

SanctuaireNotre-Dame-de-Lourdes
20 Bourget
(450) 451-4631

Théâtre de la Dame de coeur
611, rang de la carrière,
Upton
(450) 549-5828

Théâtre de la ville
180, de Gentilly,
Longueuil
(450) 670-1616

Théâtre de Marieville
1979, St-Césaire,
Marieville
(450) 460-4790

Théâtre des cascades
2, ch. du canal
Pointe-des-Cascades
(450) 455-8855

Théâtre des Hirondelles
4920, ch. des Grands-Côteaux
St-Mathieu-de-Beloeil
(450) 446-2266

Théâtre Pont-Château
283, route 201, Coteau-du-Lac
(450) 456-3224

Théâtre quatre / corps
15, boul. Maple, Châteauguay
(450) 698-3127

Agrotourisme   Agrotourism

Cidreries

Au Pavillon de la pomme
1130, boul.Laurier, Mont-St-Hilaire
(450) 464-2654

Cidrerie artisanale du Minot
376, ch. Covey-Hill, Hemmingford
(450) 247-3111

Cidrerie Coteau St-Jacques
990, Grand-Rang St-Charles, St-Paul-d'Abbotsford
(450) 379-9732

Cidrerie du verger Gaston
1074, ch. de la montagne, Mont-St-Hilaire
(450) 446-2552

Cidrerie Michel Jodoin
1130, Petit-Caroline, Rougemont
(450) 469-2676

Clos de la Montagne
330, rang de la Montagne, Mont-St-Grégoire
(450) 358-4868

Vignobles

Vignoble Clos de la Montagne
330, rang de la Montagne, Mont-St-Grégoire
(450) 358-4868

Vignoble Dietrich-Jooss
407, Grande-Ligne, Iberville
(450) 347-6857

Cider Factories

Ferme Hubert Sauvé
140, rang du Milieu, St-Thimothée
(450) 373-2979

Ferme Quinn
2495, boul Perrot Sud
Notre-Dame-de-L'Île-Perrot
(514) 453-1510

La cidrerie du village
509, Principale, Rougemont
(450) 469-3945

Les jardins d'Eden
1215, de la Montagne, St-Paul-d'Abbotsford
(450) 379-9028

Les Vergers Nature plus
990, ch. de la Montagne, Mont-St-Hilaire
(450) 446-3154

Verger et cidrerie Charbonneau
575, rang de la montagne, Mont-St-Grégoire
(450) 347-9184

Vineyards

Vignoble du Marathonien
318, route 202, Havelock
(450) 826-0522

Vignoble Morou
238, route 221, Napierville
(450) 245-7569

Érablières

Cabane à sucre Handfield
Rang des soixantes, St-Marc-sur-Richelieu
(450) 584-2226

Cabane à sucre l'Hermine
212, rang St-Charles, St-Chrysôstome
(450) 826-3358

Érablière à la feuille d'Érables
156, ch. des Sous-Bois, Mont-St-Grégoire
(450) 460-7778

Maple Grove

Le domaine St-Simon
925, 4ᵉ rang Ouest, St-Hyacinthe
(450) 798-2334

Les quatres feuilles
360, rang de la Montagne, Rougemont
(450) 469-4955

Sucrerie de la Montagne
300, rang St-Georges, Rigaud
(450) 451-0831

Sports et Loisirs   Sports & Leisure

Nature et plein air

Balad'Air
566, rang de la Montagne
Mont-St-Grégoire
(450) 358-9643

Centre de la nature de Mont-St-Hilaire
422, ch. des moulins
(450) 467-1755

Centre de plein air-les forestiers
1677, ch. St-Dominique, les Cèdres
(450) 452-4736

Centre Notre-Dame-de-Fatima
2464, boul.Perrot, Notre-Dame-de-l'île-Perrot
(514) 453-7600

Comos ULM
1435 A, rang du Cordon, Richelieu
(450) 447-5152

Ile des Patriotes
665, boul. Bord de l'Eau, Grande-Île
(450) 373-8860

Équitation

Centre d'entraînement Des Chênes inc.
43, Principale, St-Basile-le-Grand
(450) 441-9394

Centre d'équitation de la Montagne
2900, rang del la Rivière Nord
St-Mathias-sur-Richelieu
(450) 464-3147

Nature & Outdoor

Jardins
Les jardins d'Henriette
2196, ch.St-Louis
St-Lazare
(450) 455-3884

L'Escapade
5, Pagé, Rigaud
(450) 451-086ᵑ

Parc régional des Îles de St-Timothée
240, St-Laurent
St-Timothée
(450) 377-1117

Parc des îles de Boucherville
55, Île Ste-Marguerite
(450) 928-5088

Parc Safari
850, route 202, Hemmingford
(450) 247-2727

Horseback Riding

Centre de location Chez France
1800, rang de la Rivière Nord
St-Mathias-sur-Richelieu
(450) 464-1569

Centre équestre Mont-Rouge
6360, route de Rougemont
St-Jean-Baptiste
(450) 467-5418

Centre équestre St-Bruno
695, Le Grang Boulevard Ouest
St-Bruno-de-Montarville
(450) 441-6607

Le Ranch au tournant du Lac
1626, Ch. Bellevue, Carignan
(450) 447-9444

Golfs

Club de golf Atlantide
2207, Don Quichotte
Notre-Dame-de-l'île-Perrot
(514) 425-2000

Club de golf Beauchâteau
1957, ch. du Beauchâteau, Maple Grove
(450) 429-5126

Club de golf Bellevue
880, boul. Léry, Léry
(450) 692-8201

Club de golf de la Rive Sud
415, ch. Bella-Vista, St-Basile-le-Grand
(450) 653-6360

Club de golf de St-Polycarpe
855, ch. Ste-Catherine, St-Polycarpe
(450) 267-3666

Club de golf La Providence
1005, Bordeleau, St-Hyacinthe
(450) 773-1234

**Club de golf
Le Parcours du Cerf**
2500, Fernand-Lafontaine, Longueuil
(450) 468-1142

Club de golf Les Légendes
400, Bergères, St-Luc
(450) 877-5566

Pistes cyclables

**Circuits des
Îles de Bouchervilles (20Km)**
Boucherville

Circuits des Riverains (55Km)
Brossard, La Prairie, Longueuil,
Ste-Catherine, St-Lambert

**Piste de la bande du Canal
(21Km)**
Chambly, St-Jean-sur-Richelieu

Golfs

Club de golf Napierville
30, rang Cyr, Napierville
(450) 877-5544

Club de golf Ormstown
673, rang Dumas, Ormstown
(450) 829-20641

Club de golf Rivière-Beaudette
1350, ch. Ste-Claire, Rivière-Beaudette
(450) 267-3666

Club de golf Rivière-Rouge
169, route 201, Côteau-du-Lac
(450) 763-2200

Club de golf St-Anicet
690, route 132 Ouest, St-Anicet
(450) 264-3511

Club sportif et champêtre
313, route 219
Hemmingford
(450) 247-2412

Golf Riviera
150, Grand Boulevard Est
St-Bruno-de-Montarville
(450) 653-5035

Le golf de Rouville
1230, rang Nord, St-Jean-Baptiste
(450) 464-3903

Cycling Trail

**Piste du canal
de Soulanges (24Km)**
Coteau-du-Lac, Pointe-des-Cascades, St-Zotique

Piste La Campagnarde (63Km)
Acton Vale, Drummondville, Foster, Roxton Falls

Piste La Montérégiade I(22Km)
Farnham, Granby

**Piste La Montérégiade II
(18Km)**
Farnham, Iberville

Types de localités ☜ Settlement Types

Arrêt	**AR**	Stop
Bureau de poste	**BP**	Post Office
Canton	**CT**	Township
Hameau	**HAM**	Hamlet
Centre de Villégiature	**CVL**	Resort Centre
Jonction	**JCN**	Junction
Municipalité	**M**	Municipality
Territoire non-organisé	**NO**	Unorganized Territory
Paroisse	**P**	Parish
Réserve Indienne	**RI**	Indian Reserve
Secteur	**SEC**	Sector
Secteur résidentiel	**SRE**	Residential Sector
Ville	**V**	City
Village	**VL**	Village

ACA	L'Acadie	NAP	Napierville
ACT	Acton Vale	NDSHY	N.-D.-de-St-Hyacinthe
BEA	Beauharnois	NDP	N.-D.-de-l'Île-Perrot
BED	Bedford	OTP	Otterburn Park
BEL	Beloeil	PER	L'Île-Perrot
BR	Brossard	PIN	Pincourt
BRO	Bromont	PTC	Pointe-des-Cascades
BV	Boucherville	RI	Richelieu
CAN	Candiac	RIG	Rigaud
CAR	Carignan	ROS	Ste-Rosalie
CB	Chambly	SAM	St-Amable
CDR	Les Cèdres	SAS	St-Athanase
CHA	Châteauguay	SASOR	Ste-Anne-de-Sorel
COT	Coteau-du-Lac	SB	St-Bruno-de-Montréal
COW	Cowansville	SGB	St-Basile-le-Grand
CTC	Contrecoeur	SCS	St-Constant
CTG	Canton de Granby	SH	St-Hubert
DEL	Delson	SHY	St-Hyacinthe
DUN	Dunham	SJ	Ste-Julie
FAR	Farnham	SJE	St-Jean-sur-Richelieu
GP	Greenfield Park	SLB	St-Lambert
GRA	Granby	SM	St-Mathias
GRI	Grande-Île	SOR	Sorel
HUD	Hudson	STD	St-Thomas-d'Aquin
HUN	Huntingdon	STE	Ste-Catherine
IBE	Iberville	STH	Mont-St-Hilaire
IC	Île-Cadieux	STI	St-Timothée
KA	Kahnawake	STJSO	St-Joseph-de-Sorel
LAP	La Prairie	STL	St-Luc
LAZ	St-Lazare	STR	St-Rémi
LB	Lac-Brôme	TRA	Tracy
LE	Léry	TV	Terrasse-Vaudreuil
LM	LeMoyne	VAL	Salaberry-de-Valleyfield
LO	Longueuil	VAU	Vaudreuil-Dorion
MAR	Marieville	VER	Verchères
MCM	McMasterville	VL	Vaudreuil-sur-le-Lac
MEL	Melocheville	VR	Varennes
MER	Mercier	WAT	Waterloo
MG	Maple Grove		

Liste des types de voie

List of road types

Numérique — Numeric

Benni

Cédar

Demers

Édouard

129

M

Normandie

PREFACE
to the second edition

I am grateful for the opportunity to revise and update the information in the *Practical Guide to the Care of the Surgical Patient*. Many helpful comments and suggestions from you, the reader, have contributed greatly. The purpose of this manual remains unchanged: to serve as a concise, ready, quick-reference guide. The organization and outline form remain the same.

Care of the total patient, including medical aspects, is emphasized. Discussions of new drugs, such as bretylium, moxalactam, and ranitidine, are included. Indications for medications and dosages are extended and pediatric dosages are now given. Illustrations for surgical procedures are provided and laboratory data have been revised.

As an overview, the title page of each main section, which is prefaced with a brief statement about its contents, should be consulted. This information should be of great value in understanding and using this manual. Hopefully, the manual itself will continue to serve the needs of house officers, medical students, assistants, and nurses.

I am pleased with the response to the first edition and am happy to continue in this work. Many thanks to The C.V. Mosby Company, friends, and family members for their help in the preparation of this edition.

Robert L. McEntyre

Practical guide to the care of the

SURGICAL PATIENT

Robert L. McEntyre, M.D.

Former Surgical Resident,
The New York Hospital,
Cornell Medical Center,
New York, New York

SECOND EDITION

with 13 illustrations

The C. V. Mosby Company

ST. LOUIS • TORONTO • PRINCETON   1984

MOSBY

A TRADITION OF PUBLISHING EXCELLENCE

Editor: Karen Berger
Assistant editor: Sandy Gilfillan, Terry Van Schaik
Editing supervisor: Peggy Fagen
Manuscript editor: Helen Hudlin
Book design: Jeanne Bush
Cover design: Nancy Steinmeyer
Production: Mary Stueck

SECOND EDITION

Printed in the United States of America

The C.V. Mosby Company
11830 Westline Industrial Drive, St. Louis, Missouri 63146

Library of Congress Cataloging in Publication Data

McEntyre, Robert L.
   Practical guide to the care of the surgical patient.

   Bibliography: p.
   Includes index.
   1. Therapeutics, Surgical—Handbooks, manuals, etc.
I. Title. (DNLM:1. Postoperative Care—handbooks.
2. Preoperative Care—handbooks. WO 39 M478p)
RD49. M37   1985   617   84-1197
ISBN 0-8016-3211-0

TH/D/D 9 8 7 6 5 4   01/D/096

PREFACE
to the first edition

William S. Halsted introduced the surgery residency system to the United States. Ever since then, an important element of surgical training has been the passage of information from resident to resident. This manual aspires to continue that tradition by providing an ongoing reference system in the area of preoperative and postoperative care.

Practical Guide to the Care of the Surgical Patient is designed to provide those directly involved in patient care with practical information in a concise and usable form. You may wonder how to acquire consultations, what orders to write, which dosages to use, how to initiate diagnostic and therapeutic management, or how to interpret laboratory data. Suggestions and guidelines for these aspects of preoperative and postoperative care are presented. Each section is prefaced with a brief statement about its contents.

The manual was written by a resident for residents, although it is also hoped that this information will be valuable to medical students, surgeons' assistants, nurses, and others. It is not intended to substitute for the necessary in-depth reading of standard textbooks or surgical literature. Rather, it should stimulate further thinking and studying, which should thus provide a firmer understanding of the material presented.

I am indebted to all who contributed their ideas and encouragement in this work. In particular, thanks are due G. Tom Shires, Professor and Chief of Surgery, his attending staff and residents, as well as the medical students, surgeons' assistants, and nurses at The New York Hospital-Cornell Medical Center. My thanks also go to Dr. Dina Stallings, for her support over the years; to my wife, Barbara, for her constant support and typing; to my family, for their understanding and encouragement; and to many others, too numerous to mention.

Robert L. McEntyre

CONTENTS

KEY TELEPHONE NUMBERS

Because of the frequent need to contact various departments, consulting physicians, and nursing stations, this section is placed first. Each list should be completed by the individual user. In this way the manual is personalized and provides an immediate source of reference.

1. Key departments
2. Consulting physicians
3. Nursing stations
4. Other frequently called numbers

KEY TELEPHONE NUMBERS

Department	Extension	Location	Department	Extension	Location
Admitting			Surgical Pathology		
Anesthesia			Urinalysis		
Bacteriology			X-ray (diagnostic)		
Blood Bank			Angiography		
Blood Gases			Cardiac Catheterization		
Cardiac Care Unit			Lymphangiography		
Chemistry			Mammography		
Coagulation			Pediatric		
CT			Portables		
Cytology			Preoperative		
Drug Information Center			Urologic		
Drug Levels			X-ray (therapeutic)		
Echocardiography					
Echoencephalography					
EEG					
EKG					
ER					

Consulting physicians	Extension	Location
Anesthesia		
Cardiology		
Dentistry		
Endocrine		
ENT		
Fracture		
GI		
Hematology		
Infectious Disease		
Medicine		
Neurology		
OB/GYN		
Oncology		
Ophthalmology		
Pediatrics		
Pediatric Surgery		
Pulmonary		
Psychiatry		
Renal		
Surgery		
Thoracic		
Transplant		
Urology		

Department	Extension	Location
Hematology		
ICU		
Information		
IV Team		
Medical Records		
Nuclear Medicine		
Nursing		
ORs		
Paging		
Pathology		
Pharmacy		
Physical Therapy		
Pulmonary Function		
Recovery Room		
Rehabilitation		
Respiratory Therapy		
Security		
Social Service		
Sonography		
Surgery		
Surgical Library		

Other	Exten-sion	Loca-tion	Other	Exten-sion	Loca-tion
___	___	___	___	___	___
___	___	___	___	___	___
___	___	___	___	___	___
___	___	___	___	___	___
___	___	___	___	___	___
___	___	___	___	___	___
___	___	___	___	___	___
___	___	___	___	___	___
___	___	___	___	___	___
___	___	___	___	___	___
___	___	___	___	___	___

Nursing stations and extensions

1 ___	1 ___	1 ___	1 ___
2 ___	2 ___	2 ___	2 ___
3 ___	3 ___	3 ___	3 ___
4 ___	4 ___	4 ___	4 ___
5 ___	5 ___	5 ___	5 ___
6 ___	6 ___	6 ___	6 ___
7 ___	7 ___	7 ___	7 ___
8 ___	8 ___	8 ___	8 ___
9 ___	9 ___	9 ___	9 ___
10 ___	10 ___	10 ___	10 ___
11 ___	11 ___	11 ___	11 ___
12 ___	12 ___	12 ___	12 ___
13 ___	13 ___	13 ___	13 ___
14 ___	14 ___	14 ___	14 ___
15 ___	15 ___	15 ___	15 ___
16 ___	16 ___	16 ___	16 ___
17 ___	17 ___	17 ___	17 ___
18 ___	18 ___	18 ___	18 ___
19 ___	19 ___	19 ___	19 ___
20 ___	20 ___	20 ___	20 ___
21 ___	21 ___	21 ___	21 ___
22 ___	22 ___	22 ___	22 ___
23 ___	23 ___	23 ___	23 ___
24 ___	24 ___	24 ___	24 ___
25 ___	25 ___	25 ___	25 ___

Other frequently called numbers

1 ___	___	11 ___	___
2 ___	___	12 ___	___
3 ___	___	13 ___	___
4 ___	___	14 ___	___
5 ___	___	15 ___	___
6 ___	___	16 ___	___
7 ___	___	17 ___	___
8 ___	___	18 ___	___
9 ___	___	19 ___	___
10 ___	___	20 ___	___

Other frequently called numbers—cont'd

21 _____ _____	36 _____ _____
22 _____ _____	37 _____ _____
23 _____ _____	38 _____ _____
24 _____ _____	39 _____ _____
25 _____ _____	40 _____ _____
26 _____ _____	41 _____ _____
27 _____ _____	42 _____ _____
28 _____ _____	43 _____ _____
29 _____ _____	44 _____ _____
30 _____ _____	45 _____ _____
31 _____ _____	46 _____ _____
32 _____ _____	47 _____ _____
33 _____ _____	48 _____ _____
34 _____ _____	49 _____ _____
35 _____ _____	50 _____ _____

ORDERS, NOTES, AND PREPARATIONS

This section presents practical guidelines in an outline form that follows the general course of a surgical patient admitted to the hospital:

1. Admission orders
2. Preoperative orders
3. Preoperative check
4. Operative note
5. Postoperative orders
6. Postoperative check
7. Laboratory and medication preparations

It should be remembered that these are only suggestions and guidelines, since the routines may vary at different institutions.

ADMISSION ORDERS

This is a guide to the formulation of the actual orders for the patient. No single list of orders would be appropriate for every patient, but certain considerations should be made.

Disposition

List the ward and service to which the patient is being admitted (e.g.: Admit to G5-Blue surgical service).

Diagnosis

The actual diagnosis (e.g., choledocholithiasis) or the provisional diagnosis (e.g., acute appendicitis) should be noted.

Condition

Specify the patient's general condition. Simple terms such as "good," "fair," "poor," or "critical" convey the message satisfactorily.

Allergies

List any medications to which the patient has experienced an allergic reaction. Even if "allergies" are denied, ask specifically about penicillin, sulfonamides, aspirin, iodine, and tape. Also note any medications the patient must avoid (e.g., atropine in patients with glaucoma or asthma).

Obtain old chart

Patients who are returning to the hospital have records available which should be sought. Much time can be saved by consulting these for information concerning a previous admission (presentation, examinations, laboratory work, medical and surgical treatment, response, complications). Relevant information should be assessed and summarized in the appropriate part of the present admission.

Diet

Specify whether NPO, clear liquids, full, soft, regular, or special diet. Modify appropriately with regard to dentition and underlying diseases (cardiac, diabetes, peptic ulcer, renal failure, etc.). Consider forced fluids, fluid restriction, salt restriction, low fat, low cholesterol, amount of roughage, and supplements. Nutritional status should be assessed, and, when appropriate, enteral feedings or hyperalimentation should be considered. (See *Hyperalimentation* in Section seven.)

Activity

Activity appropriate for the patient's current condition should be specified (up, chair, bed rest, commode, bathroom privileges, bath, assistance). If activity is to be restricted, leg exercises, deep breathing, and other prophylactic measures should be considered.

Vital signs

Specify how frequently these observations should be made in order to adequately assess the patient (q1h, q2h, q4h, q8h).

IV fluids

Specify fluid composition and rate. Include appropriate replacement of preexisting deficits and ongoing losses, as well as maintenance requirements. (See *IV fluid management* in Section six.)

Intake and output

Accurate records of the volume and composition of fluid intake (PO, IV) and measured losses (NG, urine, fistula) are important guides in the calculation of proper fluid management.

Daily weights

Significant changes in weight and trends toward weight gain or weight loss are especially important in patients with renal, hepatic, or cardiac impairment. These patients may have edema, ascites, or congestive failure. Adjustment of fluids or diuretics or both may be indicated.

Diagnostic tests

Routine: CBC, electrolytes, glucose, BUN, PT, PTT, VDRL, type and crossmatch, chest x-ray, ECG, urinalysis. *Specific (as appropriate):* Blood gases, other chemistries, coagulation screen, cultures, cytology, endocrine, special hematology, pulmonary tests, scans, sonograms, other x-rays, etc. Arrange for the appropriate preparation of the patient when needed for specific tests (see *Laboratory and medication preparations* at the end of this section).

Drugs

Incoming medications.
Symptomatic medications:
Bowels: Order laxative or antidiarrheal when appropriate.
Fever: Order antipyretic or other cooling measures when indicated.
Pain: Appropriate analgesic may be ordered in absence of contraindications (e.g., allergy or undiagnosed abdominal pain).
Sedation: Order sedative when appropriate.
Sleep: Order bedtime hypnotic when needed.
Therapeutic medications: Consider any other specific medications that may be indicated (e.g., antibiotics, cardiac drugs, diuretics, insulin, and steroids).

Optional

NG suction or lavage.

Catheterization of urinary bladder.

Monitoring: Urine output, CVP, Swan-Ganz pressures, ECG, etc.

Preparations: Barium enema, colonoscopy, body scan, bowel, SBE, steroid (see *Laboratory and medication preparations* at the end of this section).

Wound: Cultures, irrigations, dressing changes.

Specimens: Stool guaiacs, urine glucose and acetone, cultures.

Position: Elevate head of bed, elevate extremity.

Preventive care: Turn, range of motion, elastic stockings, Ace bandages, chest physical therapy, endotracheal suctioning.

Precautions: Infection, seizure, suicide, side-rails up, etc.

Consultations: Anesthesia, cardiology, dietary, hematology, medicine, etc.

Notify MD if (specify: fever, hypotension, etc.).

The mnemonic DAVID helps one to remember the basic set of admission orders:

D: disposition, diagnosis, and diet

A: allergies and activity

V: vital signs

I: IVs, intake and output

D: daily weights, diagnostic tests, and drugs

PREOPERATIVE ORDERS

NPO after midnight.

Prepare and shave (specify operative area).

Antiseptic shower (povidone-iodine or hexachlorophene soap).

Void on call to the OR.

Premedications (may be written by anesthesiologist in some hospitals):

Sedative IM on call to OR (such as barbiturate or narcotic); dose may vary with the age, weight, and condition of the patient.

Atropine, 0.4-0.6 mg IM, on call to OR (for general anesthesia) unless the patient has fever, glaucoma, asthma, or other contraindication to the use of atropine.

Optional: Antibiotics, enemas, IV hydration, transfusion, steroids. (See *Laboratory and medication preparations* at the end of this section.)

PREOPERATIVE CHECK

Assess the results of CBC, electrolytes, glucose, BUN, PT, PTT, chest x-ray, ECG, and urinalysis and note them in the chart. Note whether operative consent, preoperative orders, and cross-match (when necessary) are in order. Follow up significant abnormal laboratory tests and revise orders when necessary.

OPERATIVE NOTE

Preoperative diagnosis
Postoperative diagnosis
Operation
Surgeon
Assistants
Anesthesia
Findings
Specimen and result of frozen section
Location of drains or tubes
Estimated blood loss
IV fluids given
Complications
Patient's condition and disposition

POSTOPERATIVE ORDERS
Disposition, operation, condition, allergies (specify)

Vital signs

Specify frequency as needed to adequately assess the patient. Usual routine is: every 15 minutes for the first hour, then every half-hour until fully recovered from anesthesia, then every hour for 4 hours, then per nursing routine if the patient's condition is stable.

IV fluids

Specify fluid composition and rate. Include replacement solutions (e.g., NG suction losses) as well as maintenance requirements. Potassium is normally included in replacement solutions but is excluded from maintenance solutions until normal renal function is established (e.g., on the first POD).

Diet

Specify according to the individual patient and operative procedure. Usual routine is: NPO until postnausea and passing flatus; then begin with clear liquids and advance to usual diet as tolerated.

Ambulation

Early ambulation is recommended whenever possible to encourage deeper respirations and to help prevent thrombophlebitis. Usual routine is: may stand to void when fully reacted; then up ad lib at least tid (if postoperative condition permits).

Turning, coughing, and deep breathing

Every hour until patient is ambulatory helps to clear secretions and open smaller airways, but excessive coughing may be detrimental in some cases (e.g., after thyroidectomy or herniorrhaphy). Aspiration of nasopharynx and trachea may be necessary for adequate pulmonary toilet.

Incentive spirometer

May be beneficial in preventing postoperative atelectasis by encouraging deep breathing.

Antiembolic stockings or Ace wraps

Advocated routinely by many surgeons to help prevent thromboembolic disease of the lower extremities in patients at risk. Others believe that early ambulation has more to recommend it when feasible.

Voiding

With normal renal function and adequate fluid intake, most patients are expected to void by 6-8 hours postoperatively, or, better still, 8-12 hours after the preoperative voiding. If a catheter is present in the bladder, a urine output of 30-60 ml/hour is usually considered adequate.

Drains, tubes, and catheters

Specify the type of drainage desired (straight or gravity drainage, suction, etc.) and if an IV fluid replacement is indicated.

Notifying house officer

Ensure notification of any unusual condition by specifying it in the order, e.g., if:

Temperature $> 38.5°$.
Pulse > 120 or < 50.
Respirations > 40.
Blood pressure $< 100/60$ or $> 180/100$.
Unable to void by 8 hours postoperatively.
Bright red blood saturates the dressing.

Intake and output

Essential in the fluid management of seriously ill patients and after major operations (see *Admission orders*).

Daily weights

Essential in managing problems in fluid balance. Generally, a postoperative patient can be expected to lose lean body mass at the rate of 0.25-0.5 kg/day during the catabolic phase (usually for about 1 week). Then the patient will gain lean body mass at about the same rate during the anabolic phase. The actual weight will be affected by the state of hydration, cardiovascular and renal status, and the presence of fever, infection, or thyroid disease.

Fractional urines

Fractional urines for glucose and acetone should be ordered every 4-6 hours in patients with diabetes mellitus or if TPN is administered. A "sliding scale" can then be ordered to determine the amount of insulin the patient should receive. It is wise to check a concomitant blood glucose specimen whenever significant glycosuria or ketonuria occurs.

Glucose	Acetone	Insulin (rough guide)
0.5%	0	0
0.5-1%	0	5 units SC
1-2%	0	10 units SC
>2%	Small	15 units SC
>2%	Moderate	Notify resident
>2%	Large	Notify resident

In the case of hyperalimentation, it may be more beneficial to add the daily insulin requirement directly to the solution to be administered.

Diagnostic tests

Depending on the patient's condition and operation, certain tests may be indicated in the recovery room. Others may be appropriate for the following day. (Examples are CBC, electrolytes, glucose, BUN, chest x-ray, and ECG.) Avoid random testing.

Drugs

Include adequate analgesic. Smaller, more frequent doses of analgesics are preferred (e.g., every 3-4 hours). Too little analgesia may result in poor ventilation due to splinting. Too much analgesia predisposes the patient to hypoventilation. Resume preoperative medications when appropriate. Are antibiotics, steroids, or insulin needed? Be certain to check for allergies.

POSTOPERATIVE CHECK

From the moment a patient leaves the operating room until he or she may be safely discharged from the hospital, the patient's well-being is of the utmost importance and should be ensured by appropriate observations and management. At the minimum, temperature, vital signs, respiratory and cardiovascular status, the condition of the dressing, whether the patient has voided, and any special complaints should be assessed and noted in the chart. Further evaluation may depend on the patient's age, the type of operation and anesthesia, and the presence or absence of underlying diseases or complications. The following is a relatively complete list of observations, although other parameters may be necessary:

Vital signs (temperature, pulse, respirations, blood pressure, CVP).
Urine output (hourly if catheterized).
Mental status (arousability, orientation).
Complaints (incisional pain, nausea, etc.).
Skin (color, turgor, warmth).
HEENT (pupils, throat, etc.).

Neck (jugular venous distention).
Chest (airway, breath sounds, rales, rhonchi).
Heart (rhythm, murmur, gallop, rub).
Abdomen (distention, tenderness, bowel sounds).
Legs (tenderness, edema, pulses).
Dressing (amount and type of drainage).
Wound (condition, if inspected).
Catheter, drains, tubes (specify type and amount of drainage).
Results of postoperative tests (CBC, chemistries, chest x-ray, etc.).
Ensure that the appropriate orders are being carried out.
Revise orders and repeat tests when indicated.
Repeat the postoperative check as necessary in order to adequately assess the patient.

LABORATORY AND MEDICATION PREPARATIONS

NPO (after midnight unless otherwise indicated)

Angiography
BMR
Biliary drainage
Bronchoscopy
Cardiac catheterization
Cholangiogram (IVC, T-tube)
Cholecystogram
Duodenoscopy
Esophagram
Esophagoscopy
ERCP
Gastric analysis
GI series
Gastroscopy
Intestinal biopsy
IVP
Laryngoscopy
Myelogram
Nephrotomogram
Small bowel series
Venogram

Fluid diet (evening and morning unless otherwise indicated)

Arteriography
Barium enema
Colonoscopy (clear liquids)
Esophageal motility (clear liquids)
Liver-spleen scan
Retrograde pyelogram

No preparation

 Cystoscopy
 Lymphangiogram
 Sonogram (abdominal, pancreatic)

Barium enema

 Before:
 Clear liquid dinner and breakfast.
 Castor oil, 30-60 ml PO, at 6 PM.
 Tap-water enema, 2000 ml, in the evening.
 Tap-water enema, 2000 ml, in the morning.
 After:
 Oil retention enema; then soapsuds enema.
 Alternative: magnesium citrate, 240 ml PO; then phosphosoda
   enema.

Colonoscopy

 Before:
 Clear liquid diet.
 Castor oil, 30-60 ml PO, at 6 PM.
 Tap-water enemas until clear, in the evening.
 Tap-water enema, 2,000 ml, in the morning.
 After:
 Resume previous diet.

Body scan (CT)

 NPO for at least 4 hours.
 No barium for at least 2 days.
 Mild sedative IM on call.
 Atropine, 0.4-0.6 mg IM, on call.
 Full bladder (patient should not void for 3-4 hours).

Bowel preparation (begin 3 days before surgery)

 1. Mechanical cleansing is the single most important con-
    sideration:
      Clear liquid or low residue diet.
      Magnesium citrate, 120-240 ml PO, daily.
      Soapsuds enemas (two) each evening.
      Tap-water enemas (one) each morning.
 2. Vitamin K, 10 mg IM, daily.
 3. Potassium chloride, 15 ml PO, bid.
 4. Vitamin C, 250 mg PO, bid.
 5. Multivitamins, 1 PO, bid.
 6. Adequate hydration the night before surgery (e.g., 1000
    ml lactated Ringer's solution IV).
 7. Oral antibiotic regimens advocated by various surgeons:
      Hunter—Columbia:
        Neomycin, 1 g PO q1h for 4 hours; then q4h for 36 hours.
        Erythromycin base, 1 g PO q6h for 36 hours.

Condon—Wisconsin:

    Neomycin/erythromycin base, 1 g of each PO at 1 PM,
2 PM, and 11 PM the day before operation.

Cohn—Louisiana State:

    Kanamycin, 1 g PO q1h for 4 hours, then q6h for a total
of 72 hours.

Others:

    Neomycin alone or in combination with bacitracin, poly-
myxin B, phthalylsulfathiazole (Sulfathalidine), or
tetracycline.

8. Systemic antibiotics recommended by other surgeons:

   Stone—Emory:

      Cephazolin, 1 g IM 12 hours before operation.

   Altemeier—Cincinnati:

      Aqueous penicillin, 1 million units, and tetracycline, 0.5
g IV, 2 hours before operation.

SBE prophylaxis

Preoperative: It is generally accepted that patients with acquired valvular disease, congenital heart disease, or prosthetic
heart valves should receive prophylactic antibiotics before surgery. The duration of preoperative administration varies, with
recommendations varying from 1 hour to 12-24 hours preoperatively. Certainly, it is most desirable that antibiotic levels are adequate at the time of surgery.

Postoperative: Again, the duration of administration varies
from 1 or 2 doses to 3 or 4 days postoperatively. Depending on
the procedure, some feel that parenteral antibiotics should be
continued until intravenous and urinary catheters are discontinued and endotracheal suctioning is no longer necessary.

The following schedules have been recommended, with the
first dose given ½-1 hour before surgery. Subsequent doses
are begun immediately after surgery or, in some cases, intra-
operatively.

1. Head and neck surgery:

    Procaine penicillin, 1.2 million units IM, *or* aqueous peni-
cillin, 2 million units IM or IV, q6h.

    Streptomycin, 1 g IM q12h.

    Alternative (if penicillin-allergic): vancomycin, 1 g IV q12h

2. Abdominal surgery:

    Ampicillin, 1 g IV or IM, q6h

    Gentamicin, 3-5 mg/kg/day IM or IV, divided q8h

    Alternatives: a cephalosporin plus gentamicin or vancomy-
cin plus gentamicin

Steroid preparation

Preoperative: The possibility of acute adrenal insufficiency occurring perioperatively should be anticipated in patients:

1. With known adrenal insufficiency from any cause.
2. Receiving adrenal steroids (currently, or for more than 1-2 weeks in the last 6-12 months).
3. About to undergo adrenalectomy.

Patients in the first two categories should receive:

Hydrocortisone, IV/IM, or cortisone acetate, IM:

100 mg at 12 midnight.
100 mg 2 hours preoperatively.
100 mg in the OR.

Postoperative: Steroid administration should be of sufficient dosage to prevent signs and symptoms of acute adrenal insufficiency, particularly fever and hypotension. Other signs include tachycardia, oliguria, disorientation, nausea, vomiting, and abdominal pain. Electrolyte disturbances usually develop in a matter of days. A guide to the dosage of steroids follows, although it should be modified, when necessary, to the individual patient's requirements.

	Hydrocortisone, IV	Cortisone, IM	Cortisone, PO
Day of operation	100 mg over first 4 hours	50 mg q12h	—
	100 mg over next 8 hours	—	—
	100 mg over next 12 hours	—	—
POD 1	100 mg q12h	50 mg q12h	—
POD 2	50 mg q12h	50 mg q12h	—
POD 3	—	25 mg q12h	25 mg q12h
POD 4	—	25 mg q12h	25 mg q12h
POD 5	—	—	25 mg q12h
POD 6	—	—	37.5 mg q12h
POD 7	—	—	37.5-50 mg

Long-term maintenance: 25-37.5 mg cortisone per day, or 20-30 mg hydrocortisone plus 0.1 mg 9α-fluorohydrocortisone per day.

MEDICATIONS

Some 270 medications commonly used in hospitals are presented in this section. Each drug is listed alphabetically by generic name. For ease in reference, an index classifying the agents according to use is presented. A complete alphabetical list of generic, chemical, and brand names is included in the index at the end of the book.

The pharmacologic information in this section was carefully selected. Currently accepted adult and pediatric dosages, routes of administration, indications, and contraindications are presented. The selection of brand names was based on personal familiarity and is not meant to recommend any of the agents described. The reader should consult an appropriate source for additional information and for any new information regarding the safe and proper use of these medications. Included in this section are:

1. Abbreviations and conversions
2. Drug classification index
3. Generic name index of medications
4. Tables
   a. Analgesics
   b. Antacids
   c. Glucocorticoids
   d. Insulins
   e. Potassium supplements (oral)

Abbreviations

ac	before meals (ante cibum)	prn	as needed (pro re nata)
ad lib	as desired (ad libitum)	q	each (quaque)
bid	twice daily (bis in die)	q1h	every hour
D5W	dextrose 5% in water	q2h	every 2 hours
g	gram	q3h	every 3 hours
h	hour	q4h	every 4 hours
hs	at bedtime (hora somni)	q6h	every 6 hours
IM	intramuscular(ly)	q8h	every 8 hours
IV	intravenous(ly)	q12h	every 12 hours
kg	kilogram	qd	every day (quaque die)
μg	microgram	qid	four times daily
MDR	minimum daily		(quater in die)
	requirement	qod	every other day
mEq	milliequivalent		(quaque alium die)
mg	milligram	RDA	recommended daily
ml	milliliter		allowance
MRC	Medical Research Council	SC	subcutaneous(ly)
OD	right eye (oculus dexter)	SL	sublingual(ly)
OS	left eye (oculus sinister)	stat	at once (statim)
OU	each eye (oculus uterque)	tbs	tablespoon
pc	after meals (post cibum)	tid	three times daily (ter in die)
PO	by mouth (per os)	tsp	teaspoon
PR	per rectum		

Conversions

10^3 grams = kilogram (kg)	1 grain = 65 milligrams
1.0 gram = gram (g)	1 teaspoon = 5 milliliters (ml)
10^{-3} gram = milligram (mg)	1 tablespoon = 15 milliliters
10^{-6} gram = microgram (μg)	1 fluid ounce = 30 milliliters
10^{-9} gram = nanogram (ng)	15 macrodrops = 1 milliliter
10^{-12} gram = picogram (pg)	60 microdrops = 1 milliliter

DRUG CLASSIFICATION INDEX

Note: Some of these drugs appear only in the tables at the end of this section.

Amebicide
  Metronidazole
Ammonia
  detoxicant
  Lactulose
Analgesics
  Acetaminophen
  Alphaprodine
  Anileridine
  Aspirin
  Codeine
  Dextromoramide
  Dipipanone
  Heroin
  Hydromorphone
  Levorphanol
  Meperidine

Methadone
Methotrimepera-
  zine
Metopon
Morphine
Oxycodone
Oxymorphone
Pentazocine
Phenacetin
Phenazocine
Piminodine
Propoxyphine
Sodium salicylate
Antacids
  Aluminum
  hydroxide
  Calcium carbonate

Magnesia magma
Magnesium
  hydroxide
Magnesium
  trisilicate
Antianemics
  Ferrous gluconate
  Ferrous sulfate
  Iron dextran
Antiarrhythmics
  Bretylium tosylate
  Lidocaine
  Ouabain
  Procainamide
  Propranolol
  Quinidine

Antiasthmatics
Aminophylline
Beclomethasone
Epinephrine
Isoproterenol
Oxtriphylline
Terbutaline
Theophylline
Antibiotics
Amikacin
Ampicillin
Carbenicillin
Cefazolin
Cephalexin
Cephaloridine
Cephalothin
Cephradine
Chloramphenicol
Clindamycin
Cloxacillin
Dicloxacillin
Doxycycline
Erythromycin
Gentamicin
Kanamycin
Lincomycin
Methicillin
Moxalactam
  disodium
Nafcillin
Neomycin
Oxacillin
Penicillin
Piperacillin
  sodium
Polymyxin B
Streptomycin
Tetracycline
Tobramycin
Vancomycin
Anticholinergics
Atropine sulfate
Flavoxate
Propantheline
Anticoagulants
Heparin
Warfarin
Anticonvulsants
Acetazolamide

Diazepam
Phenobarbital
Phenytoin
Antidepressants
Doxepin
Imipramine
Trazodone
  hydrochloride
Antidiarrheals
Diphenoxylate
Kaolin and pectin
Lactobacillus
  acidophilus
Opium tincture
Paregoric
Antidiuretic
Vasopressin
Antiemetics
Benzquinamide
Chlorpromazine
Hydroxyzine
Prochlorperazine
Promethazine
Thiethylperazine
Trimethobenza-
  mide
Antiestrogenic
Tamoxifen
Antiflatulant
Simethicone
Antifungals
Amphotericin B
Griseofulvin
Nystatin
Antigout
Allopurinol
Colchicine
Indomethacin
Phenylbutazone
Probenecid
Sulfinpyrazone
Antiheparin
Protamine sulfate
Antihistamines
Diphenhydramine
Hydroxyzine
Promethazine
Antihypertensives
Clonidine

Diazoxide
Hydralazine
Methyldopa
Nitroprusside
Phenoxybenza-
  mine
Phentolamine
Propranolol
Reserpine
Anti-inflammatory
Aspirin
Glucocorticoids
Ibuprofen
Indomethacin
Phenylbutazone
Sulfasalazine
Antilipemic
Clofibrate
Antineoplastics
Azathioprine
Mithramycin
Tamoxifen
Antiparkinson
Carbidopa
Levodopa
Antipyretics
Acetaminophen
Aspirin
Ibuprofen
Indomethacin
Antithyroid
Methimazole
Propylthiouracil
Antituberculosis
  drug
Isoniazid
Antitussives
Codeine
Hydrocodone-
  homatropine
Blood derivatives
Albumin
Antihemophilic
  factor
Fibrinogen
Calcium salts
Calcium carbonate
Calcium glubionate
Calcium gluconate

Cardiac drugs
Deslanoside
Digitoxin
Digoxin
Lidocaine
Ouabain
Procainamide
Propranolol
Quinidine

Diuretics
Acetazolamide
Ethacrynic acid
Furosemide
Hydrochlorothiazide
Mannitol
Spironolactone
Theophylline
Triamterene

Expectorants
Guaifenesin
Potassium iodide

Glucocorticoids
Cortisone
Dexamethasone
Hydrocortisone
Methylprednisolone
Prednisolone
Prednisone
Triamcinolone

Hemostatics
Aminocaproic acid
Antihemophilic factor
Factor IX complex

Histamine (H₂) antagonists
Cimetidine
Ranitidine

Hormones
Calcitonin
Glucagon
Glucocorticoids
Insulins
Levothyroxine
Liothyronine
Thyroid
Vasopressin

Insulins
Lente insulin
NPH insulin
Protamine zinc insulin
Regular (crystalline) insulin
Semilente insulin
Ultralente insulin

Keratolytic
Podophyllum resin

Laxatives
Bisacodyl
Casanthranol
Cascara sagrada
Castor oil
Dioctyl sulfosuccinate
Magnesia magma
Magnesium citrate
Mineral oil
Phenolphthalein
Psyllium hydrophilic mucoid

Miotic
Pilocarpine

Mydriatics
Atropine
Epinephrine
Homatropine

Narcotic antagonists
Levallorphan
Nalorphine
Naloxone

Oral hypoglycemics
Chlorpropamide
Tolbutamide

Parasympatholytics
Atropine
Homatropine
Propantheline

Parasympathomimetics
Bethanechol
Edrophonium

Parathyroid
Calcitonin
DHT

Potassium-removing resins
Sodium polystyrene sulfonate

Potassium supplements
Potassium acetate-bicarbonate-citrate
Potassium bicarbonate
Potassium chloride
Potassium gluconate

Sedatives and hypnotics
Chloral hydrate
Flurazepam
Meprobamate
Paraldehyde
Pentobarbital
Phenobarbital
Promethazine

Skeletal muscle relaxants
Diazepam
Pancuronium

Sulfonamides
Sulfadiazine
Sulfamethoxazole
Sulfasalazine
Sulfisoxazole

Sympatholytics
Ergotamine
Phenoxybenzamine

Sympathomimetics
Dopamine
Ephedrine
Epinephrine
Isoproterenol
Levarterenol
Pseudoephedrine
Terbutaline

Thyroid
  Levothyroxine
  Liothyronine
  Thyroid UPS
Tranquilizers
  Chlordiazepoxide
  Chlorpromazine
  Diazepam
  Haloperidol
  Hydroxyzine
  Prochlorperazine
Trichomonacide
  Metronidazole
Uricosurics
  Probenecid
  Sulfinpyrazone

Urinary germicides
  Methenamine
  Nalidixic acid
  Nitrofurantoin
Vasodilators
  Glyceryl trinitrate
  Isosorbide dinitrate
  Nifedipine
Vitamins
  Vitamin A
  Vitamin B
    Folic acid
    Nicotinic acid
  Vitamin B_1
  Vitamin B_2
  Vitamin B_6

Vitamin B_{12}
Vitamin C
Vitamin D
Vitamin D_2
Vitamin K
Others
  Beclomethasone
  Gama benzene
    hexachloride
  Lithium carbonate
  Phenazopyridine
  Phosphates,
    inorganic
  Zinc sulfate

ACETAMINOPHEN (Datril, Tylenol)
  Adults:
  1. Usual dose: 325-650 mg PO/PR q4-6h prn.
  2. Maximum recommended dosage: 2.6 g/24 hours.
  Children:
  1. 6-12 years:
     Usual dose: 240 mg PO/PR q4-6h prn.
     Maximum recommended dosage: 1440 mg/24 hours.
  2. 3-6 years:
     Usual dose: 120 mg PO/PR q4-6h prn.
     Maximum recommended dosage: 720 mg/24 hours.
  3. 1-3 years:
     Usual dose: 60-120 mg PO/PR q4-6h prn.
     Maximum recommended dosage: 720 mg/24 hours.
  4. Under 1 year:
     Usual dose: 60 mg PO/PR q4-6h prn.
     Maximum recommended dosage: 360 mg/24 hours.

Indications: Low-intensity pain; fever; as an aspirin substitute.
Action: Nonnarcotic antipyretic analgesic; para-aminophenol derivative.
Contraindication: Acetaminophen hypersensitivity.

ACETAZOLAMIDE (Diamox)

Adults:
1. Diuretic: 250-375 mg/day PO/IV single dose.
2. Glaucoma: 250 mg-1 g/day divided q4-6h.

Children:
1. Diuretic: 5 mg/kg/day single dose.
2. Epilepsy or glaucoma: 8-30 mg/kg/day divided q6-8h.

Indications: For adjunctive treatment of: glaucoma, edema caused by congestive heart failure, epilepsy (primarily petit mal).

Action: Carbonic anhydrase inhibitor (depresses hydration of carbon dioxide).

Contraindications: Sulfonamide hypersensitivity, hyponatremia, hypokalemia, hyperchloremic acidosis, marked renal or hepatic impairment, adreno cortical insufficiency, chronic noncongestive angle-closure glaucoma.

ALBUMIN, NORMAL HUMAN SERUM (Albuminar, Albumisol, Albuspan, Buminate)

Adults:
1. Shock with acute plasma volume depletion (5% solution preferred in presence of dehydration):
   Initial: 25 g (500 ml) IV rapidly.
   Repeat with 12.5-25 g (250-500 ml) in 15-30 minutes if indicated.
2. Hypoproteinemia (nephrotic syndrome, hepatic cirrhosis) (25% solution preferred in presence of edema):
   Usual dose: 0.5 g/kg IV at 1 ml/minute.
   Repeat q1-2 days until desired response achieved.

Children:
1. Shock with acute plasma volume depletion: (5% solution preferred in presence of dehydration):
   Initial: 10 ml/kg IV as rapidly as tolerated.
   Repeat dose in 15-30 minutes if indicated.
2. Hypoproteinemia: (25% solution preferred in presence of edema):
   Usual dose: 0.5 g/kg IV at 1 ml/minute.
   Repeat q1-2 days until desired response achieved.
3. Hyperbilirubinemia or erythroblastosis fetalis: (25% solution preferred):
   Usual dose: 1 g/kg IV 1 hour prior to exchange transfusion or replace 50 ml of donor plasma with 50 ml of 25% albumin.

Note:
1. 5% solution:
   Albumin content: 5 g/100 ml.
   Sodium content: 130-160 mEq/liter.
   Isotonic and isosmotic with plasma.
2. 25% solution ("salt poor"):
   Albumin content: 25 g/100 ml.
   Sodium content: 130-160 mEq/liter.
   Five times more osmotic than an equivalent volume of plasma.
3. Therapy in shock states with acute plasma volume depletion should be guided by frequent monitoring of blood pressure, pulse rate, urine output, and hemoglobin or hematocrit levels. Additional measurements include CVP, pulmonary artery wedge pressure, arterial blood pressure, ABGs and lactate levels, and other parameters available in the ICU.

Contraindications: Severe anemia, congestive heart failure.

ALLOPURINOL (Zyloprim)

Adults:
1. Initial: 100 mg PO qd. Increase by 100 mg weekly, until serum uric acid levels are less than 6 mg/100 ml or until maximum daily dosage is reached (800 mg/day).
2. Maintenance (average doses):
   a. Mild gout: 200-300 mg/day PO, divided or as single dose.
   b. Moderately severe gout: 400-600 mg/day in divided doses.
   c. Prevention of uric acid nephropathy during cancer chemotherapy: 600-800 mg/day PO in divided doses for 2-3 days, followed by usual maintenance doses.
3. Maximum recommended dosage: 800 mg/day (no more than 300 mg/dose).

Children (with secondary hyperuricemia associated with malignancies):
10 mg/kg/day PO divided q8h.

Action: Xanthine oxidase inhibitor; inhibits formation of uric acid.

Contraindication: Allopurinol hypersensitivity.

AMIKACIN (Amikin)

Adults and children with normal renal function:
15 mg/kg/day IM/IV divided q8-12h.

Newborns:
10 mg/kg as loading dose, then 7.5 mg/kg q12h.

Note:
1. Reduce dosage if renal function impaired.
2. Monitor renal function closely (creatinine, creatinine clearance).

Effective against: Many gram-negative bacilli, including *Pseudomonas, E. coli, Proteus, Klebsiella, Enterobacter, Serratia, Providencia, Acinetobacter, Citrobacter freundii,* and penicillinase-producing staphylococci.

Use: Short-term treatment of serious gram-negative and staphylococcal infections.

Action: Semisynthetic aminoglycoside derived from kanamycin; bactericidal.

Excretion: Renal 90% (primarily glomerular filtration).

Contraindication: Amikacin hypersensitivity.

AMINOCAPROIC ACID (Amicar)

Adults:
1. Initial: 5 g PO or IV slowly, followed by 1-1.25 g q1h, to achieve plasma levels of 0.130 mg/ml until bleeding has stopped, usually within 8 hours.
2. Maximum recommended dosage: 30 g/24 hours.

Children:
1. Initial: 100 mg/kg PO or IV slowly, followed by one-third initial dose qlh, to achieve plasma levels of 0.13 mg/ml until bleeding has stopped, usually within 8 hours.
2. Maximum recommended dosage: 18 g/m²/24 hours.

Indication: Excessive bleeding caused by systemic hyperfibrinolysis.

Action: Reduces fibrinolysis by inhibiting plasminogen activator substances.

Contraindication: Evidence of an active intravascular clotting process.

AMINOPHYLLINE (theophylline ethylenediamine)

Adults:
1. Crisis: 250-500 mg IV slowly q6h prn.
2. Oral: 100-200 mg PO q6h.
3. Suppository: 250-500 mg PR q6H.

Children:
1. Status asthmaticus: 5-6 mg/kg IV over 15-20 minutes, then 0.9 mg/kg/hour continuous IV infusion.
2. Maintenance: 2-5 mg/kg/dose PO q8h prn.

Indications: Bronchial asthma, status asthmaticus, congestive heart failure.

Action: Produces smooth muscle relaxation; bronchodilation; increases cardiac output; mild diuretic.

Contraindications: Aminophylline hypersensitivity, peptic ulcer disease.

AMPHOTERICIN B (Fungizone)

Adults and children:
1. *Test dose:* 0.1 mg/kg IV over 6 hours on first day of therapy.
2. Increase by: 0.25 mg/kg/day until 1 mg/kg/day is reached.

Note: Monitor hepatic, renal, and hematopoietic indices closely.
Use: Limited to serious systemic fungal infections.
Action: Polyene antibiotic; causes change in cell membrane permeability.
Contraindication: Amphotericin B hypersensitivity.

AMPICILLIN (Amcill)

Adults: 0.5-1 g PO/IM/IV q6h.
Children: 50-100 mg/kg/day PO/IM/IV divided q6h.

Indications: Similar to penicillin G but more effective against enterococci, *P. mirabilis, Salmonella, Shigella,* and *E. coli.*
Action: Semisynthetic penicillin; bactericidal, inhibits cell-wall synthesis.
Excretion: Renal (can be delayed with probenecid); high biliary excretion.
Contraindication: Penicillin hypersensitivity.

ANTIHEMOPHILIC FACTOR, HUMAN (Factor VIII, Factorate, Hemofil, Humafac)

Adults and children:
1. Surgery:
   Preoperative: 30-40 units/kg IV (minimum AHF level, 30%-40%).
   Postoperative: 20 units/kg IV q8h for 10 days (minimum AHF level, 15%-30%).
2. Overt bleeding: 20 units/kg followed by 10 units/kg q6-8h for 24 hours, then 10 units/kg q12h for 3-4 days.
3. Joint or muscle hemorrhage: 25 units/kg q12h for 2-4 days.
4. Massive wounds: Sufficient units to stop bleeding and maintain partial thromboplastin time close to normal.

Note: Individualize dosage and rate of administration based on clinical response and laboratory determinations of plasma factor VIII levels.
Indications:
1. Hemophilia A (treatment and maintenance).
2. Bleeding disorders caused by factor VIII deficiency.
Action: Lyophilized or dried concentrate of factor VIII; important in conversion of prothrombin to thrombin.
Contraindication: Bleeding disorders not associated with factor VIII deficiency.

ASCORBIC ACID (vitamin C)

Adults:
1. RDA: 60 mg.
2. Therapeutic: 100-1000 mg PO qd.

Children:
1. RDA: 30-50 mg PO qd.
2. Therapeutic: 100-300 mg PO qd.

Note: IM/IV administration available as sodium ascorbate.
Action: Antiscorbutic agent; important in connective tissue and protein formation as well as in iron absorption.
Contraindication: None.

ASPIRIN (acetylsalicylic acid, ASA)

Adults:
1. Mild pain or fever: 325-650 mg PO/PR q4h prn.
2. Rheumatoid arthritis: 2.6-5.2 g/day PO in divided doses.
3. Acute rheumatic fever: 5-8 g/day PO in 1-g divided doses.
4. Timed-release form: 1.3 g PO q8h prn.

Children (as antipyretic):
1. Usual dose: 65 mg/kg/day PO/PR divided q4-6h.
2. Maximum recommended dosage: 3.6 g/24 hours.

Note: Caution in presence of peptic ulcer, platelet disorders, anticoagulant therapy, hypoprothrombinemia, bleeding tendencies, or asthma.
Indications: Mild to moderate pain; fever; inflammation.
Action: Nonnarcotic antipyretic, antiinflammatory analgesic.
Contraindication: Salicylate hypersensitivity.

ATROPINE SULFATE

Adults:
1. Preanesthesia: 0.4-0.6 mg IM.
2. Bradycardia: 1-1.5 mg IV.
3. Adjuvant with antacids: 0.5-1 mg PO tid and hs.
4. Cholinesterase-inhibitor poisoning: 2 mg IM q8-10 minutes prn.

Children:
1. .01 mg/kg/dose PO/SC.
2. Maximum dose: 0.4 mg.

Action: Belladonna alkaloid, parasympatholytic (anticholinergic).
Contraindications: Glaucoma, prostatism, GI obstruction, asthma, fever.

AZATHIOPRINE (Imuran)

Adults and children:
1. Initial: 3-5 mg/kg/day IV/PO.
2. Maintenance: 1-3 mg/kg/day PO.

Note:
1. Monitor hematologic, renal, and hepatic status closely.
2. Oral administration preferable when possible.
Indication: As adjunct in the prevention of renal transplant rejection.
Action: Imidazolyl derivative of mercaptopurine; immunosuppressant.
Contraindication: Azathioprine hypersensitivity.

BECLOMETHASONE DIPROPIONATE (Vanceril Inhaler)

Adults: 2 inhalations tid-qid (1 inhalation = 42 μg).

Children (6-12 years old):
1-2 inhalations tid-qid (1 inhalation = 42 μg).

Indication: Chronic, steroid-dependent bronchial asthma.
Action: Topical anti-inflammatory steroid, nonsystemic.
Contraindication: Status asthmaticus (mucous plugs may block airways).

BENZQUINAMIDE (Emete-con)

Adults: 50 mg IM q3-4h prn (0.5-1.0 mg/kg/dose).

Children: Not recommended for use in children.

Indication: Nausea or vomiting associated with anesthesia and surgery.
Action: Antiemetic, antihistaminic, mild anticholinergic and sedative effects.
Contraindications: Benzquinamide hypersensitivity.

BETHANECHOL (Urecholine)

Adults:
1. Oral: 5-25 mg PO qid prn.
2. Subcutaneous: 5 mg (effective in 5-15 minutes)

Note: Antidote = atropine 0.6 mg SC.
Indications: Acute postoperative and postpartum nonobstructive urinary retention, neurogenic atony.
Action: Parasympathomimetic, increases detrusor tone.
Contraindications: Hyperthyroidism, pregnancy, peptic ulcer disease, asthma, hypotension, coronary artery disease, Parkinson's disease.

BISACODYL (Dulcolax)

Adults:
1. Tablets: 10-15 mg PO hs prn.
2. Suppositories: 10 mg PR prn.

Children (over 3 years old):
1. Tablets: 5 mg PO hs prn.
2. Suppositories: 5 mg PR prn.

Indications: Functional constipation; colon x-ray or proctoscopy preparation.

Action: Cathartic; acts directly on colonic mucosa to stimulate intestinal motility.

Contraindications: Intestinal obstruction, undiagnosed abdominal pain.

BRETYLIUM TOSYLATE (Bretylol)

Adults (ventricular fibrillation):

1. Initial: 5 mg/kg IV bolus.
2. Subsequent: 10 mg/kg IV; repeat as necessary. Continuous infusion: 1-2 mg/minute.

Children: Safety not established.

Note: Monitor ECG for further arrhythmia during use.

Indications:

1. Prophylaxis and therapy of ventricular fibrillation.
2. Other life-threatening ventricular tachycardia failing to respond to first-line antiarrhythmics such as lidocaine.

Action: Antiarrhythmic; inhibits norepinephrine release by depressing terminal excitability of adrenergic nerve.

Contraindication: None, when used for treatment of ventricular fibrillation or life-threatening refractory ventricular arrhythmias.

BUTALBITAL (Fiorinal)

Adults: 1-2 tablets or capsules PO q4h prn.

Children: Not recommended for use in children.

Composition: Butalbital 50 mg, aspirin 200 mg, phenacetin 130 mg, caffeine 40 mg.

Indication: Tension (or muscular contraction) headache.

Action: Butalbital: sedative and muscle relaxant effects; aspirin-phenacetin-caffeine: analgesic effect.

Contraindications: Hypersensitivity to barbiturates, aspirin, phenacetin, or caffeine; porphyria.

CALCIFEROL, USP (vitamin D_2, ergocalciferol)

Adults:

1. RDA: 400 units.
2. Usual therapy: 400-1600 units PO qd.
3. Hypoparathyroidism: 50,000-400,000 units PO qd.
4. Osteomalacia: 1500-5000 units PO qd.
5. Lupus vulgaris: 100,000-200,000 units, 1-3 times per week.

Children:

1. RDA: 400 units.
2. Usual therapy: 400-1600 units PO qd.

3. Infantile rickets: 1500-5000 units PO qd.
4. Refractory rickets: 50,000-1,000,000 units PO qd.

Note:
1. IM preparation available for malabsorption states.
2. Caution in presence of coronary artery disease, renal insufficiency, atherosclerosis.
3. Monitor serum calcium and magnesium levels closely.

Action: Fat-soluble antirachitic agent; important in calcium and phosphorous metabolism; requires metabolism in both liver and kidney.

Contraindication: Hypervitaminosis D.

CALCITONIN (Calcimar)

Adults: 100 MRC units SC/IM qd.

Children: Not recommended for use in children.

Indication: Hypercalcemia of Paget's disease.

Action: Synthetic parafollicular hormone; decreases bone and renal tubular calcium reabsorption; decreases volume and acidity of gastric juice.

Contraindication: Calcitonin hypersensitivity.

CALCIUM GLUBIONATE (Neo-Calglucon)

Adults:
1. Dietary supplement: 15 ml PO q8h.
2. Adjunct in chronic hypoparathyroidism: 15-45 ml PO daily.
3. Adjunct in acute hypoparathyroidism: 15-45 ml PO q8h.

Children:
1. Dietary supplement: 7.5 ml PO q8h.

Note: 45 ml supplies 1 g calcium.

Indications: Calcium deficiency states; dietary supplement.

Contraindication: Patients with renal calculi.

CALCIUM GLUCONATE

Adults:
1. Oral: 1-15 g PO daily (range).
2. IV: 5-10 ml of 10% solution IV slowly.

Children:
1. Oral: 500 mg/kg/day in divided doses.
2. IV: 200 mg/kg/dose IV slowly.

Note:
Tablets: 1 g calcium gluconate = 4.5 mEq calcium.
10% solution: 10 ml = 1 g calcium gluconate = 4.5 mEq calcium.

Indications:
1. Symptomatic hypocalcemia.
2. Adjunct in management of cardiac arrest.

Action: Cardiotonic bivalent cation.
Contraindication: Digitalis therapy.

CARBENICILLIN (Geopen, Geocillin)

Adults:
1. Moderate infections: 1-2 g IM/IV q4-6h.
2. Severe infections: 4-5 g IV q4-6h.

Children:
1. Moderate infections: 50-200 mg/kg/day IM/IV divided q4-6h.
2. Severe infections: 300-500 mg/kg/day IM/IV divided q4-6h.

Note:
1. Synergistic with gentamicin against some *Pseudomonas* strains.
2. Monitor sodium intake to avoid congestive heart failure.
3. Massive doses may result in severe hypokalemia.

Effective against: Most gram-positive bacteria, *Pseudomonas aeruginosa, Enterobacter,* indole-positive *Proteus (vulgaris, morganii, rettgeri),* selected *Serratia* and *Bacteroides.*
Action: Semisynthetic penicillin; bactericidal; inhibits cell wall synthesis.
Contraindication: Penicillin hypersensitivity.

CARBIDOPA-LEVODOPA (Sinemet)

Adults:
1. Initial: One 10/100 tablet PO tid.
   Increase dosage gradually for optimal effect.
2. Maximum recommended dosage: Eight 25/250 tablets/day.

Composition: Carbidopa 10 mg, levodopa 100 mg.
Indication: Parkinson's disease (permits lower dosage of levodopa).
Contraindications: Carbidopa or levodopa hypersensitivity, MAO inhibitor administration, narrow-angle glaucoma, melanoma.

CASANTHRANOL-DIOCTYL SODIUM SULFOSUCCINATE (Peri-Colace)

Adults: 1-2 capsules or 1-2 tbs syrup PO hs prn.

Children: 1-2 tsp syrup PO hs prn.

Note: Prolonged or frequent use may cause laxative dependence.
Indication: Uncomplicated constipation.
Action: Casanthranol, mild stimulant laxative; dioctyl sodium sulfosuccinate, stool softener.
Contraindications: Abdominal pain, nausea, vomiting.

CASCARA SAGRADA (Peristaltin)

Adults:
1. Tablets: 325 mg PO hs prn.
2. Aromatic fluid extract: 5 ml PO hs prn.

Children: 2-8 ml/dose.

Infants: 1-2 ml/dose.

Indication: Functional constipation.

Action: Mild stimulant laxative; contains anthracene compounds.

Contraindications: Cascara hypersensitivity, intestinal obstruction, undiagnosed abdominal pain.

CASTOR OIL

Adults:
1. Castor oil or castor oil aromatic: 15-30 ml PO.
2. Castor oil emulsion (Neoloid): 30-60 ml PO.

Children:
1. Castor oil or castor oil aromatic: 4-15 ml PO.
2. Castor oil emulsion: 7.5-30 ml PO.

Infants:
1. Castor oil or castor oil aromatic: 4 ml PO.
2. Castor oil emulsion: 2.5-7.5 ml PO.

Indications: When prompt and complete evacuation of the bowel is desired, e.g., x-ray preparation of the abdomen (IVP, barium enema).

Action: Strong stimulant laxative; contains triglyceride of ricinoleic acid.

Contraindications: Hypersensitivity, intestinal obstruction, undiagnosed abdominal pain, pregnancy, menstruation.

CEFAZOLIN SODIUM (Ancef, Kefzol)

Adults: 0.5-1 g IM/IV q6h (moderate to severe infections).

Children: 25-100 mg/kg/day IM/IV divided q6h.

Use: Cephalothin substitute; preferred for IM use; higher biliary concentrations; more effective against *E. coli* and *Klebsiella*.

Action: Semisynthetic cephalosporin; bactericidal; inhibits cell wall synthesis.

Contraindication: Cephalosporin hypersensitivity.

CEPHALEXIN (Keflex)

Adults: 0.25-1 g PO q6h (absorption impaired if given after food).

Children: 25-50 mg/kg/day PO divided q6h.

Note: Similar to cephalothin; lower activity against staphylococci.

Use: Gram-positive coccal infections; as a penicillin substitute if allergic to penicillin; urinary tract infections not susceptible to other agents.

See *Cephalothin sodium* for other properties.

CEPHALOTHIN SODIUM (Keflin)

Adults: 1-2 g IV q4-6h (IM very painful).

Children: 80-160 mg/kg/day IV divided q4-6h.

Effective against: Many gram-positive cocci, including most penicillinase-producing staphylococci; many gram-negative bacilli, including *E. coli, Proteus mirabilis, Klebsiella,* and *Haemophilus influenzae.*

Action: Semisynthetic cephalosporin antibiotic; bactericidal.

Contraindications: Cephalosporin hypersensitivity; not recommended in cases of immediate reactions to penicillin (urticaria, diffuse pruritus, anaphylaxis).

CEPHRADINE (Anspor, Velosef)

Adults: 250-500 mg PO/IM/IV q6h.

Children: 25-50 mg/kg/day PO/IM/IV divided q6h.

Effective against: Many gram-positive cocci, including most penicillinase-producing staphylococci; many gram-negative bacilli, including *E. coli, Proteus mirabilis, Klebsiella,* and *Haemophilus influenzae.*

Action: Semisynthetic cephalosporin antibiotic; bactericidal.

Contraindications: Cephalosporin hypersensitivity; not recommended in cases of immediate reactions to penicillin (urticaria, diffuse pruritus, anaphylaxis).

CHLORAL HYDRATE (Noctec)

Adults: 0.5-1.0 g PO/PR (hypnotic); 250 mg PO/PR (sedative).

Children: 50 mg/kg PO/PR (hypnotic); 25 mg/kg PO/PR (sedative).

Note: Use with caution during coumarin anticoagulation.

Indication: Insomnia.

Action: Sedative-hypnotic.

Contraindications: Chloral hydrate hypersensitivity, marked liver or renal impairment.

CHLORAMPHENICOL (Chloromycetin)

Adults:
1. Moderate infections: 0.5-1 g PO/IV q6h (50 mg/kg/day, divided q6h).
2. Severe infections: 100 mg/kg/day PO/IV divided q6h.

Children:
1. Moderate infections: 50-100 mg/kg/day PO/IV divided q6h.
2. Severe infections: 100 mg/kg/day PO/IV divided q6h.

Note: Monitor hematologic status closely.
Effective against: Many gram-positive and gram-negative bacteria, especially anaerobes, including *Bacteroides fragilis*. Staphylococcal resistance depends on extent of use in a particular locality.
Action: Bacteriostatic antibiotic; inhibits protein synthesis.
Contraindication: Chloramphenicol hypersensitivity.

CHLORDIAZEPOXIDE (Librium)

Adults:
1. Mild anxiety: 5-10 mg PO tid-qid.
2. Severe anxiety: 20-25 mg PO tid-qid.
3. Preanesthesia: 50-100 mg IM 1 hour before surgery.
4. Acute alcohol withdrawal: 50-100 mg IM/IV q2-4h prn.

Children: Not recommended for use in children.

Action: Benzodiazepine sedative-hypnotic.
Contraindication: Chlordiazepoxide hypersensitivity.

CHLORDIAZEPOXIDE-CLIDINIUM (Librax)

Adults: 1-2 capsules PO q6-8h.

Children: Not recommended for use in children.

Composition: Chlordiazepoxide 5 mg, clidinium 2.5 mg.
Indications: Adjunct in peptic ulcer, irritable bowel, acute enterocolitis.
Action: Chlordiazepoxide—sedative-hypnotic; clidinium—anticholinergic, spasmolytic.
Contraindications: Chlordiazepoxide or clidinium hypersensitivity, glaucoma, prostatic hypertrophy, benign bladder neck obstruction.

CHLORPROMAZINE (Thorazine)

Adults: 10-50 mg PO/IM tid-qid (varies with indication).

Children: 2 mg/kg/day PO/IM divided q4-6h prn.

Note: Extrapyramidal effects may be inhibited by antiparkinson drugs.
Indications: Acute intermittent porphyria; nausea; vomiting; agitation; hiccups.
Action: Aliphatic phenothiazine; sedative; antiemetic.
Contraindications: Comatose states; presence of large amounts of CNS depressants; bone marrow depression.

CHLORPROPAMIDE (Diabenese)

Adults: 250 mg PO qd (average daily dose).

Indication: Mild to moderate adult onset diabetes mellitus.
Action: Oral hypoglycemic agent; sulfonylurea.

Contraindications: Juvenile onset diabetes mellitus, brittle diabetes, ketosis, acidosis, pregnancy; impairment of hepatic, renal, or thyroid function.

CHOLESTYRAMINE RESIN (Cuemid, Questran)

Adults:
1. Initial: 4 g PO tid with meals.
2. Maintenance: 4 g PO tid (ac) or qid (ac and hs).

Children: 240 mg/kg/day divided q8h.

Note: Individualize dosage according to patient's needs.
Indications:
1. Adjunct to diet and weight reduction in type II hypercholesterolemia.
2. Pruritus associated with partial biliary obstruction.

Action: Anion exchange resin; produces an increased fecal bile acid excretion.
Contraindications: Cholestyramine hypersensitivity, complete biliary obstruction.

CIMETIDINE (Tagamet)

Adults: 300 mg PO/IV q6h.

Children: 20-40 mg/kg/day divided q6h.

Note: Antacids may be given if indicated for pain relief.
Indications:
1. Short-term treatment of duodenal ulcer (up to 8 weeks).
2. Pathologic hypersecretory conditions.

Action: Histamine H_2-receptor inhibitor at the parietal cell level.
Contraindication: None known.

CLINDAMYCIN (Cleocin)

Adults:
1. Oral: 150-300 mg q6h (maximum, 450 mg PO q6h).
2. IV/IM: 600-1200 mg q6h (IM: limit to 600 mg/dose).

Children:
1. Oral: 8-6 mg/kg/day PO divided q6-8h (maximum 20 mg/kg/day).
2. IV/IM: 15-25 mg/kg/day divided q6-8h (maximum 40 mg/kg/day).

Effective against: Gram-positive cocci, including penicillinase-producing staphylococci and anaerobic bacteria (especially *Bacteroides fragilis*).
Action: Semisynthetic antibiotic similar to lincomycin; bacteriostatic.
Contraindication: Clindamycin or lincomycin hypersensitivity.

CLOFIBRATE (Atromid-S)

Adults: 500 mg PO qid.

Note: May potentiate oral anticoagulants.
Indications: Hypercholesterolemia, hypertriglyceridemia.
Action: Decreases liver synthesis of cholesterol, triglycerides.
Contraindications: Pregnancy, lactation, hepatic and renal insufficiency, primary biliary cirrhosis.

CLONIDINE (Catapres)

Adults:
1. Initial: 0.1 mg PO bid. Increase gradually if necessary.
2. Maximum recommended dosage: 2.4 mg/day.

Indication: Mild to moderate essential hypertension.
Action: Antihypertensive (decreases sympathetic outflow).

CLOXACILLIN (Tegopen)

Adults: 0.25-1 g PO q6h (before meals).

Children: 50-200 mg/kg PO divided q6h.

Note: Differences from oxacillin:
1. Better absorbed than oxacillin.
2. Serum concentration twice as high.
3. 95% bound to serum proteins.
4. Less excreted in bile.
Indications: Gram-positive coccal infections, including penicillinase-producing staphylococci.
Action: Bactericidal; inhibits cell wall synthesis.
Contraindication: Penicillin hypersensitivity.

CODEINE (methylmorphine)

Adults:
1. Analgesic: 30-60 mg PO/SC q4h prn.*
2. Antitussive: 8-20 mg PO q4h prn.†

Children:
1. Analgesic: 0.5-1 mg/kg dose PO/SC q4h prn.*
2. Antitussive: 0.2-0.3 mg/kg dose PO q4h prn.†

Note:
1. Parenteral codeine, 120 mg, is equianalgesic to morphine, 10 mg.
2. Oral codeine is about two-thirds as effective as it is parenterally.
3. Antidote for overdose: See *Levallorphan* or *Naloxone*.
Indications: Mild to moderate pain; symptomatic relief of cough.
Action: Mild narcotic analgesic-antitussive.
Contraindication: Codeine hypersensitivity. See cautions for morphine.

*Codeine phosphate may be administered SC.
†Available in elixirs, liquids, and syrups containing 5-10 mg/5ml.

COLCHICINE, USP (Colchicine)

Adults:
1. Acute gouty arthritis:
   - PO: 1-1.2 mg stat; then 0.5-0.6 mg q1h until the pain is relieved or until nausea, vomiting, or diarrhea occurs (maximum recommended dosage, 10 mg/day).
   - IV: 1-2 mg stat; then 0.5 mg q3-6h (maximum recommended dosage, 6 mg/day).
2. Prophylaxis: 0.5-0.6 mg PO, 3 or more times weekly.
3. Adjunct to antigout therapy: 0.5-0.6 mg PO bid-tid.

Note:
1. Oral administration preferred when feasible.
2. Uric acid levels should not be lowered until gouty attack has subsided.

Action: Antigout agent; reduces inflammatory response; does not reduce serum uric acid levels.

Contraindications: Colchicine hypersensitivity; serious GI, renal, or cardiac disease.

DESLANOSIDE (Cedilanid-D)

Adults:
1. Digitalization:
   - IV: 1.6 mg as one injection or in two divided doses.
   - IM: 1.6 mg divided in 0.8-mg portions at two sites.
2. Maintenance: Start an oral preparation within 12-24 hours.

Children:
1. Digitalization: 12.5 μg/kg IV stat, then 6 μg/kg IV q2h × 2.
2. Maintenance: Start an oral preparation within 12-24 hours.

Note:
1. Limit parenteral digitalization to urgent situations.
2. Begin oral digitalis preparation as soon as the emergency has passed.

Indication: When rapid digitalization is necessary.

Action: Digitalis glycoside (see *Digoxin*).

Onset: 10-30 minutes (IV).

Peak: 1-2 hours; T½, 33 hours.

Contraindications: Deslanoside hypersensitivity, digitalis toxicity, ventricular tachycardia or fibrillation.

DIAZEPAM (Valium)

Adults:
1. Preoperative medication: 5-10 mg IM before surgery.
2. Anxiety: 2-10 mg PO 2-4 times daily.

3. Acute alcohol withdrawal: 10 mg IM/IV stat; then 5-10 mg in 3-4 hours if necessary.
4. Severe muscle spasm: 5-10 mg IM/IV stat; then 5-10 mg in 3-4 hours if necessary.
5. Status epilepticus: 5-10 mg IV stat; repeat every 10-15 minutes if necessary up to maximum of 30 mg.

Children:
1. Oral: 0.1-0.8 mg/kg/day divided q6-8h.
2. IM/IV: 0.04-0.75 mg/kg/day (maximum single dose 5 mg).

Note:
1. IV administration should not exceed 5 mg/minute.
2. Extreme caution advised with IV use, especially in presence of chronic lung disease or unstable cardiovascular status.

Action: Benzodiazepine derivative; sedative; anticonvulsant.
Contraindications: Diazepam hypersensitivity, glaucoma (see PDR).

DIAZOXIDE (Hyperstat)

Adults: 1 ampule (300 mg in 20 ml) IV bolus; repeat in 30 minutes if necessary.

Children: 5 mg/kg/dose (safety in children not established).

Note:
1. Associated with sodium retention, hyperglycemia, hypotension, drug interactions.
2. Monitor blood pressure, serum electrolytes, glucose, uric acid closely.
3. Begin alternative antihypertensive therapy after emergency controlled.

Indication: Malignant hypertension as an emergency.
Action: Peripheral arteriolar smooth muscle relaxation.
Peak effect: 2-5 minutes.
Duration: About 12 hours.
Contraindications: Diazoxide or thiazide hypersensitivity; hypertension caused by coarctation or AV shunt.

DICLOXACILLIN (Dynapen)

Adults: 250-500 mg PO q6h.

Children: 12.5-25 mg/kg/day PO divided q6h.

Indication: Penicillinase-producing staphylococcal infections.
Action: Penicillinase-resistant isoxazolyl penicillin; bactericidal.
Contraindication: Penicillin hypersensitivity.

DIGITOXIN (Crystodigin)

Adults:
1. Digitalization: 1 mg IV or 0.7-1.2 mg PO in divided doses over 12-24 hours.
2. Maintenance: 0.05-.15 mg PO/IV qd.

Children:
1. Digitalization: 30 µg/kg PO/IV in divided doses.
2. Maintenance: 2.5-5 µg/kg PO/IV qd.

Indications and action: Similar to digoxin.
Onset: 25 minutes to 2 hours.
Peak: 4-12 hours; T½, 4-6 hours.
See *Digoxin* for other properties.

DIGOXIN (Lanoxin)

Adults:
1. Digitalization: 0.75-1.0 mg IV or 1-1.5 mg PO in divided doses over 12-24 hours.
2. Maintenance: 0.125-0.5 mg PO/IV qd.

Children (over 2 years old):
1. Digitalization: 25-50 µg/kg PO/IM/IV in divided doses.
2. Maintenance: 10 µg/kg/day PO/IM/IV.

Note:
1. Individualize dosage according to clinical situation and response.
2. Decrease dosage in renal impairment, hypokalemia, hypercalcemia, hypothyroidism, hypoxemia, advanced heart disease, or cor pulmonale.
3. Agents used to manage digitalis-related arrhythmia include potassium, lidocaine, phenytoin, procainamide, and propranolol.

Indications: Congestive heart failure, atrial fibrillation, atrial flutter, paroxysmal atrial tachycardia, cardiogenic shock.
Onset: 15-30 minutes (IV).
Peak: 1½-5 hours; T½, 36 hours.
Action: Cardiac glycoside; inotropic effect; increases refractory period of AV node and, to a lesser extent, the SA node and conduction system.
Contraindications: Digitalis hypersensitivity or toxicity, ventricular fibrillation.

DIHYDROTACHYSTEROL (Hytakerol)

Adults:
1. Initial: .8-2.4 mg PO qd for 3-4 days (1 mg = 120,000 units).
2. Maintenance: 0.2-1.0 mg PO qd (check serum calcium).

Children:
1. Initial: 1-5 mg PO qd for 4 days.
2. Maintenance: 0.5-1.5 mg PO qd.

Note: Differences from vitamin D_2 (ergocalciferol):
1. Three times as active in promoting resorption of calcium from bone.

2. One-fiftieth as active in promoting intestinal absorption of calcium.
3. Requires hydroxylation in liver only.
4. Faster onset, shorter duration of action.
5. More expensive than vitamin D_2.

Indication: Hypocalcemia caused by hypoparathyroidism and pseudohypoparathyroidism.
Contraindications: Hypercalcemia; hypocalcemia caused by renal insufficiency and hyperphosphatemia.

DIOCTYL CALCIUM SULFOSUCCINATE (Surfak)

Adults: 240 mg PO qd.

Children: 5 mg/kg/day PO divided q6-8h.

Note: Similar to *Dioctyl sodium sulfosuccinate.*

DIOCTYL SODIUM SULFOSUCCINATE (Colace)

Adults: 100 mg PO tid.

Children: 5 mg/kg/day PO divided q6-8h.

Indications: Constipation due to hard stools, painful anorectal conditions, cardiac and other conditions; to avoid difficult or painful defecation.
Action: Softens stool by lowering surface tension.
Contraindication: None known.

DIPHENHYDRAMINE (Benadryl)

Adults: 25-50 mg PO/IM/IV q6h prn.

Children:
1. Oral: 5 mg/kg/day PO/IM divided q6h.
2. Intravenous: 2 mg/kg IV slowly for anaphylaxis.

Indications: Allergic reactions, motion sickness, parkinsonism, insomnia.
Action: Antihistaminic (H_1-receptor blocker) with antispasmodic, antitussive, antiemetic, and sedative effects.
Contraindications: Diphenhydramine hypersensitivity, asthmatic attack, narrow-angle glaucoma, prostate hypertrophy, GI obstruction, MAO inhibitor administration.

DIPHENOXYLATE-ATROPINE SULFATE (Lomotil)

Adults:
1. Initial: 2 tablets or 10 ml PO q6h.
2. Maintenance: 1 tablet or 5 ml PO q12h.

Children (2-12 years):
1. Initial: 0.3-4 mg/kg/day PO divided q12h.
2. Maintenance: 0.1 mg/kg/day PO divided q12h.

Composition (1 tablet or 5 ml liquid):
diphenoxylate 2.5 mg, atropine sulfate 0.025 mg.

Note:
1. Caution in presence of liver disease, acute ulcerative colitis, MAO inhibitor administration, addiction potential, and in young children.
2. Atropine present in subtherapeutic dose to discourage overdosage.

Indication: Adjunct in treatment of acute nonspecific diarrhea.

Action: Slows intestinal motility.

Contraindications: Diphenoxylate hypersensitivity, jaundice, pseudomembranous enterocolitis, children less than 2 years old. For atropine contraindications, see *Atropine sulfate.*

DOPAMINE (Intropin)

Adults: 200 mg in 250 ml D5W or NS (800 μg/ml) at 2-5 μg/kg/minute (low-dose range). Increase if needed to 20-50 μg/kg/min (high-dose range).

Note:
1. Correct preexisting volume deficits before administration.
2. Monitor pulse, blood pressure, CVP, urine output, peripheral perfusion closely. Titrate infusion to blood pressure.

Indications: Shock syndrome caused by myocardial infarction, trauma, sepsis, open heart surgery, renal failure, congestive heart failure.

Action: Catecholamine precursor of norepinephrine; inotropic and chronotropic agent; mild peripheral vasodilator.

Contraindications: Pheochromocytoma, uncorrected tachyarrhythmias, ventricular fibrillation.

DOXEPIN (Sinequan)

Adults:
1. Usual initial range: 10-25 mg PO tid.
2. Usual maintenance range: 25-50 mg PO tid.

Indications: Depression, anxiety.

Action: Dibenzoxepin tricyclic; decreases reuptake of norepinephrine.

Contraindications: Doxepin hypersensitivity, glaucoma, urinary retention, MAO inhibitor administration, children under 12 years old.

DOXYCYCLINE (Vibramycin)

Adults: 100 mg PO/IV bid on day 1; then 100 mg PO/IV qd.

Children: 4.4 mg/kg on day 1, then 2.2 mg/kg/day PO/IV.

Note: Main advantages over tetracycline:
1. Increased oral absorption.
2. Fewer GI side effects.
3. Does not accumulate in renal failure.

4. Twice as active against most bacteria.
5. Less frequent administration because of prolonged T½.
Indication: As for tetracycline.
Action: Broad-spectrum antibiotic; bacterostatic; inhibits protein synthesis.
Contraindication: Tetracycline hypersensitivity.

EDROPHONIUM CHLORIDE (Tensilon)

Adults:
1. Test dose: 2 mg IV; observe for cholinergic reaction.
2. Therapeutic dose: 5-10 mg IV; repeat q10 minutes 4 times if necessary.

Children:
1. Test dose: 0.5-1 mg IV; observe for cholinergic reaction.
2. Therapeutic dose: 0.2 mg/kg/dose IV, repeat q10 minutes × 4 if necessary (maximum total dose 5-10 mg).

Note:
1. Caution in presence of bronchial asthma, arrhythmias.
2. IV administration preferred over IM use.
3. Monitor ECG and blood pressure closely with paroxysmal supraventricular tachycardia.
4. Antidote for overdosage (cholinergic crisis): atropine sulfate, 1 mg IV prn.

Indications:
1. For reversal of neuromuscular block caused by curariform drugs.
2. Myasthenia gravis (diagnosis, emergency treatment).
3. Also used for paroxysmal supraventricular tachycardia.
Action: Rapid-acting cholinergic agent of short duration; produces effect by inhibition or inactivation of acetylcholinesterase.
Onset: 30-60 seconds (IV), 2-10 minutes (IM).
Duration: 10 minutes (IV).
Contraindications: Hypersensitivity to anticholinesterase agents, mechanical intestinal or urinary obstruction, paroxysmal atrial tachycardia.

EPHEDRINE-THEOPHYLLINE-HYDROXYZINE (Marax)

Adults: 1 tablet PO q6-12h.

Children: ½ tablet PO q6-12h, then 5 ml PO q6-8h.

Composition:
Ephedrine, 25 mg/tablet, 6.25 mg/5 ml.
Theophylline, 130 mg/tablet, 32.50 mg/5 ml.
Hydroxyzine, 10 mg/tablet, 2.5 mg/5 ml.
Note: Individualize dosage according to response and tolerance.
Indication: For controlling bronchospastic disorders.

Action:

Ephedrine—sympathomimetic bronchodilator and vasoconstrictor.

Theophylline—xanthine bronchodilator, mild diuretic.

Hydroxyzine—ataraxic, reduces CNS stimulation of ephedrine.

Contraindications: Hypersensitivity to individual agents, cardiovascular disease, hypertension, hyperthyroidism, early pregnancy.

EPINEPHRINE (Adrenalin)

Adults:

1. Anaphylactic shock:
   1:1,000 (aqueous): 0.3-0.5 ml in 10 ml NS IV q5-15 minutes.
2. Bronchospasm (asthma, allergic reactions):
   1:1,000 (aqueous): 0.1-0.3 ml SC/IM q15-20 minutes prn.
   1:200 (Sus-Phrine): 0.1 ml SC q4-6h prn.
3. Cardiac resuscitation (resistant ventricular fibrillation; asystole):
   1:1,000 (aqueous): 0.5-1.0 ml in 10 ml NS IV/IC q5 minutes prn.
   (Increases fibrillatory strength and may allow electrical conversion.)
4. IV infusion (for inotropic effect after volume restoration):
   1:1,000 (aqueous): 3 ml in 300 ml D5W or NS at 1 μg-4 μg/minute.

Children:

1. Anaphylaxis:
   1:1000 (aqueous): 0.01 ml/kg diluted IV.
2. Bronchial asthmatic attack:
   1:1000 (aqueous): 0.01 ml/kg/dose SC/IM q15-20 minutes prn.*
   1:200 (Sus-Phrine): 0.005 ml/kg/dose SC q8-12h prn.†
3. Cardiac resuscitation: 1:10,000 (aqueous):
   Newborn: 0.1 ml/kg/IV/IC q3-5 minutes prn.
   Children: 1-5 ml IV/IC q3-5 minutes prn.
4. IV infusion: 1:10,000 (aqueous): 4-8 μg/minute IV.

Note:

1. For IV/IC administration, dilute each 1 mg (1 ml) of 1:1000 solution in at least 10 ml of NS to prepare a 1:10,000 solution.

---

*Maximum 0.5 ml of 1:1000/dose.
†Maximum 0.15 ml/dose.

2. Caution in presence of hypertension, hyperthyroidism, or coronary, cerebral, or peripheral vascular disease.

Action: Sympathomimetic bronchodilator and vasoconstrictor; produces alpha-receptor activation with the exception of intestinal relaxation; produces beta-receptor activity with positive inotropic and chronotropic stimulation of the heart. In low doses, beta-adrenergic effects are predominant; in higher doses, alpha-adrenergic effects are observed.

Contraindications: Hypersensitivity to sympathomimetic amines, coronary insufficiency, shock (other than anaphylaxis), narrow-angle glaucoma, general anesthesia, digital nerve blocks, organic brain disease.

ERGOTAMINE TARTRATE (Ergomar)

Adults: 2 mg SL at onset of headache; repeat in ½ hour if necessary.

Children: Safety not established.

Note: Limit dosage to 6 mg/day and 10 mg/week.
Indications: Vascular headaches (migraine or cluster).
Action: Cerebral vasoconstriction.
Contraindications: Hypertension, occlusive vascular disease, coronary artery disease, hepatic and renal disease, sepsis, pregnancy.

ERYTHROMYCIN (Erythrocin)

Adults:
1. Oral: 250-500 mg q6h.
2. IV: 15-20 mg/kg/day (severe infections).

Children: 30-50 mg/kg/day PO divided q4-6h.

Note: Reduce dosage if liver impairment present.
Indications: In penicillin allergy for group A streptococcal and some pneumococcal infections or prophylaxis; Legionnaire's disease; *Mycoplasma pneumoniae* pneumonia.
Action: Macrolide; inhibits protein synthesis; bacteriostatic and bactericidal.
Contraindication: Erythromycin hypersensitivity.

ETHACRYNIC ACID (Edecrin)

Adults:
1. Oral: 25-50 mg bid (initial dose).
2. IV: 0.5-1 mg/kg/day (single dose).

Children:
1. Oral: 25 mg PO (initial dose).
2. IV: Not recommended by manufacturer, but 1 mg/kg/day (single dose) reported safe and effective.

Indications:
1. Edema (congestive heart failure, liver cirrhosis, renal disease).
2. Ascites (malignant, idiopathic, lymphedema).

Action: Blocks renal tubular reabsorption of sodium.

Onset: Within 5 minutes after IV dose.

Duration: 6-8 hours.

Contraindication: Anuria. Discontinue if increasing electrolyte imbalance, azotemia, oliguria, or severe watery diarrhea develops. Use cautiously in liver disease and cor pulmonale.

FACTOR IX COMPLEX, HUMAN (Konyne, Proplex)

Adults and children:
1. Loading dose: 60 units/kg.
2. Maintenance dose: 10 units/kg q12h. Acceptable factor IX level prior to surgery is above 20% of normal; maintain for 8-10 days postoperatively.

Note: Individualize dosage based on clinical response and laboratory determinations of plasma levels of factors II, VII, IX, and X.

Indications:
1. Hemophilia B (factor IX deficiency, Christmas disease).
2. Bleeding disorders caused by deficiency of factor II, VII, IX, or X.
3. Hemorrhagic disease of the newborn (life-threatening cases only).

Action: Lyophilized concentrate of factors II, VII, IX, and X.

Contraindications: Liver disease with suspected intravascular coagulation or fibrinolysis.

FERROUS GLUCONATE OR SULFATE

Adults: 50-100 mg elemental iron PO tid.

Children: 4-6 mg elemental iron/kg/day divided tid.

Note:
1. 300 mg ferrous gluconate provides 35 mg of iron.
2. 300 mg ferrous sulfate provides 60 mg of iron.
3. Response to therapy best indicated by rising hemoglobin levels.
4. Replacement of iron stores may require 4-8 weeks after hemoglobin normal.

Indications: Iron deficiency, iron-deficiency anemia.

Contraindication: All anemias other than iron-deficiency anemia.

FIBRINOGEN, HUMAN (Parenogen)

Adults: 2-10 g IV, slowly (1 g over 15-30 minutes).

Children: 1 g IV slowly (1 g over 30-60 minutes).

Note:
1. Individualize dosage based on clinical response and laboratory determinations of plasma fibrinogen levels.
2. Monitor coagulation status closely.

Indication: Severe fibrinogen deficiency (< 60 mg/100 ml).

Action: Lyophilized concentrate of fibrinogen; heat labile. Converted into fibrin on contact with thrombin.

Hemostatic level: 100 mg/100 ml.

Contraindication: Fibrinogen deficiency complicated by disseminated intravascular coagulation.

FLAVOXATE (Urispas)

Adults: 100-200 mg PO q6-8h.

Indications: Relief of lower urinary tract symptoms such as dysuria, urgency, nocturia, suprapubic pain, frequency, and incontinence.

Action: Synthetic antispasmodic; urinary tract spasmolytic.

Contraindications: Flavoxate hypersensitivity, GI or lower urinary tract obstruction, glaucoma.

FLURAZEPAM (Dalmane)

Adults: 15-30 mg PO hs prn.

Indication: Insomnia.

Action: Benzodiazepine derivative; hypnotic agent.

Contraindication: Flurazepam hypersensitivity.

FOLIC ACID (Folvite)

Adults:
1. MDR: 50-100 μg.
2. RDA: 0.2-0.4 mg.
3. Usual therapeutic dosage: 0.25-1 mg PO qd.
4. Macrocytic anemia (due to folate deficiency):
   Initial: 1-10 mg PO qd.
   Maintenance: 1-2 mg PO qd.

Children:
1. Usual therapeutic dosage: 0.25-1 mg PO qd.
2. Maintenance:
   Infants: 0.1 mg PO qd.
   Children up to 4 years old: 0.3 mg PO qd.
   Children 4 years old and over: 0.4 mg PO qd.

Action: B-complex vitamin; essential for nucleoprotein synthesis and erythropoiesis.

Normal serum level: 0.005-0.015 µg/ml.
Contraindication: Folate hypersensitivity.

FUROSEMIDE (Lasix)

Adults:
1. Oral: 20-80 mg once or twice daily.
2. IV: 20-40 mg once or twice daily.

Children:
1. Oral: 2 mg/kg/day.
2. IV: 1 mg/kg/day.

Note: Much larger doses may be required in azotemic patients.
Indications: Edema caused by congestive heart failure, cirrhosis, renal disease; hypertension, acute pulmonary edema; may also be used in hyperkalemia and hypercalcemia.
Action: Inhibits tubular reabsorption of sodium.
Onset: 5 minutes (IV, 1 hour (PO).
Duration: 2 hours (IV), 6-8 hours (PO).
Contraindications: Furosemide hypersensitivity, anuria, hepatic coma, pregnancy.

GAMMA BENZENE HEXACHLORIDE (Kwell)

Adults and children:
Cream or lotion: Apply liberally to infected area after bath; leave on 24 hours; then wash thoroughly. May be repeated at weekly intervals twice if necessary.
Shampoo: Apply 30 ml to infected and adjacent areas and work into lather with warm water for at least 4 minutes; rinse and dry thoroughly; repeat in 24 hours if necessary. For head and crab lice only.

Indications: Scabies and head or crab lice.
Action: Ectoparasiticide; active ingredient lindane.
Contraindication: Gamma benzene hexachloride hypersensitivity.

GENTAMICIN (Garamycin)

Adults: 3-5 mg/kg/day IM/IV divided q8h.

Children: 7.5 mg/kg/day IM/IV divided q8h.

Note:
1. Reduce dosage in renal insufficiency.
2. Monitor serum creatinine and urine creatinine clearance closely.
3. IV administration preferable in sepsis, shock, congestive heart failure.
Effective against: Most gram-negative bacteria, including *Pseudomonas, E. coli, Proteus, Klebsiella-Enterobacter-Serratia,* and staphylococci (including penicillin- and methicillin-resistant strains).

Action: Aminoglycoside; bactericidal; inhibits protein synthesis.
Therapeutic serum level: 5-7 µg/ml.
Contraindications: Gentamicin hypersensitivity; cross-aller-
genicity with other aminoglycosides.

GLUCAGON

Adults: 0.5-1 mg SC/IM/IV.

Children: 0.025-0.1 mg/kg/dose SC/IM/IV (maximum =
1 mg).

Note: The patient will usually awaken in 5-20 minutes. However, if liver glycogen stores are absent, glucose must be
given IV.
Indication: Severe hypoglycemic reactions in diabetes.
Action: Increases blood glucose through hepatic glycogen-
olysis.
Contraindication: Glucagon hypersensitivity.

GRISEOFULVIN (Grifulvin V)

Adults: 500 mg PO, divided q6-12h.

Children: 10-20 mg/kg/day PO divided q6-12h.

Note: Confirm presence of dermatophyte infection before pre-
scribing.
Indications: Chronic ringworm (tinea) infections of the skin,
hair, and nails.
Action: Fungistatic; absorbed orally; deposits in keratin; gradually exfoliated.
Contraindications: Griseofulvin hypersensitivity, porphyria,
hepatocellular disease, pregnancy.

GUAIFENESIN (Robitussin)

Adults: 200-400 mg PO q4h.

Children:
1. 6-11 years old: 100-200 mg PO q4h.
2. 2-5 years old: 50-100 mg PO q4h.

Indication: To promote expectoration of inspissated mucus.
Action: Enhances flow of less viscid respiratory tract secre-
tions.
Contraindication: Guaifenesin hypersensitivity.

GUANETHIDINE (Ismelin)

Adults:
1. Initial: 10-25 mg PO qd.
   Increase dosage q5-7 days to achieve optimal response.
2. Maintenance: 25-50 mg PO qd (average); 10-300 mg PO
   qd (range).

Children:

1. Initial: 0.2 mg/kg/day PO.
2. Increase dosage q7-10 days to achieve optimal response.
3. Maintenance: May be 5-8 times the initial dose.

Note:

1. Monitor supine and erect blood pressure to individualize dosage.
2. Discontinue 2 weeks preoperatively to minimize hypotensive reactions.

Indications:

1. Moderate to severe essential hypertension.
2. Renal hypertension (pyelonephritis, amyloidosis, renal artery stenosis).
3. To control adrenergic manifestations of hyperthyroidism.

Action: Sympathetic blocking agent; inhibits release of norepinephrine.

Onset: 2-3 days (PO).

Duration: 10 days (PO).

Contraindications: Guanethidine hypersensitivity, pheochromocytoma, severe coronary or cerebrovascular insuffiency, MAO inhibitor administration.

HALOPERIDOL (Haldol)

Adults:

1. Initial: 0.5-2.0 mg PO q8-12h.
2. Maintenance: 1 mg PO qd (average lowest dose).
3. Acute crisis: 2-5 mg IM q4-8H (or up to q1h).

Note:

1. Individualize dosage for optimal effect.
2. Extrapyramidal reactions may be minimized by antiparkinson drugs.
3. May increase anticoagulant requirements.

Indications:

1. Oral maintenance therapy of psychotic disorders.
2. Parenteral therapy of acute psychotic crises.

Action: Butyrophenone derivative; antipsychotic; antiemetic.

Contraindications: Haloperidol hypersensitivity, severe depression, Parkinson's disease.

HEPARIN SODIUM (Panheprin)

Adults:

1. Continuous IV infusion:
    Load: 5000-10,000 units IV bolus.
    Maintenance: 1000-2000 units/hour by constant infusion pump.
2. Intermittent intravenous injection:
    Load: 10,000 units IV bolus.
    Maintenance: 5000-10,000 units IV bolus q4-6h.

3. Intermittent subcutaneous injection:
   Load: 5000 units IV bolus.
   Maintenance: 8000-10,000 units SC q8h.

Children:
1. Continuous IV infusion:
   Load: 50-100 units/kg IV bolus.
   Maintenance: 100 units/kg IV drip every 4 hours.
2. Intermittent intravenous injection:
   Load: 100 units/kg IV bolus.
   Maintenance: 50-100 units/kg IV bolus q4h.

Note:
1. Individualize dosage to maintain PTT at 1½-2½ times control or clotting time at 2-3 times control, to prevent over or underheparinization.
2. The prothrombin may be prolonged by heparin administration; therefore, when switching to oral anticoagulant, measure PT either 5 hours after the last IV dose or 24 hours after the last SC dose of heparin. Heparin therapy may be discontinued when oral anticoagulant is fully effective.
3. Overheparinization may be controlled by protamine sulfate.

Indications:
1. Prophylaxis and treatment of venous thrombosis.
2. Prophylaxis and treatment of pulmonary embolism.
3. Atrial fibrillation with embolization.
4. Adjunct in treatment of disseminated intravascular coagulation.
5. Prevention of clotting in arterial and cardiac surgery.
6. Prevention of cerebral thrombosis in evolving stroke.
7. Adjunct in treatment of coronary occlusion with acute myocardial infarction.
8. Adjunct in prophylaxis and treatment of arterial embolism.
9. Adjunct in blood transfusions, extracorporeal circulation, dialysis, and blood samples.

Action: Anticoagulant effect is achieved through inactivation of thrombin and inhibition of activation of fibrin stabilizing factor; prolongs PTT, clotting time, thrombin time, PT.

Onset: Immediate (IV).

T½: About 2 hours (IV).

Contraindications: Heparin hypersensitivity, active uncontrollable bleeding. Extreme caution whenever an increased danger of hemorrhage exists: major surgery, shock, severe hypotension, diastolic pressure > 120 mm Hg, suspected intracranial hemorrhage, threatened abortion, continuous tube drainage of stomach or small intestine, salicylate administration, peptic ulcer disease, thrombocytopenia, hemophilia, subacute bacterial endocarditis.

HYDRALAZINE (Apresoline)

Adults:
1. Oral: Initial, 10 mg q6h. Increase gradually until optimum response achieved. Usual range, 4-200 mg/day, divided q6h.
2. IM/IV: 20-40 mg repeated as necessary.

Children:
1. Oral: 0.75/kg/day divided q6h. Increase gradually for optimum response.
2. IM/IV: maximum 7.5 mg/kg/day or 1.7-3.5 mg/kg/day divided q4-6h.

Note:
1. Limit parenteral administration to hypertensive crises.
2. Monitor CBC, LE cell preparations, ANA titers closely.
3. Use with caution in suspected coronary artery disease.
4. Propranolol useful to minimize reflex tachycardia and increased cardiac output.

Indications: Oral therapy of essential hypertension; parenteral therapy of hypertensive crises.

Action: Decreases arteriolar resistance by unknown nonadrenergic mechanism.

Maximum effect: 10-80 minutes (IV), 3-4 hours (PO).

Contraindications: Hydralazine hypersensitivity, coronary artery disease, mitral and valvular rheumatic heart disease.

HYDROCHLOROTHIAZIDE (Esidrix, Hydrodiuril, Oretic)

Adults:
1. Diuretic: 50-100 mg PO 1-2 times daily or 3-5 days/week.
2. Hypertension: Initial: 50-100 mg/day PO as single dose or divided q18h. Increase gradually until optimum response achieved.

Children: 2.2 mg/kg/day PO divided q12h.

Note:
1. Dosage must be individualized according to patient response.
2. Adequate potassium intake may be necessary to prevent hypokalemia.
3. Monitor serum electrolytes, uric acid, and blood glucose closely.

Indications:
1. Adjunctive treatment of edema in congestive heart failure, cirrhosis, steroid and estrogen therapy, nephrotic syndrome, acute glomerulonephritis, chronic renal failure.
2. Essential hypertension.

Action: Thiazide diuretic; inhibits tubular resorption of sodium.

Contraindications: Hydrochlorothiazide or sulfonamide hypersensitivity, anuria.

HYDROCODONE-HOMATROPINE (Hycodan)

Adults: 1 tablet or 5 ml syrup PO q4-6h prn.

Children:
1. 2-12 years old: ½ tablet or 2.5 ml PO q4-6h prn.
2. < 2 years old: ¼ tablet or 1.25 ml PO q4-6h prn.

Composition (1 tablet or 5 ml syrup): Hydrocodone 5 mg, homatropine 1.5 mg.
Indication: Symptomatic relief of cough.
Action: Centrally acting narcotic antitussive.
Contraindications: Hydrocodone or homatropine hypersensitivity, glaucoma.

HYDROMORPHONE (Dilaudid)

Adults:
1. Analgesic: 2-4 mg IM/SC/IV/PO q4-6h prn (or 3-mg suppository).
2. Antitussive: 1 mg PO q3-4h prn (tablet or syrup form, 1 mg/5 ml).

Children: Optimal dosage not established.

Note:
1. Parenteral hydromorphone, 1.5-2.0 mg, is equianalgesic to morphine, 10 mg.
2. Oral hydromorphone is almost as effective as parenteral hydromorphone.
3. Antidote for overdosage: See *Levallorphan* or *Naloxone*.
Indications: Moderate to severe, acute or chronic pain; persistent nonproductive cough.
Action: Semisynthetic narcotic analgesic and antitussive.
Contraindications: Opiate hypersensitivity; intracranial lesion associated with increased intracranial pressure; status asthmaticus. (See cautions for morphine.)

HYDROXYZINE (Atarax, Vistaril)

Adults: 25-100 mg PO/IM tid prn.

Children: 2 mg/kg/day PO divided q6-8h.

Note: May potentiate narcotics, barbiturates.
Indications: Anxiety; tension; pre- and postoperative sedation.
Action: Ataraxic, muscle relaxant, antispasmodic, antiemetic.
Contraindications: Hydroxyzine hypersensitivity, early pregnancy.

IBUPROFEN (Motrin)

Adults: Maximum dose should not exceed 2400 mg/24 hours.
Children: Not recommended for use in children.

Note: Smallest effective dose recommended to avoid potential adverse effects.

Indications: Symptomatic relief of rheumatoid arthritis or osteoarthritis. Also used for migraine headaches, menstrual cramps.

Action: Nonsteroidal anti-inflammatory, antipyretic analgesic.

Contraindications: Ibuprofen hypersensitivity; syndrome of nasal polyps, angioedema, and bronchospasm due to aspirin hypersensitivity.

IMIPRAMINE (Tofranil)

Adults: 25 mg PO/IM tid-qid.

Children: 10-75 mg PO hs (depends on weight).

Indications: Depression; childhood enuresis.

Action: Tricyclic antidepressant; potentiates adrenergic synapses by blocking reuptake of norepinephrine.

Contraindications: Imipramine hypersensitivity, myocardial infarction, MAO inhibitor use.

INDOMETHACIN (Indocin)

Adults:

1. Acute gouty arthritis: Initial: 50 mg PO tid until articular pain subsides. Then taper dose rapidly until discontinuance is possible.
2. Other indications:
   Initial: 25 mg PO bid-tid. May increase dose by 25 mg weekly until satisfactory response achieved.
   Maximum recommended dosage: 150-200 mg/24 hours. Then taper dose rapidly until discontinuance is possible.

Note:

1. Short-term administration with the lowest effective dose is recommended to avoid bone marrow toxicity and other adverse effects.
2. Monitor hematologic status and weight closely.

Indications: Short-term relief of severe symptoms caused by acute gouty arthritis, rheumatoid arthritis, rheumatoid spondylitis, osteoarthritic hip, and postpericardiotomy syndrome.

Action: Anti-inflammatory, antipyretic analgesic.

Contraindications: Aspirin or indomethacin hypersensitivity; peptic ulcer, GI lesions, hypertension, congestive heart failure, blood dyscrasias, pregnancy, lactation; children less than 14 years old.

IRON DEXTRAN (Imferon)

Adults and children:

1. Calculate total iron requirement: 150 mg iron for each g% of hemoglobin deficient, plus 400-700 mg to replace iron stores.

2. Administer IM in daily increments by Z-track technique.
3. Total daily dose should not exceed 4 ml (200 mg) for patients weighing 110 pounds or more.

Note:
1. Caution with severe liver impairment.
2. Begin with test dose of 0.5 ml and observe for adverse reactions.

Indication: Iron deficiency anemia when oral route unfeasible.

Contraindications: Iron dextran hypersensitivity; all anemias other than iron deficiency anemia.

ISONIAZID (INH)

Adults: 5 mg/kg/day PO qd (usual, 300 mg/day; severely ill, 600 mg/day).

Children: 10-20 mg/kg/day PO qd (maximum: 500 mg/day).

Note:
1. Caution in presence of liver or renal disease, convulsive disorders.
2. Isoniazid-related hepatitis increased in patients over 35 years old.
3. Monitor liver function tests closely.
4. Pyridoxine (15-50 mg/day) recommended to prevent polyneuritis in presence of malnutrition, diabetes; in adolescence.

Indications:
1. For all forms of tuberculosis in which organisms are susceptible.
2. For preventive therapy of close associates.
3. For positive tuberculin skin test reactors.

Action: Effective against actively growing tubercle bacilli.

Contraindications: Isoniazid hypersensitivity, drug-induced hepatitis, acute liver disease of any etiology, pregnancy.

ISOPROTERENOL (Isuprel)

Adults: 1 mg (5 ml) in 500 ml D5W or NS (2 μg/ml) at 1-5 μg/minute IV drip.

Note:
1. Correct preexisting hypovolemia before administering isoproterenol.
2. Monitor pulse, blood pressure, CVP, urine output, ECG closely.
3. Maintain pulse < 110-130.

Indications:
1. Shock (hypoperfusion syndrome).
2. Cardiac standstill or arrest.
3. Carotid sinus hypersensitivity.
4. Adams-Stokes syndrome.

5. Ventricular tachycardia.
6. Bronchospasm during anesthesia.
Action: Synthetic beta-sympathomimetic; inotropic and chronotropic agent. Also may cause peripheral vasodilatation.
Contraindication: Tachycardia caused by digitalis toxicity.

ISOSORBIDE DINITRATE (Isordil)

Adults:
1. SL: 5-10 mg q2-3h prn, acute attack.
2. Oral: 10-20 mg qid (prophylactic dosage).

Indication: Angina pectoris.
Action: Smooth muscle relaxation.
Contraindication: Isosorbide dinitrate hypersensitivity.

KANAMYCIN (Kantrex)

Adults and children: 7.5-15 mg/kg/day IM/IV, divided q8-12h.

Note:
1. Maximum total daily dose, 1.5 g.
2. Reduce dosage if renal impairment present.
Effective against: Staphylococci (including penicillin-resistant
strains), many gram-negative bacteria.
Use: Short-term use in serious gram-negative and staphylococcal infections; other drugs such as gentamicin, tobramycin, and amikacin are currently used more frequently
because of frequency of bacterial resistance with kanamycin.
Action: Bactericidal aminoglycoside; inhibits protein synthesis
and alters membrane permeability.
Excretion: Renal 90% (glomerular filtration), bile 1%.
Contraindication: Kanamycin hypersensitivity.

KAOLIN AND PECTIN (Kaopectate)

Adults: 30-60 ml PO q4-6h prn.

Children: 10-30 ml PO q6h prn.

Composition: Kaolin 20%, pectin 1%.
Indication: Symptomatic treatment of mild diarrhea.
Action: Adsorbent antidiarrheal agent.
Contraindications: Intestinal obstruction, undiagnosed abdom-
inal pain.

LACTOBACILLUS ACIDOPHILUS AND BULGARICUS
(Lactinex)

Adults and children:
1. Diarrhea: 4 tablets or 1 packet (1 g) added to or taken with
liquid or food (PO) q6-8h.
2. Fever blisters and canker sores: 4 tablets or 1 packet of
granules chewed and swallowed (PO) q6-8h.

Action: Antidiarrheal; restores normal intestinal flora; suppresses emergence of some pathogenic staphylococci and *Candida*.

Contraindication: None known.

LACTULOSE (Cephulac)

Adults: 30-45 ml (20-30 g) PO tid-qid.

Children: 40-90 ml (27-60 g) PO divided tid-qid.

Infants: 2.5-10 ml (1.67-6.67 g) PO divided tid-qid.

Note:
1. Results are comparable to those achieved with neomycin.
2. Lactulose is preferred in renal failure or partial deafness, because of lack of renal excretion and lack of ototoxicity.

Indication: Portal-systemic encephalopathy.

Action: Decreases blood ammonia concentration by 25%-50% as a result of acidification of colon contents and formation of ammonium ion.

Contraindication: Patients requiring a low-galactose diet.

LEVALLORPHAN (Lorfan)

Adults:
1. Respiratory depression caused by narcotic overdosage:
   1 mg (1 ml) IV initially, followed by:
   0.5 mg IV q10-15 minutes, twice if necessary.
   Maximum total dose , 3 mg.

Neonates:
1. Respiratory depression due to narcotic administration to the mother. 0.05-1 mg IV into umbilical vein after delivery. Alternately, IM or SC administration may be used.

Note:
1. Naloxone is recommended as the drug of choice for respiratory depression, especially in situations where the etiology of the respiratory depression is unclear, because naloxone does not cause further respiratory depression.
2. Ineffective in reversing respiratory depression caused by nonnarcotics.

Indication: Significant respiratory depression caused by narcotic analgesics.

Action: Synthetic narcotic antagonist; structurally related to levorphanol. Agonist and antagonist effects occur and depend primarily on the presence and dosage of the narcotic.

Onset: 1-2 minutes (IV).

Duration: 2-5 hours (parenteral).

Contraindications: Mild respiratory depression; narcotic dependence which may produce withdrawal symptoms.

LEVARTERENOL (Levophed)

Adults:
1. Initial: 4 ml (4 mg) in 1 liter D5W IV drip at 2-3 ml/minute.
2. Maintenance: 0.5-1 ml/minute to maintain systolic pressure at least 90-110 mm Hg.

Note:
1. Correct preexisting hypovolemia before administration.
2. Monitor blood pressure, CVP, urine output, and peripheral perfusion closely.

Indications: Acute hypotension resulting from pheochromo-cytomectomy, sympathectomy, spinal anesthesia, myocar-dial infarction, septicemia, blood and drug reactions.

Action: Alpha- and beta-adrenergic agent; promotes peripheral vasoconstriction; inotropic effect on the heart; vasodilata-tion of coronary arteries.

Contraindications: Hypovolemic hypotension, mesenteric or peripheral thrombosis, cyclopropane or halothane anes-thesia.

LEVORPHANOL TARTRATE (Levo-Dromoran)

Adults:
1. Analgesic: 2-3 mg SC/PO q4-8h prn.
2. Antitussive: 0.5-1 mg PO q4-8h prn.

Children: Safety not established.

Note:
1. Parenteral levorphanol, 2 mg, is equianalgesic to morphine, 10 mg.
2. Oral levorphanol is almost as effective as it is parenterally.
3. Antidote for overdosage: see *Levallorphan tartrate.*

Indications: Moderate to severe, acute or chronic pain; pre-operative sedation; also used IV as adjunct to anesthesia.

Action: Synthetic narcotic analgesic; antitussive; similar to morphine.

Peak (analgesia): 20 minutes (IV), 60-90 minutes (SC/PO).

Duration (analgesia): 6-8 hours (SC/PO).

Contraindications: As with morphine: acute alcoholism, bron-chial asthma, increased intracranial pressure, respiratory depression, anoxia. See cautions for Morphine.

LEVOTHYROXINE (Letter, Synthroid)

Adults:
1. Hypothyroidism:
   Initial: 50 μg PO qd. Increase dosage gradually at 2-4 week intervals until desired response is obtained.
   Maintenance: 100-200 μg PO qd (average).

2. Myxedema:
   Initial: 12.5-25 µg PO qd. Increase dosage gradually at 2-4
   week intervals until desired response is obtained.
   Maintenance: 100-200 µg PO qd (average).
3. Myxedema coma:
   Initial: 200-500 µg IV (without heart disease).
   Maintenance: 100-300 µg PO qd (average).

Children:
1. Initial: 3-5 µg/kg PO qd. Increase dosage gradually every 2
   weeks until desired response is obtained.
2. Maintenance: 0.1-0.3 mg PO qd (or higher).

Note:
1. Individualize dosage based on clinical response and thyroid
   function tests.
2. 0.1 mg levothyroxine roughly equivalent to 65 mg desiccated thyroid.
3. May potentiate oral anticoagulant effects, increase insulin
   requirements.

Indication: Reduced or absent thyroid function of any etiology.
Action: Synthetic crystalline L-thyroxine (T_4).
Onset: 12-48 hours.
T½: 6-7 days in euthyroid individuals.
Contraindications: Thyrotoxicosis, acute myocardial infarc-
   tion without hypothyroidism, uncorrected adrenal insuf-
   ficiency.

LIDOCAINE (Xylocaine)

Adults: 50-100 mg IV bolus; then 2-4 mg/minute continuous
   IV infusion.

Children: 0.5-1 mg/kg/dose IV bolus, then 20-40 µg/kg/
   minute.

Note: Monitor ECG for further arrhythmia during use.
Indications: Ventricular arrhythmias (VPCs, ventricular tachy-
   cardia, ventricular fibrillation), including those caused by
   digitalis toxicity.
Action: Antiarrhythmic; increases the electrical stimulation
   threshold of the ventricle during diastole.
T½: About 2 hours.
Therapeutic serum level: 2-6 µg/ml.
Contraindications: Hypersensitivity to local anesthetics of the
   amide type; Adams-Stokes syndrome; severe heart block.

LINCOMYCIN (Lincocin)

Adults: 500 mg PO q6h, or 600 mg IM/IV q8h.

Children: 30-60 mg/kg/day divided q6-8h, or 10 mg/kg/day
   IM/IV q8-12h.

Note:
1. Reduce dosage with renal or hepatic insufficiency.
2. Similar to erythromycin in spectrum and pharmacology.
Effective against: Gram-positive cocci, including most staphylococci.
Use: As penicillin substitute in penicillin allergy.
Action: Bacteriostatic antibiotic; inhibits bacterial protein synthesis.
Contraindications: Lincomycin or clindamycin hypersensitivity.

LIOTHYRONINE (Cytomel)
Adults:
1. Hypothyroidism:
   Initial: 25 μg PO qd. Increase dosage gradually q1-2 weeks.
   Maintenance: 25-75 μg PO qd (average).
2. Myxedema:
   Initial: 5 μg PO qd. Increase dosage gradually q1-2 weeks.
   Maintenance: 50-100 μg PO qd (average).
3. Simple (nontoxic) goiter:
   Initial: 5 μg PO qd. Increase dosage gradually q1-2 weeks.
   Maintenance: 25-75 μg PO qd (average).

Children:
1. Initial: 5 μg PO qd. Increase dosage gradually q3-4 days.
2. Maintenance: 25-75 μg PO qd (over 3 years old).

Note:
1. Individualize dosage based on clinical response and thyroid function tests.
2. Reduce dosage in presence of cardiac disease.
3. 25 μg liothyronine roughly equivalent to 65 mg desiccated thyroid.
4. May potentiate oral anticoagulant effects, increase insulin requirements.
Indications: Hypothyroidism, simple (nontoxic) goiter, T_3 suppression test.
Action: Synthetic L-triiodothyronine (T_3).
Onset: Rapid, usually within a few hours.
T½: About 2 days.
Contraindications: Thyrotoxicosis, acute myocardial infarction without hypothyroidism, uncorrected adrenal insufficiency.

LITHIUM CARBONATE (Eskalith, Lithane, Lithonate)
Adults:
1. Acute mania: 600 mg PO q8h.
2. Maintenance: 300 mg PO q8h.

Note:
1. Titrate dosage to clinical response and serum lithium level.
2. Monitor serum lithium levels closely; draw 8-12 hours after the preceding dose.

3. Adequate fluid and salt intake recommended to prevent toxicity.

Indications: Manic episodes of manic-depressive illness; maintenance therapy for recurrent manic-depressive episodes.

Action: Details unclear. Alters sodium transport in nerve and muscle cells.

Onset: Symptoms of mania generally controlled in 1-3 weeks of therapy.

T½: 24 hours.

Therapeutic serum level: 1.0-1.5 mEq/liter.

Contraindications: Caution in presence of renal impairment, heart disease, dehydration, sodium depletion, diuretic administration, and in children less than 12 years old.

MAGNESIA MAGMA (milk of magnesia, magnesium hydroxide suspension)

Adults:
1. Laxative: 15-30 ml PO hs prn.
2. Antacid: 5-10 ml PO pc and hs.

Children:
1. Laxative: 0.5 ml/kg/dose PO hs prn.

Indications: Functional constipation, hyperacidity.

Actions: Mild saline cathartic; antacid (1 ml neutralizes 2.7 mEq of HCl).

Contraindications: Severe renal insufficiency, intestinal obstruction, undiagnosed abdominal pain.

MAGNESIUM CITRATE

Adults: 120-240 ml PO.

Children:
1. 5-10 years old: 25% of the adult dose.
2. > 10 years old: 50% of the adult dose.

Note:
1. Each 100 ml contains about 1.75 g magnesium oxide.
2. Systemic absorption of magnesium may approach 20%.
3. Ensure sufficient fluid intake to prevent dehydration.

Indications: When prompt and complete evacuation of the bowel is desired; e.g., after upper GI series, before proctoscopy.

Action: Saline cathartic; promotes indirect peristaltic stimulation by osmotic retention of water.

Contraindication: Severe renal insufficiency.

MAGNESIUM SULFATE

Adults:
1. Maintenance requirements: 8-24 mEq/day.
2. Magnesium deficiency: 1 g (8.12 mEq) = 2 ml of 50% solution IM, q6h for 4 doses or until desired effect is achieved.
3. Severe hypomagnesemia: Up to 2 mEq/kg IM within 4 hours if necessary; or up to 40 mEq/kg in 1 liter D5W or NS IV over 3 hours.
4. Anticonvulsant: 1 g IM/IV repeated q4-6h as necessary.

Children:
1. Maintenance requirements: 2-10 mEq/day.
2. Hypomagnesemia: 0.2 mEq/kg of 25% solution q6h for 3-4 doses until desired effect is achieved.

Note:
1. Individualize dosage based on serum magnesium levels.
2. Discontinue administration if patellar reflexes are absent.
3. Caution with renal insufficiency, digitalis administration.

Indications:
1. Provision of maintenance requirements with hyperalimentation.
2. Replacement therapy for magnesium deficiency.
3. Severe hypomagnesemia.

Contraindication: Significant renal insufficiency.

MANNITOL

Adults:
1. Test dose: 12.5 g (100 ml of 15% solution) IV over 3-5 minutes.
2. Therapeutic dose: 25 g (100 ml of 20% solution) over 15-30 minutes q2-3h prn.

Children:
1. Test dose: 200 mg/kg IV over 3-5 minutes.
2. Ascites or generalized edema: 1-2 g/kg IV slow infusion over 2-6 hours.
3. Cerebral or ocular edema: 1-2 g/kg IV over 30-60 minutes.

Note:
1. Caution in presence of congestive heart failure, portal hypertension.
2. Monitor fluid and electrolyte status, CVP, and body weight closely.
3. Maximum recommended daily dose, 100 mg.

Indications: Adjunct in prophylaxis or treatment of prerenal failure, cerebral edema, hemolytic transfusion reactions, and glaucoma. Also used as vehicle for oral agents such as polystyrene sodium sulfonate (Kayexalate).

Action: Promotes osmotic diuresis and transient ECF volume expansion. Osmotic cathartic when administered orally.

Onset: Rapid diuretic and volume expansion effect (IV).
Contraindications: Renal failure, anuria.

MEPERIDINE (Demerol)

Adults: 50-100 mg IM/SC/PO q3-4h prn (maximum recommended dose, 150 mg), or 10-50 mg diluted in D5W or NS IV at 25 mg/minute q2-4h prn.

Children: 1-2 mg/kg dose IM/SC/PO q4-6 prn (maximum, 50-100 mg/dose).

Note:
1. Parenteral meperidine, 75 mg, is equianalgesic to morphine, 10 mg.
2. Oral meperidine is less than one-half as effective as parenteral meperidine.
3. Antidote for overdose: See *Levallorphan* or *Naloxone*.

Indications: Moderate to severe pain; preoperative medication; adjunct to anesthesia; analgesia during labor.
Action: Synthetic narcotic analgesic; multiple actions similar to morphine.
Onset: More rapid than morphine; 5 minutes (IV), 10 minutes (IM), 15-60 minutes (PO).
Duration: Shorter-acting than morphine; 2 hours (IV), 2-4 hours (IM/PO).
Contraindications: Meperidine hypersensitivity, MAO inhibitor administration, pregnancy before labor, lactation. See cautions for *Morphine*.

MEPROBAMATE (Equanil, Miltown)

Adults: 200-400 mg PO tid-qid.

Children: 25 mg/kg/day divided q8-12h.

Indications: Anxiety; tension.
Action: Carbamate derivative; sedative-hypnotic; affects multiple CNS sites.
Contraindications: Meprobamate hypersensitivity, acute intermittent porphyria.

METHADONE (Dolophine)

Adults:
1. Severe pain: 2.5-10 mg IM q3-4h prn, or 5-15 mg PO q4-6h prn. Higher doses may be necessary in tolerant individuals.
2. Detoxification: Administer methadone in decreasing doses over a period not exceeding 3 weeks. Dosage highly individualized at 20-150 mg/day. After stabilization on methadone (80-150 mg/day), dose may be reduced 20%-50% every 1-3 days. Methadone can be stopped in most patients by the 6th-10th day.
3. Maintenance: Administer relatively stable doses of methadone for longer than 3 weeks. Eventual goal is withdrawal

of methadone. Range 10-120 mg. Average 40-100 mg. These patients are physically dependent on methadone. Euphoria is not induced. Hospitalized methadone maintenance patients who are NPO should receive 2 injections daily IM or SC, and each dose should be about one-fourth the total oral daily dosage.
4. Narcotic abstinence syndrome: 20-40 mg PO qd. Reduce dosage as per detoxification (above).

Children: 1-1.8 mg/kg/dose IM/SC/PO q3-4h. Not recommended as an analgesic for children.

Note:
1. Parenteral methadone, 8-10 mg, is equianalgesic to morphine, 10 mg.
2. Oral methadone, 1 mg, will substitute for morphine, 4 mg, heroin, 2 mg, or meperidine, 20 mg, in the dependent patient.
3. "Significant" withdrawal symptoms include perspiration, piloerection, fever, muscle cramps, and diarrhea.
4. Antidote for overdose: See *Levallorphan* or *Naloxone;* caution in presence of drug dependency, may precipitate acute withdrawal syndrome.

Action: Synthetic narcotic analgesic with antitussive properties.
Onset: Similar to morphine; 10-15 minutes (IM), 30-60 minutes (PO).
Duration:
4-6 hours (IM)—in single doses.
22-48 hours in patients physically dependent on oral methadone.
T½: About 24 hours (on oral methadone maintenance).
Contraindications: Methadone hypersensitivity; see cautions for *Morphine*.

METHENAMINE MANDELATE (Mandelamine)

Adults: 1 g PO pc and hs.

Children: 50-60 mg/kg/day divided q8h.

Note: Maintain urinary pH < 5.5 (ammonium chloride, vitamin C, or methinonine: 3-6 g/day).
Indication: Chronic urinary tract infection.
Action: Nonspecific antibacterial agent; methenamine hydrolyzes to form ammonia and formaldehyde in acid urine; mandelic acid promotes urine acidification.
Contraindications: Renal insufficiency, gout.

METHICILLIN (Staphcillin)

Adults:
1. Moderate infections: 1 g IM/IV q4-6h.
2. Severe infections: 2-3 g IV q4h.

Children: 100-300 mg/kg/day IM/IV divided q4-6h.

Note: Reduce dosage in severe renal impairment.
Indications: Penicillin-resistant staphylococcal infections.
Action: Semisynthetic penicillin; bactericidal; inhibits cell wall synthesis; penicillinase-resistant.
Contraindication: Penicillin hypersensitivity.

METHIMAZOLE (Tapazole)

Adults:
1. Initial: 15-60 mg/day PO, divided q8-12h.
2. Maintenance: 5-20 mg/day PO, divided q8-12h (when euthyroid).

Children:
1. Initial: 0.4 mg/kg/day PO divided q8h.
2. Maintenance: 0.2 mg/kg/day PO divided q8h (when euthyroid).

Note:
1. Guide therapy by clinical response and thyroid function tests.
2. 10 mg methimazole equivalent to 100 mg propylthiouracil.
Indications:
1. Medical treatment of hyperthyroidism.
2. Preoperatively for thyroid surgery.
3. Before radioiodine therapy.
Action: Thiocarbamide derivative; similar to propylthiouracil.
Onset: Antithyroid effect noted when thyroid gland depleted of stored hormone (usually in 1-2 weeks). Euthyroidism in 6-8 weeks (average).
Contraindication: Methimazole hypersensitivity.

METHYLDOPA (Aldomet)

Adults:
1. Crisis: 250-500 mg in 100 ml D5W IV over 30-60 minutes q6h.
2. Maintenance: 250 mg PO bid-qid.

Children:
1. Crisis: 20-40 mg/kg/day IV divided q6h.
2. Maintenance: 10 mg/kg/day PO divided q8-12h.

Note: Monitor hepatic and hematologic function closely.
Indication: Moderate to severe hypertension.
Action: Inhibits dopa-decarboxylase, blocking formation of dopamine.
Contraindications: Methyldopa hyersensitivity, active hepatic disease, previous methyldopa therapy associated with liver disorders.

METRONIDAZOLE (Flagyl)

Adults:
1. Trichomoniasis: 250 mg PO tid for 7 days.
2. Amebiasis: 750 mg PO tid for 5-10 days.

Children: Amebiasis: 35-50 mg/kg/day PO for 10 days.

Note: Potentiates coumarin effects on anticoagulation.
Contraindications: Metronidazole hypersensitivity, blood dyscrasia, organic brain disease, first trimester of pregnancy.

MINERAL OIL (liquid petrolatum)

Adults:
1. Oral: 15-45 ml hs prn.
2. Rectal: 90-120 ml.

Children:
1. Oral: 5-10 ml hs prn.
2. Rectal: 30-40 ml.

Note: Caution; lipoid penumonia if aspiration occurs.
Indication: Functional constipation.
Action: Emollient cathartic; promotes lubrication of the GI tract and prevents dehydration of stools; relatively nonabsorbable.
Contraindications: Intestinal obstruction, undiagnosed abdominal pain.

MITHRAMYCIN (Mithracin)

Adults:
1. Hypercalcemia and hypercalcuria: 25 μg/kg/day IV for 3-4 days.
2. Testicular tumors: 25-30 μg/kg/day for 8-10 days.

Note:
1. Administer by IV route only.
2. Dilute daily dose in 1 liter of D5W and administer by slow IV infusion over 4-6 hours.
3. Correct electrolyte imbalance before therapy (especially hypokalemia and hypophosphatemia).
4. Extreme caution with renal, hepatic, or bleeding disorders.
5. Monitor platelet count, PT, bleeding time, renal and hepatic function closely.

Indications: Hypercalcemia and hypercalcuria when symptomatic, due to advanced neoplasms, and not responsive to conventional treatment.
Action: Inhibition of RNA synthesis and bone resorption.
Contraindications: Platelet deficiencies or abnormalities, coagulation disorders, bone marrow impairment, pregnancy.

MORPHINE SULFATE

Adults: 2-15 mg SC q4h prn (usual analgesic dose, 10 mg).

Children: 0.1-0.2 mg/kg/dose SC q4h prn (maximum analgesic dose, 15 mg).

Note:
1. Use the smallest effective dose to minimize side effects, tolerance, and dependence.
2. Analgesic effect occurs at doses in the range of 8-15 mg.
3. Antitussive effect occurs at doses in the range of 2-3 mg.
4. Antidiarrheal effect occurs at doses in the range of 4-6 mg.
5. IV administration preferred in low flow states.
6. Caution in presence of head injury, increased intracranial pressure, undiagnosed abdominal pain, biliary colic, acute pancreatitis, hepatic or renal or respiratory insufficiency, asthma, shock, prostatism, hypothyroidism, Addison's disease, pregnancy, drug dependency, and in elderly, debilitated, or very young patients.
7. Antidote for overdose: See *Levallorphan* or *Naloxone.*

Indications: Moderate to severe pain; preoperative sedation; adjunct to anesthesia; acute pulmonary edema; analgesia during labor, severe cough, or diarrhea.

Action: Narcotic analgesic; opium alkaloid; produces analgesia, sedation, depression of cough reflex; multiple other CNS, respiratory, cardiovascular, GI, and genitourinary effects. May cause histamine release.

Onset: 1 minute (IV).

Peak (analgesia): 50-90 minutes (SC), 30-60 minutes (IM), 20 minutes (IV).

Duration (analgesia): 4-7 hours (SC), 1-2 hours (IV).

Contraindications: Morphine hypersensitivity; see cautions in *Note* above.

MOXALACTAM DISODIUM (Moxam)

Adults: 2-4 g/day in divided doses IV q8-12h.

Children: 50 mg/kg IV q6-8h.

Note:
1. Doses higher than 4 g/day may risk potential bleeding event.
2. Monitor appropriate coagulation studies.
3. Reduce dosage if renal function impaired.

Effective against: Many gram-negative bacilli (including some *Pseudomonas* and *Serratia*); many gram-positive bacilli, and many anaerobes.

Action: Semisynthetic, broad spectrum beta-lactam antibiotic.

Contraindications: Moxalactam hypersensitivity. Caution with type I hypersensitivity reactions to penicillin.

NAFCILLIN (Nafcil, Unipen)

> *Adults:* 0.25 1 g PO/IM/IV q4-6h.
>
> *Children:* 25-100 mg/kg/day PO/IM/IV q4-12h.
>
> *Note:* Dosage and route depend on severity of infection.
> *Indications:* Gram-positive coccal infections (especially penicillin-resistant staphylococci).
> *Action:* Semisynthetic penicillin; bactericidal; inhibits cell wall synthesis; penicillinase-resistant.
> *Contraindication:* Penicillin hypersensitivity.

NALIDIXIC ACID (NegGram)

> *Adults:* 1 g PO q6h.
>
> *Children:* 50 mg/kg/day divided q6h.
>
> *Note:* Monitor blood count, renal and hepatic function tests periodically.
> *Indications:* Urinary tract infections due to *E. coli, Klebsiella, Enterobacter,* and *Proteus;* not effective against *Pseudomonas.*
> *Action:* Naphthyridine derivative; bactericidal; may affect bacterial DNA.
> *Contraindications:* Nalidixic hypersensitivity, convulsive disorders.

NALORPHINE (Nalline)

> *Adults:*
> 1. Severe respiratory depression due to narcotic analgesic: 5-10 mg IV; repeat q10-15 minutes twice if necessary. Maximum total dose, 40 mg.
> 2. Severe respiratory depression due to unknown agent: 5 mg IV; observe patient carefully; may repeat q10-15 minutes twice if necessary.
> 3. Diagnosis of narcotic dependence: (caution: 1-3 mg SC only: withdrawal symptoms appear within 15-20 minutes, peak at 30-45 minutes, and last 2-3 hours.) Morphine, 15-30 mg, or sodium pentobarbital, 100-200 mg, IV may be administered in cases of severe reaction.
>
> *Children:*
> 1. Severe respiratory depression due to narcotic analgesic: 0.1 mg/kg/dose IV; repeat q10-15 minutes twice if necessary.
> 2. Maximum total dose—0.3 mg/kg.
>
> *Neonates:*
> 1. Respiratory depression due to narcotic administration to the mother: 0.2 mg IV into umbilical vein after delivery.
> 2. Maximum total dose, 0.5 mg.

Note:
1. Naloxone is recommended as the drug of choice for respiratory depression, especially in situations where the etiology of the respiratory depression is unclear, because naloxone does not cause further respiratory depression.
2. Naloxone has been used to reverse respiratory depression due to nalorphine.

Action: Synthetic narcotic antagonist; structurally related to morphine. Agonist and antagonist effects occur and depend primarily on the presence and dosage of the narcotic.

Onset: 1-2 minutes (IV).

Duration: 1½-4 hours (parenteral).

Contraindications: Mild respiratory depression, when narcotic addiction may produce withdrawal symptoms (except as a diagnostic test).

NALOXONE (Narcan)

Adults:
1. Narcotic overdosage (known or suspected): 0.4 mg (1 ml) IV; repeat q2-3 minutes 3 times if necessary. Absence of significant improvement implies narcotic overdose unlikely.
2. Postoperative narcotic depression: 0.1-0.2 mg IV; repeat q2-3 minutes × 3 if necessary. Excessive dosage may reverse analgesia and increase blood pressure significantly. Too rapid reversal may cause nausea, vomiting, diaphoresis, or tachycardia.
3. Diagnosis of narcotic dependence (investigational): 0.16 mg IM; if withdrawal symptoms absent after 20-30 minutes, give 0.24 mg IV; withdrawal symptoms, when present, may appear within 5-20 minutes and may be gone within 1½ hours.

Children: Narcotic overdose (known or suspected): 0.01 mg/kg IV; repeat q2-3 minutes, up to 3 times if necessary.

Neonates: Narcotic-induced depression: 0.01 mg/kg IV; repeat q2-3 minutes, 3 times if necessary.

Note:
1. Titrate frequency and dosage to clinical response.
2. Caution in presence of narcotic dependence and cardiac irritability.
3. Excessive dosage may reverse analgesia and increase blood pressure significantly.
4. Too rapid reversal may cause nausea, vomiting, diaphoresis, or tachycardia.

Differences from nalorphine and levallorphan:
1. Naloxone has virtually no pharmacologic activity when administered alone: e.g., produces no analgesic activity, miosis,

    sedation; no respiratory or circulatory depression; no psychoticlike effects, tolerance, or physical dependence.

2. Naloxone is effective in reversing mild or moderate, as well as severe, respiratory depression due to narcotic analgesics, propoxyphene, and pentazocine.
3. Naloxone antagonizes narcotic-induced analgesia, sedation, and sleep.
4. Naloxone also antagonizes effects of other narcotic antagonists.
5. Naloxone is more potent and has a shorter duration of action.

Action: Synthetic narcotic antagonist; structurally related to oxymorphone. Essentially a pure narcotic antagonist; thought to act primarily by competitive inhibition at specific opioid receptor sites.

Onset: 1-2 minutes (IV), 2-5 minutes (IM/SC).

Duration: About 45 minutes (IV); 2-3 hours (IM/SC), depending on dosage.

Contraindication: Naloxone hypersensitivity.

NEOMYCIN SULFATE

Adults:

1. Adjunct to mechanical cleansing of large bowel:
   1 g PO qh for 4 hours; then 1 g PO q4h (not to exceed 48 hours).
2. Adjunct in treatment of hepatic coma:
   100 mg/kg/day PO, divided q6h for 1 day; then 50 mg/kg/day.

Children:

1. Diarrhea due to enteropathic *E. coli:* 50 mg/kg/day divided q6h for 2-3 days.

Note: Caution with concurrent use of other nephrotoxic or ototoxic agents.

Action: Aminoglycoside; bactericidal; inhibits protein synthesis; 97% unabsorbed; most enteric organisms susceptible.

Contraindications: Neomycin hypersensitivity, intestinal obstruction.

NIFEDIPINE (Procardia)

Adults:

1. Initial: 10 mg PO tid.
2. Usual effective dose: 10-20 mg PO tid.

Indications: Vasospastic angina; chronic stable angina.

Action: Antianginal agent; calcium channel blocker. Inhibits transmembrane influx of calcium ions into cardiac and smooth muscle. Dilates coronary arteries and inhibits coronary artery spasm.

Contraindication: Nifedipine hypersensitivity.

NITROFURANTOIN (Furadantin, Macrodantin)

Adults:
1. Usual dose: 50-100 mg PO qid.
2. Suppressive dose: 50-100 mg PO (usually taken in the evening).

Children: 5-7 mg/kg/day divided q6h.

Effective against: Certain gram-positive cocci and coliform organisms.

Indication: Urinary tract infections, especially if chronic, recurrent, or refractory to other agents.

Action: Interferes with bacterial enzyme systems; bactericidal in urinary tract concentrations.

Contraindications: Nitrofurantoin hypersensitivity, renal insufficiency, pregnant patients at term, infants under 1 month of age, G6PD deficiency.

NITROGLYCERIN (glyceryl trinitrate)

Adults:
1. 1/100 grain = 0.6 mg SL.
2. 1/150 grain = 0.4 mg SL.
3. 1/200 grain = 0.3 mg SL.

Note: Dosage and frequency must be individualized. Preferably given prophylactically 3 minutes before exertion usually leading to angina.

Indication: Angina pectoris.

Action: Smooth muscle relaxant, vasodilator.

Peak: 1.3 minutes.

Duration: 30 minutes.

Contraindication: Nitrate hypersensitivity.

NITROGLYCERIN OINTMENT 2% (Nitro-Bid Ointment)

Adults: 1-2 inches q4h applied to chest, abdomen, or anterior thighs.

Note: Reduce dosage if headache occurs.

Indication: Angina pectoris attacks, especially at night.

Action: As for nitroglycerin.

Contraindications: Nitrate hypersensitivity, severe anemia, glaucoma, increased intracranial pressure.

NITROPRUSSIDE (Nipride)

Adults: 50-100 mg/250 ml D5W at 0.5-8 μg/kg/minute via constant infusion pump.

Note:
1. Total doses should be limited to 3 mg/kg.
2. Continuous monitoring of blood pressure is essential.
3. Oral antihypertensive medication may be begun concomitantly.

4. Treatment of thiocyanate toxicity: peritoneal dialysis.
5. Treatment of cyanide intoxication: IV sodium thiosulfate.

Indication: Hypertensive emergencies.

Action: Rapid-acting IV antihypertensive agent; for immediate reduction of blood pressure; produces peripheral vasodilation.

Onset: Rapid (1-2 minutes).

Duration: Short (1-2 minutes).

Metabolism: Converted to cyanide in RBC, then to thiocyanate in liver.

Contraindications: Renal or hepatic insufficiency; compensatory hypertension (AV shunt or coarctation of aorta).

NYSTATIN (Mycostatin)

Adults:
1. Oral suspension: 4-6 ml retained in mouth qid (100,000 units/ml).
2. Oral tablets: 1-2 tablets tid (500,000 units/tablet).
3. Vaginal tablets: 1-2 tablets qd for 2 weeks (100,000 units/tablet).
4. Topical: Apply liberally to affected areas bid (100,000 units/g).

Children:
1. Oral suspension: 4-6 ml retained in mouth qid.
2. Oral tablets: 1-2 million units/day PO divided q6-8h.
3. Vaginal tablets: 1 tablet PV hs for 10 days.
4. Topical: Apply liberally to affected areas bid.

Indications: Thrush; candidiasis.

Action: Polyene antibiotic; binds to and disrupts cytoplasmic membrane.

Contraindication: Nystatin hypersensitivity.

OPIUM TINCTURE (deodorized opium tincture, laudanum)

Adults: 0.3-1 ml PO q6h prn (15 drops/ml).

Children: Not recommended for use in children.

Neonates: 1:25 diluted dose for infants born to opiate-addicted mothers.

Note:
1. Contains 1% morphine or 50 mg/5 ml. This is 25 times the amount contained in paregoric.
2. Caution in presence of asthma, prostatism, hepatic disease, or history of narcotic dependence.
3. Antidote for overdosage: See *Levallorphan* or *Naloxone*.

Indication: Symptomatic treatment of diarrhea.

Action: Antispasmodic antidiarrheal agent because of morphine content.

Contraindication: Diarrhea due to poisoning.

OUABAIN (G-strophanthin)

Adults: 0.25-0.5 mg IV; then 0.1 mg IV q1h until desired result achieved or 1 mg given within 24 hours.

Children: 5 µg/kg stat, then 1 µg/kg q30 minutes until desired result achieved, or 10 µg/kg given.

Note:
1. Limit parenteral digitalization to urgent situations.
2. Caution with PVCs or recent administration of digitalis.
3. Discontinue if nausea, vomiting, extreme bradycardia, or arrhythmia results.
4. Begin oral digitalis preparation as soon as the emergency has pased.

Indication: When rapid digitalization is necessary.

Action: Short-acting crystalline glycoside; capable of producing the same therapeutic and toxic effects as digitalis; acts more rapidly when given IV than any other cardiac glycoside.

Onset: 5-10 minutes.

Peak: ½-2 hours.

T½: 21 hours.

See Digoxin, for other properties.

OXACILLIN (Prostaphlin)

Adults:
1. Oral: 0.5-1 g q4-6h.
2. IM/IV: 1 g q4-6h.

Children:
1. Oral: 50-100 mg/kg/day divided q4-6h.
2. IM/IV: 100 mg/kg/day divided q4-6h.

Indications: Gram-positive coccal infections (especially penicillin-resistant staphylococci); *Streptococcus fecalis* is relatively resistant.

Action: Isoxazolyl penicillin; bactericidal; penicillinase-resistant.

Contraindication: Penicillin hypersensitivity.

OXTRIPHYLLINE (Choledyl)

Adults: 200 mg PO qid with meals.

Children: Pediatric syrup, 3-4 mg/kg q6h.

Note: Differences from aminophylline:
1. Oxtriphylline is less irritating to gastric mucosa.
2. More readily absorbed.
3. More stable and more soluble.
4. Less development of tolerance.
5. 100 mg oxtriphylline is equivalent to 64 mg anhydrous theophylline.

Indications: Bronchospasm due to asthma, bronchitis, emphysema.

Action: Xanthine bronchodilator; choline salt of theophylline.

Contraindication: See *Theophylline.*

OXYCODONE (dihydrohydroxycodeinone: Percocet-5, Percodan, Percodan-Demi, Tylox)

Adults: Commercially available only in combination products:

1. Percodan (oxycodone 4.88 mg, aspirin 224 mg, phenacetin 160 mg, caffeine 32 mg). 1 tablet PO q6h prn.
2. Percodan-Demi (oxycodone 2.44 mg, aspirin 224 mg, phenacetin 160 mg, caffeine 32 mg). 1-2 tablets PO q6h prn.
3. Percocet-5 (oxycodone 5 mg, acetaminophen 325 mg). 1 tablet PO q6h prn.
4. Tylox (oxycodone 4.88 mg, acetaminophen 500 mg). 1 tablet PO q6h prn.

Children (6-12 years): 1.22 mg PO q6h prn.

Not recommended for children under 6 years old.

Note:

1. Oxycodone, 5 mg, is equianalgesic to codeine, 120 mg.
2. Cautions as for other narcotic analgesics or for combined agents.
3. Antidote for overdosage: See *Levallorphan* or *Naloxone.*

Indication: For the relief of moderate to moderately severe pain.

Action: Semisynthetic narcotic analgesic.

Contraindications: Hypersensitivity to oxycodone or to combined agents.

PANCURONIUM BROMIDE (Pavulon)

Adults: 2-4 mg IV push q2-4h prn.

Children:

1. Initial: 0.1-1.15 mg/kg/dose.
2. Maintenance: 0.01 mg/kg/dose.

Note:

1. Be prepared to intubate within 2 minutes of induced effect.
2. Antagonized by acetylcholine, anticholinesterases, potassium ion.

Indications:

1. Adjunct in anesthesia to induce skeletal muscle relaxation.
2. Facilitation of management of patients on mechanical ventilators.

Action: Curariform, nondepolarizing, muscle relaxant.

Contraindications: Pancuronium or bromide hypersensitivity.

PARALDEHYDE

Adults:

1. Sedation: 4-10 ml PO/IM/PR q4-6h.
2. Anticonvulsant: 15-30 ml IV/deep IM/PR q4-6h prn.
3. Delirium tremens: 15-30 ml deep IM/PR q4-6h prn.

Children:

1. Sedation: 0.15 ml (150 mg)/kg/dose PO/IM/PR q4-6h prn.
2. Anticonvulsant: 0.15-0.3 ml/kg/dose deep IM/PR q4-6h prn.

Note:

1. Available as oral solution or in ampules, both containing 1 g/ml.
2. Oral administration is preferable whenever possible.
3. May be suspended in oil and given PR.
4. IM injection may cause sterile abscesses.
5. IV solution: 5 ml in 500 ml D5W; infuse rapidly for seizure control.

Indications: Insomnia; status epilepticus; delirium tremens; mostly used now for management of alcholism.

Action: Sedative-hypnotic; similar to barbiturates; duration of hypnosis brief; depressive after-effects minimal; respiratory depression minimal.

Contraindications: Peptic ulcer disease, esophagitis, anal inflammation, hepatic and pulmonary disease, asthma, disulfiram therapy.

PAREGORIC (camphorated opium tincture)

Adults: 5-10 ml PO q6h prn.

Children: 0.25-0.5 ml/kg PO q6h prn.

Note:

1. Contains 0.04% morphine, or 2 mg/5ml. This is 25 times less than the amount contained in opium tincture.
2. Caution in presence of asthma, prostatism, hepatic disease, history of narcotic dependence.
3. Antidote for overdosage: See *Levallorphan* or *Naloxone.*

Indications: Symptomatic treatment of diarrhea.

Action: Antispasmodic antidiarrheal agent because of morphine content.

Contraindication: Diarrhea caused by poisoning.

PENICILLIN G

Adults:

1. Aqueous forms: Rapid absorption, high transient levels.
   a. Penicillin G potassium (1.7 mEq potassium/1 million units).

    b. Penicillin G sodium (2 mEq sodium/1 million units).
2. Repository forms: Slow absorption, low persistent levels.
    a. Penicillin G procaine (Wycillin); 1 mg = 1009 units.
      600,000-1,200,000 units *IM only*, q6-12h.
      Surgical SBE prophylaxis (adults):
        600,000 units IM on day of procedure.
        600,000 units IM 1-2 hours preoperatively.
        600,000 units IM daily for 2 days.
      Slight anesthetic effect of procaine.
    b. Penicillin G benzathine (Bicillin); 1 mg = 1211 units.
      Slight anesthetic effect of benzathine.
3. (Refer to PDR for other conditions not discussed here.)

Drug of choice for: Infections caused by non-penicillinase-producing staphylococci, streptococci (group A, viridans, anaerobic), *Diplococcus pneumoniae, Neisseria gonorrhoeae* and *meningitidis,* clostridia, corynebacteria, *Listeria, Bacillus anthracis, T. pallidum, Bacteroides* (oropharyngeal strains); and actinomycosis, leptospirosis, Whipple's disease.

Note: Penicillinase-producing staphylococci, coliforms, and some strains of *C. diphtheriae* and gonococci may be resistant.

Action: Bactericidal; inhibits cell wall synthesis; acid-labile.

Contraindication: Penicillin hypersensitivity.

PENICILLIN V POTASSIUM (Pee Vee K, V-Cillin K)

Adults: 250-500 mg PO q6h.

Children: 15-60 mg/kg/day PO divided q6h.

Note:
1. Tablets contain 250 mg (400,000 units) or 500 mg (800,000 units).
2. Less active than penicillin G against gram-positive cocci, meningococci, gonococci, and *H. influenzae;* more protein-bound.

Indications: Mild to moderately severe infections caused by penicillin G–sensitive microorganisms.

Action: Potassium salt of penicillin V; bactericidal; inhibits cell wall synthesis; acid-stable.

Contraindication: Penicillin hypersensitivity.

PENTAZOCINE (Talwin)

Adults:
1. Oral: 50-100 mg q3-4h prn.
2. IM/IV: 30 mg q3-4h prn.

Children: Safety not established.

Note:
1. Parenteral pentazocine, 30 mg, equianalgesic to morphine, 10 mg.
2. Oral pentazocine, 50 mg, equianalgesic to codeine, 60 mg.
3. Antidote for overdosage: See *Naloxone.*

Indications: Moderate to severe pain; preoperative sedation; anesthesia supplement; obstetrical analgesia.

Action: Synthetic benzomorphan analgesic; nonnarcotic; promotes analgesia and sedation; also has mild narcotic antagonist properties.

Onset (analgesia): 2-3 minutes (IV), 15-20 minutes (IM), 15-60 minutes (PO).

Peak (analgesia): 15-60 minutes (IM), 1-3 hours (PO).

Duration (analgesia): Much less than morphine, 2-3 hours, due to high hepatic extraction ratio (0.5-1).

Contraindications: Pentazocine hypersensitivity; see cautions for *Morphine.*

PENTOBARBITAL (Nembutal)

Adults: 50-100 mg PO/IM hs prn.

Children: 2-3 mg/kg/dose PO/IM/PR hs prn.

Indications: Anxiety; insomnia; preanesthetic; anticonvulsant.

Action: Sedative-hypnotic; short-acting barbituric acid derivative.

Contraindications: Barbiturate hypersensitivity, prophyria.

PHENAZOPYRIDINE-HYOSCYAMINE-BUTALBITAL (Pyriduim Plus, formerly Dolonil)

Adults: 1 tablet PO qid after meals and qhs.

Children: Not recommended for use in children.

Composition:
Phenazopyridine, 150 mg (topical analgesic).
Hyoscyamine, 0.3 mg (antispasmodic).
Butalbital, 15 mg (sedative).

Note:
1. Infections, when present, require appropriate antibiotics.
2. Reddish-orange discoloration of urine may occur because of phenazopyridine.

Indication: Symptomatic relief of lower urinary tract irritability.

Contraindications: Hypersensitivity to any component; renal or hepatic insufficiencies, glaucoma, porphyria.

PHENOBARBITAL (Luminal)

Adults:
1. Sedative-hypnotic: 30-60 mg PO/PR/IM q8h prn.
2. Chronic anticonvulsant: 150-250 mg/day PO, divided q12h.

3. Status epilepticus:
     Initial: 150-400 mg IV, slowly.
     Repeat doses: 120-240 mg IV q20 minutes prn.

Children:
1. Sedation: 2-3 mg/kg/dose PO/IM/PR q8h prn.
2. Chronic anticonvulsant: 3-5 mg/kg/day PO divided q12h.
3. Status epilepticus:
     Initial: 6 mg/kg IV slowly.
     Repeat doses: 3 mg/kg IV slowly q20 minutes prn.

Note:
1. Maximum total daily dose: Adults, 1 g; children, 12 mg/kg.
2. IV administration may cause respiratory arrest or hypotension.
3. May decrease oral anticoagulant effect by inducing microsomal enzymes.

Action: Barbiturate; sedative-hypnotic; anticonvulsant.
T½: 2-6 days.
Therapeutic serum levels: 20-40 μg/ml.
Contraindications: Barbiturate hypersensitivity; porphyria; severe hepatic, renal, or pulmonary insufficiency.

PHENOLPHTHALEIN (Agoral, Ex-Lax)

Adults: 100-200 mg PO hs prn.

Children:
1. 2-5 years old: 15-30 mg.
2. 6-12 years old: 30-60 mg.

Note: May impart a red color to alkaline stools or urine.
Indication: Functional constipation.
Action: Diphenylmethane cathartic; acts primarily on colon wall to stimulate intestinal motility.
Contraindications: Phenolphthalein hypersensitivity, intestinal obstruction, undiagnosed abdominal pain.

PHENOXYBENZAMINE (Dibenzyline)

Adults:
1. Initial: 10 mg PO qd. Increase dosage gradually by 10 mg every 4 days as needed for optimal effect.
2. Maintenance: 20-60 mg PO qd (maximum, 200 mg/day).

Note:
1. Individualize dosage for optimal hypotensive effect, minimal side effects.
2. Caution in presence of coronary, cerebral, or renal insufficiency.
3. Administration should begin 4-10 days before elective pheochromocytomectomy or angiography.

4. Propranolol effective in controlling tachycardia and arrhythmias.

Indications:

1. Preoperative control of hypertension due to pheochromocytoma.
2. Maintenance therapy of hypertension in unresectable pheochromocytoma.

Action: Long-acting alpha-adrenergic blocking agent; antagonizes pressor response to catecholamines.

Onset: Slow; may require 2 weeks or more to optimize dosage.

Duration: Prolonged.

Contraindications: Phenoxybenzamine hypersensitivity; conditions where a fall in blood pressure may be undesirable.

PHENTOLAMINE (Regitine)

Adults:

1. Oral: 50 mg q4-6h.
2. IV: 5-20 mg injected slowly, or as 0.5 mg/minute infusion.
3. Pheochromocytoma test: 1-5 mg IV, slowly.

Children:

1. Oral: 5 mg/kg/day PO divided q4-6h.
2. IV: 0.1-0.5 mg/kg injected slowly.
3. Pheochromocytoma test: 0.1 mg/kg IV slowly.

Note:

1. Parenteral administration may produce severe hypotensive reactions and decreased cardiac output.
2. Caution in presence of coronary or cerebrovascular insufficiency.
3. Propranolol effective in controlling tachycardia and arrhythmias.

Indications:

1. Preoperative or intraoperative control of hypertensive crises caused by pheochromocytomas.
2. Diagnosis of pheochromocytoma: Regitine blocking test.

Action: Rapid-acting alpha-adrenergic blocking agent; competitively inhibits binding of sympathomimetic agents to alphaadrenergic receptors.

Onset: Within 30 seconds (IV).

Peak effect: Within 5 minutes (IV).

Duration: 30-60 minutes (IV).

Contraindications: Phentolamine hypersensitivity, myocardial infarction, coronary artery disease.

PHENYLBUTAZONE (Azolid, Butazolidin)

Adults:
1. Acute gouty arthritis:
    Initial: 200 mg PO tid-qid until articular inflammation sub-
        sides.
    Then taper dose rapidly and discontinue within 7-14 days.
2. Other indications: Severe symptoms:
    Initial: Up to 200 mg PO tid for the first 2-3 days. Then re-
        duce to 100 mg PO tid and discontinue within 7-10 days.
    Mild to moderate symptoms: 100 mg PO tid-qid (analgesic
        dosage).

Note:
1. Short-term administration with the lowest effective dose is
    recommended to avoid bone marrow toxicity and other
    adverse effects.
2. Reduce dose promptly as soon as symptomatic improve-
    ment occurs, usually by the third or fourth day of treatment.
3. Monitor hematologic and renal status, as well as weight,
    closely.
4. Potentiates effects of oral anticoagulants and sulfonylureas.

Indications: Short-term relief of severe symptoms due to gout,
    rheumatoid arthritis, rheumatoid spondylitis, osteoarthritis,
    psoriatic arthritis, acute superficial thrombophlebitis, and
    painful shoulder.

Action: Anti-inflammatory, antipyretic analgesic; similar to
    oxyphenbutazone and the pyrazolines. Produces sympto-
    matic relief of inflammation, fever, and pain. Also has mild
    uricosuric effect.

Contraindications: Phenylbutazone hypersensitivity, peptic
    ulcer disease, congestive heart failure, blood dyscrasias,
    renal or hepatic disease, hypertension, thyroid disease, sys-
    temic edema, polymyalgia rheumatica, temporal arthritis,
    long-term anticoagulant therapy, children under 14 years old.

PHENYTOIN (Dilantin)

Adults:
1. Anticonvulsant: 300 mg/day PO in single or divided doses.
2. Status epilepticus: 150-250 mg IV, slowly; then 100-150
    mg in 30 minutes if necessary.
3. Antiarrhythmic: 100 mg IV, slowly, q3-5 minutes until ar-
    rhythmia terminated or 1 g given.

Children:
1. Anticonvulsant: 4-8 mg/kg/day PO in single or divided doses.
2. Status epilepticus: 15 mg/kg in NS at a rate of 50 mg/
    minute.
3. Antiarrhythmic: 1-5 mg/kg IV slowly, repeat prn.

Note:
1. Dosages may require modification for therapeutic effect.
2. Do not exceed 50 mg/minute by the IV route.
3. Abrupt withdrawal of phenytoin in epileptic patients may precipitate status epilepticus.

Indications: Generalized tonic-clonic and psychomotor seizures; status epilepticus; ventricular arrhythmias, including those induced by digitalis.

Action:
  Anticonvulsant (inhibits spread of seizure activity in motor cortex).
  Antiarrhythmic (electrophysiologic effects similar to lidocaine).

$T\frac{1}{2}$: 22 hours (range, 7-42 hours).

Therapeutic serum levels: 10-20 μg/ml (allow 7-10 days of therapy).

Contraindications: Hypersensitivity to hydantoin products, sinus bradycardia, SA or AV block, Adams-Stokes syndrome.

PHOSPHATES, INORGANIC (Neutra-Phos)

Adults: 250-500 mg PO q6-8h.

Children: 250 mg PO q6-8h.

Note:
1. One capsule or 75 ml of the solution contains 250 mg phosphorus.
2. Use for hypercalcemic crisis should follow adequate rehydration and is restricted to hypophosphatemic states (e.g., hyperparathyroidism).

Indications:
1. Dietary supplement of phosphorus.
2. Adjuvant in hypercalcemic crisis.
3. Recurrent calcium oxalate stone formation.

Action: Lowers serum calcium level by altering the calcium-phosphate equilibrium toward deposition in bone and reduction of intestinal calcium absorption.

Contraindications: Hyperphosphatemia (e.g., vitamin D toxicity), renal insufficiency.

PHYTONADIONE USP (Aqua-Mephyton, Konakion, vitamin K₁)

Adults:
1. Overcoumadinization without bleeding: 2.5-10 mg PO.
2. Overcoumadinization with bleeding: 10-50 mg IV, slowly (1 mg/minute).
3. Hyperalimentation supplement: 5-10 mg IM, once weekly.

Children:
1. Hypoprothrombinemia: 5-10 mg PO/IM/IV.
2. Hyperalimentation supplement: 2-5 mg IM once weekly.

Infants (hemorrhagic disease of newborn):
1. Prophylaxis: 1 mg IM.
2. Treatment: 5-10 mg IM.

Note:
1. Although bleeding because of excessive hypoprothrombinemia may be controlled within 3-8 hours with parenteral administration of vitamin K$_1$, administration of fresh whole blood or plasma may be necessary when bleeding is severe.
2. Consider heparin administration if anticoagulation is still needed after correction of hypoprothrombinemia.
3. Monitor PT closely.
4. IV administration only indicated when other routes not feasible.
5. Ineffective in treatment of hypoprothrombinemia caused by severe liver disease or heredity.

Action: Fat-soluble vitamin; essential for liver synthesis of blood coagulation factors II, VII, IX, X. Reverses anticoagulation effect produced by coumarin and inandione derivatives. Requires presence of bile salts in GI tract for oral absorption.
Onset: 15 minutes (IV), 1-2 hours (IM/SC), 6-12 hours (PO).
Duration: 6-8 hours (IM/SC), 12-48 hours (PO).
Contraindications: Hypersensitivity to phytonadione or combined agents; liver disease if response to initial dose inadequate.

PILOCARPINE (Isopto-Carpine, Pilocar)

Adults and children:
1. Glaucoma: 1-2 drops of 1-2% solution OU 1-4 times/day.
2. Nonobstructive urinary retention: 6-8 mg PO/SC q6h.

Note:
1. Acute glaucoma may require morphine, carbonic anhydrase inhibitors, osmotic diuretics, and/or surgery.
2. Actions blocked or antagonized by atropine sulfate.

Indications:
1. Glaucoma (especially the chronic simple or wide-angle type).
2. To counteract mydriasis produced by atropine.

Action: Miotic; many parasympathomimetic effects.
Onset: 15 minutes.
Peak: 30-60 minutes.
Duration: 20 hours.
Contraindications: Pilocarpine hypersensitivity, acute or angle-closure glaucoma, GI or urinary obstruction, severe cardiac disease, asthma, myasthenia gravis in patients receiving neostigmine, progressive muscular atrophy or bulbar palsy.

PIPERACILLIN SODIUM (Pipracil)

Adults:
1. Serious infections: 3-4 g IV q4-6h.
2. Maximum recommended dose: 24 g/day.

Children: Safety not established.

Effective against: Many gram-negative and gram-positive bacteria; many anaerobic bacteria.

Action: Semisynthetic, broad-spectrum penicillin.

Contraindication: Hypersensitivity to any penicillin or cephalosporin.

PODOPHYLLUM RESIN (Podophyllin)

Adults and children:
Available as 11.5%-25% suspension in tincture of benzoin.

Note: Because of caustic burns and other difficulties, this preparation should be applied by the physician as follows:
1. Protect uninvolved skin and mucous membranes with petroleum jelly.
2. Apply podophyllum with cotton-tipped applicator and allow to dry.
3. Instruct patient to wash off the material in 6 hours, or sooner if burning develops.
4. Repeated administration may be necessary for extensive areas.

Indication: Condylomata acuminata ("venereal" warts).

Action: Topical antimetabolite; inhibits mitosis in metaphase.

Contraindications: Hypersensitivity; should be avoided during pregnancy because of possible toxic effects.

POLYMYXIN B SULFATE (Aerosporin)

Adults and children:
1. IV: 1.5-2.5 mg/kg/day, divided q12h.
2. IM: 2.5-3.0 mg/kg/day, divided q4-6h.

Note:
1. Limit total daily dose to 200 mg (1 mg = 10,000 units).
2. Reduce dosage if renal impairment present.
3. Extremely painful on IM injection.
4. See PDR for intrathecal, topical uses.

Effective against: Most gram-negative bacilli, including *Pseudomonas.*

Use: Serious gram-negative infections when other agents cannot be used.

Action: Polypeptide antibiotic; damages bacterial cytoplasmic membrane.

Contraindication: Polymyxin hypersensitivity.

POTASSIUM IODIDE (SSKI)

Adults:
1. Expectorant: 300 mg (6 drops) diluted PO tid-qid.
2. Hyperthyroidism: 50-100 mg (1-2 drops) diluted PO q8h.
3. Before thyroidectomy: 50-100 mg (1-2 drops) diluted PO q8h for 7-10 days, administered with a thionamide.

Children:
1. Expectorant: 60-250 mg diluted PO qid.
2. Before thyroidectomy: 50-250 mg diluted PO tid for 7-10 days.

Action: Expectorant; inhibits iodide binding and decreases vascularity of thyroid in hyperthyroidism.

Contraindications: Iodide hypersensitivity, hyperkalemia, tuberculosis; use as an expectorant in patients with hyperthyroidism.

PROCAINAMIDE (Pronestyl)

Adults:
1. Oral: 750-1,000 mg (15 mg/kg) followed by 250-500 mg (5 mg/kg) q3-4h.
2. IM: 0.5-1 g q6h until oral therapy is possible.
3. IV: 100 mg slowly q3-5 minutes until arrhythmia terminated for 1 g given. May also be given by continuous infusion, 2-6 mg/minute, after loading dose.

Children:
1. Oral: 40-60 mg/kg/day divided q4-6h.
2. IM: 20-30 mg/kg/day divided q6h.
3. IV: 2 mg/kg/dose slowly (maximum dose, 100 mg).

Note:
1. Limit IV use to emergencies because of hypotensive reactions.
2. Monitor blood pressure and ECG closely with IV use.
3. Differences with respect to quinidine; procainamide is safer for IV use, better absorbed orally, no development of cinchonism.

Indications: Similar to quinidine; slightly more effective than quinidine in prevention of ventricular tachyarrhythmias (VPCs, ventricular tachycardia).

Contraindications: Procainamide hypersensitivity, myasthenia gravis, AV block, hypersensitivity to local anesthetics.

PROCHLORPERAZINE (Compazine)

Adults:
1. Oral: 10 mg q6-8h prn.
2. IM: 10 mg q6-8h prn.
3. Suppository: 25 mg bid prn.

Children: 0.2-0.4 mg/kg/day PO/IM/PR divided q6-8h.

Indications: Nausea, vomiting, anxiety, tension, agitation.
Action: Piperazine phenothiazine; antiemetic; sedative.
Contraindications: Phenothiazine hypersensitivity; comatose or greatly depressed states due to CNS depressants; bone marrow depression; pediatric surgery.

PROMETHAZINE (Phenergan)

Adults: 25-50 mg IM/PO/PR q4-6h prn.

Children: 0.25-1.0 mg/kg/dose q6-12h prn.

Indications: Pre- and postoperative sedation; adjunct to analgesics; treatment of motion sickness, nausea, vomiting, and allergic reactions; adjunct in anaphylaxis.
Action: Phenothiazine; antiemetic; antihistaminic; sedative.
Contraindication: Promethazine hypersensitivity.

PROPANTHELINE BROMIDE (Probanthine)

Adults:
1. Oral: 15 mg tid with meals, 30 mg qhs (75 mg total).
2. NM/IV: 30 mg q6h initially; 15 mg q6h for maintenance.

Children: 1-2 mg/kg/day PO divided PC and qhs.

Indications: Peptic ulcer disease: irritable bowel syndrome.
Action: Parasympatholytic; inhibits GI motility; decreases gastric secretion.
Contraindications: Glaucoma, GI obstruction, prostatism, intestinal atony, toxic megacolon, hiatal hernia with reflux esophagitis.

PROPOXYPHENE HYDROCHLORIDE (Darvon, SK-65)

Adults: 65 mg PO q4h prn.

Children: Not recommended for use in children.

Note: Propoxyphene, 65 mg, is equianalgesic to codeine, 30-45# mg.
Indications: Mild to moderate pain.
Action: Mild synthetic analgesic; nonnarcotic.
Contraindications: Propoxyphene hypersensitivity.

PROPRANOLOL (Inderal)

Adults:
1. Hypertension:
    Initial: 80 mg/day PO divided q6-8h. Increase gradually until optimum response achieved. Usual range 160-480 mg/day in divided doses.
2. Angina pectoris:
    Initial: 10-40 mg PO q6-8h. Increase gradually until optimum response achieved.
    Maximum dose: 320 mg/day.

3. Arrhythmias:
   - Oral: 10-30 mg q6-8h.
   - Intravenous: 1-3 mg at 1 mg/minute q4-6h.
   - Maximum dose: 10 mg.
4. Hypertrophic subaortic stenosis: 20-40 mg PO q6-8h.
5. Pheochromocytoma:
   - Preoperatively: 60 mg/day PO divided q6-8h for 3 days, concomitantly with alpha-adrenergic blocking agents.
   - Inoperable tumor: 30 mg/day PO in divided doses.
6. Thyrotoxicosis:
   - Oral (initial): 10 mg PO q6-8h. Increase gradually until optimum response achieved. Usual range 80-160 mg/day.
   - Intravenous: 50-100 μg/minute IV drip to control tachycardia, tremor, etc.

Children:
1. Arrhythmias:
   - Oral: 0.5-1.0 mg/kg/day divided q6-8h.
   - Maximum dose: 60 mg/day.
   - Intravenous: 0.01-0.15 mg/kg/dose q6-8h.
   - Maximum dose: 10 mg/dose.
2. Thyrotoxicosis: 2.5-10.5 mg/kg/dose PO q6-8h.

Note:
1. Individualize dose and route according to indication and response.
2. Limit IV use to life-threatening arrhythmias, and monitor blood pressure, ECG, CVP, and pulmonary capillary wedge pressure carefully.
3. Preoperatively, propranolol should be tapered gradually and stopped 48 hours before surgery, except for patients with pheochromocytoma.
4. Postoperatively, oral propranolol should be restarted as soon as feasible.

Indications:
1. Hypertension (usually in combination with a thiazide diuretic).
2. Angina pectoris (when nitrates alone have failed).
3. Cardiac arrhythmias (to slow ventricular rate in supraventricular arrhythmias).
3. Hypertrophic subaortic stenosis (may decrease obstruction by reducing contractility).
5. Pheochromocytoma (after alpha-blockage with phenoxybenzamine).
6. Thyrotoxicosis (helpful in controlling tachycardia, tremor, etc.).

Action: Beta-adrenergic receptor blocking agent.

Contraindications: Propranolol hypersensitivity, bronchial asthma, sinus bradycardia, AV block, cardiogenic shock, congestive heart failure, seasonal allergy, MAO inhibitor use.

PROPYLTHIOURACIL (PTU)

Adults:

1. Initial: 100 mg PO q8h (while symptoms of hyperthyroidism persist).
2. Maintenance: 100-150 mg/day PO, divided q8h (when euthyroid).
3. Thyroid storm: 1000 mg PO or via NG tube; then 200-400 mg q6-8h.

Children:

1. Initial: 50-150 mg/day PO divided q8h (6-10 years old). 150-300 mg/day PO divided q8h (over 10 years old).
2. Maintenance: 75-200 mg/day PO divided q8h (when euthyroid).

Note:

1. Guide therapy by clinical response and thyroid function tests.
2. 100 mg propylthiouracil are equivalent to 10 mg methimazole.

Indications:

1. Medical treatment of hyperthyroidism (usually for 1-2 years).
2. Preoperatively for thyroid surgery (usually for 1-3 months).

Action: Thiocarbamide derivative; inhibits synthesis of thyroid hormones and decreases peripheral conversion of T_4 to T_3.
Contraindication: Propylthiouracil hypersensitivity.

PROTAMINE SULFATE

Adults and children: 1 mg/100 units of heparin (approximately) IV, slowly.

Note:

1. Dosage determined by estimate of the amount of circulating heparin.
2. The requirement decreases rapidly after heparin is discontinued.
3. Maximum single dose limited to 50 mg in any 10-minute period.
4. Neutralization of heparin may be transient, especially following cardiac surgery; monitor coagulation studies closely.

Indication: Overheparinization.
Action: Heparin antagonist; forms inactive complex with heparin when given with heparin; anticoagulant effect when given alone.
Contraindications: None known; overdosage may cause hemorrhage.

PSEUDOEPHEDRINE (Sudafed)

   Adults: 60/mg PO q4h prn (maximum, 360 mg/day).

   Children: 15 mg PO q4h prn (2-6 years old). 30 mg PO q4h prn (6-12 years old).

   Indications: Primarily used for symptomatic relief of nasal and sinus congestion.

   Action: Sympathomimetic; decongestant and bronchodilator effects.

   Contraindications: Use with caution in the presence of hypertension, heart disease, thyroid disease, propranolol administration, urinary retention, glaucoma.

PSYLLIUM HYDROPHILIC MUCOID (Metamucil, Serutan)

   Adults: 7 g (1 tsp) in a glass of water PO 1-3 times daily.

   Children: Reduce dosage according to age.

   Indications: Functional constipation; adjunct in uncomplicated diverticular disease of the colon.

   Action: Bulk-producing agent; increases the moisture content and mass of the stool, thereby stimulating reflex peristalsis.

   Contraindications: Active diverticulitis, intestinal obstruction, fecal impaction.

PYRIDOXINE (vitamin B_6)

   Adults:
1. RDA: 2 mg.
2. Dietary deficiency: 10-20 mg PO qd for 3 weeks.
3. Isoniazid adjunct: 100 mg PO qd (range, 50-450 mg/day).

   Infants:
1. RDA: 0.3-0.5 mg PO qd.
2. Usual therapy: 2 mg PO qd in formula.

   Indications: Dietary deficiency; isoniazid adjunct; pyridoxine-responsive anemias.

   Action: B-complex vitamin; important as a coenzyme in protein and fat metabolism. Also important in hematopoiesis and proper function of the nervous system.

   Contraindication: Pyridoxine hypersensitivity.

QUINIDINE GLUCONATE (Quinaglute)

   Adults: 1-2 tablets PO q8-12h (330 mg/tablet).

   Children: Safety not established.

   Note: Sustained-release preparation, primarily used for prevention of premature atrial, nodal, or ventricular contractions, and for maintenance of NSR following conversion of atrial fibrillation, tachycardia, or flutter.

   See *Quinidine sulfate* for other properties.

QUINIDINE POLYGALACTURONATE (Cardioquin)

Adults:
1. Conversion: 1-3 tablets PO; repeat in 3-4 hours if necessary.
2. Maintenance: 1 tablet PO q8-12h.

Children: Safety not established.

Note:
1. Each tablet contains 275 mg of quinidine polygalacturonate, equivalent to 200 mg of quinidine sulfate.
2. Claimed to cause less GI irritation than quinidine sulfate.

See *Quinidine sulfate* for indications and other properties.

QUINIDINE SULFATE

Adults:
1. Test dose: 200 mg PO; observe for idiosyncrasy.
2. Maintenance: 200-300 mg PO q6-8h.

Children:
1. Test dose: 2 mg/kg PO; observe for idiosyncrasy.
2. Therapeutic dose: 3-6 mg/kg/dose q2-3h $\times$ 5.

Note:
1. Caution with severe heart disease, congestive failure, hypotension, or digitalis intoxication.
2. Monitor blood levels and/or ECG with large oral doses or parenteral administration.
3. Cardiotoxicity QRS or QT prolongation, ventricular arrhythmias.
4. Quinidine effect enhanced by potassium, reduced by hypokalemia.

Indications: Major use is to prevent tachyarrhythmias, including premature contractions and paroxysmal atrial tachycardia, flutter, or fibrillation.

Action: Depresses myocardial excitability, conduction velocity, and contractility. Prolongs duration of effective refractory period of atrial or ventricular muscle. Decreases excitability of ectopic foci in the heart. Also has anticholinergic effect. Large oral doses may produce hypotension through peripheral vasodilation.

Therapeutic serum level: 3-6 μg/ml.

Metabolism: Liver, 70%.

Excretion: Renal, 30%.

Contraindications: Quinidine hypersensitivity or idiosyncrasy, digitalis intoxication, partial AV or complete heart block, intraventricular conduction defects, aberrant impulses, and abnormal rhythms produced by escape mechanisms.

RANITIDINE (Zantac)

Adults: 150 mg PO bid.

Children: Safety not established.

Note:
1. Antacids may be given if indicated for pain relief.
2. In patients with creatinine clearance less than 50 ml/min, the dosage is reduced to 150 mg once daily.

Indications:
1. Short-term treatment of duodenal ulcer (up to 8 weeks).
2. Pathologic hypersecretory conditions.

Action: Histamine H_2-receptor antagonist. Inhibits gastric acid secretion (basal and stimulated—food, histamine, pentagastrin).

Contraindication: None known.

RESERPINE (Serpasil)

Adults:
1. Initial: 0.25-0.5 mg PO qd for 1-2 weeks.
2. Maintenance: 0.1-0.25 mg PO qd.
3. Hypertensive crisis: Titrate response beginning with 0.5-1 mg, then 2-4mg IM q3h.

Children:
1. Maintenance: 0.02 mg/kg/day PO divided q12h.
2. Hypertensive crisis: 0.07 mg/kg/dose IM q8-24h prn.

Note: Discontinue 2 weeks preoperatively to minimize hypotensive reactions.

Indications:
1. Oral therapy of mild essential hypertension.
2. Parenteral therapy of certain hypertensive crises.

Action: Rauwolfia derivative; depletes catecholamines from sympathetic nerve endings; may also deplete catecholamines and serotonin from CNS. IM injection produces arteriolar vasodilation.

Onset: 2-3 hours (IM), 3-6 days (PO).

Duration: 10-12 hours (IM), 2-6 weeks (PO).

Contraindications: Reserpine hypersensitivity, mental depression, active peptic ulcer, ulcerative colitis, patients undergoing electroconvulsive therapy.

RIBOFLAVIN (vitamin B_2)

Adults:
1. RDA: 1.7 mg PO qd.
2. Therapeutic: 2-5mg PO tid with meals.

Children: RDA: 0.5-1.5 mg PO qd.

Indications: Riboflavin deficiency; adjunct with niacin in treatment of pellagra; may counteract bone marrow depression and optic neuritis caused by chloramphenicol medication.

Action: B-complex vitamin; water-soluble; heat-stable; photolabile; synthetically prepared. Important in metabolism of carbohydrates, proteins, and fats.

Deficiency: Angular stomatitis; cheilosis; glossitis; itching, burning, and keratosis of the eyes; photophobia. Often accompanies pellagra.

Contraindication: None.

SILVER SULFADIAZINE (Silvadene cream)

Adults and children: $1/_{16}$-inch thickness applied in sterile manner 1-2 times/day.

Note: Significant quantities of silver sulfadiazine may be absorbed.

Indications: Topical burn therapy, as an adjunct for the prevention and treatment of wound sepsis in patients with second- and third-degree burns.

Action: Broad antimicrobial spectrum; bactericidal and fungicidal; acts on cell membranes and cell walls.

Contraindications: Silvadene cream hypersensitivity; term pregnancy; premature infants; infants less than 1 month old; caution in patients with G6PD deficiency.

SIMETHICONE (Mylicon)

Adults: 40-80 mg PO pc and hs.

Children: Safety not established.

Indications: For relief of paintful symptoms due to excessive gas in the GI tract.

Action: Antiflatulent antifoaming agent due to surface-active effects.

Contraindications: Bowel obstruction, undiagnosed abdominal pain.

SODIUM POLYSTYRENE SULFONATE (Kayexalate)

Adults:

1. Oral: 10-20 g in 20-100 ml water or 20% sorbitol q4-6h.
2. Retention enema: 30-50 g in 100-200 ml D10W or 20% sorbitol q6h.

Children: 1 mEq potassium per 1 g resin. Calculate dose according to desired change. PO/PR q6h prn.

Note:

1. Flushing enemas with non-sodium-containing fluids recommended before and after retention enemas.

2. Because of sodium content, caution is recommended in patients with congestive heart failure, severe hypertension, or marked edema.
3. Monitor serum potassium, sodium, and calcium levels closely.
4. With severe hyperkalemia, other measures, including glucose-insulin infusions, diuretics, and dialysis, should be considered.

Indication: Hyperkalemia.

Action: Nonabsorbable osmotic, cation-exchange resin.

Contraindication: None.

SPIRONOLACTONE (Aldactone)

Adults: 25 mg PO 1-4 times daily.

Children: 1.7-3.3 mg/kg/day PO divided q6-8h.

Note:
1. Caution with concurrent administration of potassium salts.
2. Diuretic action may require 7-10 days of therapy.
3. Often combined with other diuretics for faster onset of diuresis.

Indications: As an adjunct in the treatment of primary hyperaldosteronism; certain edematous states; essential hypertension; hypokalemia.

Action: Aldosterone antagonist; blocks sodium and water retention; spares renal potassium loss.

Contraindications: Renal failure, hyperkalemia.

STREPTOMYCIN SULFATE

Adults:
1. Usual dosage: 1-2 g IM in divided doses q12h.
2. Severe infection: 2-4 g IM in divided doses q6-12h.

Children: 20-40 mg/kg/day IM divided q8-12h.

Note:
1. Reduce dosage if renal impairment present.
2. Avoid concurrent use of other neurotoxic or nephrotoxic agents.
3. Bacterial resistance may develop readily.

Effective against: Many gram-negative bacteria, such as *Mycobacterium tuberculosis.* Synergistic with penicillin against *Streptococcus fecalis.*

Indications:
1. As adjunct in surgical SBE prophylaxis.
2. As adjunct in the treatment of tuberculosis.

Action: Aminoglycoside antibiotic; bactericidal; inhibits protein synthesis.

Excretion: Renal (glomerular filtration).

Contraindication: Streptomycin hypersensitivity.

SULFASALAZINE (Azulfidine)

Adults:
1. Initial: 3-4 g/day PO divided q6-8h.
2. Maintenance: 500 mg PO qid.

Children:
1. Initial: 40-60 mg/kg/day PO divided q4-8h.
2. Maintenance: 30 mg/kg/day PO divided q6h.

Note:
1. Adjust dosage to each patient's response and tolerance.
2. Adequate hydratioin recommended to prevent crystalluria.
Indications: Mild to moderate ulcerative colitis; adjunct in severe ulcerative colitis.
Action: Immunosuppressant; details unclear.
Metabolism: Degrated by colonic bacteria to 5-aminosalicylate (excreted in the feces) and sulfapyridine (absorbed and excreted in the urine).
Contraindications: Sulfonamide or salicylate hypersensitivity; intestinal and urinary obstruction; porphyria; pregnancy at term or nursing.

SULFINPYRAZONE (Anturane)

Adults:
1. Initial: 100-200 mg PO bid with meals.
2. Maintenance: 200-400 mg PO bid with meals.

Note: Individualize dosage to maintain blood urate level ‹ 6 mg/100 ml.
Indication: Maintenance therapy in chronic gout.
Action: Uricosuric; decreases serum uric acid levels by potentiating the urinary excretion of uric acid; also inhibits platelet aggregation.
Contraindications: Sulfinpyrazone hypersensitivity, active peptic ulcer.

SULFISOXAZOLE (Gantrisin)

Adults: 2-4 g PO initially, then 4-8 g/day PO divided q4-8h.

Children: 75 mg/kg PO initially, then 150 mg/kg/day PO divided q4-6h.

Note: Maintain adequate fluid intake to prevent crystalluria.
Indications: Urinary tract infections caused by susceptible *E. coli, Klebsiella, Staphylococcus,* and *Proteus.* For other indications, see PDR.
Action: Bacteriostatic sulfonamide; competitively blocks bacterial synthesis of folic acid from para-aminobenzoic acid.
Metabolism: 30%-35% acetylated in the liver.
Excretion: Renal, 95% (glomerular filtration).
Contraindications: Sulfonamide hypersensitivity, pregnancy at term or nursing.

TERBUTALINE SULFATE (Brethine, Bricanyl)

Adults:
1. Oral: 2.5-5 mg q6h (maximum, 15 mg/day).
2. SC: 0.25 mg repeated in 15-30 minutes if necessary.

Note: Caution with hypertension, heart disease, hyperthyroidism, diabetes.

Indication: Acute bronchospasm.

Action: Sympathetic bronchodilator; a synthetic amine beta-2-stimulant.

Onset: 5-15 minutes (SC), 30 minutes (PO).

Contraindication: Hypersensitivity to sympathomimetic amines.

TETRACYCLINE (Achromycin)

Adults:
1. Oral: 1-2 g daily in 2-4 divided doses.
2. IM: 250 mg qd (very painful).
3. IV: 250-500 mg q12h.

Note:
1. Not recommended in children during tooth development.
2. Oral absorption impaired by antacids, iron salts, milk, and food.

Indications: Biliary tract infections (if organisms susceptible); penicillin substitute; acute intestinal amebiasis; severe acne; trachoma; *Mycoplasma* pneumonia.

Action: Broad spectrum; bacteriostatic; inhibits bacterial protein synthesis.

Distribution: Wide, including bone, liver, CNS.

Excretion: Liver, intestine, renal (glomerular filtration).

Contraindication: Tetracycline hypersensitivity.

THEOPHYLLINE (Elixophyllin Elixir)

Adults:
1. Recommended dosage: 3-5 mg/kg PO q6h.
2. Severe asthma attack: 75 ml PO q6-8h prn.
3. Maintenance: 30-45 ml PO q8h.

Children:
1. Severe asthma attack: 1 ml/kg PO q6-8h prn.
2. Maintenance: 0.4-0.6 ml/kg PO q8h.

Note: The elixir contains 80 mg theophylline per 15 ml.

Indications: Bronchial asthma, other pulmonary diseases with bronchospasm.

Action: Xanthine bronchodilator; increases cardiac output; mild diuretic.

Contraindications: Theophylline hypersensitivity, peptic ulcer disease.

THIAMINE (vitamin B$_1$)

Adults:

1. RDA: 1.5 mg PO qd.
2. Mild deficiency: 5-10 mg PO tid with meals.
3. Alcoholic withdrawal: 50 mg IM 1-2 times/day.
4. Wernicke's encephalopathy: 500-1000 mg IM initially, then 100 mg IM 1-2 times/day.

Children: RDA: 0.5-1.5 mg PO qd.

Note:

1. Oral absorption of thiamine limited to about 10 mg/day.
2. IM absorption of thiamine excellent.

Indications: Thiamine deficiency states.
Action: B-complex vitamin; essential in carbohydrate metabolism.
Deficiency: Beriberi, peripheral neuritis, peripheral neuropathy.
Contraindication: Hypersensitivity to thiamine.

THIETHYLPERAZINE (Torecan)

Adults: 10 mg PO/IM/PR q8h prn.

Children: Safety not established in children under 12 years.

Indication: Nausea, vomiting, vertigo, motion sickness.
Action: Phenothiazine antiemetic.
Contraindications: Phenothiazine hypersensitivity, severe CNS depression, comatose states, pregnancy.

THYROID USP (desiccated thyroid)

Adults:

1. Hypothyroidism:
   Initial: 50 mg PO qd. Increase dosage gradually q1 month as needed.
   Maintenance: 60-180 mg PO qd.
2. Myxedema:
   Initial: 15 mg PO qd. Increase dosage gradually q2-4 weeks as needed.
   Maintenance: 60-180 mg PO qd.

Children:

1. Initial: 30 mg PO qd. Increase by 15 mg/day each week as needed.
2. Maintenance: 60-180 mg PO qd (average).

Infants:

1. Initial: 15 mg PO qd. Increase by 15 mg/day each week as needed.
2. Maintenance: 60-180 mg PO qd (average).

Note:
1. May potentiate oral anticoagulant effects.
2. Diabetic patients may require higher doses of insulin or oral hypoglycemic agents.

Indication: Specific replacement for reduced or absent thyroid function.

Action: Provides both levothyroxine and liothyronine in natural ratio.

Contraindications: Thyrotoxicosis, acute myocardial infarction without hypothyroidism, uncorrected adrenal insufficiency.

TOBRAMYCIN (Nebcin)

Adults and children: 3-5 mg/kg/day IM/IV in divided doses q8h.

Note:
1. Reduce dosage if renal impairment present.
2. Monitor serum creatinine and urine creatinine clearance closely.
3. Peritoneal and hemodialysis effective in reducing serum level.
4. Avoid concurrent use of other neurotoxic and nephrotoxic agents.

Indications: For serious gram-negative infections, especially if caused by *Pseudomonas aeruginosa*.

Action: Aminoglycoside antibiotic; bactericidal; inhibits protein synthesis.

Excretion: Renal (glomerular filtration), minimal biliary excretion.

Contraindications: Tobramycin hypersensitivity; cross-allergenicity among aminoglycosides.

TOLBUTAMIDE (Orinase)

Adults:
1. Initial: 1-2 g PO in single or divided doses.
2. Maintenance: 0.25-3 g PO in single or divided doses.

Note:
1. Individualize dosage based on clinical response and careful monitoring of blood and urinary glucose.
2. Patients already stabilized on insulin may require reduction in insulin dosage.
3. Surgical procedures may induce hyperglycemia, requiring supplementation or replacement with insulin therapy.

Indications:
Mild to moderate, stable adult-onset diabetes mellitus.
Adjuvant to insulin therapy in certain labile diabetic patients.

Action: Sulfonylurea; oral hypoglycemic agent; stimulates synthesis and release of endogenous insulin in presence of pancreatic beta cells.

Onset: 2-4 hours.
Peak: 5-8 hours.
Duration: 24 hours.
Contraindications: Juvenile-onset, unstable, or brittle diabetes; diabetes complicated by acidosis, ketosis, or coma; diabetes in presence of fever, severe trauma, or infections; severe hepatic or renal insufficiency; peptic ulcer; pregnancy.

TRAZODONE HCl (Desyrel)

Adults:
1. Initial: 50 mg PO tid.
2. Maximum: 400 mg/day outpatient; 600 mg/day inpatient.

Children: Safety not established.

Note: Prior to elective surgery, trazodone should be discontinued for as long as clinically feasible (interaction between trazodone and general anesthetics unknown).
Indication: For treatment of depression.
Action: Antidepressant; inhibits uptake of serotonin by brain synaptosomes.
Contraindication: Trazodone hypersensitivity.

TRIAMTERENE (Dyrenium)

Adults:
1. Initial: 100 mg PO bid.
2. Maintenance: 100-300 mg/day PO.

Note: Monitor electrolyte, renal, and hematologic status carefully.
Indications: Edema due to congestive heart failure, cirrhosis, or nephrotic syndrome.
Action: Diuretic; inhibits sodium resorption in the distal renal tubule.
Contraindications: Triamterene hypersensitivity, severe renal or hepatic disease, hyperkalemia.

TRIMETHOBENZAMIDE (Tigan)

Adults:
1. Oral: 250 mg q6-8h prn.
2. Suppository: 200 mg q6-8h prn.
3. IM: 200 mg q6-8h prn.

Children: 15 mg/kg/day PO/PR/IM divided q6-8h prn.

Indications: For control of uncomplicated nausea and vomiting.
Action: Antihistaminic, antiemetic.
Contraindications: Trimethobenzamide hypersensitivity.

TRIMETHOPRIM-SULFAMETHOXAZOLE (Bactrim, Septra)

Adults:

1. Urinary tract infections: 2 tablets PO q12h for 10-14 days.
2. *Pneumocystis carinii* pneumonitis: 2 tablets PO q6h for 14 days.

Children:

1. Urinary tract infections: Trimethoprim 8 mg/kg/day PO divided q12h. Sulfamethoxazole 40 mg/kg/day PO divided q12h.
2. *Pneumocystis carinii* pneumonitis: Trimethoprim 20 mg/kg/day PO divided q6h. Sulfamethoxazole 100 mg/kg/day PO divided q6h.

Composition: Trimethoprim 80 mg, sulfamethoxazole 400 mg.
Indications: Chronic or recurrent UTIs.
Action: 1. Trimethoprim inhibits production of tetrahydrofolic acid from dihydrofolic acid.
2. Sulfamethoxazole inhibits production of dihydrofolic acid.
Excretion: Renal (glomerular filtration and tubular secretion).
Contraindications: Trimethoprim or sulfonamide hypersensitivity, pregnancy.

VANCOMYCIN (Vancocin)

Adults:

1. IV: 500 mg q6h or 1 g q12h.
2. Staphylococcal enterocolitis: 500 mg PO q6h.

Children:

1. IV: 40 mg/kg/day divided q12h.
2. Staphylococcal entercolitis: 40 mg/kg/day PO divided q6h.

Note:

1. Reduce dosage if renal impairment present.
2. Avoid concomitant use with other nephrotoxic and ototoxic agents.
3. Poorly absorbed orally.

Effective against: Most gram-positive bacteria, including penicillin- and methicillin-resistant staphylococci.
Indications: Serious penicillin-resistant staphylococcal infections; penicillin and cephalothin allergy; enterococcal endocarditis; staphylococcal enterocolitis.
Action: Glycopeptide antibiotic; bactericidal; inhibits cell wall synthesis; also damages cytoplasmic membrane.
Excretion: Renal, 80%; bile, minimal.
Contraindication: Vancomycin hypersensitivity.

VASOPRESSIN TANNATE (Pitressin Tannate in Oil)

Adults: 2.5-5 IU IM q1-3 days prn (5 units/ml).

Children: 1 ml IV/IM q1-3 days prn; may increase to 2.5-5 ml IV/dose if needed.

Indication: Diabetes insipidus caused by deficiency of endogenous ADH.

Action: Antidiuretic; increases renal tubular resorption of water.

Contraindications: Severe hypertension, severe coronary artery disease, MAO inhibitor use. Use with caution in the presence of hyperthyroidism, diabetes mellitus, propranolol administration, urinary retention, and glaucoma.

VITAMIN A

Adults:
1. RDA: 5,000 units.
2. Dietary supplement: 12,00 units PO/IM qd.
3. Severe deficiency: 100,000 units PO/IM qd for 3 days; then 50,000 units PO/IM qd for 2 weeks; then 10,000-20,000 units PO/IM qd for 2 months.

Children (1-8 years):
1. RDA: 2000-5000 units.
2. Usual therapy: 17,500-35,000 units PO/IM qd for 10 days.

Infants:
1. RDA: 1500 units.
2. Usual therapy: 7500-15,000 units PO/IM qd for 10 days.

Note:
1. Absorption of oral preparations requires presence of intestinal bile.
2. Avoid use of mineral oil during oral administration.

Indications: Vitamin A deficiency states.

Action: Fat-soluble vitamin; essential for normal function, growth, development, and integrity of epithelial tissues.

Contraindication: Hypervitaminosis A.

VITAMIN B$_{12}$ (cyanocobalamin)

Adults:
1. RDA: 6 μg.
2. Usual therapy: 10-50 μg IM/SC qd.
3. Pernicious anemia:
    Initial: 100-1000 μg IM/SC qd for 1-2 weeks.
    Maintenance: 100-1000 μg IM/SC once each month.
4. Prevention of megaloblastic anemia after gastrectomy: 100 μg IM/SC each month.
5. Schilling test:
    a. Cyanocobalamin 57 Co 0.5-1 μCi PO.
    b. Cyanocobalamin 1 mg IM 1-2 hours after radioactive dose.

Children:
1. Initial: 100 μg IM/SC qd for 1-2 weeks.
2. Maintenance: 60 μg IM/SC once each month.

Indication: Vitamin B$_{12}$ deficiency.

Action: B-complex vitamin; required for nucleoprotein and myelin synthesis, cell reproduction, normal growth and erythropoiesis, and for folic acid function; requires intrinsic factor for absorption.

Contraindication: Hypersensitivity to cobalamins or cobalt.

WARFARIN SODIUM (Coumadin, Panwarfin)

Adults:

1. Initial: 10-20 mg PO qd for 1-3 days.
2. Maintenance: 2-10 mg PO qd.

Note:

1. Individualize dosage to maintain PT at 1.5 to 2.5 times control value. This should be monitored daily during initiation of therapy and every 1-4 weeks thereafter.
2. Factors that may enhance anticoagulant effect:
   a. Systemic: vitamin K deficiency, obstructive jaundice, liver disease, diarrhea, steatorrhea, cancer, malnutrition, congestive heart failure, fever, collagen disease.
   b. Drugs that inhibit vitamin K absorption: antibiotics, cholestyramine, mineral oil.
   c. Drugs that displace warfarin sodium (Coumadin) from plasma proteins: chloral hydrate, chloramphenicol, diazoxide, ethacrynic acid, neomycin, phenylbutazone, salicylates, sulfonamides, tetracycline, and other acidic drugs.
   d. Drugs that inhibit warfarin sodium (Coumadin) metabolism: allopurinol, chloramphenicol, clofibrate, disulfiram, metronidazole, and phenylbutazone.
   e. Other: glucagon, quinidine, thyroid drugs and others.
3. Factors that may decrease anticoagulant effects:
   a. Systemic: diabetes mellitus, edema, hyperlipemia, hypothyroidism, hereditary resistance to coumarin therapy.
   b. Drugs that stimulate warfarin sodium (Coumadin) metabolism: barbiturates, chloral hydrate, estrogens, glutethimide, griseofulvin, haloperidol, meprobamate, phenytoin, rifampin.
   c. Drugs that increase the production of procoagulants: estrogens, oral contraceptives, vitamin K.
4. Factors that may cause an increased bleeding tendency:
   a. Inhibition of platelet aggregation: aspirin, dipyridamole, indomethacin, phenylbutazone.
   b. Inhibition of procoagulant factors: alkylating agents, antimetabolites, quinidine, salicylates.
   c. Ulcerogenic drugs: aspirin, indomethacin, phenylbutazone.
5. Drugs that can be used with little or no effect on PT.
   a. Analgesics: acetaminophen, codeine, propoxyphene.

    b. Sedative-hypnotics: diazepam, flurazepam, chlordiaze-poxide.

6. Preoperatively, dosage should be adjusted to maintain the PT at no more than 1.5 to 2 times control value.
7. Postoperatively, dosage should be adjusted to maintain the PT at no more than 1.5 to 2 times control values until sutures and drains are removed.
8. Overcoumadinization may be controlled by the following measures:
     a. Discontinuing Coumadin (slow control, days).
     b. Vitamin K₁ (phytonadione) PO or IV, slowly (4-8 hours).
     c. 250-500 ml of fresh frozen plasma (immediate effect).
     d. Fresh whole blood (rarely indicated).

Indications:
1. Prophylaxis and treatment of venous thrombosis and its extension.
2. Treatment of atrial fibrillation with embolization.
3. Prophylaxis and treatment of pulmonary embolism.
4. As adjunct in treatment of coronary occlusion (controversial).

Action: Coumarin anticoagulant; inhibits vitamin K-2,3 epoxide reductases; produces inhibition of liver synthesis of vitamin K-dependent factors VII, IX, X, and II in sequence.

Onset:
1. PT becomes prolonged in 1-4 days (indicates depletion of factor VII).
2. Antithrombotic activity begins in 7 days (indicates depletion of factors IX and X).

Duration: 4-5 days (indicates liver synthesis of new clotting factors).

Metabolism: Liver microsomal enzymes, the activity of which varies greatly (from 1- to 10-fold) from patient to patient.

Excretion: Renal (primarily as inactive metabolites).

Protein binding: 97% bound to plasma proteins (mostly to albumin).

Contraindications: Hypersensitivity; any hemorrhagic diathesis (see *Heparin* contraindications).

ZINC SULFATE (Orazinc, Zinc-220)

Adults: 1 capsule PO with meal or milk qd.

Note:
1. Each capsule contains 220 mg zinc sulfate, equivalent to 50 mg of elemental zinc.
2. Normal daily requirement of zinc is 10-20 mg/day.

Indications: Prophylaxis or treatment of simple zinc deficiency.

Action: Adequate zinc necessary for normal growth and tissue repair; important in enzymes needed for protein and carbohydrate metabolism.

Contraindication: None known.

TABLES

• • •

Narcotic analgesics	IM	PO	Differences from morphine, 10 mg IM
Alphaprodine (Nisentil)	45 mg	—	Very short-acting
Anileridine (Leritine)	30 mg	50 mg	High PO to IM potency
Codeine	120 mg	200 mg	High PO to IM potency
Dextromoramide (Palfium)	7.5 mg	10 mg	High PO to IM potency
Dipipanone (Pipadone)	20 mg	—	Similar to methadone
Heroin (diacetyl-morphine)	4 mg	—	Shorter-acting
Hydromorphone (Dilaudid)	1.5 mg	7.5 mg	Shorter-acting
Levorphanol (Levo-Dromoran)	2 mg	4 mg	High PO to IM potency
Meperidine (Demerol)	75 mg	300 mg	None
Methadone (Dolophine)	10 mg	20 mg	High PO to IM potency
Methotrimeperazine (Levoprome)	20 mg	—	Phenothiazine—unlike morphine sulfate
Metopon (Metopon)	3 mg	18 mg	None
Oxycodone (Percodan)	15 mg	30 mg	Shorter-acting, high PO to IM potency
Oxymorphone (Numorphan)	1 mg	6 mg	None
Pentazocine (Talwin)	60 mg	180 mg	Narcotic antagonist analgesic
Phenazocine (Prinadol)	3 mg	15 mg	Between morphine sulfate and methadone
Piminodine (Alvodine)	7.5 mg	—	None
Propoxyphene (Darvon)	—	240 mg	Similar to codeine but more toxic in high doses

Modified from Honde, R.W.: The management of pain. In Clark, R. L., and others, editors: Oncology 1970 (proceedings of the Tenth International Cancer Congress, Houston, 1970), Chicago, 1971, Year Book Medical Publishers, Inc., vol. 3, p. 489.

Nonnarcotic analgesics	PO	Differences from aspirin, 650 mg PO
Acetaminophen (Tylenol)	650 mg	Similar to phenacetin, less potential renal toxicity
Codeine	32 mg	Weak narcotic, high analgesic potential, relatively low addiction liability
Pentazocine (Talwin)	30 mg	Weak narcotic antagonist, high analgesic potential
Phenacetin	650 mg	Similar to aspirin but with limited anti-inflammatory properties
Propoxyphene (Darvon)	65 mg	Weak narcotic, low analgesic potential, low addiction liability
Sodium salicylate	1,000 mg	Similar to aspirin

Modified from Honde, R. W.: The management of pain. In Clark, R. L., and others, editors: Oncology 1970 (proceedings of the Tenth International Cancer Congress, Houston, 1970), Chicago, 1971 Year Book Medical Publishers, Inc., vol. 3, p. 489.

Antacids	Buffering capacity (mEq/15 ml)	Sodium content (mEq/15 ml)
1. Aluminum hydroxide (Amphojel)	29	0.8
2. Aluminum hydroxide— magnesium hydroxide		
(Maalox, Maalox Plus*)	49	0.7
(Mylanta*)	37.5	0.4
(Mylanta II*)	75	1.0
(Riopan)	33	0.1
3. Aluminum hydroxide— magnesium trisilicate		
(Gelusil)	20	1.0
4. Calcium carbonate (Dicarbosil, Tums)	19.5	0

*Also contains simethicone.
Note: Information on indications, dosages, and adverse effects follows on p. 102.

Indications and dosages:
1. Peptic ulcer disease:
   Acute stage: 30-60 ml of liquid antacid PO q1-2h while awake for 2 weeks.
   Healing stage: 15-30 ml of liquid antacid 1 and 3 hours after eating and hs for 2 months.
   Occasional pain: 15-30 ml of liquid antacid PO prn.
2. Reflux esophagitis: As for peptic ulcer disease.
3. Prophylaxis for stress ulcers (head trauma, severe infection, shock, steroid administration): 30 ml PO or via NG tube q1-2h.

Note:
1. Liquid antacids generally more effective than tablets.
2. 60 ml of antacid is more effective than 15 ml of the same antacid.
3. Larger doses of antacids associated with increased side effects.
4. Use antacid low in sodium if salt-restriction necessary (congestive heart failure, renal insufficiency).
5. Aluminum hydroxide antacids preferred in renal failure and hypoparathyroidism.

Action: Helpful in reducing ulcer pain; promotion of ulcer healing controversial.

Adverse effects:
1. Aluminum hydroxide: Constipating; may cause hypophosphatemia by binding phosphate in GI lumen. Also binds orally administered antibiotics, chlorpromazine, and thyroxine.
2. Calcium carbonate: Constipating; large doses may cause hypercalcemia and hypercalcuria. Limit dosage to 8 g/day (16 tablets).
3. Magnesium hydroxide: Large doses may cause severe osmotic diarrhea, hypermagnesemia (15% absorbed). Contraindicated in renal failure.
4. Magnesium trisilicate: Large doses may cause diarrhea; silicate renal stones reported following prolonged use; contraindicated in renal failure.

Contraindications: Magnesium-containing antacids contraindicated in renal failure; antacids generally not recommended with tetracycline administration.

Glucocorticoids	Equivalent dosages*	Route	Anti-inflammatory	Mineralo-corticoid	Initial dosage (mg/day) High	Initial dosage (mg/day) Moderate
1. Cortisone acetate†	25 mg	PO/IM	0.8	0.8	—	100-150
2. Dexamethasone (Decadron)	0.75 mg	PO/IV	20-30	0	7.5-15	3-4.5
3. Hydrocortisone† (Hydrocortisone tablets) (Solu-Cortef)	20 mg	PO, IM/IV	1.0	1.0	—	80-120
4. Methylprednisolone (Medrol) (Depo-Medrol) (Solu-Medrol)	4 mg	PO, IM, IM/IV	3-5	0	40-80	16-24
5. Prednisone	5 mg	PO	3-5	0.8	50-100	20-40
6. Prednisolone (Meticortelone) (Prednisolone tablets)	5 mg	IM/IV, PO	3-5	0.8	50-100	20-40
7. Triamcinolone (Aristocort) (Triamcinolone tablets)	4 mg	Topical, PO	3-5	0	40-80	16-24

*Equivalent dosages not always consistent with recommended dosages.
†Complete spectrum of glucocorticoid activity.
Note: Information on side effects and contraindications follows on p. 104.

Note: (numbers in this note correspond to entries in the table on p. 103):

1. Biologic activity apparently contingent on conversion to hydrocortisone. Used in Addison's disease, drug-induced adrenal insufficiency.
2. Side effects: low incidence of hyperglycemia; excessive mental stimulation and increased appetite. Used for: diagnosis of Cushing's syndrome (suppression test), adrenal tumor versus hyperplasia, cerebral edema.
3. Preferred for Addison's disease, drug-induced adrenal insufficiency.
4. May also be used in massive doses, 15-30 mg/kg/day, for septic shock, aspiration pneumonia, fat embolism, systemic lupus erythematosus (SLE), allergic states, ulcerative colitis.
5. Used for adrenal insufficiency; SLE and other various inflammatory conditions (see PDR). Short-acting and least expensive.
6. Enhanced anti-inflammatory activity.
7. Side effects: increased incidence of muscle cramps, muscle wasting, weakness, mental depression, headache, facial flushing, and anorexia.

Contraindications: Peptic ulcer, psychoses, acute glomerulonephritis, herpes simplex of the eyes, vaccinia or varicella, exanthematoses. Cushing's syndrome, infections not controlled with antibiotics, systemic fungal infecions, tuberculosis.

Insulins	Onset (hours)	Peak (hours)	Duration (hours)
Fast			
Regular (crystalline)	0.5	2-4	6
Semilente	1.0	4-8	12
Intermediate			
NPH	2.0	8-12	24
Lente	2.0	8-12	24
Long			
Protamine zinc	6.0	12-24	36
Ultralente	6.0	18-24	36

Note: Acute hyperglycemia may occur as a result of infection, surgery, trauma, steroid therapy, and pregnancy.

Indications:
1. Juvenile-onset diabetes mellitus.
2. Adult-onset diabetes mellitus (diet failure).
3. Acute hyperglycemia (see note above).
4. Hyperosmolar nonketotic coma.
5. Ketoacidosis.

Complications:
1. Hypoglycemia (food omitted, exercise, insulin overdosage, propranolol).
2. Rebound hyperglycemia (Somogyi effect).
3. Insulin allergy (urticaria, pruritus, intermittent use of insulin).
4. Insulin resistance (production of insulin-neutralizing antibodies).
5. Lipodystrophy (may result in unpredictable absorption).

Potassium supplements (oral)	Potassium content
1. Potassium acetate-bicarbonate-citrate	
Potassium Triplex	5 ml = 15 mEq potassium
2. Potassium bicarbonate	
Klorvess Effervescent Tablets	1 tablet = 20 mEq potassium
K-Lyte	1 tablet = 25 mEq potassium
3. Potassium chloride	
Kaon-Cl Tablets	1 tablet = 6.67 mEq potassium
Kay Ciel Elixir	15 mg = 20 mEq potassium
Slow-K	1 tablet = 8 mEq potassium
4. Potassium gluconate	
Kaon Elixir	15 ml = 20 mEq potassium
Kaon Tablets	1 tablet = 5 mEq potassium

Note: Most of the above potassium preparations require dilution with 60-90 ml water or juice. The exceptions are Kaon Tablets, Kaon-Cl Tablets, and Slow-K; these are taken in tablet form without prior dilution and have been associated with GI ulcerations, bleeding, and perforation. They also contain smaller amounts of potassium than the other preparations. They are included here only for the sake of completeness and are not recommended.

Indications: Hypokalemia, which may be due to diuretic therapy, digitalis intoxication, low dietary intake of potassium, loss of potassium due to vomiting or diarrhea, diabetic acidosis, metabolic alkalosis, corticosteroid therapy, familial periodic paralysis.

Adverse effects:

1. With all potassium preparations: the danger of hyperkalemia.
2. Gastric irritation if taken undiluted orally (nausea, vomiting, and diarrhea).
3. Small bowel ulcerations with tablets of potassium preparations.

Contraindications: Renal failure, Addison's disease, acute dehydration, hyperkalemia.

SIGNS, SYMPTOMS, AND DISEASES

The purpose of this section is to present some practical guidelines to signs, symptoms, and diseases that may be encountered in the surgical patient. The contents are alphabetically arranged, and each topic is concisely outlined for quick review. For pre- and postoperative orders, one should consult Section Two for general format and suggestions. The format of the entries in this section is generally as follows:

1. Etiology
2. Signs and symptoms
3. Diagnostic tests
4. Differential diagnosis
5. Therapeutic guidelines

Entries in this section were selected for various reasons. Some are presented because of their emergency nature and the necessity of providing a quick reference on initial evaluation and therapy. *Surgical emergencies* discussed include acute abdomen, GI hemorrhage, hemorrhagic shock, burns, hyperparathyroid crisis, and bleeding problems. *Medical emergencies,* which can occur in any surgical patient or in the postoperative state, include acute myocardial infarction, cardiac arrest, cardiogenic shock, pulmonary embolism, thyroid storm, acute hypoparathyroidism, adult respiratory distress syndrome, and acute oliguria. *General information* topics provide lists of reference information often easily forgotten. *Summaries* of some of the more uncommon syndromes may be of interest. Of course, not every topic can be presented in a manual such as this, and for those not included the reader should refer to other sources.

OVERVIEW OF CONTENTS

General information
Acid-base abnormalities
Anemias
Bleeding problems
Burns
Fevers
Hypercalcemic crisis
Infections
Shock
Transfusion reactions

Head and neck
Acute parotitis
Diabetes insipidus
Hyperparathyroidism, primary
Hyperthyroidism
Hypothyroidism
Multiple endocrine
adenomatosis syndrome
Thyroid nodule
Thyroid storm

Respiratory system
Adult respiratory distress
syndrome
Aspiration pneumonia
Atelectasis
Pneumonia
Pneumothorax

Cardiovascular system
Acute myocardial
infarction
Cardiac arrest
Cardiogenic shock
Hypertension
Pulmonary edema
Pulmonary embolism

Gastrointestinal system
Esophagus
Achalasia
Stomach
Dumping syndrome

Duodenum
Perforated peptic ulcer
Small bowel
Small bowel obstruction
Appendix
Appendicitis
Large bowel
Large bowel obstruction
Ulcerative colitis
Volvulus
Biliary tract
Acute cholecystitis
Biliary colic
Cholangitis
Choledocholithiasis
Chronic cholecystitis
Liver
Viral hepatitis
Pancreas
Acute pancreatitis
Zollinger-Ellison
syndrome
Other
Abdominal abscess
Abdominal angina
Acute abdomen
GI hemorrhage
Medical cause of acute abdomen
Acute intermittent
porphyria
Diabetic ketoacidosis
Fitz-Hugh and Curtis
syndrome

Genitourinary system
Hematuria
Oliguria
Urinary tract infection

Extremities
Deep venous thrombosis

ABDOMEN, ACUTE

The following lists were developed to provide a differential diagnosis of the acute abdomen, useful in emergency room situations. A careful history, physical examination, blood count, urinalysis, and chest and abdominal x-ray films are most important. See the individual entries for further information.

Right upper quadrant
Appendicitis (ascending)
Cholangitis
Cholecystitis
Choledocholithiasis
Fitz-Hugh and Curtis syndrome
Hepatic abscess
Hepatitis
Hepatomegaly
Myocardial infarction
Pancreatitis
Peptic ulcer disease
Pericarditis
Pleurisy (diaphragmatic)
Pneumonia (basal)
Pulmonary embolism
Pyelonephritis
Renal colic
Subphrenic abscess
Thoracic aneurysm
(dissecting)
Right lower quadrant
Appendicitis
Cholecystitis (acute,
perforated)
Diverticulitis
Ectopic pregnancy
(ruptured)
Endometriosis
Epididymitis
Gastroenteritis
Hip pain (referred)
Intestinal obstruction
Leaking aortic aneurysm
Mittelschmerz
Pelvic inflammatory
disease
Peptic ulcer (perforated)
Psoas abscess
Rectus hematoma
Regional enteritis
Renal colic
Salpingitis
Torsion of ovarian cyst
or tumor
Urinary tract infection
Left upper quadrant
Gastritis
Myocardial infarction
Pancreatitis
Peptic ulcer disease
Pericarditis
Pleurisy (diaphragmatic)
Pneumonia (basal)
Pulmonary embolism
Pyelonephritis
Renal colic
Splenic infarct or rupture
Subphrenic abscess
Thoracic aneurysm
(dissecting)
Left lower quadrant
Diverticulitis
Ectopic pregnancy
(ruptured)
Endometriosis
Epididymitis
Hip pain (referred)
Intestinal obstruction
Leaking aortic aneurysm
Mittelschmerz
Pelvic inflammatory
disease
Psoas abscess
Rectus hematoma
Renal colic
Salpingitis
Torsion of ovarian cyst
or tumor
Urinary tract infection
Diffuse
Abdominal angina
Aortic aneurysm
(ruptured)
Appendicitis (early)
Colitis
Diabetic ketoacidosis
Gastroenteritis
Intestinal obstruction
Leukemia
Mesenteric lymphadenitis
Mesenteric thrombosis
Pancreatitis
Peritonitis
Porphyria
Sickle cell crisis
Tabes dorsalis
Uremia

ABDOMINAL ABSCESS

Types

Subphrenic, subhepatic, lesser sac, paracolic, cul-de-sac, perivisceral.

Etiology

Peritonitis, perivisceral inflammation (appendicitis, etc.).
Foreign material, necrotic tissue, collections of fluid.
Surgery (biliary, gastric, pancreatic).

Signs and symptoms

Gradual worsening, pallor, weakness.
Anorexia, distention, vomiting.
Fever, tachycardia, leukocytosis.
Increasing abdominal mass.
Rectal tenderness and fullness.

Diagnostic tests

CBC with differential, liver function tests.
Abdominal x-ray, chest x-ray, sonogram, liver scan.
Laparotomy may be necessary for diagnosis.

Therapeutic guidelines

May resolve conservatively with antibiotics, but spontaneous rupture is catastrophic. Discontinue antibiotics to expedite diagnosis. Surgical drainage is necessary if progressive sepsis occurs.

ABDOMINAL ANGINA

Etiology

Intestinal ischemia caused by gradual atherosclerotic stenosis or occlusion of one or more visceral arteries (celiac, superior mesenteric, inferior mesenteric). Usually occurs in elderly patients with widespread evidence of atherosclerosis.

Signs and symptoms

Postprandial epigastric pain, aggravated by large meals.
Weight loss caused by reduction of intake.
Altered bowel habits (constipation, diarrhea, malabsorption).
May be associated with flatulence, bloating, and distention.
Abdominal tenderness may be minimal.
Vascular bruits, decreased pulses, hypertension.

Diagnostic tests

Flush aortography or selective mesenteric angiography may reveal high-grade, isolated stenoses.

Complications

Intestinal infarction, perforation.

Therapeutic guidelines

Arterial reconstruction (endarterectomy, reimplantation, or bypass graft).

ACHALASIA (Cardiospasm)
Etiology

Idiopathic degeneration of the esophageal myenteric plexus.
Trypanosomiasis (Chagas' disease).
Effect: esophageal aperistalsis, impaired esophagogastric sphincter relaxation.

Signs and symptoms

Progressive dysphagia, regurgitation of recently ingested foods.

Diagnostic tests

Chest x-ray: esophageal fluid level, mediastinal widening, absent gastric bubble.
Esophagram: esophageal dilation, conically narrow cardio-esophageal junction.
Esophagoscopy: rule out malignancy or other organic stricture.
Manometry: esophageal aperistalsis, methacholine stimulates a forceful, sustained contraction of the esophagus.

Differential diagnosis

Scleroderma, strictures (benign and malignant).

Complications

Aspiration pneumonia, esophageal cancer.

Therapeutic guidelines

Pneumatic or hydrostatic dilation of lower esophageal sphincter.
Heller esophagomyotomy or a modification of this approach.
Antireflux procedure recommended in presence of esophageal reflux.

ACIDOSIS, METABOLIC
Etiology

1. *Hyperchloremic acidoses:*
   a. *Loss of bicarbonate:*
      Severe diarrhea.
      Small bowel fistula.
      Ureterosigmoidostomy.
      Carbonic anhydrase inhibitors.
      Renal tubular acidosis.
   b. *Administration of acids:*
      Hydrochloric acid, ammonium chloride.
      Arginine hydrochloride (as with TPN).

2. *High anion-gap acidoses:*
   Caused by increased unmeasured anions.
   Reflects accumulation of organic acids.
   Normal anion gap = $(Na + K) - (Cl + HCO_3) = 8$ mEq/liter ± 4.
   > 8 mEq/liter implies increased anion gap.
   a. *Retention of acids:*
      Renal failure.
   b. *Production of acids:*
      Lactic acidosis.
      Ketoacidosis.
      Salicylate intoxication.
      Methyl alcohol intoxication.
      Ethylene glycol intoxication.
      Paraldehyde intoxication.

Complications

Decreased myocardial contractility.
Decreased myocardial response to catecholamines.
Decreased vascular response to catecholamines.
Predisposition to cardiac arrhythmias.
Predisposition to hyperkalemia.

Compensatory mechanism

Pulmonary hyperventilation (reduction of P_{CO_2}).

Diagnostic tests

Low arterial pH.
Low serum bicarbonate.

Therapeutic guidelines

1. Treat the underlying cause of the acidosis.
2. Ensure adequate tissue perfusion.
3. Administer bicarbonate if acidosis is severe.
4. Follow serum electrolytes, bicarbonate, and arterial pH closely.

ACIDOSIS, RESPIRATORY
Etiology

Retention of CO_2 (decreased alveolar ventilation).
Respiratory depression:
   Narcotic administration.
   CNS injury.
Pulmonary disease:
   Airway obstruction.
   Atelectasis.
   Emphysema.
   Pleural effusion.
   Pneumonia.

Compensatory mechanism

Renal:
Retention of bicarbonate.
Excretion of acid salts.
Increased ammonia formation.
Chloride shifts into red cells.

Diagnostic tests

Low arterial pH.
Elevated arterial P_{CO_2}.

Therapeutic guidelines

1. Treat the underlying cause of the acidosis.
2. Improve ventilation:
   Ensure adequate airway and tracheobronchial hygiene.
   Encourage deep breathing and coughing.
   Prevent inspissation of secretions (hydration, humidified air).
3. Avoid oversedation.
4. Adequate chloride (prevent metabolic alkalosis).

ALKALOSIS, METABOLIC

Aggravated by hypokalemia.

Etiology

1. *Chloride-responsive alkaloses* (urine Cl^- < 10-20 mEq/liter):
   Loss of hydrochloric acid:
   Gastric suction or vomiting.
   Villous adenoma of colon.
   Congenital chloride-losing diarrhea.
   Diuretic administration.
   Posthypercapneic alkalosis.
2. *Chloride-resistant alkaloses* (urine Cl^- > 10-20 mEq/liter):
   Gain of bicarbonate (IV or PO).
   Severe chronic hypokalemia.
   Primary hyperaldosteronism.
   Cushing's syndrome.

Compensatory mechanism

Renal excretion of bicarbonate.
Hypoventilation (retain carbon dioxide: limited by oxygen demand).

Diagnostic tests

Elevated arterial pH, elevated serum bicarbonate.

Therapeutic guidelines

1. Treat the underlying cause of the alkalosis.
2. Administer sodium chloride for chloride-responsive types.

3. Administer potassium chloride for chloride-resistant types.
4. Discontinue bicarbonate administration.

ALKALOSIS, RESPIRATORY
Etiology

Hyperventilation (reduced Pco_2):
   Psychogenic causes (anxiety).
   Hypermetabolic states (fever, thyrotoxicosis).
   Excessive mechanical ventilation.
   Pregnancy.
   Cirrhosis.
   Cardiac diseases.
   Pulmonary diseases.
   Brainstem lesion.
   Early salicylate intoxication.

Compensatory mechanism

Renal excretion of bicarbonate.

Diagnostic tests

Elevated arterial pH, low arterial Pco_2.

Therapeutic guidelines

1. Treat the underlying cause of the alkalosis.
2. Sedate for anxiety.
3. Increase $Fico_2$ (rebreathing mask, readjust ventilator).
4. Administer calcium gluconate IV for tetany.
5. Administer potassium chloride for hypokalemia.

ANEMIAS
Classification

Increased red cell losses:
1. *Hemorrhage:*
   Acute (see *Shock, hemorrhagic*).
   Chronic: iron deficiency.
2. *Hemolysis:*
   a. *Intracorpuscular defects:*
      Hereditary spherocytosis.
      Hereditary elliptocytosis.
      Sickle cell anemia.
      Thalassemia.
      G6PD deficiency.
   b. *Extracorpuscular defects:*
      Autoimmune hemolytic disease.
      Toxic, bacterial, physical destruction.
      Erythroblastosis fetalis.
      Malaria.
      Sequestration (hypersplenism).

Decreased red cell production:
1. *Nutritional deficiencies:*
   Iron, folic acid.
   Vitamin B_{12}.
   Pyridoxine.
2. *Marrow replacement* (myelophthisic anemias):
   Tumors.
   Tuberculosis.
3. *Marrow injury* (aplastic anemias):
   Medications.
   Irradiation.
4. *Endocrine deficiency:*
   Pituitary.
   Thyroid.
   Adrenal.

RBC indices

Macrocytic:
Vitamin B_{12} deficiency (pernicious anemia).
Folate deficiency (malabsorption, pregnancy).
Chronic liver disease.
Hypothyroidism.
Tapeworm infestation.

Normocytic:
Acute hemorrhage.
Hemolytic anemias.
Bone marrow failure.
Chronic diseases.
Renal failure.
Endocrine disorders.

Hypochromic-microcytic:

Anemia	Serum iron	TIBC	Marrow iron stores	Marrow sideroblasts
Iron deficiency	↓	↑	0	0
Thalassemia	N or ↑	N	N or ↑	N or ↑
Chronic disease	↓	↓	↑	↓
Sideroblastic	↑	↓	↑ ↑	↑ ↑

Anemia workup

1. CBC (severity of anemia).
   Peripheral smear (evidence of red cell destruction).
   Reticulocyte count (evidence of red cell production).
   Indices (MCV, MCH, MCHC).
   If chronic hemorrhage is suspected, check:
      Urinalysis for occult blood.

Stool guaiac for occult blood.
NG aspirate for occult blood.
Bleeding history (e.g., menstrual).
2. If hypochromic-microcytic indices, check:
   a. Serum iron.
   b. TIBC.
   c. Transferrin saturation.
   d. Bone marrow (iron stain).
   e. Hemoglobin electrophoresis.
3. If macrocytic, check:
   a. Serum B_{12} level.
   b. Serum folate level.
   c. Liver function tests.
   d. Thyroid function tests.
4. If normocytic, check:
   a. Coombs' test.
   b. Haptoglobin.
   c. Bone marrow.
   d. Renal function tests.
5. If serum B_{12} level low, check:
   a. Shilling urinary vitamin B_{12} excretion test.
6. Other tests:
   a. Bilirubin.
   b. Osmotic fragility.
   c. Plasma hemoglobin.
   d. Platelet count.
   e. Reticulocyte count.
   f. Sedimentation rate.
   g. Sickle cell preparation.
   h. Stool urobilinogen.
   i. Urine hemoglobin.
   j. Urine urobilinogen.

SPECIFIC ANEMIAS
Acquired hemolytic anemia

Etiology:
Malignant lymphoma.
Systemic lupus erythematosus.
Idiopathic.

Diagnostic tests:
Indirect bilirubin increased.
Urine and stool urobilinogen increased.
Hemoglobinemia, hemoglobinuria.
Haptoglobin level decreased.
Reticulocytes increased.
Bone marrow: erythroid hyperplasia.
Coombs' test positive.

Anemia of chronic disease

Etiology:
Infections (tuberculosis, bronchiectasis, lung abscess, empyema, bacterial endocarditis, brucellosis).
Malignancies.
Chronic liver disease.
Collagen diseases.
Uremia.

Diagnostic tests:
Anemia usually mild.
Normocytic, normochromic.
Serum iron decreased.
TIBC normal or decreased.
Transferrin saturation normal or decreased.
Bone marrow: sideroblasts decreased; iron stores normal or increased.

G6PD deficiency

Etiology:
Inherited chronic hemolytic anemia (X-linked).
Many subtypes exist.
Precipitated by various drugs (primaquine, nitrofurantin, vitamin K, sulfonamides, fava beans, etc.).

Diagnostic tests:
Spot test (erythrocyte enzyme assay).
Methemoglobin reduction test.
Brilliant cresyl blue reduction test.

Hereditary elliptocytosis

Etiology:
Autosomal dominant inheritance.
Chronic mild hemolytic anemia.

Diagnostic tests:
Elliptocytes (oval) (25%-90% of red cells).
May have:
  Anemia (mild to moderate).
  Bilirubin increased.
  Reticulocytes increased.
  Haptoglobin decreased.

Therapeutic guidelines:
Splenectomy if splenomegaly is present.

Hereditary spherocytosis

Etiology:
Intrinsic red cell membrane defect.
Abnormal permeability to sodium.
Autosomal dominant inheritance.

Diagnostic tests:
Hyperchromic-microcytic anemia.
Spherocytes present on peripheral smear.
Reticulocytes increased.
Bone marrow: erythroid hyperplasia.
Indirect bilirubin increased.
Stool urobilinogen increased.
Haptoglobin level decreased.
Osmotic fragility increased (incubate specimens).

Therapeutic guidelines:
Splenectomy

Iron deficiency

Etiology:
Chronic blood loss (menstruation, occult).
Nutritional deficiency.
Decreased absorption (gastrectomy, achlorhydria).
Increased requirements (pregnancy, lactation).

Diagnostic tests:
MCV, MCHC, MCH decreased.
Serum iron decreased.
TIBC increased.
Transferrin saturation decreased.
Bone marrow: normoblastic hyperplasia; hemosiderin decreased; sideroblasts decreased.
Reticulocytes: normal or decreased.

Therapeutic guidelines:
Ferrous sulfate, 300 mg PO tid. (Absorption may improve with ascorbic acid.)

Intravascular hemolysis

Etiology:
Sepsis.
Autoimmune phenomena.

Diagnostic tests:
Plasma hemoglobin increased for 6-8 hours.
Plasma haptoglobin level decreased for 2-3 days.
Urine hemoglobin increased for 1 day.
Serum bilirubin increased inversely to liver function.

Pernicious anemia

Etiology:
Intrinsic factor deficiency (decreased vitamin B_{12} absorption).

Signs and symptoms:
Weakness, sore tongue, paresthesias, anorexia, weight loss, dyspnea.

Diagnostic tests:
Anemia usually severe.
MCV increased.
Reticulocytes normal or increased.
Thrombocytopenia, leukopenia.
Hypersegmented neutrophils.
Histamine-fast achlorhydria.
Vitamin B_{12} level decreased.
Serum iron increased during relapse.
Indirect bilirubin increased.
Urine and stool urobilinogen increased.
LDH increased.
Alkaline phosphatase increased.
Cholesterol decreased.
Bone marrow: erythroid hyperplasia and immaturity.
Shilling test diagnostic.

Therapeutic guidelines:
Vitamin B_{12} injections.

Sideroblastic anemias

Red cell precursors contain nonheme iron granules.

Etiology:
Hereditary (pyridoxine-responsive):
   X-linked.
   Autosomal recessive.
Acquired:
   Idiopathic (pyridoxine-resistant).
   Neoplastic, inflammatory, hematologic, metabolic.
   Drugs or toxins.

Diagnostic tests:
Severe hypochromic-microcytic anemia.
Serum iron increased.
TIBC decreased.
Transferrin saturation increased.
Bone marrow: ringed sideroblasts; normoblastic or megaloblastic hyperplasia.

Therapeutic guidelines:
Pyridoxine (vitamin B_6), 50-200 mg PO qd.
Discontinue possible offending drugs.
Iron therapy contraindicated.

Sickle cell anemia

Trait (10% of American blacks):
Hemoglobin S 20%-40%.
Hemoglobin A 60%-80%.
Hemoglobin F < 2%.
Sickle preparation positive.

Disease (hemoglobin electrophoresis):
Hemoglobin S 80%-100%.
Hemoglobin F < 20%.
Hemoglobin A absent.
Sickle cell preparation positive.
Reticulocytes, WBC, platelets increased.
Bone marrow: hyperplasia.
Osmotic fragility decreased.
Bilirubin (indirect) increased.
Urine and stool urobilinogen increased.

Therapeutic guidelines (symptomatic only):
Blood transfusions.
Treat folate deficiency, infections, etc., as indicated.

Thalassemia ("Mediterranean" anemia)

Minor (heterozygous):
Hypochromic-microcytic anemia.
Reticulocytes increased.
Serum iron increased.
Osmotic fragility decreased.
Hemoglobin electrophoresis:
  Hemoglobin A_2 increased (3%-6%).
  Hemoglobin F_2 increased (2%-10%).

Major (homozygous, Cooley's anemia, target cell anemia):
Hemoglobin F 10%-90%.
Hemoglobin A decreased.
MCV and MCHC markedly decreased.
Reticulocytes increased.
Bone marrow: erythroid hyperplasia.
Serum iron increased.
Indirect bilirubin increased.
Urine and stool urobilinogen increased.
Osmotic fragility decreased.

Therapeutic guidelines:
Folic acid.
Transfusions.
Splenectomy.

APPENDICITIS, ACUTE
Signs and symptoms

Normal sequence:
1. Vague, crampy periumbilical or epigastric pain (referred); usually unrelated to ingestion of food or bowel dysfunction.
2. Shift of pain to RLQ with involvement of parietal peritoneum.
3. Anorexia—most patients lose the desire to eat or drink.
4. Nausea and vomiting (variable).

Exceptions:
1. RLQ pain may be the first symptom.
2. Some patients may have prodrome of indigestion, diarrhea, or constipation.
3. Pain may localize to the right flank with retrocecal appendicitis.
4. Pain may localize to the pelvis with pelvic appendicitis.

Temperature is usually normal early on, then rises to 100-101 F. High fever may occur with perforation.

Leukocytosis is typically mild with left shift in the differential count. High elevation may occur with perforation.

Urinalysis may reflect dehydration because of anorexia or vomiting (high specific gravity, ketonuria). Both red and white cells may be present if the inflammatory process involves the ureter.

Abdominal examination may reveal:
RLQ tenderness—the most important finding.
Localized guarding, rigidity, or direct rebound.
Referred rebound (Rovsing's sign).
Hyperesthesia of the skin in the RLQ.
Psoas sign with involvement of psoas musculature.
Obturator sign with involvement of pelvic wall.

Rectal examination may reveal tender mass on the anterior or right lateral rectal wall.

Pelvic examination may confirm the above findings.

Barium enema may reveal an extrinsic pelvic mass if abscess formation has occurred.

Complications

Perforation with abscess formation or peritonitis.

Differential diagnosis

Acute cholecystitis.
Carcinoma of cecum or
    ascending colon.
Cecal diverticulitis.
Gastroenteritis.
Meckel's diverticulitis.
Mesenteric lymphadenitis.
Mittelschmerz.
Pelvic inflammatory disease.
Perforated duodenal ulcer.
Regional enteritis.
Renal colic.
Tubal pregnancy.

Therapeutic guidelines

Preoperative: NPO; IVs; ± NG suction; ± antibiotics.
Postoperative: NPO (or NG suction) until flatus or feces.
Antibiotics, when indicated, are continued.

ASPIRATION PNEUMONIA
Etiology

Vomiting and inhalation of gastric contents can occur during induction of anesthesia and with emergency intubation of unconscious patients, unless special precautions are taken with these procedures. The severity of pneumonitis is proportional to the acidity (pH < 2.5) and amount of gastric acid aspirated. Atelectasis, necrosis, and hemorrhagic consolidation may occur.

Signs and symptoms

Dyspnea, tachypnea, cyanosis, and generalized bronchospasm occur.
Tachycardia, hypotension, and cardiac arrest may develop.
Auscultation may reveal rales, rhonchi, and diffuse expiratory wheezing.
Chest x-ray: unilateral or bilateral infiltrates.
ABG: Pao_2 decreased, $Paco_2$ normal or decreased.

Therapeutic guidelines

1. Ensure adequate airway: suction pharynx and trachea vigorously; bronchoscopy indicated primarily for aspiration of particulate matter.
2. Provide adequate oxygen as determined by respiratory parameters. Endotracheal intubation, mechanical ventilation, and PEEP may be necessary.
3. Hydration: as determined by blood pressure, urine output, hematocrit, and CVP.
4. Bronchodilators: useful if bronchospasm is present.
5. Glucocorticoids: controversial; if used they should be given early, IV, and in high doses.
6. Antibiotics: use is best determined by clinical course and sputum cultures. Common infecting organisms are anaerobes, gram-negative bacilli, and *Staphylococcus aureus.*

ATELECTASIS
Etiology

Atelectasis, or alveolar collapse, is the most common postoperative pulmonary problem. It occurs in the immediate postoperative period (12-24 hours) and rarely beyond the third day. The precise etiology is unknown, although inspiratory insufficiency, bronchial obstruction, and surfactant deficiency are likely mechanisms. Decreased compliance, decreased lung volume, and increased shunting are the result.

Signs and symptoms

Sudden onset of fever, tachycardia, and tachypnea.
Auscultation: basilar rales, decreased breath sounds, bronchial breathing.
Chest x-ray: platelike atelectasis, consolidation.
ABG: Pao_2 decreased, $Paco_2$ normal or decreased.

Differential diagnosis

Other causes of early postoperative fevers, e.g.:
Pneumonia: obtain sputum culture, Gram stain.
Urinary tract infection: obtain urinalysis, culture.
Wound infection (streptococcal or clostridial in first 24 hours).

Complications

Bacterial pneumonitis, pneumonia, lung abscess.

Therapeutic guidelines

1. Preoperative prophylaxis; encourage deep breathing and coughing exercises; patients should cease smoking if possible for at least 2 weeks before surgery.
2. Postoperative prophylaxis: encourage deep breathing, coughing, changes in body position, and early ambulation. Incentive spirometer to encourage development of maximal inspiration. Narcotic administration: low doses, frequent intervals.
3. The treatment of atelectasis is an extension of postoperative prophylaxis:
   a. Hydration, expectorants, or mucolytic agents to loosen secretions.
   b. Bronchodilators to reduce bronchospasm if present.
   c. Nasotracheal or transtracheal suctioning to encourage coughing.
   d. Bronchoscopy, if required, to aspirate tracheobronchial tree.

BILIARY COLIC
Etiology

This is perhaps the best-known symptom of cholelithiasis. It is caused by a small gallstone attempting to pass through the cystic, hepatic, or common bile ducts. Sudden distention and strong muscular contraction of the biliary tree proximal to the obstruction cause the characteristic signs and symptoms.

Signs and symptoms

Sudden, severe midepigastric pain, often radiating to the shoulder, back, or right subscapular area. The pain may occur after a large meal and usually subsides spontaneously in a few hours. The onset is usually more acute and the pain more paroxysmal and severe than with cholecystitis; it is often more unremitting and of longer duration than pain in intestinal colic. Early nausea and vomiting are common, and collapse may occur.

Abdominal examination may reveal right rectus muscle spasm and tenderness during episodes of pain. Between attacks, physical signs are usually minimal. Typically, fever, leukocytosis, and elevated bilirubin or amylase are absent.

Diagnostic tests

See laboratory tests for *cholecystitis*.

Differential diagnosis

See *cholecystitis*.

Therapeutic guidelines

See *cholecystitis*.

BLEEDING PROBLEMS
Etiology

Congenital (hemophilia).
Liver disease (alcohol).
Malignancy (prostate, leukemia).
Sepsis (disseminated intravascular coagulation).

Differential diagnosis

Anticoagulation (heparin, Coumadin [warfarin], aspirin).
Defibrination (DIC, sepsis, shock).
Fibrinolysis (prostate, lung, pancreatic cancer).
Surgical bleeding (obvious versus occult).
Thrombocytopenia (massive transfusion).
Transfusion reaction (small transfusion).

Signs and symptoms

Petechiae (platelet or capillary defect), ecchymoses.

Diagnostic tests

Rapid screen:
PTT (heparin, hemophilia).
PT (Coumadin, DIC, fibrinolysis, liver dysfunction).
Platelet count (massive transfusion).
Bleeding time (platelets abnormal, Von Willebrand's).
Thrombin time (heparin, defibrination, fibrinolysis).

Fibrinogen (if thrombin time prolonged).
Verify accuracy of crossmatch.

ANTICOAGULATION
Overcoumadinization

Diagnostic test:
PT increased.

Therapeutic guidelines:
Discontinue Coumadin.
Fresh-frozen plasma.
Vitamin K, 10 mg IM (if liver function normal).
Monitor for continued blood loss.

Overheparinization

Diagnostic tests:
PTT increased.
Clotting time increased.

Therapeutic guidelines:
Discontinue heparin slowly.
Protamine sulfate, 2 mg per 100 units heparin, IV drip.
Monitor for continued blood loss.

Aspirin (may cause diffuse wound bleeding)

Therapeutic guidelines:
Discontinue aspirin.

DEFIBRINATION (see *Disseminated intravascular coagulation*)

FIBRINOLYSIS (usually transient)
Etiology

Usually occurs in association with DIC.
May occur after cardiac resuscitation and in severe postpros-
tatectomy bleeding.

Diagnostic tests

Clot retraction.
Euglobulin lysis time.

Therapeutic guidelines

Support vital parameters.
Aminocaproic acid, 5 g IV/PO (unless DIC present).
Then 1 g IV/PO q1h (maintenance).
Heparin if DIC also present.

HEMOPHILIA (affects sons of X-linked recessive carriers)
Etiology:
Hereditary disorder.

Diagnostic tests

Bleeding time increased.
Coagulation time increased.
Prothrombin time increased.
PTT increased.

Therapeutic guidelines

Type A (factor VIII deficiency):
Cryoprecipitate, 30-40 units IV, or:
Fresh-frozen plasma.
Type B (factor IX deficiency):
Fresh-frozen plasma, or:
Banked blood (has stable factor).

HEMORRHAGE (see also *Shock, hemorrhagic*)
Therapeutic guidelines

Stop blood loss (pressure tamponade, cold packs, operative
hemostasis).
Support patient as necessary (fluids, transfusion, etc.).

THROMBOCYTOPENIA
Etiology

Acquired defect is usual cause (idiopathic thrombocytopenic
purpura, leukemia, marrow metastasis, systemic lupus erythematosus, etc.).
Congenital defects (rare).

Therapeutic guidelines

Platelet transfusion (at least 10 units).
Steroids, splenectomy if ITP.

TRANSFUSION REACTION (see *Transfusion reactions*, pp. 200-202)

VITAMIN K DEFICIENCY
Etiology

Cirrhosis, lymphoma, ileitis.
Duodenal or jejunal diverticula.

Diagnostic tests

PT increased.

Therapeutic guidelines

Vitamin K administration (if liver function normal).

VON WILLEBRAND'S DISEASE
Etiology

A deficiency of a factor VIII-like substance with thrombas-
themia; autosomal dominant inheritance.

Diagnostic tests

Bleeding time prolonged.
Platelet adhesiveness decreased.
Factor VIII deficiency.

Therapeutic guidelines

Cryoprecipitate, 1 unit/10 kg body weight; then 10-15 ml/kg.

UNKNOWN CONDITION
Etiology

Liver disease (hypoprothrombinemia).
Transfusion reaction (hemolysis).
Massive transfusion of ACD blood.
Dextran administration.
DIC.
Hemophilia.
Always rule out inadequate hemostasis.

Diagnostic tests

Rapid screen series (see pp. 124-125).

Emergency measures

Fresh blood or plasma.
Platelet concentrates if thrombocytopenic.
Vitamin K administration if PT prolonged.
Corticosteroids IV if thrombocytopenia or drug reaction is suspected.
Calcium gluconate, 10 ml of 10% solution IV, slowly, if massive transfusion and hypocalcemia is present.
Fibrinogen, 2-6 g of 1%-2% solution IV, if hypofibrinogenemic.
Antihemophilic concentrate for hemophilia.

BURNS
Types

1. *First-degree:* superficial epidermis; erythema; caused by ultraviolet light exposure.
2. *Second-degree:* deeper epidermis; blisters; usually caused by flash or scald burns.
3. *Third-degree:* epidermis destroyed; painless; may be caused by flame, immersion, etc.

Resuscitation guidelines for > 20% second- or third-degree burns
Day 1

1. *Ensure adequate airway;* assess for obstruction and smoke inhalation. Early intubation preferred over tracheostomy for impending upper airway obstruction.
2. *Oxygenate from humidified source;* percent determined by respiratory parameters, presence of smoke inhalation.

3. *Start Ringer's lactate IV using formula as guide:*
    Parkland Formula:
      4 ml/kg body weight × percent of second- and third-degree burn = Ringer's lactate (ml).
      (For example, 14,000 ml Ringer's lactate may be needed for a 70-kg person with 50% second- and third-degree burns.)
      Give one half of the calculated volume in the first 8 hours postburn.
      Give one half of the calculated volume in the next 16 hours.
      Establish a urine output of 30-70 ml/hour.
      Adjust therapy according to clinical response.
    Brooke Formula:
      Weight in kilograms × percent burned × 0.5 ml = colloid.
      Weight in kilograms × percent burned × 1.5 ml = Ringer's lactate.
      2000 ml D5W.
4. *Insert Foley catheter;* monitor urine output hourly.
5. Use *NG tube* to prevent aspiration and gastric dilation. Monitor gastric aspirate for obvious or occult blood. Instill antacids hourly to help prevent acute superficial erosions.
6. *Initial laboratory tests and procedures:*
    CBC.
    Serum electrolytes, BUN.
    ABG.
    Urinalysis.
    Chest x-ray.
    ECG.
    ±Carboxyhemoglobin level.
    ±Sickle preparation.
    ±Blood alcohol level.
    ±Drug levels.
    ±Fiberoptic bronchoscopy.
    ±Xenon lung scan.
    Monitored variables:
    Temperature and vital signs.
    Cardiac monitor.
    Urine output and specific gravity.
    CVP.
    PAD pressure.
    Pulmonary capillary wedge pressure.
    Intra-arterial blood pressure.
    ±Cardiac outputs, stroke volumes, etc.
    ±A-aDo$_2$ gradient.
    ±Quantitative burn wound biopsy culture.
    ±Other cultures (urine, sputum, blood).
    ±Creatinine clearance.

7. *Tetanus prophylaxis:*
   No prophylaxis if immunized within last year.
   Tetanus toxoid, 0.5 ml, if last immunization 1–10 years ago.
   Hypertet, 250-500 units, plus tetanus toxoid, 0.5 ml, if last
   immunization over 10 years ago.
8. *Gram-positive prophylaxis:* Penicillin or erythromycin for
   3-4 days.
9. *Sedation:* Give morphine IV in small frequent doses as
   necessary for sedation after replacement of volume losses.
10. *Wound:* Culture, cleanse, debride, and irrigate the wound.
    Provide topical chemotherapy to suppress bacterial popu-
    lation and prevent bacterial conversion of second-degree
    burns to third-degree injuries.
11. *Escharotomy:* Decompression incisions for circumferential
    third-degree burns. Evaluate capillary refill, neurologic
    status, and Doppler flow sounds.
12. *Other:*
    Edema: Elevate extremity; monitor movement, sensation,
    capillary refill, Doppler blood flow.
    Early physical therapy to preserve range-of-motion.
    Bronchodilators: usually aminophylline for bronchospastic
    disorders.
    Mechanical ventilation if respiratory failure imminent.
    PEEP if hypoxia persists despite high F_{IO_2}.
    Subeschar needle clysis for third-degree burn wound sepsis.

Days 2-5

1. *Monitoring:* Continue close monitoring of vital signs, urine
   output, and cardiac, pulmonary, and renal status.
2. *Fluids:* Patients with < 40% burns usually have complete
   repair of capillary leak injury after the first 24 hours. Thus,
   if ECF losses have been adequately replaced by this time,
   fluid administration can be decreased. Dextrose 5% in water
   may be all that is required (for evaporative water loss).
   Maintain serum sodium at 140 mEq/liter, and serum potassium in normal range. Patients with > 40% burns have only
   partial repair of capillary leak injury after 24 hours. ECP
   loss may continue requiring additional crystalloid or colloid: 3ml/kg for each 10% over 20% burn to maintain urine
   output of 30-100 ml/hour.
3. *Blood:* Aside from the effect of hemodilution caused by
   IV hydration, burn injury may reduce red cell mass, usually
   by day 5-7. Transfuse with packed cells to maintain hematocrit at 35%-40%.
4. *Diet:* Begin enteral feedings (oral or Silastic feeding tube)
   as soon as the patient can tolerate adequate volumes. Proceed gradually to avoid gastric distention, vomiting, and
   diarrhea. Maintain stabilization of weight or weight gain

by high caloric (4500 calories/day) and high protein (150 g/day) sources when patient is tolerating diet well. Caloric requirements: 25 calories/kg of body weight + 40 calories/kg of body weight × percent burn. IV hyperalimentation may be necessary but is not without its complications.

5. *Wound:* Inspect burn surface daily during hydrotherapeutic cleansing of burn wound. Debride loose eschar and necrotic tissue; unroof abscess pockets.

6. *Infection:* Continue prevention and/or treatment of infection. Culture wound, urine, and blood at least every other day.

7. *Digitalis prophylaxis:* Controversial; some burn specialists recommend slow digitalization when electrolytes are stable, in order to avoid cardiac failure and pulmonary edema when burn edema is resorbed into the vascular system.

8. *Other:* Consult other references regarding enzymatic debridement, tangential excision, deep excision, and skin grafting.

CARDIAC ARREST

Irreversible brain damage may occur in less than 4 minutes.

Etiology

Ventricular fibrillation, asystole, electromechanical dissociation.

Precipitating causes:

Hypoxia.	Drug effect or idiosyncrasy.
Myocardial infarction.	Vagovagal reflex.
Shock.	Manipulation of the heart.
Hyperkalemia.	Air embolism.
Anesthetic overdosage.	Hypothermia.
Heart block.	Electrocution.

Diagnostic tests

Premonitory signs: arrhythmia, bradycardia, hypotension.
Pathognomonic signs: absent pulses, absent heart sounds.
Associated signs: dilated pupils, apnea, cyanosis.

Therapeutic guidelines

Immediately:

1. Place patient supine on a hard, flat surface.
2. Open the airway by extending the neck and pulling the mandible forward.
3. Ventilate (mouth-to-mouth, mask, or endotracheal tube) 2-4 quick full breaths initially, then 12 breaths per minute. Obstruction implies foreign body: turn patient to side, initiate manual removal. Several blows to the back may be necessary to remove an impacted foreign body, or laryn-

goscopy may be used. Emergency cricothyroid puncture and insertion of a 6-mm tube may be necessary if the above maneuvers fail. Gastric distention may be treated by NG suction in order to improve ventilation.

4. Establish effective heartbeat. A sharp blow to the patient's sternum may stimulate the heart to beat if carried out immediately. Otherwise, begin external cardiac compression, 60 times per minute. Check pulses, pupils, and ECG. Internal cardiac compression is indicated for penetrating wounds of the heart, cardiac tamponade, tension pneumothorax with mediastinal displacement, chest or spinal deformities, and severe emphysema with a barrel-type chest.

5. Promote venous return and combat shock by elevating the legs or placing the patient in the Trendelenburg position, and give IV fluids as indicated. Placement of a large-bore venous catheter into an internal jugular or subclavian vein is valuable for CVP monitoring, fluid administration, or in case a transvenous pacemaker catheter electrode has to be inserted.

6. Treat hypotension with dopamine, 200 mg (1 ampule) in 250 ml saline; initial infusion 2-5 μg/kg/minute. Alternatively, metaraminol, 100 mg, or levarterenol, 8 mg, may be added to one of the infusion bottles.

7. Treat metabolic acidosis with sodium bicarbonate, 1 mEq/kg or one 50-ml ampule (44.6 mEq) IV. Repeat one-half the dose at 10-minute intervals or as indicated by blood gases and pH. Caution against excessive sodium bicarbonate because of metabolic alkalosis, hyperosmolarity.

8. If pulses are still absent, suspect ventricular fibrillation and immediately give an external DC defibrillating shock of 200-400 watt-seconds for 0.25 second with one electrode firmly applied to the skin over the apex of the heart and the other over the sternal notch. Check ECG for further treatment:

   a. *Ventricular fibrillation:* Defibrillate again with 400 watt-seconds. If ventricular fibrillation persists, give epinephrine, 0.5-1 ml (1:1000) or 5-10 ml (1:10,000) IV or IC, and continue cardiopulmonary resuscitation to allow the epinephrine to circulate through the heart. Then defibrillate again. In addition, administer lidocaine, 75 mg IV push. If the above are unsuccessful, administer propranolol, 1 mg IV, followed by another defibrillating shock. If the ventricular fibrillation is caused by digitalis toxicity, phenytoin, 100 mg IV, can be given instead of lidocaine.

   b. *Asystole:* Continue cardiopulmonary resuscitation and give isoproterenol, 2 mg in 500 ml D5W by IV infusion, to raise the ventricular rate to 60-70 bpm. Calcium chloride, 5-10 ml (10% solution) IV or IC, can also be given to initiate cardiac contractions or to increase the force of cardiac contractions, unless the patient has

been digitalized. Transvenous pacing may be necessary when asystole, complete heart block, or sinus brady-cardia persists.
c. *Electromechanical dissociation:* QRS complexes are regular, but the pulse and blood pressure remain unobtainable. Treatment is the same as for asystole. In addition, atropine, 0.4-1 mg IV, may be given for progressive bradycardia. Infusions of saline or plasma may be useful if signs of volume deficit are present.
9. Hypothermia may be considered if neurologic changes have occurred or the arrest is prolonged.
10. When cardiac, pulmonary, and CNS functions have been restored, monitor carefully for shock and complications of the precipitating cause. Support ventilation and circulation. Observe carefully for recurrent fibrillation, asystole, and other arrythmias. Consider the use of assisted circulation in selected cases.

CARDIOGENIC SHOCK
Etiology

The most common etiology is coronary artery disease and acute myocardial infarction; 10%-15% of patients with myocardial infarction develop cardiogenic shock; 20% of patients with cardiogenic shock are hypovolemic because of reduced fluid intake, vomiting, or other causes and require fluid replacement.

Signs and symptoms

The patient may be unable to give an accurate history but may show clinical signs of cardiovascular collapse: pallor, diaphoresis, and cool, cyanotic skin; empty peripheral veins; labored respirations; restlessness, agitation, apathy, lethargy, confusion, or coma.
Further examination may reveal:
Systolic blood pressure < 80-90 mm Hg
Pulse rate > 100 bpm.
Urine output < 30 ml/hour.

Diagnostic tests

ECG: acute myocardial infarction or acute coronary insufficiency.
CVP: rises briskly during fluid replacement.
Left ventricular end-diastolic pressure: high.
Cardiac output: low.

Differential diagnosis

Massive pulmonary embolism.
Dissecting aortic aneurysm.
Cardiac tamponade.

Therapeutic guidelines

1. Initial lab tests should include CBC, electrolytes, glucose, BUN, creatinine, CPK, SGOT, LDH, ABG and pH, urinalysis, ECG, and chest x-ray.
2. *Monitoring:*
   Cardiac (ECG) monitor.
   Arterial blood pressure.
   CVP.
   Swan-Ganz catheter.
   Urinary catheter.
3. Check chest x-ray, ECG, and ABGs to establish diagnosis and rule out other causes of shock, such as cardiac tamponade, which requires pericardiocentesis.
4. Position: flat in bed, unless severe dyspnea or pulmonary edema present. Apply Ace bandages from toes to groin and elevate lower extremities to return venous blood into the circulation.
5. Adequate airway and oxygenation: intubate if necessary and support ventilation with a volume-cycled respirator. Maintain Pao_2 at 70 mm Hg or higher, $Paco_2$ 35-40 mm Hg.
6. If initial CVP and PAD or PWP are low, correct hypovolemia with IV infusions of crystalloid, colloid, or blood, depending on the history, serum chemistries, and hemoglobin or hematocrit.
7. If initial CVP and PWP are high in the absence of pulmonary edema, vasodilator therapy with phentolamine, sodium nitroprusside, or isoproterenol may be administered to lower systemic peripheral vascular resistance.
8. If pulmonary edema is present, with high CVP and PAD or PWP, the patient should be digitalized with a rapidly acting digitalis agent such as digoxin, ouabain, or deslanoside. Vasodilator drugs may also be helpful if peripheral vascular resistance is high.
9. Arrhythmias must be controlled rapidly, since they decrease cardiac output and perpetuate the shock. Maintain adequate oxygenation, electrolyte balance, and administer antiarrhythmic agents when indicated.
10. Hypotension that does not respond to the above measures may require sympathomimetic agents such as dopamine or isoproterenol.
11. Treat metabolic acidosis with sodium bicarbonate IV to maintain an arterial pH of at least 7.30. Check ABGs; avoid metabolic alkalosis.
12. Maintain proper electrolyte balance with emphasis on preventing or correcting abnormalities in serum sodium and potassium.
13. Digitalis, as previously mentioned, is indicated for pulmonary edema caused by congestive heart failure.

14. Diuretics, such as furosemide or ethacrynic acid, are effective in pulmonary edema if adequate renal blood flow is present and if the patient is not sodium-depleted. Monitor renal function closely.
15. Corticosteroids may be beneficial in preventing infarct extension and promoting vasodilation.

    If an adequate response to the above measures is not achieved, mechanical assistance or, in some cases, surgery may be considered.

    Always be ready to modify treatment on the basis of changes in the patient's clinical condition.

CHOLANGITIS, ACUTE
Etiology

Bacterial infection of an obstructed biliary tree.

Usually precipitated by stones, stricture, neoplasm, pancreatic cysts, duodenal diverticula, or invasion by parasites.

Signs and symptoms

Charcot's triad: spiking fever and chills, continuous RUQ or midepigastric pain, jaundice. Skin and sclera may be icteric.

Diagnostic tests

Elevated serum bilirubin and alkaline phosphatase.

Leukocytosis (15-20,000).

Blood cultures may reveal causative organism: *E. coli, Enterobacter, Proteus,* clostridia.

Complications

Intrahepatic abscesses, liver failure, biliary cirrhosis, pancreatitis.

Hypotension and CNS depression may occur with acute suppurative cholangitis.

Therapeutic guidelines

NPO; NG suction; IV hydration.

Antibiotics effective against intestinal organisms (e.g., ampicillin, gentamicin, clindamycin).

Early surgical exploration and T-tube drainage if acute suppurative cholangitis is suspected.

CHOLECYSTITIS, ACUTE
Etiology

Inflammation of the gallbladder usually caused by obstruction of cystic duct by gallstone. Acalculous cholecystitis may be found in 2%-5%.

Signs and symptoms

Colicky pain may begin in midepigastrium or RUQ. Pain may radiate to the right shoulder, back, or subscapular area. May be associated with nausea, vomiting, anorexia. With peritoneal inflammation the pain localizes to the RUQ. Patient may have previous history of biliary colic, fatty food intolerance.

Abdominal examination may reveal:

RUQ tenderness.

Unilateral rectus guarding.

Murphy's sign.

Palpable, tender gallbladder.

Diminished bowel sounds.

Low-grade fever, tachycardia, and leukocytosis.

Diagnostic tests

Serum bilirubin may be elevated 2-3 mg/100 ml.

Serum amylase may be slightly elevated.

Abdominal x-ray: gallstones radiopaque in 10%-15%.

IVC: visualization of gallbladder excludes diagnosis.

Double-dose OCG: nonvisualization of gallbladder (95% diagnostic).

Differential diagnosis

Appendicitis (ascending).

Coronary artery disease.

Fitz-Hugh and Curtis syndrome.

Hepatitis (alcoholic, viral).

Pancreatitis.

Peptic ulcer disease.

Pyelonephritis.

Renal colic.

Right lower lobe pneumonia.

Complications

Empyema, gangrene, or perforation of the gallbladder; pancreatitis.

Therapeutic guidelines

NPO; NG suction; IV hydration.

Administer antibiotics if infection exists.

Correct coagulation defect if present.

Cholecystectomy (early [72 hours], versus late [6 weeks]) cholecystostomy.

Common duct exploration if indicated (see *Choledocholithiasis*).

CHOLECYSTITIS, CHRONIC
Etiology

Repetitive inflammation of the gallbladder, resulting in fibrosis and nonfunction. Associated with gallstones in nearly every case.

Signs and symptoms

The history usually involves chronic or episodic complaints of biliary colic, dyspepsia, fatty food intolerance, indigestion, heartburn, flatulence, nausea.

Diagnostic tests

1. Abdominal x-ray: gallstones radiopaque in 10%-15%.
2. Oral cholecystogram: gallstones and/or nonfunctioning gallbladder.
   Requires:
   a. Compliance in taking pills.
   b. Absorption from small intestine.
   c. Conjugation in liver.
   d. Excretion in bile.
   e. Concentration in gallbladder.
   f. Bilirubin less than 3 mg/100 ml.
3. IVC if malabsorption exists.
   Requires:
   a. Patency of biliary ducts to visualize.
   b. Bilirubin less than 3-4 mg/100 ml.

Differential diagnosis

Pancreatitis.
Peptic ulcer disease.
Coronary artery disease.
Others (see *Acute cholecystitis*).

Complications

Acute cholecystitis, common duct stones, adenocarcinoma of the gallbladder.

Therapeutic guidelines

Medical: Low-fat diet.
             Chenodeoxycholic acid (experimental).
Surgical: Cholecystectomy.

CHOLEDOCHOLITHIASIS
Etiology

Gallstones present in the extrahepatic biliary tree, usually associated partial or intermittent biliary obstruction.

Signs and symptoms

Biliary colic present in 90%.
Jaundice present in 80%, usually intermittent.
Episodic cholangitis with bacterial invasion.
Tea-colored urine; clay-colored stools.
Pruritus with prolonged obstruction.
Abdominal examination may reveal tender hepatomegaly with cholangitis; the gallbladder is usually not palpable.

Diagnostic tests

Bilirubin: may rise within 24 hours, 2-3 mg/100 ml, fluctuates.
Alkaline phosphatase elevated early.
5'-Nucleotidase elevated early.
Gamma-glutamyl transpeptidase elevated early.
SGOT and SGPT mildly elevated.
24-hour urinary urobilinogen elevated.
Fecal urobilinogen low.
Abdominal x-ray: stones radiopaque in 10%-15%.
IVC may be successful if bilirubin less than 3-4 mg/100 ml:
Common bile duct dilated; calculi present.
Failure of contrast to enter duodenum.

Differential diagnosis

Obstructive jaundice caused by neoplasm.
Intrahepatic cholestasis.
Primary hepatocellular disease.
Other causes of RUQ pain.

Complications

Acute pancreatitis.
Hepatic failure.
Intrahepatic abscesses.
Secondary biliary cirrhosis.
Suppurative cholangitis.

Therapeutic guidelines

NPO, NG suction, IV hydration.
Administer antibiotics if infection exists.
Vitamin K IM if PT prolonged.
Exploration of the common bile duct with removal of calculi:
Absolute indications:
1. Palpable stones (99% reliable).
2. Jaundice with cholangitis (97% reliable).
3. IVC positive for stones (85% reliable).
4. Common duct dilation (35% reliable).
Relative indications:
1. Obstructive jaundice.
2. Biliary duct fistula.
3. Small stones in gallbladder.

    4. Single-faceted stone in gallbladder.
    5. Pancreatitis.

COLON CANCER
Types

Polypoid, nodular, ulcerating, scirrhous, colloid.

Spread

Direct extension (4 cm distal, 7 cm proximal).
Lymphatic (regional nodes).
Hematogenous (venous to liver, lung, bones).
Gravitational seeding (peritoneum, Blumer's shelf, ovary).
Implantation at operation.

Duke's classification (modified)

Types	Regional nodes	Five-year survival
A : confined to mucosa	Negative	80%
B₁ : confined to muscularis	Negative	66%
B₂ : penetrates muscularis	Negative	54%
C₁ : confined to bowel wall	Positive	43%
C₂ : penetrates bowel wall	Positive	22%
D : distant metastases	Positive	14%

Signs and symptoms

Right colon: RLQ pain, anemia, anorexia, weight loss.
Left colon: obstruction, pencil stools, hematochezia.
Rectum: bright red blood, tenesmus.
Physical examination: palpable mass, hepatomegaly, ascites, caput medusae.
Rectal examination: mass, guaiac-positive stools.
Proctosigmoidoscopy with biopsy.

Diagnostic tests

Biopsy, barium enema with air-contrast studies.

Complications

Obstruction, hemorrhage, perforation.

Therapeutic guidelines

Preoperative:
Routine blood tests, liver function tests, IVP, barium enema, UGI.
Metastatic work-up: liver scan, bone scan.
Cardiac, pulmonary, renal status.
Bowel preparation (see Section Two).
IV hydration or transfusion as necessary.
Foley catheter in OR.

Operative:
Explore for intra-abdominal spread.
Resect by no-touch isolation technique.
Palliation: may improve quality of survival.
APR: for low rectal cancer.
Adjunctive therapy:
5-Fluorouracil.
Preoperative radiation.

COLOSTOMY
Purposes

1. Decompress obstructed colon.
2. Divert feces in preparation for resection (inflammation, obstruction, trauma).
3. Distal colon and rectum removed.
4. Protect distal anastomosis from infection.

Types

Loop colostomy (lowest mortality).
End colostomy.
Double-barreled.
Single-barreled.

Complications:

Stenosis (if colostomy not matured).
Prolapse, necrosis, retraction, paracolostomy hernia.
Perforation, diarrhea, fecal impaction, skin irritation.
Complication rate: 20% (15% of which require operative correction).

DEEP VENOUS THROMBOSIS (see also *Pulmonary embolism*)
Etiology

Virchow's triad:
Stasis (bed rest, venous obstruction).
Hypercoagulability (polycythemia, estrogen administration).
Venous injury (fractures, soft tissue trauma).

Types

DVT (predisposes to pulmonary embolus).
Superficial migrating (lymphoma, pancreatic or prostatic cancer).

Signs and symptoms

Local tenderness, warmth, and pain with movement.
Swelling (caused by obstruction of venous return).
Tenderness (calf, popliteal fossa, inguinal).
Pratt's sign (tenderness on compression of calf against tibia).
Homan's sign (tenderness on dorsiflexion of the foot).

Phlegmasia alba dolens (thrombosis of iliofemoral veins).
Phlegmasia cerulea dolens (thrombosis of venous collaterals).

Diagnostic tests

Venogram (phlebography): most consistently accurate.
Venous flow studies (Doppler): noninvasive.
Radioactive fibrinogen scan: positive during thrombus formation.
Impedance plethysmography.

Differential diagnosis

Superficial thrombophlebitis.
Acute lymphangitis.
Rupture of gastrocnemius, adductor, or quadriceps muscles.
Edema as a result of cardiac, renal, or hepatic disease.
Neuropathy or disk disease.

Complications

Pulmonary embolism.
Chronic venous insufficiency.
Varicose veins.
Venous gangrene.
Postphlebitic syndrome.

Therapeutic guidelines

Prophylactic measures:
Encourage leg exercises, deep breathing exercises in bed.
Early ambulation, elevation, adequate hydration.
Anticoagulation in high-risk patients:
Aspirin, 325 mg PO bid.
Warfarin (adjust by PT).
Minidose heparin (5000 units SC q8-12h).

Therapeutic measures:
Bed rest (prevent thrombus dislodgement).
Elevation, elastic supports (decrease swelling).
Heparinization, 7-10 days (prevent thrombus extension).
Coumadinization, 6-12 weeks.
Early thrombectomy in iliofemoral thrombosis.

DIABETES INSIPIDUS
Etiology

ADH is normally produced in the anterior hypothalamus, stored in the posterior pituitary, and released in response to osmotic stimuli. It acts by promoting water reabsorption in distal renal tubules. ADH insufficiency may lead to severe water loss by the lack of this mechanism. Generally, hyponatremia does not occur because aldosterone continues to promote sodium reabsorption. Secondary causes of diabetes insipidus are damage of the neurohypophysis from trauma, neoplasms, sarcoidosis, eosinophilia granuloma, or local infections. Primary causes may be familial or idiopathic.

Signs and symptoms

Sudden polyuria and polydipsia.
Urine output may increase to 5-10 liters/day.
Specific gravity may decrease to 1.001-1.005.
Urine osmolality may decrease to 50-200 mOsm/liter.
Serum sodium and osmolality are only slightly increased at first, but with persisting polyuria both parameters may increase ($Na^+ > 150$, osmolality = 295 ± 15 mOsm).

Differential diagnosis

Excessive water intake (psychogenic or iatrogenic).
Acute tubular necrosis (diuretic phase).
Diabetes mellitus (high specific gravity because of glycosuria).
Nephrogenic diabetes insipidus (distal tubules unresponsive to ADH).
Diencephalic diabetes insipidus.

Diagnostic tests

Water restriction:

Observe changes in urine volume and concentration.
Avoid more than 3%-5% weight loss (circulatory collapse).
Normal: Urine flow decreases to 30 ml/hour or less (depending on amount of fluid restriction).
  Urine osmolality increases to > 800 mOsm/liter.
  Specific gravity increases to > 1.020.
Diabetes insipidus: Urine volumes remain considerably greater than 30 ml/hour.
  Urine osmolality remains at 50-200 mOsm/liter.
  Specific gravity remains at 1.000-1.005; with extreme dehydration, however, may reach 1.008-1.014.

Vasopressin:

Aqueous vasopressin: 5 IU SC, lasts about 2 hours.
Normal: Antidiuresis (watch for iatrogenic syndrome of inappropriate ADH).
Diabetes insipidus: Antidiuresis.

Therapeutic guidelines

1. Vasopressin tannate in oil, 2.5-5 IU IM every 1-3 days as needed (monitor urine output).
2. Aqueous vasopressin, 5 IU SC: diagnostic, affords close control, but is rapidly inactivated.
3. Chlorothiazides: may decrease urine volumes by 33%-50% by paradoxic effect.

4. DDAVP: Synthetic analogue of arginine vasopressin, taken once or twice daily by nasal insufflation. Considered to be the drug of choice for chronic treatment of mild to severe neurohypophyseal diabetes insipidus.

DIABETES MELLITUS (see also *Diabetic ketoacidosis*)

Diabetes mellitus imposes special considerations on both the patient and the surgeon. Hyperglycemia can result from diabetes itself, or it may be the result of glucose intolerance exacerbated by stress, surgery, anesthesia, infection, etc. Immediate effects of hyperglycemia may be dehydration and electrolyte abnormalities caused by osmotic diuresis. Acidosis can lead to vomiting and Kussmaul respirations, with further metabolic derangements. Coma may be the result of hyper- or hypoglycemia. Long-term effects of diabetes include neuropathy, retinopathy, nephropathy, and vasculopathy. Most diabetics can be managed with one of three regimens, or a combination thereof:

1. Diet: 30-35 calories/kg/day (ideal body weight).
2. Oral hypoglycemics: tolbutamide, chlorpropamide, acetohexamide.
3. Insulin: NPH or lente (intermediate-acting).

This entry deals with the pre- and postoperative management of diabetic patients.

Baseline laboratory studies

Fasting blood sugar.
Glucose tolerance test.
Serum electrolytes $\pm$ ketones.
CBC.
Urinalysis.
ABG.
Renal function tests.

Six-hour insulin management

Regular insulin may be administered at 6-hour intervals on a sliding scale determined by double-voided urine samples. The following is a guide to such a scale:

Sugar	Acetone	Insulin
<½%	0	0
½-1%	0	5 units
1-2%	0	10 units
>2%	Small	15 units
>2%	Moderate	Call MD
>2%	Large	Call MD

Reminder: **Regular insulin**
Onset: 20-30 minutes
Peak: 2-4 hours
Duration: 6-8 hours

Increasing amounts of acetone call for the administration of extra insulin; however, one should remain alert for signs of hypoglycemia.

Therapeutic guidelines

The following guidelines apply to pre- and postoperative management of diabetic patients undergoing major operations. Since patients with severe hyperglycemia and acidosis are at increased risk, insulin is indicated preoperatively, though in smaller than usual doses. Note that the anesthesiologist must be aware of preoperative insulin dosages and fluid administration. Intraoperative blood samples for glucose and acetone are desirable.

1. Diabetes mellitus controlled with NPH insulin:

   Preoperative:

   NPO after midnight.

   IV: 5% or 10% glucose in water or saline at 125-150 ml/hour.

   Insulin: one-half usual dose of NPH insulin SC in AM.

   Postoperative:

   IV: 5% or 10% glucose in water or saline at 100-125 ml/hour.

   Insulin: one-half usual dose of NPH insulin SC in PM.

   Check urine and serum glucose and ketones q4-6h.

   Supplement with crystalline insulin SC as needed.

   Resume management with NPH insulin when feasible.

2. Diabetes mellitus controlled with oral hypoglycemics:

   Preoperative:

   Chlorpropamide: discontinue the morning before operation.

   Tolbutamide: discontinue the evening before operation.

   NPO past midnight.

   IV: 5% or 10% glucose in water or saline at 125-150 ml/hour.

   Check urine and serum glucose and ketones q4-6h.

   Give crystalline insulin SC as needed.

   Postoperative:

   IV: 5% or 10% glucose in water or saline at 100-125 ml/hour.

   Check urine and serum glucose and ketones q4-6h.

   Give crystalline insulin SC as needed.

   Resume mangement with oral hypoglycemics when feasible.

3. Uncontrolled diabetes mellitus without ketosis:

   Preoperative:

   Establish adequate diabetic control:

   IV (serum glucose > 250 mg/100 ml): saline infusion.

   (serum glucose < 250 mg/100 ml: 5% glucose in water or saline.

Correct preexisting fluid deficits and electrolyte abnormalities.

Check urine and serum glucose and ketones q4-6h.

Give crystalline insulin SC as needed.

Postoperative:

IV: 5% glucose in water or saline at 100-125 ml/hour.

Check urine and serum glucose and ketones q4-6h.

Give crystalline insulin SC as needed.

4. Diabetic ketoacidosis (see *Diabetic ketoacidosis*).

DIABETIC KETOACIDOSIS
Etiology

Lack of insulin results in a starvation state with hyperglycemia and progressive ketonemia. Acidosis leads to compensatory hyperventilation. Dehydration is caused by glycosuria and osmotic diuresis with a loss of water and electrolytes. Dehydration is furthered by the acidosis, which produces anorexia and vomiting.

Signs and symptoms

Severe, continuous, diffuse abdominal pain, often gradual in onset, although may be acute and mimic an abdominal emergency. Nausea and vomiting frequently occur with the pain. Patient may have recent onset of polydipsia and fatigue. May have personal or family history of diabetes mellitus.

Examination may reveal abdominal tenderness or rigidity. Air hunger and heavy labored breathing (Kussmaul respirations) correlate with degree of acidosis and reduction in serum bicarbonate. Breath may have fruity odor. Dehydration with low urine output and hypotension may be evident. Fever and leukocytosis may be present.

Diagnostic tests

Elevated levels of ketones and glucose in both serum and urine.

Metabolic acidosis with low pH and low serum bicarbonate.

Elevated anion gap (see *Acidosis, metabolic*).

Serum osmolality increased because of hyperglycemia.

Elevated BUN because of dehydration and protein catabolism.

Hemoconcentration as a result of dehydration.

Differential diagnosis

Hyperosmolar nonketotic coma.

Hypoglycemia.

Insulin reaction.

Lactic acidosis.

Renal failure.

Salicylate poisoning.

Therapeutic guidelines

1. If the patient is comatose and the diagnosis is in question, draw blood tests and administer 50 ml of 50% glucose IV.
2. Ensure adequate hydration rapidly, usually with NS.
3. After diagnosis is established, administer crystalline insulin both IV and SC.
4. Follow serum electrolytes, blood glucose, BUN, acetone, and pH closely.
5. Add potassium chloride to IVs when urine output is adequate.
6. Monitor blood pressure, CVP, urine output, and ECG.
7. Administer sodium bicarbonate for severe acidosis only.
8. Once the blood glucose approaches 200-300 mg/100 ml, change IVs to 5% glucose with appropriate electrolytes.
9. Other: NG suction; establish precipitating cause; continue appropriate fluid and insulin therapy.

DISSEMINATED INTRAVASCULAR COAGULATION
(see also *Bleeding problems*)
Synonyms

Acquired hypofibrinogenemia.
Defibrination syndrome.
Consumptive coagulopathy.

Etiology

Intravascular coagulation caused by thromboplastic materials released from tissues. Results in consumption of coagulation factors and platelets. Some protection may be afforded by secondary fibrinolysis.

Precipitated by many disease processes:
1. Gram-negative sepsis (endotoxin effect on platelets).
2. Gram-positive sepsis (meningococcemia).
3. Shock (surgery, trauma, anaphylaxis).
4. Hemolytic transfusion reaction.
5. Extracorporeal circulation.
6. Disseminated carcinoma (prostate, lung, pancreas).
7. Lymphomas and leukemia.
8. Thrombotic thrombocytopenia.
9. Perinatal hemorrhage.
10. Pediatric complication.
11. Rickettsial infection.
12. Snake bite.

Diagnostic tests

Fibrin split products: increased.
Fibrinogen level: < 100 mg/100 ml.
Platelet count: $< 50,000/mm^3$.
Factor V: $< 20\%$.

Thrombin time: prolonged.
PTT: > 50 seconds.
PT: > 16 seconds.
Blood smear: microangiopathic, schistocytes.

Therapeutic guidelines

1. Attack primary cause first (e.g., drainage and antibiotics for sepsis).
2. Maintain capillary flow (IV fluids—replace ECF losses).
3. Failing heart: digitalis, isoproterenol.
4. Increasing hematocrit: plasma expander.
5. Replacement therapy: platelets, fresh-frozen plasma.
6. Heparin: if bleeding is unmanageable by replacement therapy.
7. Support: bicarbonate, oxygen if indicated.

DUMPING SYNDROME
Etiology

Impaired ability of stomach to regulate its rate of emptying (e.g., after surgery for duodenal ulcer). Hyperosmotic load in jejunum decreases ECF abruptly.

Signs and symptoms

Palpitations, diaphoresis, weakness, dyspnea, flushing, nausea, abdominal cramps, belching, vomiting, diarrhea, syncope.

Diagnostic tests

Characteristic symptoms follow the ingestion of hypertonic solutions (e.g., ice cream).

Differential diagnosis

Reactive hypoglycemia (3-4 hours after meals, relieved by eating sugar).

Therapeutic guidelines

1. *Diet therapy:*
   Multiple small feedings.
   Avoidance of high-carbohydrate foods.
   Restrict fluid intake during meals.
2. *Surgery:* Insert antiperistaltic 10-cm segment of jejunum between the gastric remnant and the duodenum. Vagotomy recommended to prevent marginal ulceration.

ELECTROCARDIOGRAPH SIGNS
(see also *Angina, Arrhythmia, Myocardial infarction*)

Digitalis effect: concave S-T segment.
Digitalis excess: SA or AV block, paroxysmal atrial tachycardia with block, tachycardia.

Digitalis toxicity: PVCs, bigeminy, trigeminy, ventricular tachycardia, ventricular fibrillation, atrial fibrillation (ectopic pacemakers stimulated).

Emphysema: decreased voltage, RAD caused by RV strain.

Hypercalcemia: short Q-T interval.

Hyperkalemia: peaked T waves, wide QRS, wide flat P, absent P waves.

Hypermagnesemia: Q-T prolongation, AV block, cardiac arrest.

Hypocalcemia: prolonged Q-T interval.

Hypokalemia: flattening of T waves, S-T depression, appearance of U waves.

Pericarditis: S-T segment elevation.

Pulmonary embolus: S_1Q_3, S-T depression in II; T inversion in V_1-V_4; sudden right or left axis deviation; acute right bundle branch block.

Pulmonary infarction: S-T depression, right bundle branch block in V_1.

Subendocardial infarction: flat S-T depression.

Ventricular strain: (right) S-T depression in V_2; (left) ST depression in V_5.

FEVER, POSTOPERATIVE (see also *Infections*)

Minor: dehydration, metabolic disturbance.

Significant: temperature > 38.5 or lasting more than 6 hours.

First 24 hours: atelectasis, metabolic and endocrine effects, wound infection caused by clostridia (necrotizing fasciitis) or streptococci.

Twelve hours to POD 4: atelectasis, pneumonia, urinary tract infection.

POD 4-5: wound (*Staphylococcus*, enteric organisms).

Any time: deep venous thrombosis.

Mnemonic (Remember the "5 W's")

Wind (atelectasis): first 24 hours.

Water (UTI): third day after catheterization.

Wound (infection): POD 5-7.

Walk (phlebitis): anytime.

"Wonder" drugs (hypersensitivity reactions, etc.)

Therapeutic guidelines

1. Obtain appropriate laboratory tests and cultures.
2. Antibiotics if indicated (check appropriate cultures).
3. Antipyretics if indicated: acetaminophen, alcohol sponge, cooling blanket.

FEVER OF UNKNOWN ORIGIN
Definition

At least 3 weeks of fever.
Temperature above 38.3 C daily.
One week of intensive investigation.

Etiology

Infections (40%):
Granulomatous.
Bacterial.
Subacute bacterial endocarditis.
Others.

Neoplasms (20%):
Liver metastases.
Hypernephroma.
Hodgkin's disease.

Collagen diseases (20%):
Systemic lupus erythematosus.
Acute rheumatic fever.
Rheumatoid arthritis.
Giant cell arteritis.

Miscellaneous (10%):
Drug fever (sulfonamides, penicillin).
Multiple pulmonary emboli.
Sarcoidosis.
Factitious (malingering).

Diagnostic failure (10%):
Hypersensitivity reaction.
Viral infection.

Diagnostic tests

Laboratory:
Cultures (blood, bone marrow, tissue biopsy).
Enzymes (liver function tests).
Serology (ASO, ANA, latex fixation, febrile agglutinins).

X-rays:
Chest.
Bones.
Contrast:
   IVP.
   Arteriography (abdominal).
   Lymphangiography.
   Angiocardiography.
   Upper GI.
   Small bowel.
   Barium enema.

Scans:
Liver.
Lung.
Bone.

Tissue examination:
Biopsies (liver, bone marrow, lymph nodes, lung, pleura, skin, muscle, kidney, temporal artery, masses).
Laparoscopy.
Laparotomy.
Thoracotomy.

Therapeutic guidelines

Trials as indicated:
Antipyretics.
Antibiotics.
Antituberculous drugs.
Antiamebic drugs.
Heparin.
Steroids.
Antimetabolites.

FITZ-HUGH AND CURTIS SYNDROME (Perihepatitis)
Etiology

A complication of pelvic inflammatory disease, presumably resulting from migration of bacterial organisms from the fallopian tubes to the surface of the liver. Inflammation of Glisson's capsule causes hepatic tenderness and enlargement and leads to the development of fibrinous, or "violin-string," adhesions between the liver surface and the anterior abdominal wall. Causative organisms include *Neisseria gonorrhoeae, Streptococcus, Staphylococcus,* and *Diplococcus pneumoniae.* Syndrome occurs in approximately 1%-10% of adults and up to 30% of adolescents with salpingitis.

Signs and symptoms

RUQ abdominal pain may mimic acute cholecystitis.
Recent history of pelvic pain, vaginal discharge, fever.
Examination may reveal RUQ tenderness, guarding, and hepatic friction rub.
Pelvic examination may demonstrate adnexal and cervical motion tenderness.
Fever and leukocytosis may be present.

Diagnostic tests

Intracellular diplococci are usually present on cervical smears.
Oral cholecystogram may not visualize during the acute stage.
Mild liver function abnormalities may be present (elevated SGPT).

Differential diagnosis

    Acute cholecystitis.
    Acute viral hepatitis.

Therapeutic guidelines

1. Sexually active females with hepatic tenderness should undergo pelvic examination to check for the presence of salpingitis.
2. Cervical Gram stain and cultures are most important. Blood cultures for *Neisseria gonorrhoeae,* liver function tests, and a serologic test for syphilis should also be obtained.
3. Evaluate for other causes of hepatic dysfunction when indicated.
4. IV penicillin and IV ampicillin are current antibiotics of choice.

GASTROINTESTINAL HEMORRHAGE
UPPER GI (above ligament of Treitz)
Etiology

    Peptic ulcer disease (duodenal more frequently than gastric).
    Acute mucosal erosions (caused by salicylates, alcohol, anti-coagulants).
    Esophageal varices (portal hypertension).
    Hiatus hernia (hemorrhage usually occult).
    Mallory-Weiss syndrome (induced by vomiting).
    Gastric malignancy (carcinoma, lymphoma).

Signs and symptoms

    Hematemesis (red color implies esophageal or proximal stomach bleeding; coffee grounds implies distal stomach or duodenal bleeding).
    Melena or hematochezia (if massive hemorrhage).
    Massive bleeding: pallor, diaphoresis, tachycardia, hypotension, oliguria, azotemia, shock.
    Splenomegaly or ascites (portal hypertension).
    Liver disease (icterus, spider angiomas, palmar erythema).
    Lymphadenopathy (malignancy).
    NG aspiration (confirm and assess bleeding).

Assess

    Postural blood pressure and pulse.
    Urine output (Foley catheter).
    CVP or Swan-Ganz catheter (to assess fluid replacement).
    Serial hematocrits (24 hours for complete equilibration).
    NG tube (empty gastric contents; check for occult blood; lavage with iced saline).
    BUN (upper GI bleeding versus prerenal azotemia).
    Coagulation studies (PT, PTT, platelets, etc.).

Bowel sounds (blood is cathartic).
Stool frequency and guaiacs.

Initial resuscitation

IV: lactated Ringer's solution.
NG tube: remove blood and acids, lavage with saline.
Blood transfusion if hemorrhage massive.
Platelet transfusion, vitamin K, fresh-frozen plasma if indicated.

Establish diagnosis

Endoscopy (especially for gastritis, varices, and Mallory-Weiss
  syndrome).
Selective arteriography (visualization requires 3-5 ml/minute
  bleeding).
UGI series (especially for ulcers, varices, and hiatus hernia).
Percutaneous splenoportography.
Isotopic studies.
Splenic pulp manometry.
Balloon tamponade.
Laparotomy.

Additional treatment

1. *Pitressin (vasopressin) drip:* for varices, mucosal ulcers,
   Mallory-Weiss syndrome.
2. *Sengstaken-Blakemore tube for varices:*
   a. Test balloons for leakage under water.
   b. Insert both balloons into stomach.
   c. Inflate gastric balloon first (300 cc air).
      Then pull back and attach to helmet.
   d. NG tube in proximal esophagus for saliva (prevent aspi-
      ration).
   e. Check position of gastric balloon by x-ray.
   f. If bleeding continues, withdraw NG tube and inflate
      esophageal balloon to 40 mm Hg pressure.
      Then replace NG tube.
   g. In case of respiratory distress, cut across the Sengstaken
      tube with scissors (rapid deflation).
   h. If bleeding is controlled by tamponade:
      Deflate the esophageal balloon after 24 hours.
      Leave the gastric balloon on ¾-pound traction for another
        24 hours.
      Then take gastric balloon off traction and deflate.
      Remove NG tube.
      Leave uninflated Sengstaken tube in place for another
        24 hours.
   i. If bleeding recurs, reinflate the balloons.
   j. If no bleeding occurs, remove Sengstaken tube ½ hour
      after the patient has swallowed 2 ounces of mineral
      oil to facilitate its removal.

3. *Acute stress bleeding:*
   Anticholinergics (shunt blood from mucosa to submucosa).
   Vitamin A (protects against stress bleeding, important for
       mucus production, important for gastric cell proliferation).
   Gastric alkalination (titrate to pH 7.0)
   Intragastric Levophed (levarterenol) (8 mg/100 ml).
   Arteriography with selective Pitressin drip (0.4 mg/ml).
   Hyperalimentation (decreases stress bleeding and provides
       essential amino acids for cell regeneration).
4. *Surgery:* If bleeding persists or rebleeding occurs.

LOWER GI (below ligament of Treitz)
Etiology

Hemorrhoids (blood on surface of stool).
Carcinoma (obvious or occult hemorrhage).
Diverticulosis (hemorrhage may be massive).
Ulcerative colitis (hemorrhage may be massive).
Polyps (single or multiple polyps).
Diverticulitis (mild or moderate hemorrhage).
Regional enteritis (occult or massive hemorrhage).
Mesenteric thrombosis (abdominal pain).
Meckel's diverticulitis (brick-red stool, children).
Intussusception (currant jelly stool, children).
Other: drug reaction, blood dyscrasias, AV malformations.

Signs and symptoms

Melena or hematochezia (bright red blood).
Rectal examination (color of blood, presence of hemorrhoids,
    rectal mass).
Abdominal mass (intussusception, carcinoma, diverticulitis).
Generalized tenderness (inflammatory bowel disease, mesen-
    teric thrombosis).

Assess

Vital signs (as in upper GI hemorrhage).
NG tube to rule out upper GI hemorrhage.
Proctosigmoidoscopy (hemorrhoids, cancer, polyps, diverti-
    cula, colitis).
Fiberoptic colonoscopy.
Selective arteriography (visualization requires 2-3 ml/minute
    bleeding).
Barium studies (cancer, diverticulosis, etc.).

Therapeutic guidelines

Fluid resuscitation.
Transfusion as indicated.
Fresh-frozen plasma, vitamin K, platelets as indicated.
Selective Pitressin or epinephrine drip if indicated.
Surgery if bleeding persists or recurs.

HEMATURIA
PRERENAL HEMATURIA
Etiology

Thrombocytopenia (toxins, blood dyscrasias, idiopathic).
Coagulopathy (congenital, anticoagulant administration).
Sickle cell disease or trait.
Scurvy, hereditary telangiectasia.

Diagnostic tests

CBC, differential, platelets, sickle preparation, coagulation profile.
Drug intake, family history, nutritional status.

RENAL HEMATURIA
Etiology

Congenital (polycystic disease, medullary sponge kidney).
Trauma (renal contusion, laceration, fracture).
Inflammation (glomerulonephritis, pyelonephritis, tuberculosis).
Neoplasm (hamartoma, hypernephroma).
Calculi (renal).
Obstruction (hydronephrosis).
Vascular (renal infarction, renal vein thrombosis, hypertension, AVM).
Toxic (papillary necrosis).

Diagnostic tests

Urinalysis, microscopic, cultures, cytology, AFBs.
β_1,c globulin, ASO titers, LE preparation, ANA.
IVP, retrograde tomograms, angiography, biopsy.

POSTRENAL HEMATURIA
Etiology

Congenital (urethral valves, stricture).
Trauma (stricture).
Inflammation (periureteritis, cystitis, prostatitis, urethritis, radiation).
Neoplasm (transitional cell, prostate, hemangioma).
Calculi (vesical, ureteral).

Diagnostic tests

Cystoscopy, urine cytology, biopsy of suspicious lesions.
3-Glass test (glass 1, urethra; glass 2, bladder; glass 3, prostate).

HEMORRHAGIC SHOCK

1. The most common cause is trauma.
2. Mortality with adequate treatment should be < 4%.

3. *First aid* includes pressure tamponade over visible bleeding sites, then operative hemostasis when needed.
4. *The best position* for the patient may be with legs elevated and trunk supine, since the traditional Trendelenburg (head down) position may adversely affect respiratory status.
5. *Initial fluid resuscitation* includes IV fluids with a balanced electrolyte solution such as lactated Ringer's solution. This should be administered at a rapid rate (up to 1-2 liters in the first 45 minutes) until the CVP is adequate and blood pressure restored. If blood pressure and pulse are still not adequately restored, suspect continued or occult bleeding: this is the time for immediate transfusion of type-specific, crossmatched blood.
6. *Blood* is necessary to maintain an effective oxygen-carrying capacity. Every effort should be directed toward maintaining the hematocrit at least at 30%-35% in most cases. Packed red cells plus a plasma substitute may be the best combination. Adverse effects include transfusion reaction, adult respiratory distress syndrome with massive transfusion (use microaggregate filter), acidosis (give bicarbonate if severe), hypocalcemia (give calcium replacement if transfusion exceeds 400-500 ml/hour).
7. *Albumin* may be used as a *transient* plasma expander (1-2 hours). It increases plasma oncotic pressure and spares muscle catabolism. It is free of the risk of hepatitis. Caution if posttraumatic pulmonary insufficiency develops.
8. *Dextrans* may also be used as transient plasma expanders. They decrease blood viscosity and may improve microcirculatory flow. Adverse effects include interference with platelet function, altering of coagulation mechanisms, interference with the crossmatching of blood, and renal tubular damage if oliguric. Blood for typing and crossmatching must be drawn before the use of dextrans. Do not administer more than 1 liter/day.
9. *Buffers:* It is most important to correct acidosis by attacking the primary cause first (provide adequate ventilation, restore adequate perfusion). Sodium bicarbonate may be used for severe metabolic acidosis. THAM may also be used, but the prospect of a respiratory arrest should be kept in mind. Buffers are most often indicated after cardiac or respiratory arrests.
10. *Oxygen* therapy and ventilatory support may be indicated if dyspnea, tachypnea, or hypoxemia persists after adequate replacement of hemoglobin. Check ABGs before and during use for adjustment of oxygen administration.
11. *Antipyretics:* Increased temperature contributes to cellular metabolic effects of shock. Use aspirin, acetaminophen, or hypothermia blanket as indicated.

12. *Diuretics:* If oliguria persists despite adequate volume replacement, the use of mannitol or furosemide may improve urine output. More specific benefit is derived in cases where a large pigment load (e.g., hemoglobin) is presented to the kidneys.
13. *Pain* is best treated by small IV doses of narcotics, rather than by SC or IM administration, because of the low perfusion in hemorrhagic shock.
14. Other measures might include digitalis for congestive heart failure, intraarterial infusions for rapid replacement of intravascular volume, hypothermia to lower tissue metabolism, and renal hypothermia to protect against renal ischemic damage.

HEPATITIS, VIRAL

	Hepatitis A	Hepatitis B
Incubation period	14-45 days	50-180 days
Route of infection	Predominantly fecal-oral	Predominantly parenteral
Clinical onset	Usually abrupt	Usually insidious
Symptoms	Fatigue, anorexia, jaundice	Fatigue, anorexia, jaundice
Duration of transaminase elevation	1-3 weeks	1-6 months
Immunoglobulins (IgM levels)	Elevated	Usually normal
Severity of disease	Usually mild	Variable, occasionally severe
Complications	Rare	Present in 5%-10%
Mortality	Low (0.1%)	1%-2%
HBsAg	Absent	Present
Duration of immunity	Probably lifetime	Probably lifetime
Therapy	Supportive	Supportive
Gamma-globulin prophylaxis	ISG regularly prevents jaundice	HBIC probably useful

Hepatitis A prophylaxis

ISG: 0.02 ml/kg IM, as soon as possible after exposure, preferably within 7 days. Indicated for household contacts and needle exposure of patients with hepatitis A.

Hepatitis B prophylaxis

HBIG: 0.06 ml/kg IM, as soon as possible after exposure, preferably within 7 days. Repeat injection in 28-30 days after exposure. Recipient and source should be tested for hepatitis B antigen and antibody. Indicated for percutaneous puncture, ingestion, or spill on fresh wound of documented hepatitis B material; spouse of hepatitis B patient.

Note

Posttransfusion viral hepatitis may be hepatitis A, B, or non-A/non-B.

HYPERCALCEMIA
Etiology

The possible causes of hypercalcemia include:

Hyperparathyroidism (primary).
Metastatic cancer.
Thiazide administration.
Multiple myeloma.
Sarcoidosis.
Vitamin D intoxication.
Milk-alkali syndrome.
HPT (tertiary).

Leukemia.
Hyperthyroidism.
Adrenal insufficiency.
Immobilization (Paget's disease).
Diuretic phase of acute tubular necrosis.
Acromegaly.

Signs and symptoms

Known pathophysiologic consequences of hypercalcemia include:

CNS: impaired mentation, depression, mental deterioration, confusion, lethargy, psychosis, coma.
Eye: corneal calcification ("band" keratopathy).
Cardiovascular: short Q-T interval, bradycardia, tachycardia, digitalis sensitivity, arrhythmias, hypertension.
GI: anorexia, nausea, vomiting, constipation, abdominal pain, peptic ulcer, pancreatitis.
Genitourinary: polyuria, polydipsia, nephrolithiasis, nephrocalcinosis, uremia.
Musculoskeletal: muscular weakness, hyperactive reflexes, bone pain, fracture, osteitis fibrosa cystica.
Metabolic: acidosis with hyperchlorhydria and decreased serum bicarbonate caused by decreased tubular resorption of bicarbonate.

Diagnostic tests

Serum calcium: elevated repeatedly; assessed in relation to serum proteins.
Serum phosphorus: low in HPT unless renal failure present; high in vitamin D intoxication and metastatic cancer.
Acidosis: may be present in HPT.
Alkalosis: may be present in pseudohyperparathyroidism.
PTH level: inappropriately elevated in HPT.
Alkaline phosphatase: elevated in HPT with bone disease, as well as in liver disease and Paget's disease.
Serum protein electrophoresis: M spike of multiple myeloma; diffuse hyperglobulinemia of sarcoidosis, increased alpha-2 and beta globulins in HPT.
Hypokalemia, hypomagnesemia: association with hypercalcemia, nonspecific.

Thyroid function studies for hyperthyroidism.

Urinary calcium: normal is usually 70-200 mg/24 hours.

Urinary hydroxyproline: elevated in HPT and other conditions.

Urinary Bence-Jones protein: present in about half the patients with multiple myeloma.

Urinary cortisol for adrenal insufficiency.

Bone marrow: evidence of myeloma, leukemia, or lymphoma.

X-rays:

    Chest: fibronodular infiltrate, hilar adenopathy with sarcoidosis.

    Abdomen: renal calculi, nephrocalcinosis with HPT.

    Hand: subperiosteal resorption of distal phalanges in HPT.

    Skull: "punched-out" lesions with multiple myeloma.

    Metastatic series: osteolytic lesions (e.g., breast cancer).

IVP (after rehydration): nephrolithiasis with HPT; hypernephroma.

Barium swallow: displacement of esophagus by a parathyroid adenoma.

ECG: short QT interval.

Cortisone suppression test (prednisone, 60 mg/day, or equivalent, for 10 days):

    Respond:

        Metastatic cancer.   Vitamin D intoxication.

        Multiple myeloma.   Milk-alkali syndrome.

        Sarcoidosis.   Adrenal insufficiency.

    Resistant:

        HPT.

Complications

Progressive uremia with renal failure and hypertension.

Progressive dehydration and shock.

Coma and death.

Digitalis toxicity.

Therapeutic guidelines

See *Hypercalcemic crisis* for medical management.

See *Hyperparathyroidism* for surgical management.

HYPERCALCEMIC CRISIS

The medical management for hypercalcemic crisis is presented here. For signs and symptoms, differential diagnosis, and work-up, see *Hypercalcemia*.

Therapeutic guidelines

1. Restrict calcium intake: avoid dairy products and antacids containing calcium.
2. Saline infusion with 0.9% solution to restore ECF volume and establish diuresis of at least 1500 ml/day. Up to 4-10 liters/day of saline may be required.

Action: Sodium increases calcium excretion by competing for resorption in the distal renal tubule.

Effect: Rapid.

Note:

Caution in presence of cardiac or renal insufficiency.

Avoid fluid overloading: check intake, output, daily weights, CVP.

Monitor serum calcium, phosphorus, potassium, magnesium, and BUN.

Replace potassium and magnesium as necessary.

3. Furosemide: 20-40 mg IV q2-4h until serum calcium < 12 mg/100 ml.

Action: Increases calcium excretion and prevents volume overloading.

Effect: Rapid.

Note:

Should only be used after volume loading; caution with renal insufficiency.

Avoid rapid volume depletion and ECF contraction.

May also cause potassium and magnesium depletion.

Up to 50-100 mg/hour have been used to establish vigorous diuresis.

4. Phosphates: 500 mg PO/NG qid (initial dose).

Action: Increased deposition of calcium and phosphorus in skeletal and extracellular sites. Oral phosphorus also decreases intestinal absorption of calcium.

Effect: Rapid decline in serum calcium.

Note:

Should only be used after volume loading; contraindicated in the presence of renal insufficiency.

Especially useful if serum phosphorus is low.

Oral preparation used for chronic nonoperative urgent control of primary hyperparathyroidism or for malignancy.

Adverse effects: vomiting, diarrhea, metastatic calcification, renal failure.

IV primarily used for emergent and life-threatening hypercalcemia.

Dose: 1.5 g of phosphorus in 500-1000 ml 5% dextrose IV q6-12h.

Complications: diffuse metastatic calcification, acute renal failure, renal cortical necrosis, and fatal shock may occur.

5. Mithramycin: 15-25 μg/kg in 1 liter of saline IV over 3-6 hours.

Action: Lowers serum calcium by inhibiting bone resorption; this effect is said to occur at a lower dose than its cytotoxic effects.

Effect: Lowering of serum calcium usually occurs within 48 hours, but it may require several days for calcium to return to normal. Duration of effect may be from several days to several weeks.

Note:

Can be used when saline/furosemide regimen cannot be applied.

Especially useful for emergent or life-threatening hypercalcemia caused by enhanced bone resorption. Most frequently used for:

PTH-producing carcinomas, osteolytic metastases.

Vitamin D intoxication.

Lymphoproliferative disorders.

Non-PTH-secreting tumors (e.g., myeloma).

Adverse effects: thrombocytopenia, hepatocellular and renal damage, hemolysis; toxic effects are dose-related.

6. Magnesium sulfate: up to 2 mEq/kg IV over 8-12 hours, or in divided doses IM.

Indication: When severe hypomagnesemia accompanies hypercalcemia.

Note: 1 g of 20% solution = 8 mEq/ml.

7. Corticosteroids: 40-80 mg/day of prednisone (or its equivalent).

Effective for hypercalcemia caused by Addison's disease, vitamin D intoxication, sarcoidosis, multiple myeloma, lymphoma, some leukemias, breast cancer, or hypernephromas.

Ineffective for primary HPT, squamous cancer of lung.

Action: Antagonizes peripheral action of vitamin D (decreases GI absorption of calcium, bone turnover, and renal tubular resorption).

Effect: May take 1-2 weeks for effect to be apparent.

Adverse effects: Hypernatremia with prednisone; Cushing's syndrome.

8. Dialysis (hemodialysis or peritoneal dialysis): indicated for emergent hypercalcemia caused by primary HPT and for life-threatening hypercalcemia when the etiology is not apparent.

9. Calcitonin: 50-100 units IM.

Indicated as an adjunct in the treatment of hypercalcemia.

Effects: Variable, mild, and transient.

Adverse effects: Allergic reactions may occur.

10. Indomethacin: 50 mg PO tid.

Indicated experimentally for hypercalcemia caused by malignancy not amenable to surgical therapy.

Action: May decrease bone resorption, because of inhibition of synthesis of type E prostaglandin, which has been implicated in some solid tumors.

HYPERKALEMIA
Etiology

Renal failure, adrenal insufficiency, severe acidosis, increased tissue breakdown (crush injury, extensive infection, massive hemolysis).

Worsened by acidosis, hyponatremia, and hypocalcemia.

Signs and symptoms

Weakness, paresthesias, areflexia, muscular or respiratory paralysis.

GI: nausea, vomiting, cramps, diarrhea.

Cardiovascular: bradycardia, hypotension, ventricular fibrillation, cardiac arrest.

ECG: peaked T waves, ST depression, prolonged PR intervals, diminished to absent P waves, widening of QRS complexes.

Diagnostic tests

Check electrolytes, calcium, ECG, ABG, and pH.

Therapeutic guidelines

1. Stop all potassium intake (IV and PO). Monitor ECG.
2. Calcium gluconate: 5-10 ml of 10% solution IV, slowly (unless patient is receiving digitalis preparation).
3. Sodium bicarbonate: 45 mEq (or 1 mEq/kg) IV, slowly.
4. Glucose infusion: 200-300 ml of 20% solution over 30-60 minutes.
5. Insulin (added to glucose infusion): 1 unit of insulin per 5 g glucose.
6. Kayexalate: 20-50 g in 100-200 ml of 20% sorbitol PO q4-6h, or 50 g in 200 ml of 20% sorbitol as retention enema prn.
7. Hemodialysis or peritoneal dialysis if necessary.

HYPERMAGNESEMIA (see also *Magnesium*)
Etiology

Severe renal insufficiency, hypovolemia, or stress (surgery, trauma, burns).

Signs and symptoms

Hypotension, nausea, vomiting, weakness, loss of deep tendon reflexes, lethargy, coma.

ECG: Q-T prolongation, AV block, cardiac arrest.

Therapeutic guidelines

1. Restrict magnesium intake (especially antacids containing magnesium).
2. Replace volume deficits and correct acidosis when present.
3. Calcium gluconate: 5-10 ml of 10% solution IV, slowly (caution in presence of digitalis administration).
4. Hemodialysis or peritoneal dialysis if necessary.

HYPERNATREMIA (see also *Sodium*)
WATER DEHYDRATION
Etiology

Unreplaced losses, increased output (fever, tracheostomy, granulating surface, diabetes insipidus, high-output renal failure).
Lack of water intake.
Solute loading (salt solutions, mannitol, high protein intake).
Hormones (aldosterone, cortisone, estrogens, testosterone).

Signs and symptoms

Thirst: high specific gravity; oliguria; hemoconcentration; dry, sticky mucous membranes; fever; hypotension.

Therapeutic guidelines

Milliliters of D5W needed = 4 × body weight (kg) × mEq change in sodium desired.
Water deficit = 1 liter for each 3 mEq sodium above normal.
Add 500 ml water for each 100 mg/100 ml glucose elevation.
Replace one-half the deficit in first 12 hours.

SODIUM EXCESS (edema)
Etiology

Renal failure (unable to excrete solute load, salt retention), congestive heart failure, cirrhosis, allergic state.

Signs and symptoms

Edema implies at least 400 mEq of sodium excess (3 liters of fluid).
Weight gain.

Diagnostic tests

Serum sodium is usually normal, but total body sodium is increased.
Hematocrit may be low. Check albumin level.

Complications

Congestive heart failure, pulmonary edema, impaired wound healing.

Therapeutic guidelines

Restrict sodium: 1000 mg/day.
Diuretics: e.g., furosemide, 20-40 mg PO as needed, or spironolactone, 25-50 mg PO (if hypokalemic).
Albumin if hypoproteinemic.

HYPERPARATHYROIDISM, PRIMARY
Etiology

Excessive secretion of PTH may be caused by:
1. Parathyroid adenoma (75%-90%):
   Single adenoma (70%-85%).
   Multiple adenomas (2%-5%).
2. Parathyroid hyperplasia (10%-25%) (controversial: reports indicate up to 65% multiglandular disease).
3. Parathyroid carcinoma (<1%).

Pathophysiology

Increased levels of PTH lead to hypercalcemia because of increased resorption of calcium from bone and kidney. Hypophosphatemia occurs because of decreased tubular resorption of phosphate. Polyuria results from a decrease in renal concentrating ability.

Signs and symptoms

The three most common presentations include:
1. Asymptomatic hypercalcemia.
2. Renal colic caused by nephrolithiasis.
3. Marked hypercalcemia with progressive muscle weakness, mental deterioration, and uremia (see *Hypercalcemia*).

Recent reports describe previous neck irradiation in up to 30% of patients with primary HPT.

Diagnostic tests

Serum calcium elevated repeatedly; assessed in relation to serum proteins.

Serum phosphorus decreased.

Serum PTH inappropriately elevated by radioimmunoassay.

In addition, there may be:

Serum chloride > 102 mEq/liter.

Serum alkaline phosphatase increased in presence of bone disease.

Urine calcium and phosphorus increased.

Barium swallow may reveal indentation of esophagus caused by pressure from a large parathyroid adenoma (rare).

X-ray of extremities: subperiosteal resorption in distal phalanges.

ECG: shortened QT interval.

Glucocorticoid administration fails to suppress hypercalcemia caused by HPT.

Differential diagnosis

See *Hypercalcemia*.

Complications

See *Hypercalcemia*.

Therapeutic guidelines

1. Preoperative evaluation should establish firm diagnosis of HPT. Indirect laryngoscopy is recommended to document vocal cord function.
2. Primary neck exploration usually includes:
    Excision of parathyroid adenoma.
    Subtotal (3½ glands) parathyroidectomy for:
        Parathyroid hyperplasia.
        Multiple endocrine adenomatosis syndrome.
        Familial HPT.
        Secondary HPT.
    En bloc resection of parathyroid carcinoma.
3. Secondary neck exploration for persistent or recurrent hypercalcemia may be preceded by studies aiming to localize residual hyperfunctioning parathyroid tissue: selective venous catheterization and radioactive thyroid scanning combined with parathyroid arteriography.
4. Postoperative complications include hemorrhage, hypocalcemia, hypoparathyroidism, recurrent laryngeal nerve injury, and recurrent HPT.

HYPOCALCEMIA (see also *Calcium, Hypoparathyroidism, acute*)
Etiology

Surgically significant causes of hypocalcemia include:
    Hypoparathyroidism (see individual entry).
    Alkalosis (hyperventilation, vomiting, fistulae).
    Acute pancreatitis.
    Renal failure.
    Hypoproteinemia.
    Hypomagnesemia.

Signs and symptoms

Earliest symptoms are paresthesias of lips, fingers, and toes.
CNS: irritability, depression, confusion, papilledema.
Hyperactive tendon reflexes, muscle and abdominal cramps.
Chvostek's sign: facial muscle contraction elicited by tapping over the facial nerve; present in 10% of normal population.
Trousseau's sign: carpal spasm elicited by occluding blood flow to the forearm for 3-5 minutes.
Tetany: carpopedal spasm, tonic-clonic convulsions, laryngospasm.

Therapeutic guidelines

1. Treat the underlying cause first.
2. Correct existing electrolyte and acid-base imbalances.
3. See *Hypoparathyroidism, acute,* for calcium administration.

HYPOKALEMIA (see also *Potassium*)
Etiology

Renal (diuretics, adrenal steroids, renal tubular disease).
GI losses (NG suction, vomiting, fistulae, diarrhea).
Intracellular shift (alkalosis, glucose, insulin).
Postoperative fluids without potassium.

Signs and symptoms

Weakness, hyporeflexia, paralytic ileus, paresis, flaccid paralysis.
Cardiac: arrhythmias, increased sensitivity to digitalis.
ECG: flattening of T waves, S-T depression, appearance of U waves.

Diagnostic tests

Check serum and urine electrolytes. Consider ECG, arterial pH.
Urinary potassium < 15 mEq/day implies extrarenal cause.
Urinary potassium > 30 mEq/day implies probable renal cause.

Complications

Increased sensitivity to digitalis; arrhythmia; alkalosis.
Renal tubular damage (hypokalemic nephropathy).

Therapeutic guidelines

1. Oral potassium supplementation preferred (less danger of hyperkalemia).
   Potassium-rich foods: bananas, tomatoes, oranges, fruit juices.
   If alkalotic: potassium chloride (10% solution, 1.3 mEq/ml) preferred.
   If acidotic: potassium gluconate (1.3 mEq/Ml) or triplex (3 mEq/ml) preferred.
2. IV potassium, usually given in saline solution, should not be administered faster than 40 mEq/hour or in a concentration greater than 40 mEq/liter without ECG monitoring.
3. Digitalis dosage should be decreased to avoid toxicity.
4. Monitor ECG during rapid replacement. Recheck serum potassium.

HYPOMAGNESEMIA
Etiology

Acute tubular necrosis in diuretic phase, GI losses, parenteral therapy without magnesium, malabsorption, delerium tremens, liver cirrhosis, acute pancreatitis, diabetic acidosis during treatment, primary aldosteronism, chronic alcoholism, burns (late stage).

Signs and symptoms

Weakness, muscle fasciculation, tremor, hyperactive tendon reflexes, occasionally a positive Chvostek sign, and tetany. There may be agitation, delerium, convulsions, coma, and cardiac arrhythmias.

Therapeutic guidelines

Magnesium replacement:

1. Maintenance requirements: 8-24 mEq/day.
2. Mild deficiency: 8 mEq (one 2-ml ampule of 50% solution) IM q6h for 4 doses, or until desired result is achieved.
3. Severe deficiency: up to 2 mEq/kg IM within 4 hours if necessary, or up to 40-80 mEq in 1 liter D5W or saline IV over 4 hours.

Note:

1. Individualize dosage based on serum magnesium levels.
2. Discontinue administration if patellar reflexes are absent.
3. Caution with renal insufficiency, digitalis administration.
4. Monitor urine output, heart rate, blood pressure, respiration, and ECG when large doses are given IV.
5. Correct associated potassium and calcium abnormalities when present.

HYPONATREMIA

The main causes of hyponatremia are presented below, along with suggested treatment. Signs and symptoms, in general, may include nausea, vomiting, hypertension, increased intracranial pressure, convulsions with sodium < 120 mg/100 ml, edema with sodium retention, and oliguric renal failure.

In addition to measurement of serum sodium, it is important to check serum glucose, BUN, and urine sodium.

DILUTIONAL HYPONATREMIA

Example: GI losses replaced with water alone.
Result: Total body sodium is decreased.

Therapeutic guidelines

Replace volume losses with isotonic saline.

WATER INTOXICATION

Example: Excessive consumption or administration of water.
Result: Total body sodium is normal.

Therapeutic guidelines

Restrict water intake. If severe and symptomatic, a small amount of 3% or 5% sodium chloride solution may be given IV, slowly.

INADEQUATE FREE WATER CLEARANCE

Example: Congestive heart failure, hepatic cirrhosis, nephrosis.
Result: Total body sodium is increased.

Therapeutic guidelines

Restrict water and sodium intake.
Digitalis and/or diuretics may be indicated.

SYNDROME OF INAPPROPRIATE ADH
Signs and symptoms

Hyponatremia.
Serum osmolality: decreased.
Urine osmolality: decreased.
Urine sodium: increased.
Renal and adrenal function: normal.
No clinical evidence of volume depletion.

Therapeutic guidelines

All abnormalities disappear with adequate restriction of water.

HYPOPARATHYROIDISM, ACUTE (Postoperative)
Etiology

Transient following thyroidectomy or subtotal parathyroidectomy.
Permanent following total parathyroidectomy.

Pathophysiology

Inadequate secretion of PTH leads to hypocalcemia by reducing the rate of calcium resorption from bone and kidney. Hyperphosphatemia occurs because of increased tubular resorption.

Signs and symptoms

Earliest symptoms are paresthesias of lips, fingers, and toes.
CNS: irritability, depression, confusion, papilledema.
Hyperactive tendon reflexes, muscle and abdominal cramps.
Chvostek's sign: facial muscle contraction elicited by tapping over the facial nerve; present in 10% of normal population.
Trousseau's sign: carpal spasm elicited by occluding blood flow to the forearm for 3-5 minutes.
Tetany: carpopedal spasm, tonic clonic convulsions, laryngospasm.

Diagnostic tests

Serum calcium low; assessed in relation to serum proteins.
Serum phosphorus elevated despite normal renal function.
PTH level low.
ECG: prolonged QT interval.

Complications

Cataracts, calcification of basal ganglion, convulsions, mental deterioration, and psychosis in chronic hypoparathyroidism.

Differential diagnosis

Alkalosis (hyperventilation, vomiting, alkali administration).
Hypoproteinemia (normal ionized calcium level).
Hypomagnesemia (malabsorption, alcoholism).
Renal failure.
Pancreatitis.

Therapeutic guidelines

1. Draw blood for calcium, phosphorus, magnesium, potassium.
2. Rapid management of acute symptomatic hypocalcemia:
   Calcium gluconate: 1 g (10 ml of a 10% solution) IV, slowly (1 g of calcium gluconate provides 4.5 mEq of calcium).
   Repeat dose with cardiac monitor if necessary.
   Caution in patients receiving digitalis.
   Correct magnesium and potassium deficits when present.
3. Intermediate management:
   Calcium gluconate, 1-2 g in 1000 ml D5W q8h.
4. Continued management with oral calcium:
   Usual dose: 1.5-2 g elemental calcium per day.
   Note: 1 g elemental calcium can be obtained with 11 g calcium gluconate, 8 g calcium lactate, or 5.5 g calcium chloride.
5. Vitamin D (when needed):
   Vitamin D_2 (calciferol), 50,000-100,000 units PO qd.
   Alternative: DHT, 1-1.5 mg PO qd.
6. Optional: low-phosphorus diet, aluminum hydroxide preparation.
7. Goal: maintain serum calcium of 8.5-9 mg/100 ml.
8. Monitor serum calcium and magnesium levels.

HYPOTHYROIDISM
Etiology

Thyroidectomy, radioactive iodine therapy, alpasia; replacement by nonfunctional goiter, adenoma, or thyroiditis; hypopituitarism, idiopathic.

Signs and symptoms

General effects: cold intolerance, weight gain, fatigue, apathy, headaches, dementia, hoarse voice.
Skin: pale, thick, doughy.
Hair: dry, brittle, coarse.
Head and neck: loss of lateral one-third of eyebrows, periorbital edema, enlarged tongue, goiter (some cases).

Respiratory system: dyspnea, effusions.

Cardiovascular system: congestive heart failure, decreased cardiac output, effusions.

GI system: constipation, distention, achlorhydria, pernicious anemia.

Neurologic: slow, prolonged reflexes.

Females: decreased libido, anovulation, menorrhagia.

Males: decreased libido, impotency, oligospermia.

Diagnostic tests

Decreased T_4 and/or T_3, hypercholesterolemia (>300 mg/100 ml).

Decreased BMR.

Decreased ^{131}I uptake.

Anemia.

ECG: bradycardia, decreased voltage, flat T waves.

EEG: slow alpha activity, decreased amplitude.

Check pituitary studies (TSH).

Therapeutic guidelines

1. Mild hypothyroidism: maintenance doses of thyroid hormone (see below).
2. Severe hypothyroidism: Small initial doses, e.g., 15 mg/day of thyroid hormone. Increase by 15-30 mg q1-3 weeks as necessary to achieve optimum results (usually 90-100 mg/day).
3. Rapid replacement of thyroid hormone may be given when necessary with levothyroxine IV or with liothyronine orally. Glucocorticoids should then be given to prevent adrenal insufficiency.
4. Equivalent maintenance doses:
   Thyroid USP, 90-180 mg/day
   Levothyroxine, 100-200 μg/day (Synthroid)
   Liothyronine, 50-100 μg/day (Cytomel)

INFECTIONS (See also *Fever* entries)

1. Organism.
2. Infection.
3. Susceptibility (may vary with institution, location).

GRAM-POSITIVE COCCI
Streptococci

Groups A, B, C, G: pharyngitis, scarlet fever, rheumatic fever, cellulitis, erysipelas, fasciitis.

Microaerophilic: burrowing ulcers.

Streptococcus viridans: subacute bacterial endocarditis 70%.

Streptococcus fecalis: SBE 25%, urinary tract infection.

Therapeutic guidelines:
First choice: penicillin G.
Second choice: a cephalosporin, erythromycin.
Third choice: clindamycin.
Fourth choice: vancomycin.

Staphylococci

Abscesses, cellulitis, wound infections, bacteremia, endocarditis, penumonia, enteritis, enterocolitis.

Therapeutic guidelines:
Penicillin-susceptible:
First choice: penicillin G.
Second choice: a cephalosporin or vancomycin.
Penicillin-resistant:
First choice: oxacillin, methicillin, or nafcillin.
Second choice: a cephalosporin or vancomycin.

Pneumococci

Pneumonia, septicemia.

Therapeutic guidelines:
First choice: penicillin G.
Second choice: a cephalosporin, chloramphenicol, erythromycin, or clindamycin.

GRAM-POSITIVE RODS
Clostridia

Gas gangrene (myonecrosis), anaerobic cellulitis, septicemia, intraabdominal abscesses, urogenital infections, tetanus.

Therapeutic guidelines:
Surgical debridement, hyperbaric oxygen.
First choice: penicillin G.
Second choice: a cephalosporin, erythromycin, or chloramphenicol.

Diphtheroids

Wound contaminants, septicemia, prosthetic valve infections.

Therapeutic guidelines:
First choice: penicillin G.
Second choice: a cephalosporin, erythromycin, or tetracycline.

Listeria

Opportunistic infections, septicemia.

Therapeutic guidelines:
First choice: ampicillin alone or with streptomycin.
Second choice: chloramphenicol, erythromycin, or tetracycline.

GRAM-NEGATIVE COCCI

Gonococci

Genital infections, arthritis, meningitis, pharyngitis, ophthalmitis, endocarditis, septicemia.

Therapeutic guidelines:
First choice: penicillin G or a cephalosporin.
Second choice: tetracyline, erythromycin, or chloramphenicol.

Meningococci

Meningitis, arthritis, Waterhouse-Friderichsen syndrome.

Therapeutic guidelines:
First choice: penicillin G or a cephalosporin.
Second choice: chloramphenicol or erythromycin.

GRAM-NEGATIVE RODS (see also *Shock, septic*)

Escherichia coli

Urinary tract infections, septicemia, endocarditis, intraabdominal abscess, peritonitis.

Therapeutic guidelines:
First choice: ampicillin.
Second choice: a cephalosporin, tetracycline, chloramphenicol, gentamicin, kanamycin, polymyxin (for UTIs).

Klebsiella-Enterobacter (Aerobacter)

Friedlander's pneumonia, UTIs, intraabdominal infections, gram-negative pneumonia.

Therapeutic guidelines:
First choice: a cephalosporin for *Klebsiella;* carbenicillin for *Enterobacter.*
Second choice: chloramphenicol, tetracycline, gentamicin, or kanamycin.

Proteus

Genitourinary infections, burns, and wound infections.

Therapeutic guidelines:
First choice: ampicillin or carbenicillin.
Second choice: a cephalosporin, chloramphenicol, gentamicin, or kanamycin.

Pseudomonas

Superinfections, necrotizing wound and pulmonary infections.

Therapeutic guidelines:
First choice: gentamicin alone or with carbenicillin.
Second choice: amikacin, tobramycin, or polymyxin.

Serratia

Opportunistic infections, septicemia, endocarditis, genitourinary infections.

Therapeutic guidelines:
First choice: carbenicillin.
Second choice: gentamicin, kanamycin, or chloramphenicol.

Salmonellae

Gastroenteritis, septicemia, typhoid fever, osteomyelitis, abscesses, cholecystitis.

Therapeutic guidelines:
First choice: chloramphenicol.
Second choice: ampicillin or trimethoprim-sulfamethoxazole.

Mima-Herellae

Opportunistic infections

Therapeutic guidelines:
Kanamycin plus tetracycline.

Haemophilus

Therapeutic guidelines:
First choice: ampicillin.
Second choice: chloramphenicol or tetracycline.

ANAEROBES
Bacteroides

Septicemia, abscesses

Therapeutic guidelines:
First choice: clindamycin or chloramphenicol.
Second choice: cefazolin (20%-40% resistant).
Third choice: carbenicillin (5%-20% resistant).
Fourth choice: tetracycline (30%-50% resistant).
Fifth choice: high-dose penicillin G (20% resistant).

Actinomyces

Actinomycosis

Therapeutic guidelines:
First choice: penicillin G.
Second choice: a cephalosporin or tetracycline.

FUNGI
Candida albicans

Oral thrush, vaginitis, septicemia, endocarditis.

Therapeutic guidelines:
Oral thrush: mouth care, nystatin gargles.
Fungemia: amphotericin B.

Histoplasmosis, coccidioidomycosis, blastomycosis

Generalized fungal infections

Therapeutic guidelines:
Amphotericin B.

LARGE BOWEL OBSTRUCTION
Etiology

Mechanical occlusion of the bowel lumen because of:

Carcinoma.	Adhesions.
Diverticulitis.	Intussusception.
Volvulus.	Fecal impaction.
Hernia.	Chronic ulcerative colitis.

As fluid and gas accumulate proximal to the obstruction, distention of the large bowel occurs. In the presence of a competent ileocecal valve, cecal perforation is a major concern. In contrast to small bowel obstruction, ECF volume deficits progress more slowly. Stasis of feces and fluid proximal to the obstruction leads to rapid bacterial proliferation. With closed-loop obstruction, vascular compromise results and may lead to strangulation obstruction with areas of gangrene and perforation.

Signs and symptoms

Classic symptoms include progressive constipation, abdominal distention, and crampy lower abdominal pain. Alternating diarrhea and constipation suggest partial obstruction. As time passes, nausea and vomiting become prominent. With exhaustion or vascular compromise, steady abdominal pain develops.

Examination early on may reveal a discrete mass suggestive of carcinoma or diverticular abscess. Peristaltic rushes are a very important physical finding. Later on, progressive abdominal distention, tympany, and diminished bowel sounds occur.

Rectal examination may demonstrate a nontender rectal mass and the presence of occult blood, suggestive of carcinoma. A tender pelvic mass suggests an inflammatory lesion.

Diagnostic tests

Abdominal x-rays show distention of the colon proximal to the obstruction. Cecal distention > 10-12 cm or air within the bowel wall suggests impending perforation.

Sigmoidoscopy should be performed early in the course, since carcinoma or volvulus may be demonstrated. Sigmoidoscopy may be both diagnostic and therapeutic in sigmoid volvulus. A rectal tube should be left in place for decompression.

Barium enema may show the site of the obstruction and help determine the etiology, although it may not differentiate between carcinoma and diverticulitis as well as might be expected.

Blood tests may show elevation of the white count, amylase, and LDH.

Differential diagnosis

Metastatic cancer.
Ogilvie's syndrome.
Endometriosis.

Therapeutic guidelines

Preoperative:
1. NPO; NG suction with Levine or sump tube.
2. Fluid resuscitation and correction of electrolyte abnormalities.
3. Urine output (Foley catheter) should be established.
4. Transfusion if necessary.
5. IV antibiotics.

Postoperative:
1. NG suction should be continued until bowel sounds are present and the patient is passing flatus or feces.
2. Antibiotics, when indicated, are given a full course.
3. IV fluids are administered appropriately.
4. Vital signs, urine output, CVP, CBC, electrolytes should be monitored closely.

MULTIPLE ENDOCRINE ADENOMATOSIS
MEA I (Werner's syndrome)

Hyperparathyroidism, pituitary tumor, pancreatic tumor (Zollinger-Ellison insulinomas). (May also have adrenal and thyroid tumors.)

MEA II (Sipple's syndrome)

HPT, pheochromocytoma, medullary cancer of the thyroid.

MEA IIB (variant of MEA II)

Pheochromocytoma, medullary cancer of the thyroid, absence of HPT, marfanoid habitus, multiple neuromas.

Note

See specific entries for *Hyperparathyroidism, Pheochromocytoma, Zollinger-Ellison syndrome.*

MYOCARDIAL INFARCTION (see also *Electrocardiogram, Shock*)
Etiology

Insufficient coronary arterial blood flow resulting in ischemia and necrosis of a portion of the myocardium. Associated with coronary atherosclerosis in 90% of cases. Other causes include dissecting aortic aneurysm, coronary artery embolism, polyarteritis nodosa, radiation therapy, neoplastic invasion, acute severe hemorrhage, acute hypoxia, and administration of excessive doses of sympathomimetic agents. The infarction may be transmural (anterior, inferior, or posterior) or subendocardial.

Signs and symptoms

Typical symptoms involve acute onset of excruciating substernal constant chest pain that is unrelieved by nitroglycerin. The pain may radiate to the arms, neck, jaw, or the upper abdomen. It may be associated with nausea, vomiting, breathlessness, hiccuping, and loss of consciousness. Pain lasting longer than 24 hours may be caused by infarct extension, pericarditis, or pulmonary infarction. May be painless in 15%-20%.

Examination often reveals ashen-gray pallor, profuse diaphoresis, and cold skin. The pulse is usually rapid unless AV block is present, and the blood pressure falls. Fever often develops, and a pericardial friction rub may occur. Atrial (S_4) and ventricular (S_3) gallops and basal rales may be auscultated.

Diagnostic tests

ECG (transmural infarction):
1. Hyperacute T waves are often the earliest electrocardiographic sign.
2. ST elevation (> 2 mm) in one or more leads occurs within 24 hours.
3. T-wave inversion evolves within days to weeks.
4. Q waves may occur rapidly but develop maximal changes only after several days.

Enzymes increase from 1.4 to 10 times the normal value:
CPK: rises in 2-4 hours, peaks at 18-36 hours, returns to normal in 3-5 days.
SGOT: rises in 8-12 hours, peaks at 18-36 hours, returns to normal in 3-5 days.
LDH: rises in 8-48 hours, peaks at 3-6 days, returns to normal in 8-14 days.
Note: Elevated enzyme levels may be of questionable value up to 5 days postoperatively. CPK (MG band) and LDH (LDH_1 and LDH_2) isoenzymes may be of value, however.

Leukocytosis, transient hyperglycemia, and elevated sedimentation rate are often present.

Check chest x-ray, ABG, CVP, urine output.

Differential diagnosis

Severe angina pectoris.
Massive pulmonary embolism.

Dissecting aortic aneurysm.
Nonspecific pericarditis.
Cardiac tamponade.
Mediastinal emphysema.
Reflux esophagitis.
Acute cholecystitis.
Acute peptic ulcer.
Acute pancreatitis.
Other abdominal causes.

Complications

Mortality: 30%, untreated; 15% with best treatment.
Arrhythmias: 90% in first 3 days (usually PVCs).
Cardiogenic shock in 10%-15%.
Acute left-sided congestive heart failure.
Hypertension.
Thromboembolic complications.
Papillary muscle dysfunction and rupture.
Septal rupture.
Myocardial rupture.
Ventricular aneurysm.
Post–myocardial infarction syndrome.

Therapeutic guidelines

1. CCU, 5-7 days (monitor for arrhythmia, shock, and other complications).
2. Ward, 2-3 weeks (monitor, rest, heal).
3. Oxygen, vital signs q1h, Ace wraps or antiembolic stockings.
4. Bed rest (bedside commode permitted when stable).
5. Analgesic: morphine sulfate, 3-5 mg IV or 8-15 mg SC/IM.
6. Sedation: diazepam, chlordiazepoxide, phenobarbital, or chloral hydrate.
7. Antiemetic (if needed): diphenhydramine, 25-50 mg IM/PO.
8. Bowel care: dioctyl sodium sulfosuccinate or mineral oil, milk of magnesia.
9. Diet: liquids day 1, soft diet thereafter (low salt).
10. Nitroglycerin prn after stabilization of infarct.
11. Arrhythmias:
    PVCs: lidocaine, 50-100 mg IV bolus; then 2-4 mg/minute IV drip.
    Ventricular tachycardia: thump chest, give lidocaine as above or defibrillate.
    Sinus bradycardia (< 50 bpm): atropine, 0.4-0.6 mg IV; consider isoproterenol.
12. For cardiac arrest and cardiogenic shock, see individual entries.

OLIGURIA, ACUTE

The three main types of acute oliguria are presented below.
The normal ranges of daily urine measurements are as follows:

Physical properties

Volume	800-1500 ml
pH	5.0-7.0
Osmolality	500-800 mOsm/kg H_2O

Electrolyte concentration

Sodium	50-160 mEq
Potassium	30-90 mEq
Calcium	10-15 mEq
Magnesium	3-25 mEq
Chloride	50-140 mEq
Phosphate	30-50 mEq
Sulfate	30-50 mEq

Nonelectrolyte concentration

Urea	250-400 mM
Creatinine	1-1.6 g
Organic acids	10-30 mM

PRERENAL OLIGURIA
Etiology

Decreased renal blood flow (may be caused by water or ECF
deficits).

Clinical setting: maximal sodium and water conservation plus
stress:

Hypovolemia (hemorrhage, GI loss, excessive renal loss,
sequestered loss).

Hypotension (cardiogenic or septic shock, myocardial infarction).

Hyponatremia.

Signs and symptoms

Urine output < 20-30 ml/hour.
Urine specific gravity > 1.015.
Urine sediment: normal, few hyaline and granular casts.
BUN: increase because of tubular resorption.
BUN–plasma creatinine ratio > 15:1.
Urine–plasma urea ratio > 15:1.
Urine–plasma creatinine ratio > 15:1.
Urine–plasma osmolar ratio > 1.5.
Urine sodium < 10-20 mEq/liter.
Urine osmolality > 500 mOsm/kg H_2O.
CVP: normal or low (unless congestive heart failure present).
PWP: low (unless CHF present).

Therapeutic guidelines

Fluid challenge (unless CHF present):

200 ml of appropriate fluid over 30 minutes.

250 ml of salt-poor albumin over 1 hour.

200 ml of appropriate fluid over 30 minutes.

RENAL FAILURE (acute tubular necrosis)

Etiology

Vasomotor factors:

Hypovolemia (shock, trauma, burns).

Central or cardiogenic shock.

Septicemia (endotoxic shock).

Nephrotoxic agents:

Hemoglobin (hemolysis, transfusion reactions, cold agglutinins).

Myoglobin (electrocution, seizures, ethanol, crush injury).

Medications (aminoglycosides, polymyxins, cephaloridine, methoxyflurane).

Radiopaque dyes.

Heavy metals (mercury, lead, arsenic, bismuth).

Carbon tetrachloride.

Other factors:

Poststreptococcal glomerulonephritis.

Polyarteritis, vasculitis.

Intrarenal precipitation (sulfonamides, urates, calcium, myeloma protein).

Infections (acute pyelonephritis, necrotizing papillitis).

Signs and symptoms

Urine output < 20-30 ml/hour (unless nonoliguric failure).

Oliguria does not respond to volume expansion or diuretics.

Note: Urine specimens should be obtained before administration of diuretics.

Urine specific gravity < 1.010.

Urine sediment:

ATN: renal tubular epithelial cells; coarse, granular casts.

Glomerulonephritis: many red cells and red cell casts.

Infection: many white cells and bacteria on Gram stain.

Partial obstruction: few red and white cells with hyaline or finely granular casts.

BUN and plasma creatinine both increase.

BUN–plasma creatinine ratio < 10:1.

Urine–plasma urea ratio < 10:1.

Urine–plasma creatinine ratio < 10:1.

Urine–plasma osmolar ratio < 1.2 (impaired response to ADH).

Urine sodium > 20-40 mEq/liter (impaired tubular resorption).

Urine osmolality < 320 mOsm/kg H_2O.

CVP: normal or increased.

PWP: normal or increased.

Mortality

High, as a result of sepsis, upper GI hemorrhage.

Phases

1. *Oliguria* (may be absent or persist 1-10 days). May be complicated by azotemia, hyperkalemia, acidosis, and CHF.
2. *Diuresis* (may be the first sign of renal failure). Urine output > 500 ml/day. BUN continues to rise until the recovery of functional glomerular filtration.

Therapeutic guidelines

Oliguric phase:

1. Identify and treat the underlying cause.
2. Correct preexisting volume contraction if present.
3. Restrict fluid to insensible losses (5-7 ml/kg/day water), urinary, and GI losses.
4. Restrict sodium, potassium, and protein intake.
5. Give adequate carbohydrate, 100-200 mg/day, to inhibit protein catabolism.
6. Maintain accurate intake and output balance, including daily weights to prevent fluid overload.
7. Observe closely for sepsis. Obtain frequent cultures. Avoid urinary catheterization unless absolutely necessary. Early specific antibiotic therapy when indicated.
8. Prophylactic antacid therapy with aluminum hydroxide.
9. Reduce dosages of digitalis, aminoglycosides, based on cretinine clearances. Obtain drug levels when indicated.
10. Monitor BUN, serum creatinine and electrolytes, hematocrit, creatinine clearance, daily weights, and ECG closely.
11. Early dialysis for uremia, hyperkalemia, metabolic acidosis, hypermagnesemia, and volume overload.

Diuretic phase:

1. Accurate fluid and electrolyte replacement of insensible, urinary, and GI losses.
2. Monitor renal function tests, serum electrolytes, and daily weights closely.
3. Continue judicious restriction of protein until BUN and creatinine show signs of improvement.

POSTRENAL FAILURE
Etiology

Mechanical obstruction of urine outflow:

Ureteral obstruction: calculi, clots, papillary necrosis, surgical ligature, fungal or pyrogenic factors, edema caused by instrumentation or infection, retroperitoneal fibrosis, metastatic tumor.

Bladder neck obstruction: prostate hypertrophy, foreign body, metastatic tumor, functional or neurogenic factors.

Note: Unilateral occlusion of one ureter will not cause oliguria if the contralateral kidney is normal and unobstructed.

Signs and symptoms

Anuria suggests the obstruction is complete and bilateral.
Alternating oliguria and polyuria suggest intermittent obstruc-
tion.
Examine patient for distended bladder, tender kidneys.
BUN: may increase because of diffusion of urea.
BUN–creatinine ratio > 10:1
Urinalysis: absence of proteinuria and abnormal urinary sedi-
ment.
Plain abdominal film may show calculi.
IVP if ureteral obstruction is suspected.
Renal arteriogram or renal scan if renal artery obstruction is
suspected.

Therapeutic guidelines

1. Decompression to prevent permanent renal damage/infec-
   tion:
     Foley catheter or suprapubic cystostomy
     Ureteral catheter or ureterostomy
     Nephrostomy if indicated
2. Antibiotics if indicated.
3. Monitor for postobstructive diuresis—massive salt and water
   losses caused by impaired tubular resorption of sodium
   and water.

PANCREATITIS, ACUTE
Types

Edematous.
Hemorrhagic.

Etiology

Cholelithiasis or alcoholism are the most common causes.
Other causes include surgical trauma, hyperparathyroidism,
aminoaciduria, hyperlipidemia, hemochromatosis, vascular
stasis, toxins, and medications.

Signs and symptoms

Progressive, severe upper abdominal pain, radiating around
or through to the back at the midline.
The pain may be deep, constant, or colicky; aggravated by
lying supine, improved by sitting up.
Associated with early vomiting or retching, nausea, anorexia,
fever, and tachycardia.
Hypotension and shock may occur with hemorrhagic pancreatitis.

There may be a previous history of pancreatitis, gallstones, alcoholism, hyperlipidemia, etc.

Examination may reveal upper abdominal tenderness, with varying degrees of guarding and rebound tenderness.

Absent bowel sounds (paralytic ileus).

Fever, tachycardia, leukocytosis.

Mild jaundice (biliary tract obstruction, hemolysis).

Flank ecchymosis (Grey-Turner sign).

Periumbilical ecchymosis (Cullen's sign).

Pleural effusion and ascites.

Complications

Shock (from retroperitoneal and intraluminal fluid sequestration, ascites, and vomiting).

Acute renal failure (acute tubular necrosis).

Carpopedal spasm (hypocalcemia caused by fat necrosis with formation of calcium soaps).

Pancreatic pseudocyst formation (appears after 1-2 weeks).

Pancreatic abscess formation (appears after 2-3 weeks).

Rupture or thrombosis of major vessels.

Infection (pancreatic abscess, cholangitis, pneumonia).

Omental fat necrosis.

Perforation of adjacent viscus.

Respiratory failure (tachypnea and hypoxia).

Diagnostic tests

Serum amylase elevated.

Urine amylase elevated.

Urine amylase–creatinine clearance ratio increased.

Serum and urine lipase elevated.

Serum calcium decreased.

Transient hyperglycemia and glycosuria.

CBC: leukocytosis and hemoconcentration.

Check: electrolytes, glucose, BUN, creatinine, calcium, protein, magnesium, bilirubin.

Abdominal x-ray: jejunal "sentinel loop" (in 50%) ileus, colon cutoff sign.

Pancreatic calcification suggests chronic pancreatitis.

Chest x-ray: pneumonitis and pleural effusion (in 50%).

OCG: nonvisualization may occur even if biliary tract normal.

IVC: nonvisualization less common unless biliary tract disease exists.

Ascitic and pleural fluid may contain blood and amylase.

Laparotomy may be necessary for a differential diagnosis.

Differential diagnosis

Acute cholecystitis.
Choledocholithiasis.
Perforated peptic ulcer.
Mesenteric thrombosis.

Myocardial infarction.
Acute renal failure.
Acute appendicitis.
High small bowel obstruction.

Therapeutic guidelines

1. NPO; NG suction.
2. Adequate crystalloid replacement and maintenance fluids; colloid if indicated.
3. Monitor CVP, urine output, hemocrit, vital signs closely.
4. Check: chest x-ray and ABG if respiratory distress develops.
5. Analgesics: meperidine (causes less sphincter spasm than morphine or other opiates).
6. Blood transfusion for hemorrhagic pancreatitis.
7. Insulin for significant hyperglycemia.
8. Calcium gluconate for severe hypocalcemia.
9. Antibiotics for pancreatic abscesses, cholangitis, pneumonia, or other infection.
10. Anticholinergic (atropine, 0.2-1.0 mg IM q4-6h).
11. Sedation if indicated (diazepam).
12. Surgery (if indicated) may include:
    Peritoneal lavage.
    Drainage of pancreatic bed.
    Resection of necrotic tissue.
    Distal pancreatectomy.
    Cholecystostomy, gastrostomy, feeding jejunostomy.

PAROTITIS (Postoperative)
Incidence

1/1000 postoperative cases; bilateral in 10%-15%.

Risk

75% are 70 years old or older.
Major abdominal surgery, fractured hips.
Severe trauma; debilitated, patients with carcinoma.

Etiology

Poor oral hygiene, dehydration, anticholinergic drugs (atropine).

Pathophysiology

Transductal inoculation of bacteria (usually staphylococcus).
Bacterial invasion of Stenson's duct; then parenchyma (abscesses).
Spread to deep fascial planes, auditory canal, skin of face.

Signs and symptoms

Onset: few hours to weeks postoperatively, with parotid pain, swelling, tenderness, cellulitis, fever, and leukocytosis.
Ability to express and culture pus from Stenson's duct.

Differential diagnosis

Benign postoperative swelling caused by straining, belladonna, or neuromuscular depolarizing drugs.

Preventive measures

Adequate hydration, proper oral hygiene.

Therapeutic guidelines

1. Irradiation if less than 1 day of swelling (analgesia).
2. Broad-spectrum antibiotic against staphylococci.
3. Surgical drainage if progresses longer than 3 days.

PERFORATED PEPTIC ULCER
Etiology

Free perforation of a duodenal or gastric ulcer is a catastrophic event, one of the classic causes of the acute surgical abdomen. Gastric acid in contact with the peritoneal surface is an important factor in the pain pattern and associated symptoms. Internal fluid sequestration occurs rapidly and may be massive because of the chemical burn produced by gastric acid on the peritoneum. Signs of ECF volume deficit follow, including peripheral vasoconstriction, diaphoresis, tachycardia, hypotension, oliguria, and shock. Massive hemorrhage is uncommon but may be present in up to 8%. With posterior perforation, the pain is more toward the back, less well localized, and anterior abdominal wall signs are absent.

Signs and symptoms

Free perforation of a duodenal or gastric ulcer causes sudden, epigastric pain, nausea, and retching or vomiting. Shoulder pain may be present with phrenic irritation. The pain spreads rapidly and may localize to the RLQ, mimicking acute appendicitis. Symptoms may improve temporarily. A history of peptic ulcer pain is useful but may be absent in 10%-20%.
Examination may reveal a scaphoid, boardlike, rigid abdomen with rebound tenderness, absent liver dullness, and absent bowel sounds. Temperature may be subnormal. Tachycardia and signs of shock may be present.

Diagnostic tests

Upright chest x-ray (or left lateral decubitus): free air in 75%.
Upper GI series with Gastrografin (meglucamine diatrizoate) if free air not demonstrated.
Elevated hematocrit, white count, amylase, and LDH.

Differential diagnosis

Acute pancreatitis.
Acute cholecystitis with perforation.
Intestinal obstruction.
Perforated diverticulitis.
Perforated appendicitis.

Therapeutic guidelines

Preoperative:
1. NPO; NG suction via Levine or sump tube.
2. IV fluid resuscitation and correction of electrolyte abnormalities.
3. Adequate urine output should be established.
4. Transfusion if indicated.
5. IV antibiotics.

Postoperative:
1. NG decompression until passing flatus or feces.
2. IV fluids.
3. Antibiotics if indicated.
4. Vital signs, urine output, CVP, CBC, electrolytes should be monitored closely.

PNEUMONIA
Etiology

Organisms that colonize the upper respiratory tract may reach the alveoli by inhalation or aspiration: *Streptococcus pneumoniae* (pneumococcal or lobar pneumonia) 90%; other bacteria, *Mycoplasma,* fungi, and viruses.

Signs and symptoms

Shaking chill, fever, productive cough, pleuritic pain, tachypnea.
Nasal flaring, dullness, tubular breath sounds, coarse rales.
Chest x-ray: infiltrates, densities, or opacifications of segments or lobes:
   Lobar pneumonia (pneumococcus).
   Upper lobe *(Klebsiella).*
   Several abscesses and infiltrates (staphylococcus).
   Small abscesses *(Pseudomonas).*
   Infiltrate with effusion (streptococcus).
Polymorphonuclear leukocytosis.
Leukopenia if overwhelming infection.

Diagnostic tests

Sputum Gram stain and culture, blood cultures.
Transtracheal aspiration useful in obtaining excellent sputum samples in patients unable to produce sputum and for anaerobic cultures.

Rarely, needle aspiration, bronchial brushings, and open-lung biopsy may be indicated.

Differential diagnosis

Atelectasis, pulmonary embolism, congestive heart failure.

Complications

Pleural effusion, empyema, abscess formation, meningitis, arthritis, endocarditis.

Therapeutic guidelines

1. Encourage deep breathing and coughing; nasotracheal suction if unable to cough.
2. Administer chest physical therapy with postural drainage for thick secretions.
3. Ensure adequate hydration, expectorants, humidified air.
4. Give analgesics for pleuritic pain (avoid depressing cough reflex if possible).
5. Give oxygen therapy if cyanotic or dyspneic; caution in carbon dioxide-retaining patients.
6. Give antipyretics if increased metabolic demands resulting from fever endanger the patient.
7. Do NG decompression if necessary for gastric dilation or ileus.
8. Drain empyema if present.

Antibiotics for infections:

1. Pneumococcal (90%): penicillin or a cephalosporin.
2. Staphylococcal (1%-5%): a penicillinase-resistant penicillin or cephalothin.
3. *Klebsiella* (1%-5%): cephalothin alone or with aminoglycoside.
4. *Haemophilus* (1%): ampicillin or tetracycline.
5. *Proteus*: ampicillin, cephalosporin, or aminoglycoside.
6. *Pseudomonas*: aminoglycoside alone or with carbenicillin.
7. *Bacteroides*: chloramphenicol or clindamycin.
8. *Mycoplasma*: tetracycline or erythromycin.

PNEUMOTHORAX
Etiology

The most common causes are traumatic and idiopathic (spontaneous).

Complication of chronic obstructive pulmonary disease, abscess, tuberculosis, cancer.

Signs and symptoms

Sudden dyspnea, hyperpnea, pleuritic pain, cyanosis, and shock.

Increased resonance, decreased breath sounds, mediastinal shift.

Chest x-ray: air in pleural space, collapsed lung.

Differential diagnosis

Myocardial infarction, pulmonary embolism, acute pericarditis.

Types

1. Open (puncture in visceral pleura large, not sealed off).
2. Closed (puncture in visceral pleura sealed off, self-limited).
3. Tension (puncture in visceral pleura small but does not seal off; acts like a flap valve).

Complications

Scarring, hydrothorax, empyema, recurrent pneumothorax.

Therapeutic guidelines

1. Small pneumothorax ($<$ 10%-15%) without tension: observe carefully.
2. Indications for chest tube thoracostomy:
   Unilateral pneumothorax $>$ 15%.
   Pneumothorax associated with pulmonary disease.
   Bilateral pneumothorax of any size.
   Recurrent pneumothorax.
   Tension pneumothorax.
   Hemopneumothorax.
3. Monitor carefully with chest x-rays.
4. Indications for open thoracotomy, pleural abrasion:
   Persistent air leak beyond 7-10 days.
   Recurrent pneumothorax.

PORPHYRIA, ACUTE INTERMITTENT
Etiology

An inherited metabolic defect in heme synthesis. Acute attacks may be provoked by certain medications or by pregnancy, menstruation, infection, alcohol, or lead. By increasing ALA synthetase, large quantities of ALA and PBG are formed and excreted in the bile and urine.

Signs and symptoms

Recurrent attacks of severe abdominal pain, vomiting, and constipation.

Pain may mimic appendicitis or intestinal obstruction, but the pain is out of proportion to physical findings. Association with muscular weakness, mental symptoms, and family history may lead to the correct diagnosis.

Examination may reveal minimal abdominal findings.

Multiple surgical scars may be present on the abdomen.

Muscular weakness, decreased reflexes, and abnormal behavior may be evident.

Tachycardia and moderate hypertension are characteristic.

Fever and leukocytosis suggest concomitant infection.

Diagnostic tests

Qualitative urinary porphobilinogen (Watson-Schwartz test): positive.

Quantitative urinary ALA and PBG should be obtained for confirmation.

Differential diagnosis

Appendicitis.

Bowel obstruction.

Cholecystitis.

Pancreatitis.

Peptic ulcer.

Renal colic.

Heavy metal poisoning.

Therapeutic guidelines

1. No specific therapy is available at the present time.
2. Chlorpromazine, 50-100 mg, may produce rapid improvement of abdominal and muscle pain.
3. Glucose, 10-15 mg/hour orally or IV, may be very effective.
4. Adequate hydration and correction of electrolyte abnormalities should be ensured.
5. Mechanical ventilation may be necessary for respiratory paralysis.
6. Use of barbiturates, sulfonamides, estrogens, and alcohol should be avoided.
7. Narcotic use should be limited because of addiction risk.

PULMONARY EDEMA, ACUTE
Etiology

Acute pulmonary edema of *cardiac* origin may be caused by one of the following, which produce increased pulmonary capillary pressure:
1. Left ventricular failure:
   Myocardial infarction.
   Acute decompensation of chronic left ventricular failure—valvular, hypertensive, or cardiomyopathic.
2. Mitral stenosis.
3. Volume overload.

Noncardiac pulmonary edema may result from:
1. Increased permeability of the capillary membrane:
   Adult respiratory distress syndrome.
   Gram-negative sepsis.
   Disseminated intravascular coagulation.
   Idiosyncrasy or hypersensitivity reaction.
   Noxious inhalants (smoke or gas).

Oxygen toxicity.
Radiation pneumonitis.
Uremia.
2. Decreased plasma oncotic pressure:
Hypoalbuminemia.
3. Lymphatic obstruction:
Silicosis.
Lymphangitic carcinomatosis.
4. Uncertain etiology:
Neurogenic pulmonary edema.
Postanesthetic pulmonary edema.
High-altitude pulmonary edema.
Acute pulmonary embolism.
Heroin overdose.

Note: For purposes of this section, only pulmonary edema of *cardiac* origin will be discussed.

Signs and symptoms

The excessive transudation of serous fluid, appearing first in the interstitial spaces of the lungs and later in the alveolar spaces, gives rise to a spectrum of findings:
1. Dyspnea with rapid shallow breathing, apprehension, and diaphoresis; may progress to severe orthopnea with production of pink, frothy sputum and cyanosis.
2. Rales may be absent at first, then numerous and moist.
3. Chest x-ray may show linear shadows (Kerley's B lines), thickening and loss of definition of blood vessels, perihilar haze, butterfly pattern, pleural effusion, and, finally, confluent shadows of uniform density.
4. Pao_2 progressively decreases.
5. $Paco_2$ may be low during tachypnea, then increase with respiratory failure.
6. pH may decrease if edema is severe (metabolic and respiratory acidosis).
7. Total lung capacity decreases.
8. PAD and PWP are elevated.

Therapeutic guidelines (for acute pulmonary edema of cardiac origin)

1. *Establish diagnosis:* Check ABG and pH, intake and output, trend in daily weights, urine output, chest x-ray, ECG, as well as CBC, electrolytes, etc. This can be done while therapy is being initiated.
2. *Measures to improve ventilation:*
Sitting position in chair or feet dangling over side of bed.
Oxygen therapy as determined by respiratory parameters and presence of preexisting lung disease.

3. *Measures to reduce pulmonary capillary pressure:*
   Morphine sulfate, 3-5 mg IV q3-6h (helps to relieve anxiety, decrease tachypnea, promote venous pooling, and decrease venous return); caution with hypotension, bronchial asthma, chronic obstructive pulmonary disease, intracranial bleeding.
   Diuretics: furosemide, 40 mg, or ethacrynic acid, 50 mg IV (reduces intravascular pressure and secondarily reduces pulmonary capillary pressure).
   Restricted fluid and sodium intake.
   Rotating tourniquets q15-20 minutes (reduces venous return).
   Phlebotomy (250-500 ml): if fluid-overloaded and hypotension not present; usually reserved for severe or refractory pulmonary edema.
   Vasodilators (nitrates, phentolamine, hydralazine, nitroprusside): when venous and/or arterial resistance need further reduction.
4. *Measures to increase myocardial contractility:*
   Digitalization: especially for left ventricular failure and/or rapid atrial fibrillation; caution in cases of acute myocardial infarction.
   Catecholamines (dopamine, isoproterenol, etc.): in low doses for short-term therapy of severe pulmonary edema resistant to standard therapy.
   Glucagon: may be useful in presence of beta blockade (propranolol administration).
5. *Other measures:*
   Aminophylline: for acute pulmonary edema complicated by bronchospasm.
   Mechanical ventilation: when respiratory failure is imminent.
   PEEP: if severe hypoxia persists with adequate mechanical ventilation.
   Swan-Ganz monitoring as a guide to optimal therapy.
   Antiarrhythmic therapy when indicated.
   Antihypertensive agents if indicated.

PULMONARY EMBOLISM
Etiology

Major causes of pulmonary thromboembolism include:
   Deep venous thrombosis.
   Acute myocardial infarction.
   Chronic congestive heart failure.
   Atrial fibrillation.
   Cardiomyopathies.

Risk factors are many, including:

Previous pulmonary embolism.	Prolonged immobility.
Postsurgical.	Old age.
Posttrauma.	Obesity.
Postpartum.	Polycythemia.
Malignancy.	Oral contraceptives.

Signs and symptoms

Massive embolism to the main pulmonary artery or one of its major branches leads to acute dilation of the right ventricle and pulmonary artery, with signs of acute right ventricular failure and cardiovascular collapse. Smaller emboli in patients with preexisting cardiopulmonary disease may also precipitate serious problems. The reliability of signs and symptoms in pulmonary embolism has been questioned, but these may include sudden dyspnea, tachypnea, substernal chest pain, and cough. If pulmonary infarction develops (12-24 hours later), there may be pleuritic chest pain, hemoptysis, and fever.

Initial examination may reveal a patient in obvious distress, with severe apprehension, labored breathing, cyanosis, and signs of cardiovascular collapse. There may be an accentuated pulmonary second sound, right ventricular heave, S_3 gallop, rales, tachycardia, and an irregular pulse. With pulmonary infarction, signs of pulmonary consolidation, pleural friction rub, and fever develop. Extremities should be examined for signs of thrombophlebitis.

Diagnostic tests

CBC: leukocytosis (up to 15,000, left shift may be absent).

Triad of increased LDH, bilirubin, and normal SGOT (rare).

Fibrin split products may be present.

ABGs: Pao_2 and $Paco_2$ are typically decreased.

ECG: S_1Q_3 pattern, right ventricular strain (T inversion V_1-V_3), right bundle branch block, P pulmonale (tall P waves II, III, aV$_F$), right axis shift, Q waves in II, III, aV$_F$, sinus tachycardia, atrial fibrillation, or flutter.

Chest x-ray (findings may be minor or nonspecific): elevation of hemidiaphragm, pleural effusion, hyperlucent areas, right ventricular enlargement, dilated pulmonary arteries, pulmonary infarction.

Lung scan if normal excludes diagnosis; an abnormal perfusion scan, however, may result from many other causes, but the ventilation scan should be normal.

Pulmonary arteriography is the definitive diagnostic procedure but is dangerous; it is usually reserved for difficult diagnostic cases, such as when heparin therapy is a relative contraindication or before pulmonary embolectomy.

Swan-Ganz catheterization: CVP and PAD pressures elevated; pulmonary capillary wedge pressure normal or low.

Differential diagnosis

Acute myocardial infarction.
Congestive heart failure.
Pneumonia.

Complications

Secondary thrombus with further blockage of pulmonary vessels.
Pulmonary infarction.
Secondary infection of infarcted lung tissue.
Recurrent pulmonary embolism.
Chronic pulmonary hypertension.
Sudden death from saddle embolus.

Therapeutic guidelines

1. Oxygen in adequate amounts, determined by respiratory parameters.
2. Heparinization (in absence of absolute contraindication), usually for 7-10 days; then oral anticoagulation for at least 4-6 months.
3. Thrombolytic drugs such as streptokinase or urokinase.
4. Vena caval interruption is indicated by:
    Recurrent pulmonary embolus despite adequate anticoagulation.
    Anticoagulation is contraindicated.
    Recurrent septic emboli from pelvis.
5. Surgical embolectomy is indicated for massive pulmonary embolism to main pulmonary arteries with shock and hypoxia refractory to medical therapy.
6. Other measures:
    Antiarrhythmic therapy if indicated.
    Analgesic for pleuritis, e.g., meperidine, 50-100 mg q3-4h.
    IM injections should be avoided during anticoagulation therapy.
7. Prophylactic measures:
    Ace bandages or antiembolic stockings.
    Active leg exercises and breathing exercises.
    Early ambulation postsurgically.
    Low-dose heparin (5000 units SC q8-12h) in high-risk patients.

RESPIRATORY FAILURE (ARDS)
Synonyms

ARDS: Adult respiratory distress syndrome.
Hemorrhagic lung, postperfusion lung.

Posttraumatic pulmonary insufficiency.
Shock lung, Vietnam lung, wet lung.

Etiology

Aspiration pneumonia (damaged epithelium from low pH gastric contents).
Fat embolism (long bone fractures).
Fluid overload (especially if renal failure is present).
Inhaled toxic agents (smoke, phosgene, nitrogen dioxide).
Ischemic pulmonary injury (hemorrhagic shock).
Massive CNS injury (hypoventilation).
Microatelectasis (recumbency, operation, anesthesia, narcotics).
Oxygen toxicity (damaged pulmonary endothelial cells).
Pulmonary contusion, edema, embolism, infarction, infection.
Pulmonary microembolism:
    Soft tissue trauma from surgery or accident.
    Multiple transfusions.
    Disseminated intravascular coagulation.
Sepsis (endotoxin-damaged pulmonary capillaries).
Shock (septic, anaphylactic, hemorrhagic, cardiogenic).
Viable leukocytes in fresh whole blood.

Signs and symptoms

Worsened by underlying pulmonary insufficiency.
First stage (interstitial edema):
    Dyspnea, tachypnea mild to moderate.
    Hypocapnia may be present because of increased ventilation.
    Hypoxia easily corrected by oxygen therapy.
    Chest x-ray: diffuse ground-glass appearance.
Second stage (alveolar edema):
    Dyspnea, tachypnea marked.
    Signs of CNS hypoxia develop.
    Labored breathing ensues.
    Hypercapnia because of fatigue, ventilation/perfusion abnormalities.
    Chest x-ray: diffuse alveolar filling process.
    Functional residual capacity decreased.
    Compliance decreased.
    Ventilation/perfusion abnormalities worsen.
    Arteriovenous shunting increases.
    Diffusion capacities are impaired.
    Increased vascular permeability (leaking of fluid, protein, cells).
    Hyaline membranes form from conversion of fibrinogen to fibrin.

Complications

Pulmonary infection.
Progressive pulmonary damage.
Pulmonary fibrosis.

Therapeutic guidelines

Prophylactic measures:

Avoid aspiration, fluid overloading.
Micropore filters for multiple blood transfusions.
Avoid oxygen toxicity (check ABGs frequently).
Treat sepsis early (drainage, antibiotics).
Maintain adequate hemoglobin level.
Use frozen, washed red cells when possible.

General measures:

Accurate fluid balance (to prevent overload).
Correct coagulation abnormalities appropriately.
Consider tracheostomy, parenteral hyperalimentation.
Antibiotics for bacterial infections.
Dialysis for renal failure.
Steroids (prednisone or methylprednisolone, 1 g/day) for:
  Aspiration pneumonia.
  Fat embolism.
  Septic shock.

Specific measures:

Oxygenation (may require high FIO_2 for adequate PaO_2).
Intubation if steady downhill course is demonstrated with hypoxia, hypercapnia, lactic acidosis, or shock. General indications include:

1. Inability to effectively handle secretions.
2. Upper airway obstruction.
3. Prevention of aspiration.
4. Mechanical ventilation.

Ventilation with volume-regulated respirator if:

1. Vital capacity $< 10\text{-}15$ ml/kg.
2. Inspiratory force < -25 cm H_2O.
3. A-a $DO_2 > 300$ torr (with $FIO_2 = 1$).
4. VD/VT $> 60\%$.
5. $PaO_2 < 70$ torr (on 40% mask).
6. $PaCO_2 > 48$ torr (unless chronic hypercapnia).
7. pH < 7.25.
8. Respiratory rate $> 35\text{-}40$ per minute.

Ventilator settings (readjust as indicated):

1. Expiratory resistance: off.
2. FIO_2: 40%-60%.
3. Normal pressure limit: 40 mm Hg.
4. Peak flow: 40 liters/minute.
5. Sensitivity: 0-2 while machine is off.
6. Rate: 12-14/minute (check $PaCO_2$).

7. Sighs: 6 per hour.
8. Sigh pressure limit: 50 mm Hg.
9. Sigh volume: 1100 ml (10-15 ml/kg).
10. Temperature gauge: 4-5 (nebulized mixture).
11. VT: 10 ml/kg.

SEPTIC SHOCK
Etiology

Septic shock can be caused by any microorganism capable of producing infection. For purposes of this presentation, however, only gram-negative sepsis will be considered. The bacteria usually encountered include *E. coli, Klebsiella, Proteus, Pseudomonas, Bacteroides,* and *Serratia.* Frequent sources of infection are listed immediately below. Patients at high risk for gram-negative infection include those with underlying cardiac, pulmonary, hepatic, and renal disease, diabetes mellitus, advanced malignancy, and those who are immunosuppressed or taking steroids.

Genitourinary (operation, instrumentation).
Lung (tracheostomy, ventilators).
GI (peritonitis, abscess, biliary tract).
Skin (burns, infections).
Catheters (IV, hyperalimentation).
Septic abortions.
Postpartum infections.

Signs and symptoms

The triad of mild hyperventilation, respiratory alkalosis, and altered sensorium may be the earliest sign of gram-negative infection. The WBC is usually elevated but may be normal or low with a shift to immature forms. A falling platelet count (< 150,000) may also occur early on. Chills, fever, hypotension, rapid deterioration of pulmonary function, and respiratory failure are common. The hemodynamic pattern depends on the volume status of the patient before sepsis:

Volume status	Normovolemic	Hypovolemic
Hemodynamic pattern	Hyperdynamic	Hypodynamic
Blood pressure	Low	Low
Cardiac output	High	Low
Blood volume	Normal or high	Low
CVP	Normal or high	Low
Peripheral resistance	Low	High
Extremities	Warm and dry	Cold and cyanotic
AV O_2 difference	Small	Large

Therapeutic guidelines

1. *Early surgical debridement or drainage* is most important, as soon as vital parameters are stabilized.

2. *Fluid replacement:*
   Crystalloid infusion (monitor urine output, sensorium, CVP, blood pressure, PAD, PWP, cardiac output, etc.).
   Blood (hematocrit at least 30%-35%).
3. *Antibiotics* (as indicated by previous culture reports), or:
   Cephalothin, 6-8 g/day IV, divided q4-6h.
   Gentamicin, 3-5 mg/kg/day IV, divided q8h.
   Clindamycin or chloramphenicol if *Bacteroides* suspected.
   Modify therapy as indicated by clinical data.
4. *Early pulmonary support:* Airway, ventilation, humidified oxygen (see *Respiratory failure*).
5. *Steroids:* Controversial. Inotropic effect on heart, mild peripheral vasodilation, may stabilize lysosomal and cellular membranes. Methylprednisolone, 15-30 mg/kg IV over 5-10 minutes. Repeat once in 2-4 hours if needed.
6. *Vasopressors:* Replace volume deficits first. Dopamine is advocated in low-dose infusion ($< 30 \mu g/kg/minute$) for its inotropic and chronotropic effects, low potential for tachyarrhythmias, and ability to enhance renal blood flow. Avoid vasoconstrictors.
7. *Digitalis:* For congestive heart failure or atrial fibrillation. Ensure correction of hypokalemia.
8. *Experimental:*
   GIK: glucose 1 mg/kg, insulin 1.5 units/kg, potassium 15 mEq by IV infusion.
   Nitroglycerin ointment.
   Hyperalimentation.

SMALL BOWEL OBSTRUCTION
Etiology

Mechanical occlusion of the small bowel lumen may be caused by:

Adhesions.	Tumors.
Hernias.	Strictures.
Intussusception.	Extrinsic masses.
Gallstone ileus.	Volvulus.
Bezoars.	

As fluid and gas accumulate proximally, distention of the small bowel occurs. This leads to peristaltic waves and further distention caused by increased intestinal secretion. Dehydration and electrolyte abnormalities occur from both internal sequestration and vomiting. Pathophysiologic changes occurring with dehydration include oliguria, azotemia, hemoconcentration, tachycardia, low CVP, reduction of cardiac output, hypotension, and hypovolemic shock. With increased intraluminal pressure, bowel wall edema and impairment of venous return can occur, leading to further fluid and electrolyte sequestration. With closed-loop obstruction, gangrene and perforation may occur with the liberation of toxic materials from necrotic and bacterial sources.

Signs and symptoms

Progressive, severe, crampy abdominal pain, followed by nausea, vomiting, obstipation, and distention. When these symptoms are succeeded by continuous severe abdominal pain, strangulation with peritonitis should be suspected.

Examination may reveal abdominal distention, visible peristaltic waves, tenderness, and dehydration. Later, peritoneal signs and further dehydration may develop.

Bowel sounds may be hyperactive with rushes and tinkles during crampy pain; silence suggests strangulation or adynamic ileus.

Rectal examination may reveal a tender pelvic mass; occult blood may signify a mucosal ischemic process.

Tachycardia and hypotension may result from hypovolemia or peritonitis.

Fever and leukocytosis suggest strangulation or perforation.

Diagnostic tests

Abdominal x-rays may demonstrate gas pattern proximal to the obstruction, with air-fluid levels in the upright or decubitus position and absence of gas in the large bowel.

Hematocrit increases with hypovolemia because of vomiting and "third space" losses.

Urinalysis reflects dehydration with high specific gravity and acetonuria.

Electrolyte and acid-base abnormalities may occur early, especially with proximal SBO.

Serum amylase may increase to twice normal.

Differential diagnosis

Adynamic ileus.
Appendicitis.
Ascites.
Cholecystitis.
Large bowel obstruction.
Mesenteric vascular occlusion.
Pancreatitis.
Peptic ulcer.

Therapeutic guidelines

Preoperative:
1. NPO; NG suction or long tube decompression.
2. Fluid resuscitation and correction of electrolyte abnormalities.
3. Bladder catheterization to monitor urine output.
4. Other: antibiotics, CVP, Swan-Ganz (when indicated).

5. Early surgery (before strangulation develops) is associated with a much lower morbidity and mortality.

Postoperative:

1. NG suction is continued until bowel sounds are present and the patient is passing flatus or feces.
2. Antibiotics, when indicated, are given a full course.
3. IV fluids are administered appropriately.
4. Vital signs, urine output, CVP, CBC, electrolytes should be monitored closely.

THYROID NODULE

The risk of cancer in the 1-cm thyroid nodule may be as high as 15% in adults and up to 50% in children.

Benign

Follicular adenoma.
Papillary adenoma.
Hürthle cell "adenoma."

Malignant

Papillary: 60%-73%
Follicular: 13%-18%
Anaplastic: 10%-15%
Medullary: 5%-6%
Others include Hürthle cell carcinoma, lymphoma, lymphosarcoma, melanoma, and metastatic cancer from other sites (breast, kidney, bronchus).

Signs and symptoms

1. Symptoms of hyper- or hypothyroidism.
2. Rapid, painless increase in size suggests anaplastic cancer.
3. Rapid, painful increase in size suggests hemorrhage into a cyst or adenoma, or subacute thyroiditis.
4. Medication history may reveal use of goitrogens such as iodine excess (expectorants, antiasthmatics).
5. Irradiation of the head, neck, or mediastinum in infancy or childhood is associated with an increased incidence of papillary cancer.
6. Familial goiters may be caused by enzyme deficiencies and subsequent chronic TSH stimulation.
7. Family history of medullary carcinoma of the thyroid or other endocrinopathy (multiple endocrine adenomatosis II: medullary cancer, pheochromocytoma, hyperparathyroidism).
8. Late signs and symptoms of malignancy:
   a. Obstruction with dyspnea and dysphagia.
   b. Hoarseness from tumor invasion of the recurrent laryngeal nerve.

  c. Cervical lymphadenopathy caused by regional metastases.
  d. Nontraumatic bone pain or pulmonary symptoms as a result of distant metastases (primarily bone and lung).

Signs of malignancy

1. Firm or hard, irregular, nontender, solitary nodule.
2. Fixation of the gland with limitation of movement of the thyroid on swallowing.
3. Cervical lymphadenopathy.
4. Hoarseness because of vocal cord paralysis (confirmed by indirect laryngoscopy).
5. Horner's syndrome.
6. A dominant cold nodule in a multinodular goiter.

Diagnostic tests

1. Establish the status of thyroid function:
   a. Serum thyroxine level.
   b. T_3 resin uptake.
   c. TSH level.
2. Antithyroid antibody (positive in Hashimoto's thyroiditis).
3. Serum calcitonin level elevated (medullary cancer).
4. Cervical x-rays: tracheal distortion or compression.
5. Chest x-ray: look for any lung metastases.
6. Bone survey: osteolytic metastases.
7. Radioactive iodine–uptake and scanning studies: Define the degree of uptake or suppression of individual nodules. Hyperfunctioning (hot) nodules usually are not malignant, but follicular carcinomas may retain the ability to accumulate iodine. Other malignancies may be coincidental. Hypofunctioning (cold) nodules have a 20%-30% chance of being malignant.
8. Sonography: A solid mass that does not regress on thyroid suppression therapy is an indication for surgery. Confirmation of cystic lesion may allow simple needle aspiration.
9. Needle biopsy: While this technique may be useful when thyroiditis is suspected, it is not generally recommended by most surgeons in the diagnosis of thyroid cancer, since negative biopsies may not be representative.

Differential diagnosis

Adenomatous goiter.
Benign adenomas or cysts.
Autoimmune thyroiditis (Hashimoto's thyroiditis).
Subacute thyroiditis (de Quervain's thyroiditis).
Acute suppurative thyroiditis.

Therapeutic guidelines

Thyroid suppression therapy: This may be indicated in patients with hypofunctioning (cold) nodules, unless there is high suspicion of carcinoma. It will frequently suppress the TSH-dependent adenomatous goiter and struma lymphomatosa, but this may require 3-6 months for adequate evaluation. Regression of the nodule requires continual administration of thyroid hormone to prevent recurrence. Failure to cause regression of the nodule is an indication for surgery.

Surgical indications:
1. Solitary nodule (controversial).
2. Nodule suspicious for cancer.
3. Dominant cold nodule in a multinodular goiter.
4. Biopsy that confirms presence of cancer.
5. Elevated serum calcitonin level.
6. History of local radiation in childhood.
7. Persistence or recurrence of a mass following aspiration of a cyst.
8. Failure of the nodule to regress on suppression therapy.
9. Solid mass on sonography.

Preoperative:
1. The patient should be in a euthyroid state.
2. Hyperphysiologic doses of thyroid hormone are given for at least 1 week to suppress TSH and shrink the thyroid gland.
3. Iodine, propylthiouracil, and propranolol are used primarily for hyperthyroidism (Graves' disease, toxic adenoma, etc.).

Operative:
1. In biopsy of a thyroid nodule for suspected malignancy, total lobectomy and isthmusectomy is often the procedure of choice. The concern here is to excise an adequate margin of tissue and the fact that reoperation may be hazardous.
2. Indications for total or near-total thyroidectomy include:
   a. Multicentricity.
   b. Previous irradiation.
   c. Invasive follicular cancer.
   d. Operable anaplastic cancer.
   e. Medullary thyroid cancer.
   f. Lymphoma.
3. Limited or modified neck dissections are performed when indicated. Occasionally, radical neck dissections are performed.

Postoperative:
1. Postoperatively, most patients with benign tumors, papillary cancer, or follicular cancer should receive suppressive doses of thyroid hormone.

2. For metastatic disease caused by papillary or follicular cancer, radiation therapy or radioactive iodine to ablate residual thyroid tissue may be useful.
3. With anaplastic carcinoma, radiation therapy and suppressive doses of thyroid hormone have been recommended. Chemotherapy is under investigation.
4. For medullary cancer of the thyroid, radiation therapy may be useful for local metastases. Serum calcitonin levels should be followed for recurrence of tumor.

THYROID STORM
Etiology

Hyperthyroidism (Graves' disease, toxic goiter, etc.) *plus stress:* surgery (inadequate preparation), trauma, infection, diabetic ketoacidosis, toxemia of pregnancy, etc.

Signs and symptoms

The effects reflect abrupt, marked sympathetic stimulation:
CNS: tremor, anxiety, irritability, psychosis, delirium, stupor, coma.
Cardiovascular: marked tachycardia, arrhythmia, high-output cardiac failure.
GI: nausea, vomiting, diarrhea, abdominal pain.
Metabolism: hyperpyrexia, diaphoresis.

Complications

Hypotension, respiratory insufficiency, prostration, death (20%).

Preventive measures

Iodide therapy and antithyroid medication preoperatively.
Avoid atropine (parasympatholytic effects).

Therapeutic guidelines

1. Propylthiouracil, 1000 mg PO or via NG tube; then 200-400 mg q6-8h (to suppress further synthesis of thyroid hormones and decrease peripheral conversion of T_4 to T_3).
2. Sodium iodide, 1-2 g IV drip over 24 hours (to retard the release of stored hormone). Administer 1-2 hours after propylthiouracil so that the iodide load is prevented from entering new hormone synthesis.
3. Propranolol, 1-2 mg IV (test dose, monitor blood pressure and ECG); then 50-100 μg/minute IV drip to control tachycardia, tremor, etc. (blocks sympathetic effects).
4. IV fluids providing adequate:
Volume: to replace increased insensible losses.
Glucose: to replete liver glycogen and conserve body tissue.
Electrolytes: to prevent hyponatremia.
Supplemental vitamins: because of hypermetabolic state.

5. Steroids in large doses (controversial unless adrenal insufficiency present): hydrocortisone, 200-600 mg/day IV (or equivalent).
6. Digitalis if congestive heart failure or atrial fibrillation present.
7. Cooling mattress and acetaminophen to reduce body temperature.
8. Oxygen (humidified) to improve tissue oxygenation and meet high metabolic demand.
9. Monitor ECG and CVP or pulmonary capillary wedge pressure during propranolol and fluid resuscitation.
10. Treatment of precipitating factors, e.g., infection.

TRANSFUSION REACTIONS
HEMOLYTIC REACTION
Etiology

Incompatible blood (usually a clerical error).

Signs and symptoms

Usually apparent when 50 ml of blood have been given:
    Acute fever, chills, rigor, burning at infusion site.
    Chest or back pain, headache, flushing.
    Hypotension, hemoglobinuria, continued bleeding or oozing.

Complications

Shock may occur within 1 hour.
Acute renal failure.
Disseminated intravascular coagulation.

Therapeutic guidelines

Discontinue transfusion immediately; keep IV open with saline.
Recheck the labeling of donor blood and patient.
Repeat crossmatch between donor and patient.
Centrifuge sample of patient's blood and examine for free plasma hemoglobin.
Monitor urine output and check for free hemoglobin.
If an acute hemolytic reaction is determined:
1. NS, 500 ml IV over 1 hour.
2. Sodium bicarbonate, 25 mEq IV (alkalinizes urine).
3. Check CVP for further fluid replacement of D5½NS.
4. Maintain urine output at least 60 ml/hour with furosemide (40-80 mg IV) or mannitol (25 g IV).
5. If oliguric despite fluids and diuretics, treat as for acute renal failure.
6. If DIC occurs, use fresh-frozen plasma and heparin.

PYROGENIC REACTIONS
Etiology

1. Hypersensitivity to donor white cells, platelets, or plasma proteins (previously transfused or multiparous patients).
2. Bacterial contamination of donor unit (gram-negative).

Signs and symptoms

Fever, headache, tachycardia.
Progression to sepsis if unit contaminated.

Therapeutic guidelines

1. Discontinue transfusion; evaluate for hemolytic reaction.
2. If hemolysis is not present, begin antipyretics (acetaminophen, 650 mg PO).
3. Premedication with an antipyretic or the use of washed red cells may be appropriate if pyrogenic reactions recur with future transfusions.
4. Culture and Gram-stain donor unit; give appropriate treatment for sepsis if present.

URTICARIAL REACTIONS
Etiology

Hypersensitivity to donor antigen (patients with multiple transfusions).

Signs and symptoms

Hives, urticaria.

Therapeutic guidelines

1. Discontinue transfusion.
2. Diphenhydramine, 50 mg IM/IV.
3. Observe for anaphylaxis.
4. Pretreat patients with histories of urticarial reactions with diphenhydramine or use washed red cells.

CONGESTIVE HEART FAILURE
Etiology

Hypervolemia (especially with underlying cardiac disease).

Signs and symptoms

See *Congestive heart failure.*

Therapeutic guidelines

1. See *Congestive heart failure.*
2. Discontinue transfusion.
3. Avoid use of whole blood; use packed cells (slowly), monitor CVP.

ANAPHYLACTIC REACTIONS
Etiology

Antigen-antibody reaction in a sensitized individual.
Involves release of chemical mediators such as histamine.

Signs and symptoms

Respiratory: wheezing, dyspnea, choking, cyanosis.
Skin: urticaria, erythema, angioedema, pruritus.
GI: nausea, vomiting, diarrhea, abdominal pains.
Cardiovascular: vascular collapse, hypotension, diaphoresis, syncope.

Therapeutic guidelines

1. Discontinue transfusion.
2. Epinephrine, 0.5 ml (1:1000 solution) SC/IV.
3. Diphenhydramine, 50 mg IM/IV.
4. Oxygen by mask or nasal catheter if indicated.
5. Aminophylline, 500 mg IV drip, for bronchospasm.
6. Other measures may include intubation, tracheostomy, and vasopressors when indicated.
7. Further transfusions may require washed red cells.

OTHER REACTIONS

Dilutional thrombocytopenia (massive transfusions).
Cardiac arrhythmias (massive transfusion of chilled blood).
Citrate toxicity (rare, caused by hypocalcemia).
Hyperkalemia (banked blood transfusions).
Air embolism (10 ml may be fatal if patient is seriously ill).
Hemosiderosis (200-250 mg iron in 500 ml blood).
Microembolism (use micropore filters).

DELAYED REACTIONS

Delayed hemolytic reactions (3-14 days).
Alloimmunization to erythrocytes, leukocytes, platelets.
Posttransfusion purpura (4-40 days).
Infectious disease transmission:
Hepatitis (0.5%)—see individual entry.
Malaria (rare).
Syphilis (rare).
Cytomegalovirus.
Infectious mononucleosis.
Brucellosis.

ULCERATIVE COLITIS
Etiology

Not known, but immunologic factors are implicated.

Signs and symptoms

Rectal bleeding, mucopurulent diarrhea, tenesmus, rectal urgency.

Crampy abdominal pain and LLQ tenderness.

Fever, weight loss, dehydration.

Rectal: fissures, spasticity, tenderness.

Anemia, leukocytosis, elevated sedimentation rate.

Fluid and electrolyte imbalances.

Complications

Skin: erythema nodosum, erythema multiforme, etc.

Joint: arthralgia, arthritis, ankylosing spondylitis.

Eye: uveitis.

Cor: pericarditis.

GI: hepatobiliary lesions.

Colon: perforation, megacolon, malignancy (5%).

Rectal: fissures, fistulas, abscesses.

Blood: iron deficiency anemia, hypoalbuminemia.

Malnutrition and growth retardation.

Diagnostic tests

Sigmoidoscopy: dull, hyperemic, friable mucosa.

Abdominal x-ray: may reveal megacolon.

Barium enema:

Mucosal irregularities.

Effacement of haustrations.

Narrowing and shortening of large intestine.

Pseudopolyps (severe cases).

Stricture (contraction versus malignancy).

Differential diagnosis

Ischemic colitis, regional enteritis.

Colon cancer, diverticulitis, amebiasis.

Therapeutic guidelines

1. *Mild attack:* Sulfonamides, topical corticosteroids are effective.
2. *Severe attack:*

   NPO; appropriate replacement and maintenance fluids IV.

   NG suction if colonic dilatation present.

   IV corticosteroids or ACTH therapy.

   Antibiotics, potassium supplements, blood transfusion when indicated.
3. *Surgery indications:*

   Perforation of the colon.

   Hemorrhage if persistent and massive.

   Toxic megacolon persisting 48-72 hours.

Severe attacks unresponsive to medical therapy.
Carcinoma suspected or established.
Severe arthritis, uveitis, or dermatopathy.

URINARY TRACT INFECTION

Etiology

E. coli, Klebsiella-Enterobacter, Proteus vulgaris, P. mirabilis, Pseudomonas aeruginosa, Streptococcus fecalis.

Risk factors

Urinary retention following surgery, anesthesia, immobilization.
Instrumentation or catheterization.
Obstruction and stasis.
Vesicoureteral reflux.
Foreign bodies (catheters, stones).
Tumors.
Trauma.
Diabetes, debilitation, chronic illness.

Spread

Ascending route (cystitis, pyelonephritis).
Descending route.
Hematogenous route (renal carbuncle).
Lymphogenous route (from cervicitis, colitis).
Direct extension (from pelvic abscesses).

Signs and symptoms

Commonly asymptomatic but may include:
Lower tract: frequency, dysuria, nocturia, pyuria, hematuria, mild fever, suprapubic tenderness.
Upper tract: flank pain, prostration, leukocytosis, high fever, chills, CVA tenderness.

Complications

Gram-negative bacteremia.
Perinephric or cortical abscesses.
Renal calculi or insufficiency.

Diagnostic tests

Urine culture:

Female: < 10,000 bacteria/ml: 2% chance of infection. 10,000-100,000 bacteria/ml: reculture, look for same organism. > 100,000 bacteria/ml: 80% chance of infection.
Male: bacterial counts in excess of 10,000 are more likely to indicate UTI.
The culture result may be adversely affected by:
1. Improper collection of the sample.
2. Inappropriate culture medium.
3. Hydration state of the patient.

4. Acidity of the urine sample.
5. Presence of total obstruction.
6. Urethral contaminants.

Urinalysis:
   Infection may be present without pyuria (50%).
   Some patients with pyuria will not have bacteriuria (33%).

Gram stain (uncentrifuged specimen): One or more bacteria per high-power field indicates the presence of at least 100,000 bacteria/ml.

X-ray: Examine urinary tract if more than one episode of UTI occurs in a female, and after the first episode of infection in a male (obtain evidence of obstruction, vesicoureteral reflux, pyelonephritis, etc.).

Therapeutic guidelines

1. Adequate hydration, analgesia, and rest.
2. Antibiotics as indicated by Gram stain or culture.
3. Common urinary antiseptics include:
   Sulfisoxazole, 1 g PO qid.
   Ampicillin, 500 mg PO qid.
   Penicillin G, 400,000-800,000 units PO qid ac.
   Nitrofurantoin, 100 mg PO qid (minimizes risk of resistant fecal flora).
   Trimethoprim-sulfamethoxazole (Bactrim, Septra), 2 tablets PO bid for 10-14 days.
   Nalidixic acid, 1 g PO qid (indole-positive *Proteus*).
   Cephalothin alone or with gentamicin (for acute pyelonephritis).
   Methenamine, 500 mg, plus ascorbic acid, 500 mg PO qid (chronic suppression).
4. Follow with urinalyses, cultures at appropriate intervals:
   After initiation of therapy.
   Following completion of therapy.

VOLVULUS
SIGMOID (80%-85%)
Etiology

Large bowel obstruction caused by rotation of a redundant sigmoid loop with narrow mesentery, causing a closed-loop obstruction. Incidence is higher in elderly, bedridden patients, usually with chronic constipation and excessive laxative use.

Signs and symptoms

Crampy lower abdominal pain with nausea, vomiting, and obstipation.
Abdominal tenderness, frequently with a palpable tympanitic mass.

Absence of feces on rectal examination.

Gangrenous changes lead to signs of peritonitis with fever, tachycardia, leukocytosis, and progressive dehydration.

Diagnostic tests

Abdominal flat plate: large closed-loop collection of gas and fluid with "bent inner tube" or "omega" sign (convexity of loop lies away from site of obstruction).

Sigmoidoscopy may reveal the point of obstruction. Signs of gangrene preclude insertion of colon tube.

Barium enema: "bird's beak" sign (pointing to the site of obstruction).

Complications

Strangulation of bowel.

Therapeutic guidelines

1. Nonoperative detorsion using lubricated long rectal tube via sigmoidoscopy, then elective resection and primary anastomosis within 7 days.
2. Emergency resection with colostomy for strangulation.

CECAL (10%-15%)
Etiology

Small bowel obstruction caused by rotation of hypofixated ileum, cecum, and proximal ascending colon, causing a closed-loop obstruction.

Signs and symptoms

Severe midabdominal pain followed by nausea, vomiting, obstipation, and abdominal distention.

Tympanitic mass extends from RLQ to RUQ.

Diagnostic tests

Abdominal x-ray: SBO, single air-fluid level in epigastrium or LLQ, "coffee bean" shape with apex pointing toward RLQ.

Therapeutic guidelines

1. Cecal detorsion and fixation of cecum by cecopexy or cecostomy (if not strangulated).
2. Right hemicolectomy with ileotransverse colostomy (if strangulated).

TRANSVERSE COLON (rare)

SPLENIC FLEXURE (rare)

ZOLLINGER-ELLISON SYNDROME
Etiology

Excessive secretion of gastrin may be caused by:
Non-beta islet cell carcinoma of the pancreas (60%).
Solitary adenoma of the pancreas (25%).
Pancreatic hyperplasia or microadenomatosis (10%).
Solitary submucosal tumor of the duodenum (5%).

Pathophysiology

An endocrine tumor; gastrinoma, secretes excessive amounts of gastrin causing hypertrophy of the parietal cell mass and hypersecretion of gastric acid (6-8 liters/day). Effects of the acid include severe peptic ulcer diathesis, diarrhea, and steatorrhea caused by mucosal injury, inactivation of pancreatic lipase, and precipitation of bile salts. It is associated with other endocrine tumors (MEA-I) approximately 25% of the time.

Signs and symptoms

Severe peptic ulcer disease often unrelieved by antacids. Severe diarrhea and/or steatorrhea with weight loss. Vomiting, melena, and hematemesis may occur. Recurrent ulceration after ulcer operation. May be associated with other endocrine tumors, especially hyperparathyroidism and pituitary tumors. Examination may reveal evidence of weight loss, epigastric tenderness, and hepatomegaly caused by metastatic tumor.

Complications

Hemorrhage, perforation, obstruction, marginal ulceration.

Diagnostic tests

Gastric analysis: basal acid > 15 mEq/hour, or > 100 mEq/12 hours.
Serum gastrin > 600 pg/ml. Elevated further in response to calcium or secretin infusions but not by protein test meal.
UGI series: ulceration in duodenal bulb or distal to it; large gastric folds caused by mucosal hyperplasia.
Small bowel series: evidence of mucosal damage, blunting of duodenal and jejunal valvulae conniventes; jejunal ulcers.
Angiography: pancreatic tumor flush in 30%; identification of liver metastasis.
Check for HPT (serum calcium, PTH), other endocrine tumors, and occult metastasis (liver).

Differential diagnosis

Gastric or duodenal ulcer.
Gastric outlet obstruction.

Pernicious anemia.
Retained antrum following ulcer surgery.
Nontropical sprue.
Watery diarrhea, hypokalemic alkalosis syndrome.
Crohn's disease of duodenum or jejunum.

Therapeutic guidelines

Preoperative: Correction of fluid and electrolyte disorders; cimetidine and antacids.

Surgical:
Total gastrectomy to remove end-organ, the parietal cell mass.
Simple excision of solitary pancreatic or duodenal gastrinomas.

Postoperative: Vitamin B_{12} injections monthly; follow serum gastrin levels.

LABORATORY TESTS

Included in this section are many of the laboratory tests that are performed in most hospitals. These are often accompanied by a list of "differential diagnoses," one of which may be causing the variation from normal. Normal values may vary somewhat, depending on the individual laboratory as well as on the method used. Some data in this section are based on material from Wallach, J.: Interpretation of diagnostic tests, ed. 3, Boston, 1978, Little, Brown & Co.

ACETONE (Serum)

> *Normal values:*
> Qualitative: negative
> Quantitative: 0.3-2.0 mg/100 ml

ACID PHOSPHATASE (Serum)

> *Normal values:*
> 1.0-5.0 units (King-Armstrong)
> 0.5-2.0 units (Bodansky)
> 0.5-2.0 units (Gutman)
> 0-1.5 units (Shinowara)
> 0.1-0.63 units (Bessey-Lowry)
> *Elevated in:*
> Prostate cancer
> Idiopathic thrombocytopenic purpura
> Bone (tumor, hyperparathyroidism, Paget's disease)
> Liver (hepatitis, obstructive jaundice, cirrhosis)

ALDOLASE (Serum)

> *Normal value:*
> 3-8 units/ml
> *Elevated in:*
> Acute myocardial infarction
> Acute hepatitis (90%, increased tenfold)
> Burns
> Prostate cancer
> Other cancer (29%)
> Muscular dystrophy

ALKALINE PHOSPHATASE (Serum)

> *Normal values:*
> 5.0-13.0 units (King-Armstrong)
> 2.0-4.5 units (Bodansky)
> 3.0-10.0 units (Gutman)
> 2.2-8.6 units (Shinowara)
> 0.8-2.3 units (Bessey-Lowry)
> 30-85 mIU/ml (IU)
> *Elevated in:*
> Increased deposition of calcium in bone:
> Bone (metastases, sarcoma)
> Hyperparathyroidism (osteitis fibrosa cystica)
> Healing fractures
> Paget's disease
> Liver (biliary obstruction, chlorpropamide)
> Hyperthyroidism
> Hyperphosphatemia
> IV albumin

Myocardial infarction
Pulmonary infarction
Decreased in:
  Hypervitaminosis D
  Milk-alkali syndrome
  Scurvy
  Hypophosphatemia
  Hypothyroidism
  Pernicious anemia (33%)

ALKALINE PHOSPHATASE, LEUKOCYTE (LAP)

Normal value:
  Total score, 14-100

AMMONIA

Normal values:
  Blood: 75-196 μg/100 ml
  Plasma: 56-122 μg/100 ml
Elevated in:
  Liver failure:
    Acute hepatic necrosis
    Terminal cirrhosis
    Hepatectomy
    Portacaval bypass

AMYLASE (Serum)

Normal value:
  80-160 Somogyi units/100 ml
Elevated in:
  Acute pancreatitis:
    Increases in 3-6 hours
    Peaks in 1 day (up to 40 times normal)
    Persists 2-3 days, then lipase should be checked
    Urine levels lag by ½ day
  Perforated peptic ulcer
  Partial gastrectomy
  Pancreatic duct obstruction
  Acute alcoholism
  Mumps, other salivary gland diseases
  Acute cholecystitis
  Small bowel obstruction with strangulation
  Mesenteric thrombosis
  Aortic aneurysm rupture
  Tubal pregnancy rupture
Decreased in:
  Fulminant pancreatitis

ASCORBIC ACID (Blood)

Normal value:
0.4-1.5 mg/100 ml

ATYPICAL LYMPHOCYTES

Absent in normal serum.
Elevated in:
Viral:
Infectious mononucleosis (check heterophil agglutination)
More than 50% lymphocytes, many atypical
Infectious hepatitis
Mumps
Lympatic leukemia
Syphilis (some phases)

BASE, TOTAL (Serum)

Normal value:
145-160 mEq/liter

BASOPHILS

Normal value:
0.5%
Elevated in:
Chronic myelogenous leukemia
Polycythemia
Myeloid metaplasia
Hodgkin's disease
Postsplenectomy

BICARBONATE (Serum)

Normal value:
24-26 mEq/liter
Elevated in:
Vomiting
Pyloric obstruction
Duodenal obstruction
Respiratory acidosis
Decreased in:
Diabetic acidosis
Fasting
Severe diarrhea
Hyperchloremic acidosis
Nephritis
Respiratory alkalosis

BILE ACIDS (Serum)

Normal value:
0.3-3.0 mg/100 ml

BILIRUBIN (Serum)

Normal values:
Total: 0.1-1.0 mg/100 ml
Direct: 0.0-0.2 mg/100 ml
Indirect: 0.1-0.8 mg/100 ml
Elevated in:
Liver cell damage
Biliary duct obstruction
Hemolysis
(Fasting 48 hours may increase bilirubin by 240%)

BLEEDING TIME

Ivy: < 5 minutes
Duke: 1-5 minutes

BLOOD GASES (Arterial)

Normal values on room air:
pH: 7.35-7.45
Po_2: 75-100 mm Hg
Pco_2: 35-45 mm Hg
CO_2: 24-30 mEq/liter
O_2 sat: 96%-100%

BLOOD VOLUME

Males: 75 ml/kg
Females: 67 ml/kg

BONE MARROW ASPIRATION

Normal myeloid-erythroid ratio (3:1-4:1):
Aplastic anemia
Myelosclerosis
Multiple myeloma
Elevated in:
Infections (leukocytosis)
Leukemoid reaction
Myeloid leukemias
Decreased in:
Agranulocytosis
Megaloblastic anemias
Normoblastic anemias
Polycythemia vera

BURR CELLS

Absent in normal serum.
Present in:
Acquired hemolysis:
Uremia

Thrombocytopenic purpura
Microangiopathy (hemolytic anemia)
Mechanical hemolysis:
    Prosthetic heart valves
    Rheumatic heart disease
Disseminated intravascular coagulation

CALCITONIN (Serum)

Absent in normal serum.
Elevated in:
    Medullary carcinoma, > 100 pg/ml

CALCIUM (Serum)

Normal values:
    8.5-10.5 mg/100 ml
    4.5-5.5 mEq/liter
Elevated in:
    Hyperparathyroidism (primary, tertiary)
    Metastatic cancer
    Milk-alkali syndrome
    Vitamin D intoxication
    Multiple myeloma
    Sarcoidosis
    Immobilization (Paget's disease)
    Adrenal insufficiency
    Hyperthyroidism
Decreased in:
    Hypoparathyroidism (surgery, idiopathic, pseudohypopara-
        thyroidism)
    Malabsorption of calcium and vitamin D (obstructive jaun-
        dice)
    Decreased albumin (cachexia, nephrotic syndrome)
    Chronic renal failure
    Acute pancreatitis with fat necrosis
    Bone (osteomalacia, rickets)

CALCIUM, IONIZED

Normal value:
    2.1-2.6 mEq/liter

CARBON DIOXIDE COMBINING POWER

Normal value:
    24-30 mEq/liter

CARBON DIOXIDE CONTENT

Normal value:
    24-30 mEq/liter

CARBON DIOXIDE TENSION (Pco_2)

> *Normal value:*
> 35-45 mm Hg

CARBON MONOXIDE

Symptoms present with > 20% saturation

CARBOXYHEMOGLOBIN

> *Normal value:*
> Up to 5% of total

CARCINOEMBRYONIC ANTIGEN (CEA)

Useful for following patients postoperatively and detecting
early recurrence of:
Bladder cancer
Colon cancer
Hepatoma
Teratoblastoma

CAROTENE (Serum)

> *Normal value:*
> 50-300 μg/100 ml

CEREBROSPINAL FLUID (CSF)

Appearance: clear, colorless, nonclotting
Bilirubin: 0
Cell count: < 10 (all monocytes)
Chloride: 120-130 (20 mEq/liter higher than in blood)
CO_2: 25 mEq/liter
Gamma globulin: 5%-12% of total protein
Glucose: 45-80 mg/100 ml (20 mg/100 ml less than in blood)
Potassium: 2.2-3.3 mEq/liter
Sodium: 142-150 mEq/liter
pH: 7.35-7.40
Total protein: 15-45 mg/100 ml
Urea nitrogen: 5-25 mg/100 ml

CERULOPLASMIN (Serum)

> *Normal value:*
> 23-44 mg/100 ml

CHLORIDE (Serum)

> *Normal value:*
> 97-106 mEq/liter
> *Elevated in:*
> Dehydration
> Diabetes insipidus
> Acute renal failure

Renal tubular acidosis
Acetazolamide administration
Aspirin intoxication
Decreased in:
Chronic obstructive pulmonary disease
Congestive heart failure
Diaphoresis
Diarrhea
Pyloric obstruction
Primary aldosteronism
Adrenal cortical insufficiency
Diabetic acidosis
Thiazide administration
Chronic renal failure

CHOLESTEROL (Serum)

Varies with age, sex, and other factors
Normal values:
"Normal": 130-300 mg/ml
Optimal: 170-240 mg/100 ml
Esters: 68%-76% of total cholesterol
Elevated in:
Biliary obstruction
Pancreatic disorders (diabetes mellitus, pancreatectomy, pancreatitis)
Hypothyroidism
Nephrosis
Pregnancy
Idiopathic
Decreased in:
Hepatic failure
Hyperthyroidism
Malnutrition
Anemia
Cortisone
ACTH therapy

COAGULATION TIME (Lee-White)

Normal values:
5-15 minutes (glass tubes)
19-60 minutes (siliconized tubes)

COOMBS' (Antiglobulin) TEST

Direct (patient's red cells coated with antibody):
Positive:
Autoimmune hemolytic anemia
Cephalothin therapy (75%), especially with increased BUN
Erythroblastosis fetalis

Indirect (patient's serum contains antibody):
  Positive:
    Previous transfusion
    Acquired hemolytic anemia

COPPER (Serum)

Normal values:
  Male: 70-140 µg/100 ml
  Female: 85-155 µg/100 ml

CORTISOL (Plasma)

Normal value:
  6-16 µg/100 ml (diurnal variation)

CREATINE (Serum)

Normal value:
  0.7-1.5 mg/100 ml

CREATINE PHOSPHOKINASE (CPK)

Normal value:
  0.12 Sigma units/ml
Elevated in:
  Striated muscle necrosis, acute atrophy
  Acute myocardial infarction
  Muscle trauma
  Exercise
  Postoperative state (for 5 days, increases with electrocautery)
  Brain infarction (50%)
  IM injections: may increase by 2-6 times

CREATININE

Normal value:
  0.6-1.4 mg/100 ml
Elevated in:
  Renal failure (prerenal, renal, postrenal)
  Diet (roast meat)
  Muscle disease
  BUN–creatinine ratio > 10:1:
    GI bleeding
    Catabolic state
    Steroids
    Prerenal failure
    High-protein diet
  BUN–creatinine ratio < 10:1:
    Renal failure
    Liver failure
    GI losses increased
    Decreased protein diet

CRYOGLOBULINS (Serum)

Normal value:
0
Positive:
Systemic lupus erythematosus
Raynaud's disease
Multiple myeloma
Leukemia

EOSINOPHILS

Normal value:
2%-3%
Elevated in:
Allergy (asthma, hay fever, urticaria, medications)
Radiation therapy
Skin (pemphigus, dermatitis)
Hematopoietic disease
Infections (scarlet fever, erythema multiforme)
Parasites (trichinosis, echinococcosis)

ERYTHROCYTE SEDIMENTATION RATE (ESR)

Normal values:
Male: 0-15 mm/hour
Female: 0-20 mm/hour
Elevated in:
Infection
Inflammation
Trauma
Necrosis
Collagen disorders (rheumatic fever, rheumatoid arthritis)
Amyloidosis
Nephrotic syndrome
Hodgkin's disease
Lymphosarcoma

ETHANOL

Normal values:
< 0.01 in normal serum
Elevated in:
Marked intoxication: 0.3%-0.4%
Alcoholic stupor: 0.4%-0.5%
Coma: > 0.5%

FATTY ACIDS, TOTAL (Serum)

Normal value:
190-420 mg/100 ml

FIBRINOGEN (Plasma)

Normal value:
200-400 mg/100 ml

FIBRINOGEN SPLIT PRODUCTS

Normal value:
Positive at greater than 1:8 dilution (staphylococcal clumping)

FIBRINOLYSINS

Normal value:
0
Increases with metastatic prostate cancer (12%)

FOLIC ACID (Serum)

Normal value:
5-21 ng/ml
Decreased in:
Insufficient caloric intake
Malabsorption
Aminopterin for leukemia (antagonistic)
Hemolytic diseases (increased production)
Myeloproliferative diseases
Carcinomas

FTA-ABS

See *Serologic tests for syphillis*

GAMMA-GLUTAMYL TRANSPEPTIDASE (Serum)

Normal values:
Male: 8-37 mU/ml at 30° C
Female: 5.3-24 mU/ml at 30° C
An excellent measure of extrahepatic biliary obstruction
Elevated in:
Liver disease (parallels changes in alkaline phosphatase, LAP, and 5'-nucleotidase, but is more sensitive)
Acute hepatitis (elevation less marked than transaminases, but is the last to return to normal)
Chronic hepatitis (increases more than in acute hepatitis)
Cirrhosis (some elevation occurs; elevations 10-20 times the cirrhotic level suggest carcinoma of the liver)
Primary biliary cirrhosis (marked elevation)
Obstructive jaundice (increases faster and more than alkaline phosphatase and LAP)
Liver metastases (increases before positive liver scan; parallels alkaline phosphatase)
Acute pancreatitis (always elevated)

Chronic pancreatitis (increases during active inflammation and with involvement of the biliary tract)

Renal disease (lipoid nephrosis, renal carcinoma)

Acute myocardial infarction (increases in 50% of patients by day 4-5)

Heavy use of alcohol, barbiturates, or phenytoin (most sensitive indication of alcoholism)

GASTRIC ANALYSIS

1-hour basal acid

< 2 mEq: normal, gastric ulcer, gastric cancer
2-5 mEq: normal, gastric ulcer, duodenal ulcer
> 5 mEq: duodenal ulcer
> 20 mEq: Zollinger-Ellison syndrome

Histamine or betazole stimulation

0 mEq: achlorhydria, gastritis, gastric cancer
1-20 mEq: normal, gastric ulcer, gastric cancer
20-35 mEq: duodenal ulcer
35-60 mEq: duodenal ulcer, high normal, Zollinger-Ellison syndrome
> 60 mEq: Zollinger-Ellison syndrome

Basal-stimulation ratio

< 20%: normal, gastric ulcer, gastric cancer
20%-40%: gastric ulcer, duodenal ulcer
40%-60%: duodenal ulcer, Zollinger-Ellison syndrome
> 60%: Zollinger-Ellison syndrome

GASTRIN (Serum)

Normal value:
5-290 pg/ml

GLUCAGON (Plasma)

Normal value:
0.4-1.4 ng/ml

GLUCOSE (Fasting)

Normal values:
Blood, true: 60-100 mg/100 ml
Plasma or serum, true: 70-115 mg/100 ml
Elevated in:
Diabetes
Hemochromatosis
Cushing's disease
Acromegaly
Epinephrine disorders (pheochromocytoma, stress, emotion, burns)

Pancreatitis (acute more than chronic)
ACTH therapy
CNS disorders (convulsions, subarachnoid hemorrhage)
Decreased in:
Pancreatic disorders (islet cell tumor, hyperplasia, pancreatitis, glucagon deficiency)
Cancer (adrenal, gastric)
Liver disorders (hepatitis, cirrhosis, tumor)
Endocrine disorders (hypopituitarism, hypothyroidism, early diabetes, Addison's disease)
Surgery (postgastrectomy, gastroenterostomy)
Medications (insulin, sulfonylureas)
Diet (malnutrition)

GLUCOSE-6-PHOSPHATE DEHYDROGENASE (G6PD)

Normal value:
5-15 units

HAPTOGLOBIN (Serum)

Normal value:
30-160 mg/100 ml
Binds free hemoglobin and transports it to the liver for destruction and formation of bilirubin
Elevated in:
Biliary obstruction (33%)
Steroids
Androgens
Increased ESR
Decreased in:
Hemoglobinemia caused by hemolysis (intravascular, extravascular, intramedullary)
Cirrhosis
Genetically absent in 1% of the population

HEPATITIS-ASSOCIATED ANTIGEN (HAA)

Also called serum hepatitis (SH) antigen.
Positive:
Acute viral hepatitis:
With history of parenteral exposure (63%)
No history of parenteral exposure (30%)
Chronic active hepatitis (10%-30%)
Habitual drug users (2%)
Healthy Americans (0.1%)
Appears in blood 2 weeks to 4 months after infection
Precedes increase in hepatocellular enzymes
May disappear in days to weeks after first detection

HETEROPHIL AGGLUTINATION

Normal value:
1:56
(Sheep red cells agglutinate with patient's serum)
Positive:
Infectious mononucleosis ($> 1:224$)
Rule out recent injection of horse serum
May take 1-2 weeks to develop

HYDROXYBUTYRIC DEHYDROGENASE (HBDH)

Normal value:
120-260 units/ml
Elevated in:
Acute myocardial infarction
Muscular dystrophy
Megaloblastic anemias

17-HYDROXYCORTICOSTEROIDS (Plasma)

Normal value:
8-18 μg/100 ml

ICTERUS INDEX (Serum)

Normal value:
2-8 units

INSULIN (Plasma)

Normal values:
24 μU/ml (radioimmunoassay)
Fasting: 6-26 μU/ml
Glucose load test: < 120 μU/ml

IRON (Serum)

Normal values:
Male: 80-160 μg/100 ml
Female: 60-135 μg/100 ml
Elevated in:
Increased iron intake (hemosiderosis, hemochromatosis)
Decreased red cell formation:
Thalassemia
Decreased vitamin B_6
Pernicious anemia relapse
Increased red cell destruction: hemolytic anemias
Acute liver damage (depends on amount of necrosis)
Decreased in:
Iron deficiency anemia
Infection
Chronic diseases

Nephrosis (lose transferrin in urine)
Pernicious anemia in remission

IRON BINDING CAPACITY (Serum)

Normal value:
   250-410 μg/100 ml
   Percent saturation: 20%-55%

ISOCITRATE DEHYDROGENASE (ICD)

Normal value:
   50-180 Sigma units/ml

17-KETOSTEROIDS (Plasma)

Normal value:
   25-125 μg/100 ml

LACTIC ACID (Blood)

Normal values:
   6-16 mg/100 ml
   0.6-1.8 mEq/liter
Elevated in:
   Alkalosis
   Shock (prognostic value)
   Hypoxia:
      Cellular
      Respiratory disease
      Oxygen transport (anemia)

LACTIC DEHYDROGENASE (LDH)

Normal values:
   0-300 mIU/ml (30° C) (Wroblewski modified)
   150 units/ml (Wroblewski)
   80-120 units/ml (Wacker)
Elevated in:
   Acute myocardial infarction (for 10-14 days) LDH_{1-2}
   Pulmonary embolus and infarction LDH_3
   Hepatic LDH_5:
      Prodromal stage
      Greatest at the onset of jaundice
      Chlorpromazine administration
      Carbon tetrachloride
      Cirrhosis
      Biliary obstruction
   Pernicious anemia LDH_1
   Prostate cancer LDH_5
   Cancer:
      Leukemia (60%-90%)
      Lymphoma (60%) LDH_3
   Muscle disease

Decreased in:
Radiation

LACTOSE (Plasma)

Normal value:
< 0.5 mg/100 ml

LIPASE (Serum)

Normal value:
0-1.5 units/ml (Cherry-Crandall)
Elevated in:
Acute pancreatitis (may remain elevated after amylase normal)
Perforated peptic ulcer
Pancreatic duct obstruction (stone, opiates, codeine)

LIPIDS, TOTAL (Serum)

Normal value:
450-850 mg/100 ml

LIPOPROTEINS
Types

I: Rarest, exogenous, familial
Increased triglycerides and chylomicrons
Rule out diabetes mellitus
II: Common, essential, familial
Increased cholesterol and beta-lipoproteins
Rule out obstructive liver disease
III: Uncommon, CHO-induced
Increased triglycerides, cholesterol, and pre-beta, increased-beta diabetes
Rule out liver disease
IV: Commonest, endogenous, CHO-induced
Increased triglycerides and pre-beta
Rule out diabetes mellitus
V: Uncommon, endogenous and exogenous
Increased triglycerides, cholesterol, and pre-beta and chylomicrons
Rule out myeloma, diabetes, pancreatitis

LUTEINIZING HORMONE (LH) (Plasma)

Normal values:
Male: < 11 mIU/ml
Female:
Premenopausal: < 25 mIU/ml
Midcycle: > 3 times base level
Postmenopausal: > 25 mIU/ml

LYMPHOCYTES

Normal value:
24%-44%
Elevated in:
Infections (mononucleosis, hepatitis, mumps, tuberculosis)
Lymphatic leukemia

MAGNESIUM (Serum)

Normal values:
1.5-2.5 mEq/liter
1.8-3.0 mg/100 ml
Elevated in:
Renal failure
Antacids containing magnesium
Diabetic coma
Hypothyroidism
Adrenalectomy
Decreased in:
GI losses
Renal losses
Alcoholism
Hyperthyroidism
Hypoparathyroidism
Hyperaldosteronism
Diuretics
Decreased serum magnesium may cause hypocalcemia, hypo-
kalemia

MEAN CORPUSCULAR HEMOGLOBIN (MCH)

Normal value:
27-32 pg

MEAN CORPUSCULAR HEMOGLOBIN CONCENTRATION
(MCHC)

Normal value:
32%-36%
Increased only in hereditary spherocytosis

MEAN CORPUSCULAR VOLUME (MCV)

Normal value
82-92 μm^3
Elevated in:
Macrocytic anemias:
Megaloblastic anemias:
GI (pernicious anemia, postgastrectomy, fish tapeworms,
sprue)
Antimetabolite therapy
Physiologic (infancy, pregnancy)

Decreased in:
Microcytic anemias:
Iron deficiency:
Insufficient intake
Insufficient absorption
Increased requirement
Chronic blood loss
Decreased vitamin B_6
Thalassemia major
Normocytic anemias:
Acute hemorrhage or hemolysis
Decreased red cell formation:
Chronic infection
Uremia
Cancer
Hypoplastic anemia
Myelophthisis

METHEMOGLOBIN

Normal value:
0.03-0.13 g/100 ml

MONOCYTES

Normal value:
0-4%
> *10%:*
Monocytic leukemia
Hodgkin's disease
Lymphomas
Ulcerative colitis
Regional enteritis
Collagen diseases
Myeloproliferative diseases
(*Not* infectious mononucleosis: see *Atypical lymphocytes*)

NEUTROPHILS

Normal value:
46%-66%
Elevated in:
Infections
Tissue necrosis (myocardial infarction, tumor, burns)
Acute hemorrhage or hemolysis
Myeloproliferative diseases
Toxins (uremia, acidosis, mercury, protein)
Physiologic (exercise, stress, menstruation, labor)
Decreased in:
Sepsis (overwhelming)
Radiation
Leukemia (aleukemic)

Shock (anaphylactic)
Medications (sulfonamides, antibiotics, analgesics, marrow depression, arsenicals, antithyroids)

NITROGEN, NONPROTEIN (Serum)

Normal value:
15-35 mg/100 ml

5'-NUCLEOTIDASE

Normal values:
2-9 mU/ml
0.3-3.2 units/ml (Bodansky)
Elevated in:
Biliary obstruction (highly specific)

OSMOLALITY (Serum)

Normal value:
285-295 mOsm/liter
(Freezing point determination)
Elevated in:
Water loss (diabetes insipidus, diabetes mellitus)
Increased solute intake
Decreased solute excretion (chronic renal failure: azotemia, hypernatremia)
Positive sodium balance (increased aldosterone)
Decreased in:
Decreased serum sodium
Increased water intake
Syndrome of inappropriate ADH (bronchogenic cancer, hypothyroidism, CNS)
Diuretics
Low-salt diet
Postoperative state (excess water)

OSMOTIC FRAGILITY OF ERYTHROCYTES

Normal values:
Begins in 0.45%-0.39% NaCl
Completes in 0.33%-0.30% NaCl
Elevated in (↑ fragility):
Hereditary spherocytosis
Hemolytic anemias (acquired, hereditary, ABO incompatibility)
Thermal injury
Decreased in (↓ fragility):
Iron deficiency anemia
Thalassemia
Sickle cell anemia
Postsplenectomy

Liver disease
Jaundice

OXYGEN (Blood)

Normal values:
Capacity: 16-24 vol % (varies with hemoglobin)
Content:
Arterial: 15-23 vol %
Venous: 10-16 vol %
Saturation:
Arterial: 94%-100% of capacity
Venous: 60%-85% of capacity
Tension: 75-100 mm Hg (on room air, depends on age)

PARTIAL THROMBOPLASTIN TIME (PTT)

Normal value:
(Activated) 22-37 seconds   (Best coagulation screening test)
Elevated in:
Heparin effect
Defect in factors I, II, V, VIII, IX, X, XI, XII

Pco_2

Normal value:
35-45 mm Hg

pH (blood)

Normal values:
Arterial: 7.35-7.45
Venous: 7.36-7.41

PHOSPHATE, INORGANIC (Serum)

Normal value:
3.0-4.5 mg/100 ml

PHOSPHOLIPIDS (Serum)

Normal value:
150-350 mg/100 ml

PHOSPHORUS (Serum)

Normal value:
2.5-4.5 mg/100 ml
Elevated in:
Hypoparathyroidism
Hypervitaminosis D
Milk-alkali syndrome
High small bowel obstruction
Bone (fracture, multiple myeloma, Paget's disease, metastases)

Acromegaly
Addison's disease
Myelogenous leukemia
Decreased in:
Hyperparathyroidism (hyperplasia versus adenoma)
Hypovitaminosis D (rickets, osteomalacia, steatorrhea)
Malabsorption (celiac sprue)
Increased insulin (adenoma, injections)
Diabetes mellitus
Essential hypophosphatemia

PLASMA CELLS (rare in normal peripheral smears)

Elevated in:
Plasma cell leukemia
Multiple myeloma
Serum reaction
Infectious mononucleosis
Some viral illnesses

PLASMA VOLUME

Normal values:
Male: 44 ml/kg
Female: 43 ml/kg

PLATELET COUNT

Normal value:
150,000-450,000 per mm^3
Elevated in:
Malignancy (disseminated, advanced)
Myeloproliferative diseases
Postsplenectomy
Collagen diseases
Iron deficiency anemia
Acute infection
Cirrhosis
Pancreatitis
Decreased (< 60,000) in:
Idiopathic thrombocytopenic purpura
Thrombotic thrombocytopenic purpura
Hypersplenism
Leukemia
Infection
Radiation
Nitrogen mustards
Chloramphenicol

POTASSIUM (Serum)

Normal value:
3.5-5.0 mEq/liter
(See *Hyperkalemia* and *Hypokalemia*)

PREGNANCY TEST (Receptor assay)

Immunoassay of HCG (urine, serum, plasma)
Positive:
Pregnancy (95% positive by 10-14 days after expected menstrual period)
Hydatidiform mole
Choriocarcinoma

PROGESTERONE

Normal values:
Follicular phase: < 1.0 ng/ml
Luteal phase: > 2.0 ng/ml

PROLACTIN

Normal value:
< 20 ng/ml

PROTEIN-BOUND IODINE (PBI)

Normal value:
3.6-8.8 μg/100 ml

PROTEINS (Serum)

Normal values:
Total: 6.0-8.0 g/100 ml
  Albumin: 3.5-5.5 g/100 ml
  Globulin: 2.5-3.5 g/100 ml
Electrophoretic fractions:
  Albumin: 3.5-5.5 g/100 ml
  Globulin: 52%-68% of total
  d_1: 0.2-0.4 g/100 ml
    2%-5% of total
  d_2: 0.5-0.9 g/100 ml
    7%-14% of total
  B: 0.6-1.1 g/100 ml
    9%-15% of total
  γ: 0.7-1.7 g/100 ml
    11%-21% of total

PROTHROMBIN TIME (PT) (One-stage)

Same as control (12.4-14.0 seconds)
Elevated in:
Liver damage (hepatitis, cirrhosis)
Fat malabsorption (obstructive jaundice, colitis)

Vitamin K deficiency
Medications (Coumadin [warfarin sodium], salicylates)
Factor deficiency (I, II, V, VII, X)

PYRUVIC ACID (Plasma)

Normal value:
1.0-2.0 mg/100 ml

RETICULOCYTE COUNT

Normal value:
0.5%-1.5% of erythrocytes
Elevated in:
Increased red cell production:
Acute blood loss or hemolysis
After iron therapy for iron deficiency anemia
After treatment of megaloblastic anemia

SCHILLING TEST

1. Fasting state (NPO)
2. 0.5 μCi cyanocobalamin ^{60}Co PO
   1000 μg vitamin B_{12} IM (flushing dose)
3. 24-hour urine collection
   > 7% radioactivity, normal
   0.3% radioactivity, pernicious anemia versus malabsorption

SEROLOGIC TESTS FOR SYPHILIS (STS)

FTA-ABS: most sensitive and specific, reserved for problem
cases.
VDRL: routine screening, becomes positive 7-10 days after
chancre appears.
Percent of reactive patients:

	Primary	Secondary	Late	Latent
FTA-ABS	85%	99%	95%	95%
VDRL	78%	97%	77%	74%

SEROTONIN

Normal values:
Platelet suspension: 0.1-0.3 μg/ml blood
Serum: 0.10-0.32 μg/ml

SEROUS FLUIDS (Pleural, pericardial, ascites)

Specific gravity: 1.010-1.026
Total proteins: 3-4 g/100 ml
Albumin: 50-70 g/100 ml
Globulin: 30-40 g/100 ml
Fibrinogen: 0.3-4.5 g/100 ml
pH: 6.8-7.6

SERUM HEPATITIS (SH) ANTIGEN

See *Hepatitis-associated antigen*

SERUM PROTEIN ELECTROPHORESIS (SPEP)
Monoclonal

IgG: 65% (Bence-Jones protein)
IgA: 16%
IgM: 15% (multiple myeloma)
Bence Jones: 9% (light-chain, multiple myeloma)
IgE: rare (heavy-chain disease)
IgO: rare

Polyclonal

Collagen disease
Liver disease
Chronic infection

SGOT

Normal values:
0.19 mIU/ml (30° C) (Karmen modified)
15-40 units/ml (Karmen)
5-40 units/ml (Sigma-Frankel)
Elevated in:
Acute myocardial infarction
Hepatic disease
Muscle diseases, trauma, injury
Acute pancreatitis
Biliary disease with opiates (increased SGOT, SGPT, CPK)
Cholecystectomy
Mesenteric infarction
Pulmonary infarction
Brain infarction
Medications (oxacillin, erythromycin, opiates)

SGPT

Normal values:
0.17 mIU/ml (30° C) (Karmen modified)
6-35 units/ml (Karmen)
5-35 units/ml (Sigma-Frankel)
Parallels SGOT, but:
Increases *more* in liver necrosis and acute hepatitis
Increases *less* in:
Acute myocardial infarction
Chronic hepatitis
Cirrhosis
Liver metastases
Congestive heart failure

SICKLE CELLS

Sickle cell disease
Sickle cell trait
Confirm with hemoglobin electrophoresis, genetic studies

SODIUM (Serum)

See *Hypernatremia* or *Hyponatremia*
Normal value:
136-145 mEq/liter

STAINABLE IRON (Hemosiderin) IN BONE MARROW

Elevated in:
Hemolytic anemia
Pernicious anemia
Hemochromatosis and hemosiderosis
Uremia
Chronic infection
Chronic pancreatic insufficiency
Decreased in:
Anemia (iron deficiency, hemorrhage)
Collagen diseases
Infiltration of marrow
Uremia
Chronic infection

STOOL

Occult blood (carcinoma of the colon, etc.)
Urobilinogen
Elevated in:
Hemolytic anemias
Decreased in:
Complete biliary obstruction
Severe liver disease
Oral antibiotics
Aplastic anemia
Neutrophils: shigellosis, salmonellosis, colitis from *E. coli*,
ulcerative colitis
Monocytes: typhoid
Color:
Clay (biliary obstruction)
Tarry ($>$ 100 ml in UGI)
Red (blood, beets, tomatoes)
Black (blood, iron, bismuth)

SULFATES, INORGANIC (Serum)

Normal value:
0.8-1.2 mg/100 ml (as sulfur)

SULKOWITCH TEST

Positive: Urine calcium increased
Negative: Urine calcium decreased

T_3 (Serum, radioimmunoassay)

Normal value:
50-210 ng/100 ml

T_3 (RU)

Normal value:
24%-36%
Elevated in:
Hyperthyoidism
Medications:
Steroids
Androgen
Heparin
Coumadin (warfarin sodium)
Aspirin
Butazolidine
Penicillin
Dilantin (phenytoin)
Decreased in:
Hypothyroidism
Medications:
Estrogens
Iodine
Propylthiouracil

T_4 (Serum, radioimmunoassay)

Normal value:
4.8-13.2 μg/100 ml

T_4 (RU)

Normal value:
4%-11%

TESTOSTERONE

Normal values:
Male (adult): 0.30-1.0 μg/100 ml
Male (adolescent): > 0.10 μg/100 ml
Female: 0-0.1 μg/100 ml

THROMBIN TIME

Within 5 seconds of control
Elevated in:
Disseminated intravascular coagulation

THYROXINE, FREE (Serum)

Normal value:
1.0-2.1 ng/100 ml

THYROXINE-BINDING GLOBULIN (TBG) (Serum)

Normal value:
10-26 μg/100 ml

THYROXINE IODINE T$_4$ (Serum)

Normal value:
2.9-6.4 μg/100 ml

TOTAL IRON-BINDING CAPACITY (TIBC)

Normal value:
250-410 μg/100 ml
Elevated in:
Iron deficiency anemia
Acute and chronic blood loss
Hepatitis
Late pregnancy
Decreased in:
Hemochromatosis
Cirrhosis
Thalassemia
Uremia
Nephrosis
Rheumatoid arthritis

TRANSFERRIN SATURATION (Serum)

Normal value:
205-374 mg/100 ml
20%-55% saturation
Elevated in:
Hemosiderosis
Hemochromatosis
Thalassemia
Decreased in:
Anemia:
Iron deficiency
Infection
Uremia
Rheumatoid arthritis

TRIGLYCERIDES (Serum)

Normal value:
10-150 mg/100 ml

Elevated in:
    Familial hyperlipidemia
    Liver disease
    Nephrotic syndrome
    Hypothyroidism
    Diabetes mellitus
    Pancreatitis
    Acute myocardial infarction (peaks in 3 weeks)
Decreased in:
    Abetalipoproteinemia
    Malnutrition

UREA NITROGEN (BUN)

Normal values:
    Blood: 10-20 mg/100 ml
    Serum or plasma: 11-23 mg/100 ml
Elevated in:
    Renal failure:
        Prerenal (hypovolemia, dehydration, congestive failure, shock)
        Renal (acute tubular necrosis)
        Postrenal (BUN–creatinine ratio > 10:1)
    Catabolism (normal creatinine)
    GI bleeding
    Acute myocardial infarction
    Stress (steroids)
Decreased in:
    Overhydration
    Liver failure (decreased protein synthesis)
    Pregnancy (increased protein synthesis)
    Low-protein diet
    Nephrotic syndrome

URIC ACID (Serum)

Normal values:
    Male: 2.5-8.0 mg/100 ml
    Female: 1.5-6.0 mg/100 ml
Elevated in:
    Gout, or 25% of relatives
    Renal failure
    Nucleoprotein destruction:
        Leukemia
        Multiple myeloma
        Polycythemia
        Lymphoma
        Disseminated cancer
        Hemolytic anemia
    Diet (high protein)
    Medications (thiazides, furosemide)

Decreased in:
    Xanthine oxidase inhibitor (allopurinol)
    Uricosuric (colchicine)
    ACTH therapy

URINE ADDIS COUNT

Normal values:
    RBC: < 1 million/24 hours
    Casts: < 100,000/24 hours
    WBC plus epithelial cells: < 2 million/24 hours

URINE ALDOSTERONE

Normal value:
    2-12 mg/24 hours
Elevated in:
    Hyperaldosteronism (primary or secondary)
Decreased in:
    Adrenal insufficiency
    Panhypopituitarism

URINE AMYLASE

Normal value:
    260-950 units/24 hours (Somogyi)

URINE CALCIUM

Normal value:
    < 150 mg/24 hours on low-calcium diet
Elevated in:
    Hyperparathyroidism
    Increased calcium intake
    Immobilization
    Bone (metastases, multiple myeloma, osteoporosis)
    Hypervitaminosis D
    Renal tubular acidosis
    Idiopathic

URINE CATECHOLAMINES

Normal values:
    Epinephrine: < 10 μg/24 hours
    Norepinephrine: < 100 μg/24 hours
Elevated in:
    Pheochromocytoma
    Neuroblastoma
    Ganglioneuroma
    Ganglioblastoma
    Medications:
        Tetracyclines
        Aldomet (methyldopa)
        Epinephrine

Vitamin B complex
(Avoid all medications for at least 1 week)

URINE COLOR

Red:
Phenolphthalein, urates, bile
Beets, blackberries, food dyes
Dark:
Hemoglobin, urobilinogen, porphyrins, aspirin, melanogen, phenols, Flagyl (metronidazole)
Blue:
Methylene blue, *Pseudomonas*
White cloud:
Oxalic acid (oxalosis), glycolic acid

URINE CREATININE

Normal value:
1.0-1.6 g/24 hours

URINE CREATININE CLEARANCE

Normal value:
90-150 ml/minute

URINE C & S

$> 10^5$ implies urinary tract infection in 85%
Check urine WBC, Gram stain
May be sterile but have pyuria:
Dehydration
Mechanical inflammation
Chemical inflammation
Renal tuberculosis

URINE ELECTROLYTES

Normal values:
Na^+: varies with intake, hydration
Cl^-: 110-250 mEq/day (chief anion of urine)

URINE FERRIC CHLORIDE SCREENING

Positive indicates phenylketonuria

URINE GLUCOSE

Normal values:
Qualitative: 0
Quantitative: < 0.3 g/24 hours
TmG male: 300-450 mg/minute
TmG female: 250-350 mg/minute
Hyperglycemia (diabetes, renal diabetes):
Pituitary (ACTH)
Adrenal (steroids, epinephrine)

Thyroid
Liver
CNS
Multiple sclerosis
Medications:
Vitamin C
Glucuronic acid
Aspirin
Anesthetics
Tranquilizers

URINE GRAM STAIN

80%-95% the reliability of C & S
10% false positives

URINE HEMOGLOBIN

Normal value:
0
Elevated in:
Hematuria (with hemolysis in urine)
Renal infarction
Intravascular hemolysis:
Antibodies (transfusion, acquired hemolytic anemia, paroxysmal nocturnal hemoglobinuria)
Burns
Malaria
Strenuous exercise
Sulfonamides
Other: pus, iodides, bromides

URINE 5-HIAA

Serotonin metabolite
Normal value:
2-10 mg/24 hours
Elevated in:
Carcinoid syndrome (> 40 mg/day)
Bananas
Phenothiazines
Lugol's solution

URINE 17-HYDROXYCORTICOIDS

Normal value:
4-14 mg/24 hours

URINE KETONES (Acetone, beta-hydroxybutyric and acetoacetic acids)

Normal value:
Qualitative, 0

Elevated in:
Metabolic:
Diabetes mellitus
Renal glycosuria
Fever
Hyperthyroidism
Pregnancy
Diet (starvation, high fat)

URINE 17-KETOSTEROIDS

Normal value:
8-25 mg/24 hours
Elevated in:
Adrenal cortex (hyperplasia, adenoma, cancer)
Pituitary (ACTH)
Stress
Testosterone:
Interstitial cell tumor of testes
Arrhenoblastoma of ovary

URINE METANEPHRINES

Normal values:
Total: 24-288 μg/24 hours
Metanephrine: 24-96 μg/24 hours
Normetanephrine: 72-288 μg/24 hours

URINE MICROSCOPIC EXAMINATION

Normal values:
< 1-2 RBC per high-power field
< 1-2 WBC per high-power field
< 1-2 epithelial cells per high-power field
Occasional hyaline casts in low-power field

URINE MYOGLOBIN

Normal value:
0
Elevated in:
Crush syndrome
Ischemia (acute myocardial infarction, arterial occlusion)
Exertion
Muscle disease

URINE OSMOLALITY

Normal value:
500-1200 mOsm/liter

URINE pH

Normal value:
4.6-8.0 (depends on diet)

URINE PORPHYRINS

Normal value:
50-300 μg/24 hours

URINE PROTEIN

Normal values:
Qualitative: 0
Quantitative: 0-0.1 g/24 hours
Elevated in:
Albumin
Globulins
Bence-Jones proteins

URINE SPECIFIC GRAVITY

Normal value:
1.003-1.030
1.003: dilution
1.010: isosmotic with plasma
1.020-1.030: concentration, refrigeration of urine, proteinuria
1.040-1.050: radiographic contrast medium

URINE UROBILINOGEN

Normal value:
0-4 mg/24 hours
(Urobilinogen made in colon by bacteria)
Elevated in:
Hemolysis
Cirrhosis
Hepatitis
Cholangitis
Decreased in:
Complete biliary obstruction

URINE VANILLYLMANDELIC ACID (VMA)

Normal value:
< 9 mg/24 hours
Elevated in:
Pheochromocytoma
Neuroblastoma
Ganglioneuroma
Ganglioblastoma
Rule out:
Coffee, tea, chocolate, vanilla, fruits and vegetables
Aldomet (methyldopa), MAO inhibitors

URINE WBC (Pyuria)

> 10 implies bacteriuria in 90%
50% of patients with bacteriuria have > 10 WBC per high-power
field

VDRL

See *Serologic tests for syphilis*

VITAMIN A (Serum)
Normal value:
20-80 μg/100 ml

VITAMIN B$_{12}$ (Serum)
Normal value:
200-800 pg/ml
Decreased in:
Intrinsic factor deficiency: pernicious anemia (Schilling test,
gastrectomy, hypothyroidism)
Malabsorption
Fish tapeworm *(Diphyllobothrium latum)*
Insufficient dietary intake

VITAMIN C (Blood)
Normal value:
0.4-1.5 mg/100 ml

VITAMIN D (Blood)
Normal value:
0.7-3.3 IU/100 ml

VITAMIN E (Blood)
Normal value:
0.5-2.0 mg/100 ml

SURGICAL PROCEDURES

This section is intended to present several basic surgical procedures more as "reminders" for those already competent in performing them than for the novice. Those who have not received adequate training are advised to pursue further instruction.

1. Central venous catheter insertion
2. Chest tube thoracostomy
3. Lumbar puncture
4. Peritoneal lavage

Fig. 1. Anatomic landmarks for CVP line insertion. (From Surratt, P. M., and Gibson, R. S.: Manual of medical procedures, St. Louis, 1982, The C. V. Mosby Co.)

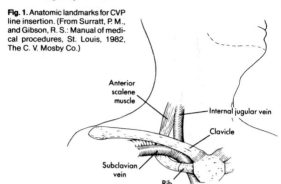

Anterior scalene muscle

Internal jugular vein

Clavicle

Subclavian vein

Rib

CENTRAL VENOUS CATHETER (subclavian approach) (Fig. 1)

Alternate routes: antecubital, internal jugular, supraclavicular:

1. Patient supine and in the Trendelenburg position to dilate subclavian veins. Place padding between shoulder blades to improve access to the midpoint of the clavicle. During catheter placement, it is helpful to stretch the vein by having the patient face away from the site, with the ipsilateral shoulder depressed maximally inferior.
2. Prepare the skin with acetone to defat the surface and paint the skin with povidone-iodine solution. Drape using sterile technique.
3. Local anesthesia to include skin, subcutaneous tissue, and periosteum at the midpoint of the undersurface of clavicle.
4. Insert needle-catheter setup through a point two finger-breadths below the middle of the clavicle. Aim toward the suprasternal notch. (Some may prefer a trial puncture with a 19-gauge needle to locate the position of the subclavian vein—between the clavicle and the first rib.) (Fig. 2, *A*)
5. Maintain suction in the syringe while advancing the needle.
6. Blood return indicates a successful puncture. Advance the needle 2-3 mm, then confirm position in the vein by aspirating blood.
7. Hold needle firmly in position and advance the radiopaque inner catheter into the superior vena cava.
8. Withdraw the needle, holding the inner catheter in place. Lock the needle in the protective cover. Then attach the IV tubing and reconfirm successful puncture by lowering the IV bottle and noting backflow of blood. (Fig. 2, *B* and *C*)

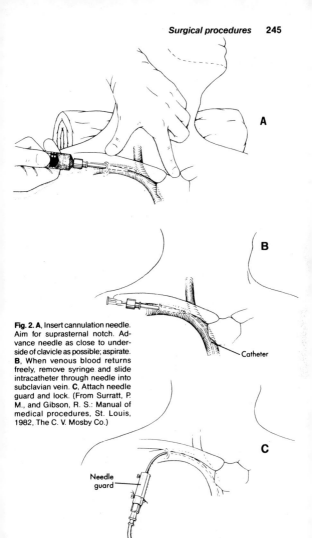

Fig. 2. A, Insert cannulation needle. Aim for suprasternal notch. Advance needle as close to underside of clavicle as possible; aspirate. **B,** When venous blood returns freely, remove syringe and slide intracatheter through needle into subclavian vein. **C,** Attach needle guard and lock. (From Surratt, P. M., and Gibson, R. S.: Manual of medical procedures, St. Louis, 1982, The C. V. Mosby Co.)

Catheter

Needle guard

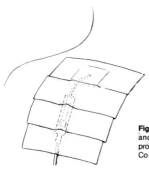

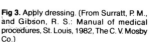

Fig 3. Apply dressing. (From Surratt, P. M., and Gibson, R. S.: Manual of medical procedures, St. Louis, 1982, The C. V. Mosby Co.)

9. Never pull the inner catheter back through the needle, since this could shear off the catheter tip and produce a catheter embolus to the heart. If necessary, remove the catheter and needle simultaneously.
10. Suture the catheter and needle in place using nonabsorbable material. Apply an occlusive dressing, using gauze, tincture of benzoin, and adhesive tape. (Fig. 3)
11. Check CVP.
12. Set IV at slow infusion until chest x-ray is obtained to check catheter position and rule out pneumohydrothorax.

CHEST TUBE THORACOSTOMY

1. Patient in supine position, arm abducted.
2. Prepare and drape using sterile technique.
3. Local anesthesia to skin and periosteum on top of the rib desired (avoid neurovascular bundle under the rib).
4. Site: the sixth intercostal space in the midaxillary line avoids major nerves and underlying muscles.
5. Skin incision, 2-3 cm in length, carried just through to the intercostal muscles.
6. Using a clamp, supported firmly by a hand on the chest wall, dissect bluntly through the intercostal muscles and through the parietal pleura into the pleural cavity.
7. Insert a sterile gloved finger into the cavity to make a space for the chest tube. (Fig. 4)
8. Insert the chest tube using a curved hemostat into the chest cavity. (Fig. 5)
9. Withdraw the hemostat and connect the chest tube to water-seal drainage.
10. Suture the skin incision around the chest tube and secure the chest tube in place with suture material. (Fig. 6)

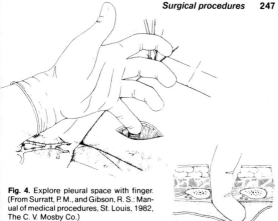

Fig. 4. Explore pleural space with finger. (From Surratt, P. M., and Gibson, R. S.: Manual of medical procedures, St. Louis, 1982, The C. V. Mosby Co.)

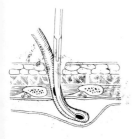

Fig. 5. Insert chest tube with curved hemostat. (From Surratt, P. M., and Gibson, R. S.: Manual of medical procedures, St. Louis, 1982, The C. V. Mosby Co.)

Fig. 6. Secure chest tube with sutures tied twice around tube. (From Surratt, P. M., and Gibson, R. S.: Manual of medical procedures, St. Louis, 1982, The C. V. Mosby Co.)

Fig. 7. Apply dressings and secure tube with tape. (From Surratt, P. M., and Gibson, R. S.: Manual of medical procedures, St. Louis, 1982, The C. V. Mosby Co.)

11. Dress wound around the tube. (Fig. 7)
12. Obtain chest x-ray to check position of tube.

LUMBAR PUNCTURE
Contraindication: papilledema (disk margins blurred; may produce herniation through incisura)

1. Patient lying on side, knee-chest position, neck fully flexed, lumbar spine close to the edge of the bed. (Fig. 8)
2. Prepare and drape using sterile technique.
3. Local anesthesia to skin and subcutaneous tissues.
4. A 21-gauge lumbar puncture needle is advanced toward the umbilicus in a midline position, even with the iliac crests, until the subarachnoid space is entered (fluid appears through trocar when stylet is removed). (Fig. 9)
5. If fluid does not appear, replace stylet; then reposition needle until fluid does appear.
6. Check opening pressure. (Fig. 10) Check closing pressure after collecting specimens.
7. Collect specimens. (Fig. 11)
   Tube 1: glucose, protein, electrolytes, VDRL.
   Tube 2: cytology.
   Tube 3: cell count.
   Tube 4: fungal, cryptococcal antigen.
   Tube 5: bacterial (Gram stain, culture).
8. Patient should remain flat for 12 hours following the procedure to prevent headache or stiff neck.

PERITONEAL LAVAGE
1. Patient in supine position.
2. Prepare and drape abdomen using sterile technique.
3. Local anesthesia. Avoid scars (bowel may adhere to anterior abdominal wall). (Fig. 12)

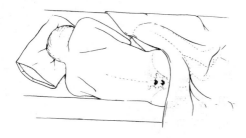

Fig. 8. Lateral decubitus position. (From Surratt, P. M., and Gibson, R. S.: Manual of medical procedures, St. Louis, 1982, The C. V. Mosby Co.)

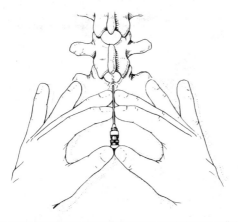

Fig. 9. Insert spinal needle into subcutaneous tissue and advance needle into subarachnoid space. (From Surratt, P. M., and Gibson, R. S.: Manual of medical procedures, St. Louis, 1982, The C. V. Mosby Co.)

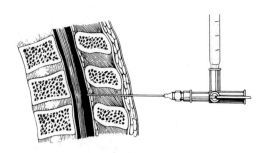

Fig. 10. Measure opening pressure. Note position of stopcock. (From Surratt, P. M., and Gibson, R. S.: Manual of medical procedures, St. Louis, 1982, The C. V. Mosby Co.)

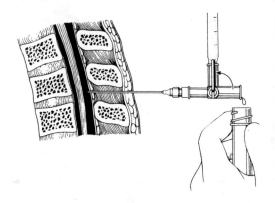

Fig. 11. Collect cerebrospinal fluid specimens. (From Surratt, P. M., and Gibson, R. S.: Manual of medical procedures, St. Louis, 1982, The C. V. Mosby Co.)

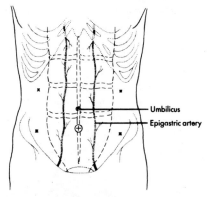

Fig. 12. Anatomic landmarks for peritoneal lavage. (From Surratt, P. M., and Gibson, R. S.: Manual of medical procedures, St. Louis, 1982, The C. V. Mosby Co.)

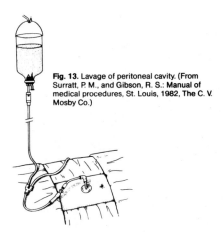

Fig. 13. Lavage of peritoneal cavity. (From Surratt, P. M., and Gibson, R. S.: Manual of medical procedures, St. Louis, 1982, The C. V. Mosby Co.)

4. Midline position, 2-4 cm below umbilicus, avoids major blood vessels. However, bowel may float to the top. Therefore, use 2-3 cm skin incision carried down through linea alba. Surgeon and assistant pick up peritoneum and a small incision is made in it.
5. Insert catheter into hole in peritoneum.
6. If fluid does not return at once through the catheter, instill lavage solution via IV drip (400-500 ml). (Fig. 13)
7. Roll patient from side to side to lavage internal surfaces.
8. Lower IV tubing and bottle to obtain specimen.
9. Remove tubing and suture wound (unless catheter is to be left in place).
10. Tap is positive if:
    RBC > 100,000/mm³.
    WBC > 500/mm³.
    Amylase, bile, or bacteria are present.

HYPERALIMENTATION

Indications

Pre- and postoperative malnutrition, especially when GI tract abnormalities are present.

Enteric fistulas, especially of the upper GI tract.

Short bowel syndrome.

Malabsorption syndrome.

Inflammatory bowel disease.

Sepsis.

Multiple trauma.

Severe burns.

Acute renal failure.

Support during chemotherapy.

Neurologic disorders that preclude oral nutrition.

Contraindications

Terminally ill patients.

When enteral feeding is both feasible and safe.

Patients in good nutritional status.

Composition (in approximately 1 liter)

Crystalline amino acids: 39 g (180 kcal).

Dextrose: 250 g (850 kcal).

Sodium: 19 mEq.

Potassium: 41 mEq.

Calcium: 4.7 mEq.

Magnesium: 8 mEq.

Chloride: 20 mEq.

Acetate: 22 mEq.

Phosphate: 29 mEq.

Vitamin B complex: 2 ml.

Ascorbic acid: 500 mg.

Rate

Begin constant infusion at 50 ml/hour (1200 ml/day).

Gradually increase to tolerance (3-4 liters/day).

Preoperative: decrease the rate by one-half the day before surgery to prevent stress glucose intolerance.

During surgery, leave at one-half rate.

Postoperative: leave at one-half rate for 24 hours; then increase rate gradually as before.

Additives

Modified formulations may be required for patients with cardiac, renal, and hepatic disease; diabetes mellitus; and other underlying diseases.

Changes in sodium, potassium, calcium, magnesium, addition of insulin, and any other modifications should be ordered through the pharmacy.

Give any additional fluids by separate IV infusions.

The patient should also receive:

Vitamin K_1, 10 mg IM weekly.

Folic acid, 5 mg IM weekly.

Vitamin B_{12}, 1000 μg IM monthly.

The patient may also require administration of:

A soybean fat emulsion weekly to prevent essential fatty acid deficiency.

Iron for iron deficiency.

Trace minerals.

Insulin.

Precautions

Avoid contamination of the hyperalimentation bottle, IV tubing, and catheter. This may occur in inadvertent disconnection, blood sampling, CVP readings, and the administration of blood products or drugs.

Avoid complications by controlling or correcting cardiovascular instability and metabolic derangements before the institution of hyperalimentation.

Complications

Sepsis (caused by contamination of solution, tubing, or catheter).

Catheter placement (pneumothorax, hemothorax, subclavian artery injury, arrhythmias, air or catheter embolism, thrombophlebitis, thrombosis).

Endocrine: hyperosmolar nonketotic hyperglycemia.

Volume, concentration, and compositional imbalances.

Metabolic:

Excessive plasma level of amino acids.

Hyperchloremic acidosis.

Hypophosphatemia.

Essential fatty acid deficiency.

Trace element deficiency.

Others.

Monitoring parameters*

Variable	Suggested frequency Phase I†	Phase II†
Growth variables		
Body weight	Daily	Daily
Body length (in infants)	Biweekly	Biweekly
Head circumference (in infants)	Weekly	Weekly
Metabolic variables		
Blood measurements		
Plasma electrolytes (Na, K, Cl)	Daily	2-3× weekly
Blood urea nitrogen	3× weekly	2× weekly
Plasma osmolarity	Daily	2-3× weekly
Plasma total calcium, inorganic phosphorus, magnesium	3× weekly	2-3× weekly
Blood glucose	Daily	2-3× weekly
Plasma transaminases, alkaline phosphatase, and bilirubin	3× weekly	1-2× weekly
Plasma total protein and fractions	2× weekly	Weekly
Blood acid-base status	Daily	2-3× weekly
Hemogram	Weekly	Weekly
Blood ammonia	1-2× weekly	1-2× weekly
Urine measurements		
Glucose	4-6× daily	2× daily
Specific gravity or osmolarity	2-4× daily	Daily
General measurements		
Volume of infusate	Daily	Daily
Oral intake (if any)	Daily	Daily
Urinary output	Daily total and each voiding	Daily
Extrarenal losses (if any)	Daily	Daily
Prevention and detection of infection		
Clinical observation (activity, temperature, etc.)	Daily	Daily
WBC count and differential	As indicated	As indicated
Blood culture and culture of infusate and filter	As indicated	As indicated

*From Winters, R. W.: Evaluation of the patient in total parenteral nutrition, Action, Mass., 1974, Publishing Sciences Group, Inc., p. 48.
†Phase I, when patient is adjusting; phase II, when patient is stable.

INTRAVENOUS FLUID MANAGEMENT

Some of the ground rules of intravenous fluid management are presented in this section. Because of the limitations of space in a book of this size, an abbreviated approach was used. More thorough coverage of this subject can be found in standard reference books.

Proper management of IV fluids, though still a controversial subject in some areas, may be simplified by the following general principles:

1. *Replace* existing volume deficits with a solution that is equivalent in volume, concentration, and composition to the fluid that was lost.
2. *Maintain* internal homeostasis with a solution that is equivalent in volume, concentration, and composition to sensible and insensible losses.

A rational approach to achieving the above goals requires a knowledge of the following areas:

1. The normal capacity of body fluid compartments:
   Total body water: 60% of body weight.
   ECF: 20% of body weight.
   Plasma volume: 5% of body weight.
   Interstitial fluid: 15% of body weight.
   ICF: 40% of body weight.
2. The normal composition of body fluid compartments:
   ECF:
   Plasma:
   Cations: Na^+, 142 mEq/liter; K^+, 4 mEq/liter; Ca^{++}, 5 mEq/liter; Mg^{++}, 3 mEq/liter.
   Anions: Cl^-, 103 mEq/liter; HCO_3^-, 27 mEq/liter; $SO_4^=$ and $PO_4^=$, 3 mEq/liter.
   Interstitial fluid:
   Cations: Na^+, 144 mEq/liter; K^+, 4 mEq/liter; Ca^{++}, 3 mEq/liter, Mg^{++}, 2 mEq/liter.
   Anions: Cl^-, 114 mEq/liter; HCO_3^-, 30 mEq/liter; $SO_4^=$ and $PO_4^=$, 3 mEq/liter.
   ICF:
   Cations: Na^+, 10 mEq/liter; K^+, 150 mEq/liter; Mg^{++}, 40 mEq/liter.
   Anions: $HPO_4^=$ and $SO_4^=$, 150 mEq/liter; HCO_3^-, 10 mEq/liter.
3. The initial rate and composition of IV fluids are guided by adequate clinical assessment. For example:
   History:
   Estimate fluid deficit:
   How much vomiting, diarrhea, drainage, fever, urine output?
   Loss of weight?
   Acute or chronic?
   Physical examination:
   Mental status.
   Temperature.
   Pulse rate.
   Respiratory rate.
   Blood pressure (sitting and lying).

Neck veins (full or collapsed).
Heart (rhythm, gallops).
Lungs (clear or congested).
Abdomen (evidence of inflammatory process).
Extremities (collapsed veins or edema).
Skin (dry, diaphoretic, turgor).
Laboratory:
Urinalysis (specific gravity, acetone).
CBC (hemoconcentration, anemia, infection).
Serum sodium (normal, high, or low).
Serum potassium (normal, high, or low).
Serum chloride (acidotic, alkalotic).
Serum bicarbonate (acidotic, alkalotic).
Blood glucose (hyper- or hypoglycemic).
BUN (hydration status, renal failure).
ABG (type of acidosis or alkalosis).
Other: creatinine, calcium, magnesium, ECG, chest x-ray.
Other:
CVP.
PWP.
Urinary catheter.
Response to fluid trial.

4. Normal content of GI secretions (average):

	ml/day	Na*	K*	Cl*	HCHO₃*	pH
Salivary	1500	10	26	10	30	
Gastric:						
pH > 4.0	2000	100	10	100	0	> 4.0
pH < 4.0	1500	60	10	130	0	< 4.0
Duodenum	100-2000	140	5	80	0	
Bile	50-800	145	5	100	35	7.8
Pancreas	100-800	140	5	75	115	8.0-8.3
Small bowel	3000	140	5	104	30	7.8-8.0
Ileostomy:						
Recent	500-2500	130	20	110	30	
Adapted	100-400	50	10	60	15-30	
Cecostomy	400	80	20	50	30	
Feces	100	60	30	4	< 15	
Sweat	500-4000	30-70	< 5	30-70	0	

*Unit: mEq/liter.

5. Normal daily losses of water:
Sensible losses: 800-1500 ml/day.
Insensible losses: 600-800 ml/day (increase by 10% for each degree of fever).

6. The composition of frequently used IV solutions (see p. 260):

IV solution	Na (mEq/liter)	K (mEq/liter)	Ca (mEq/liter)	Cl (mEq/liter)	Lactate (mEq/liter)	Calories per liter	mOsm per liter
5% Dextrose Injection, USP	0	0	0	0	0	170	252
10% Dextrose Injection, USP	0	0	0	0	0	340	505
0.9% Sodium Chloride Injection, USP	154	0	0	154	0	0	308
Sodium Lactate Injection, USP (M/6 Sodium Lactate)	167	0	0	0	167	54	334
2.5% Dextrose & 0.45% Sodium Chloride Injection, USP	77	0	0	77	0	85	280
5% Dextrose & 0.2% Sodium Chloride Injection, USP	34	0	0	34	0	170	321
5% Dextrose & 0.33% Sodium Chloride Injection, USP	56	0	0	56	0	170	365
5% Dextrose & 0.45% Sodium Chloride Injection, USP	77	0	0	77	0	170	406
5% Dextrose & 0.9% Sodium Chloride Injection, USP	154	0	0	154	0	170	560
10% Dextrose & 0.9% Sodium Chloride Injection, USP	154	0	0	154	0	340	813
Ringer's Injection, USP	147.5	4	4.5	156	0	0	309
Lactated Ringer's Injection, USP	130	4	3	109	28	9	273
5% Dextrose in Ringer's Injection	147.5	4	4.5	156	0	170	561
Lactated Ringer's with 5% Dextrose	130	4	3	109	28	180	525

BIBLIOGRAPHY

Angel, J. E., publisher: Physicians desk reference, ed. 37, Oradell, N.J., 1983, Medical Economics Co.

Ballinger, W. F., Collins, J. A., Drucker, W. R., and others: Manual of surgical nutrition, ed. 1, Philadelphia, 1975, W. B. Saunders Co.

Beeson, P. B., McDermott, W., and Wyngaarden, J. B., editors: Textbook of medicine, ed. 15, Philadelphia, 1979, W. B. Saunders Co.

Condon, R. E., and Nyhus, L. M., editors: Manual of surgical therapeutics, ed. 5, Boston, 1981, Little, Brown and Co.

Conn, H. F., editor: Current therapy, Philadelphia, 1983, W. B. Saunders Co.

Conn, H. F., and Conn, R. B., editors: Current diagnosis, ed. 6, Philadelphia, 1983, W. B. Saunders Co.

Costrini, N. V., and Thompson, W. M., editors: Manual of medical therapeutics, ed. 23, Boston, 1983, Little, Brown and Co.

Dunphy, J. E., and Way, L. W., editors: Current surgical diagnosis and treatment, ed. 5, Los Altos, 1981, Lange Medical Publishers.

Goldberger, E.: Treatment of cardiac emergencies, ed. 3, St. Louis, 1982, The C. V. Mosby Co.

Goodman, L. S., Gilman, A., and Gilman, A. G., editors: The pharmacological basis of therapeutics, ed. 6, London, 1980, The Macmillan Co.

Hardy, J. D., editor: Textbook of surgery, ed. 5, Philadelphia, 1977, J. B. Lippincott Co.

Harrison, T. R., Adams, R. D., Braunwald, E., and others, editors: Principles of internal medicine, ed. 8, New York, 1977, McGraw-Hill Book Co.

Kinney, J. M., Egdahl, R. H., and Zuidema, G. D., editors: Manual of preoperative and postoperative care, ed. 2, Philadelphia, 1971, W. B. Saunders Co.

Sabiston, D. C., editor: Textbook of surgery, ed. 11, Philadelphia, 1977, W. B. Saunders Co.

Schwartz, S. I., Lillehei, R. C., Shires, G. T., and others, editors: Principles of surgery, ed. 3, New York, 1977, McGraw-Hill Book Co.

Shires, G. T., Carrico, C. J., and Canizaro, P.C.: Shock, ed. 1, Philadelphia, 1973, W. B. Saunders Co.

Sokolow, M., and McIlroy, M. B.: Clinical cardiology, ed. 3, Los Altos, Calif., 1981, Lange Medical Publishers.

Thorbjarnarson, B.: Surgery of the biliary tract, ed. 2, Philadelphia, 1982, W. B. Saunders Co.

Wallach, J.: Interpretation of diagnostic tests, ed. 3, Boston, 1978, Little, Brown & Co.

Williams, R. H., editor: Textbook of endocrinology, ed. 6, Philadelphia, 1981, W. B. Saunders Co.

ABBREVIATIONS

A-a Do$_2$	alveolar-arterial oxygen diffusion
ABG	arterial blood gas
ac	before meals
ACD	acid citrate dextrose
ACTH	adrenocorticotropic hormone
ADH	antidiuretic hormone
ad lib	as desired
AFB	acid-fast bacteria
AHF	antihemophilic factor
ALA	aminolevulinic acid
ANA	antinuclear antibody
AODM	adult-onset diabetes mellitus
APC	atrial premature contraction
APR	abdominoperineal resection
ASD	atrial septal defect
ASO	antistreptolysin O
ATN	acute tubular necrosis
AV	atrioventicular
AVM	ateriovenous malformation
bid	twice daily
BMR	basal metabolic rate
bpm	beats per minute
BUN	blood urea nitrogen
CBC	complete blood count
CCU	cardiac care unit
CEA	carcinoembryonic antigen
CHF	congestive heart failure
cm	centimeter
CNS	central nervous system
COPD	chronic obstructive pulmonary disease
CPK	creatine phosphokinase
C & S	culture and sensitivity
CSF	cerebrospinal fluid
CT	computerized tomography
CVA	costovertebral angle
CVP	central venous pressure
DC	direct current
DDAVP	desmopressin acetate
DHT	dihydrotachysterol
DIC	disseminated intravascular coagulation

diff	differential (count)
DNA	deoxyribonucleic acid
D5½NS	dextrose 5%, ½ normal saline
DVT	deep venous thrombosis
ECF	extracellular fluid
ECG	electrocardiogram
EEG	electroencephalogram
ENT	ear, nose, and throat
ERCP	endoscopic retrograde cholangiopancreatography
ESR	erythrocyte sedimentation rate
FIco$_2$	fraction of inspired CO$_2$
Fio$_2$	fraction of inspired oxygen
FTA-ABS	fluorescent treponemal antibody absorption
FUO	fever of unknown origin
g	gram
g%	gram percent
GFR	glomerular filtration rate
GI	gastrointestinal
GIK	glucose-insulin-potassium
G6PD	glucose-6-phosphate dehydrogenase
gtt	drop
h	hour
HAA	hepatitis-associated antigen
HBDH	hydroxybutyric dehydrogenase
HBIG	hepatitis B immune globulin
HBsAg	hepatitis B surface antigen
HCG	human chorionic gonadotropin
HEENT	head, eye, ear, nose, and throat
5-HIAA	5-hydroxyindoleacetic acid
hs	at bedtime
IC	intracardiac
ICD	isocitrate dehydrogenase
ICF	intracellular fluid
ICU	intensive care unit
IF	intrinsic factor
IM	intramuscular
ISG	immune serum globulin
ITP	idiopathic thrombocytopenic purpura
IU	international unit
IV	intravenous
IVC	intravenous cholangiogram
IVP	intravenous pyelogram
JGA	juxtaglomerular apparatus
JODM	juvenile-onset diabetes mellitus
kg	kilogram
LAP	leukocyte alkaline phosphatase
LATS	long-acting thyroid stimulator
LBO	large bowel obstruction
LDH	lactic dehydrogenase

LE	lupus erythematosus
LFT	liver function test
LH	luteinizing hormone
LLQ	left lower quadrant
LR	lactated Ringer's
LUQ	left upper quadrant
LVED	left ventricular end-diastolic
LVFP	left ventricular filling pressure
LVH	left ventricular hypertrophy
M	molar
MAO	monoamine oxidase
MAT	multifocal atrial tachycardia
MBC	maximal breathing capacity
MCH	mean corpuscular hemoglobin
MCHC	mean corpuscular hemoglobin concentration
MCV	mean corpuscular volume
MEA	multiple endocrine adenomatosis
mEq	milliequivalent
mg	milligram
mIU	milli-international unit
ml	milliliter
mm	millimeter
mM	millimole
mOsm	milliosmole
mU	milliunit
μg	microgram
μU	microunit
N	normal
NCS	no concentrated sweets
NG	nasogastric
NPO	null per os (nothing by mouth)
NS	normal saline
NSR	normal sinus rhythm
OB/GYN	obstetrics and gynecology
OCG	oral cholecystogram
OD	right eye
OR	operating room
OS	left eye
OU	both eyes
$Paco_2$	partial pressure of carbon dioxide in arterial blood
PAD	pulmonary artery diastolic
PAH	para-aminohippurate
Pao_2	partial pressure of oxygen in arterial blood
pap	Papanicolaou
PAT	paroxysmal atrial tachycardia
PBG	porphobilinogen
PBI	protein-bound iodine
pc	after meals
Pco_2	carbon dioxide tension

PDR	*Physicians' Desk Reference*
PEEP	positive end-expiratory pressure
PFT	pulmonary function test
pg	picogram
PKU	phenylketonuria
PO	per os
Po$_2$	oxygen tension
POD	postoperative day
PR	per rectum
prn	as needed
PT	prothrombin time
PTH	parathyroid hormone
PTT	partial thromboplastin time
PVC	premature ventricular contraction
PWP	pulmonary wedge pressure
q	every
qAM	every morning
qd	every day
qid	four times daily
RAD	right axis deviation
RBBB	right bundle branch block
RBC	red blood (cell) count
RDA	recommended daily allowance
RHD	rheumatic heart disease
RLQ	right lower quadrant
RNA	ribonucleic acid
RPF	renal plasma flow
RTA	renal tubular acidosis
RU	resin uptake
RUQ	right upper quadrant
RVH	right ventricular hypertrophy
SA	sinoatrial
sat	saturation
SBE	subacute bacterial endocarditis
SBO	small bowel obstruction
SC	subcutaneous
SGOT	serum glutamic-oxaloacetic transaminase
SGPT	serum glutamic-pyruvic transaminase
SH	serum hepatitis
SL	sublingual
SLE	systemic lupus erythematosus
SPEP	serum protein electrophoresis
stat	at once
STS	serologic tests for syphilis
T½	serum half-life
T$_3$	triiodothyronine
T$_4$	thyroxine
TBW	total body water
THAM	tromethamine

TIA	transient ischemic attack
TIBC	total iron-binding capacity
tid	three times daily
TmG	tubular maximum for glucose
TPN	total parenteral nutrition
TSH	thyroid-stimulating hormone
TTP	thrombotic thrombocytopenic purpura
TVP	transvenous pacemaker
UGI	upper gastrointestinal
UPJ	ureteropelvic junction
UTI	urinary tract infection
V$_A$	minute alneolar ventilation
V$_D$	dead space volume
VD	venereal disease
VDRL	Venereal Disease Research Laboratories
VMA	vanillylmandelic acid
vol%	volume percent
V$_T$	tidal volume
WBC	white blood (cell) count
Z-E	Zollinger-Ellison
$>$	greater than
$<$	less than
$\geq$	greater than or equal to

INDEX

NOTES

NOTES

NOTES

NOTES

NOTES

NOTES

NOTES

NOTES

NOTES

NOTES

NOTES

The
CROCHETER'S
·COMPANION·

Nancy Brown

INTERWEAVE.
interweave.com

Editor
Sarah Rutledge Gorman

Technical Editor
Kay Mariea

Art Director
Liz Quan

Cover + Interior Designer
Adrian Newman

Illustrators
Marjorie C. Leggitt
Kathie Kelleher

Production Designer
Katherine Jackson

Interweave Press LLC
A division of F + W Media Inc.
201 East Fourth Street
Loveland, CO 80537
interweave.com

Printed in China by RR Donnelley.

Library of Congress Cataloging-in-Publication Data

Brown, Nancy, 1943-
The crocheter's companion / Nancy Brown.
pages cm
Includes bibliographical references and index.
ISBN 978-1-59668-829-2 (spiral bound)
1. Crocheting--Handbooks, manuals, etc. I. Title.
TT820.B85 2013
746.43'4--dc23

                                   2012032331

10 9 8 7 6 5 4 3 2 1

PREFACE

Crochet, a craft enjoyed in "Grandma's" day, is making a comeback in the contemporary fashion world and is gaining in popularity with the young and not-so-young alike. The love of the traditional, the delight in the homemade, and the creation of beautiful heirloom treasures comprise the true spirit of crochet and are the force behind this comeback.

This book was designed as a tool to be kept in your crochet bag, along with your other supplies. It is a quick reference for converting crochet hook sizes, understanding British terminology, deciphering international symbols, and much more.

The Crocheter's Companion can teach a novice the basic stitches, and help any crocheter work through a completed project. It is an easy-to-use how-to guide for learning new stitches and getting tips on finishing, and it offers many suggestions for special additions to your projects. Although written with the beginner-to-intermediate crocheter in mind, the experienced crocheter will also find many advanced techniques and helpful hints.

May this book inspire you to discover the fascinating art of crochet and bring you many hours of creative satisfaction, enjoyment, and pleasure.

Nancy Brown

TABLE OF CONTENTS

TOOLS, YARNS, AND GAUGES

TOOLS
Crochet hooks

Crochet hooks are the only tools you really need. Hooks are inexpensive, and if you purchase a full range of sizes, you will always have the right hook available for the project.

Crochet hooks are made in a variety of materials, including wood, plastic, aluminum, bamboo, and steel. The choice of material is a personal preference. Hooks also come in many sizes, designed for use with different weights of yarn.

A crochet hook is a type of needle with a hook on one end that is used to draw the yarn or thread through loops. Crochet hooks for use with yarn are usually aluminum or plastic, while crochet hooks for use with thread are made of steel and have smaller hook heads and shorter shanks.

Even though a crochet hook appears to be nothing more than a straight stick with a hook on one end, there are five distinct and necessary parts.

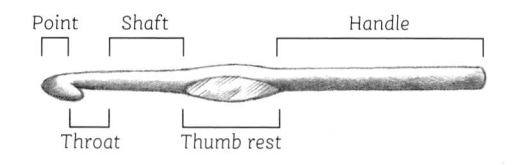

A Tunisian crochet hook is longer than most crochet hooks. It has a crochet hook on one end with a stopper or an extender cable to keep the required number of loops on the other end.

Hooks come in various sizes, according to the thickness of the needle. They are measured in millimeters (mm) or fractions of an inch. Sizes are indicated by letters, numbers, or millimeters, and the project instructions will specify the correct size required for the pattern.

Unfortunately, there is no standardization of crochet hook sizing between manufacturers. One manufacturer's size B may differ slightly from another's. Below is a comparison of sizes and types.

Comparative crochet hook sizes (from smallest to largest)

STEEL			ALUMINUM OR PLASTIC		
U.S.	UK	Metric (mm)	U.S.	UK	Metric (mm)
14	6	.6		14	2
13	5½			13	
12	5	.75	B	12	2.5
11	4½		C	11	3
10	4	1	D	10	
9	3½		E	9	3.5
8	3	1.25	F	8	4
7	2½	1.5	G	7	4.5
6	2	1.75	H	6	5
5	1½		I	5	5.5
4	1	2	J	4	6
3	1/0		K	2	7
2	2/0	2.5			
1	3/0	3			
0					
00		3.5			

Crocheter's supply kit

Your needlework bag should always contain the following tools:

- Crochet hooks of various sizes
- Hook/needle gauge
- Pencil and paper
- Row counter
- Safety pins
- Scissors
- Scraps of different-colored yarns or threads (*very handy for use as markers*)
- Sewing needles and basting threads
- Straight pins
- Tape measure
- Tapestry needles (*large-eyed, several sizes*)

YARNS

Yarn is a long continuous strand composed of either natural or man-made fibers or filaments. It is used for crochet projects and other fiber arts.

Crochet thread is specially formulated, usually from mercerized cotton, for crafting decorative crochet items like doilies or filet crochet. Crochet thread produces fabric of fine gauge that can be stiffened with starch.

Many different yarns may be used for crochet. Cotton is the most common, followed by wool and synthetic blends. Novelty yarns such as chenille, velour, and Lurex, as well as ribbons of all sorts, are fun to crochet with and can add wonderful depth to plain stitches. Cords, twines, and raffia are also suitable for crochet.

Yarns also vary in size, twist, and texture. The yarn you choose should complement the stitch you intend to work in. For example, for fancy stitches, textured yarns are usually less suitable than smooth ones. Complicated or textured patterns also show best when worked in lighter colors.

Yarns are usually selected for crochet based on the characteristics of the yarn fibers, such as wool for warmth, cotton or bamboo for lightweight garments, nylon for durability, or cashmere and alpaca for softness. Acrylic yarns are typically the least expensive. Study the characteristics of different types of yarn and crochet thread to learn which are best suited to particular types of garments. Angora or wool might make a warm sweater, but rugs need heavier yarn; and doilies or snowflake ornaments require cotton thread. For best results, use the type of yarn or thread recommended in the pattern directions.

Ply

Yarn "ply" indicates the number of strands that have been twisted together. You can see this by untwisting the end of the yarn. A single ply (also called a "singles") is one strand of spun yarn. Twisting two or more singles together forms plied yarn: A two-ply yarn is formed by two singles, a three-ply yarn by three singles, and so on. The thickness of a given yarn is determined by the individual thickness

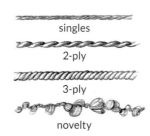

singles

2-ply

3-ply

novelty

of the plies, not the number of plies. A tightly twisted four-ply yarn may be thinner than a loosely spun singles. Plying two different yarns together may form novelty yarns, as can plying strands of the same yarn together at different speeds, thereby forming nubs and slubs.

Weight

The thickness or weight of the yarn is a significant factor in determining the gauge of your crochet project. (For an explanation of gauge and tension, see page 12.)

It is now common practice for yarn manufacturers to use a "yarn weight classification" system. This is a standard designation for the size (or diameter) of the yarn, not a reference to how much a yarn "weighs." The "yarn weight" required for a project and the amount of yarn needed to complete the project will be specified in the pattern instructions.

Yarns are generally categorized into seven groups according to weight: lace, superfine, fine, light, medium, bulky, and super bulky. A symbol should appear on the ball of yarn to indicate the group in which the yarn has been categorized.

However, older terms, such as fingering weight, sport and baby weight, DK, worsted, and chunky are still commonly used in pattern instructions.

fingering

sport/baby

DK

worsted

chunky

Dye lots

The dye lot specifies a group of skeins that were dyed together and thus have precisely the same color. Skeins with a dye lot are usually dyed after the yarn has been spun. They are dyed in huge lots, each of which is assigned a dye lot number. It is very important to purchase enough yarn, or slightly more than enough, to complete your project. Always make certain all skeins have the same dye lot number on the label. Although the color in two different lots may look the same in the skein, you will likely see a difference in the finished product.

Skeins that are labeled "no dye lot" are spun from fiber that has already been dyed. These yarns are purchased from the dye house in very large quantities and spun into different weights. There is usually a production date on these skeins. For your project, purchase enough yarn with the same date.

Yarn labels and bands

Yarn for crochet is usually sold in skeins or balls, although it may be wound onto spools or cones.

These skeins and balls are usually sold with a yarn label or band that describes: the yarn brand name; the fiber content; the color name and/or number; dye lot number or a statement that the yarn is a "no dye lot" yarn; the yarn weight classification; yarn weight in ounces and/or grams; the length of the skein in yards and/or meters; a knitting and/or crochet gauge; and laundering or cleaning instructions. This information on the yarn label is helpful in selecting the type of yarn and number of skeins needed for a project.

It is helpful to save a yarn label for each project in case you need to purchase additional skeins or want to reference instructions on care and cleaning.

Substituting yarns

Almost any yarn can be substituted for any other yarn, provided it can be worked to the specified gauge. Be careful when substituting yarns of different weights. You may get the same gauge using a smaller hook with a bulky yarn when the pattern calls for worsted, but the look and feel of the fabric may not be what you want. Select a yarn similar in weight and texture to the yarn in the materials list.

Yarn label symbols

100% virgin wool, superwash, machine washable

100% virgin wool

Suggested needle size or hook

Suitable for knitting machines

Hand wash only

Do not wash

Special cleaning

Dry clean with perchlorethylene or benzene

Do not dry clean

Yarn label symbols continued

Machine washable, gentle cycle maximum 30°C (86°F)

Do not bleach

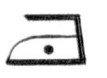

Iron at low setting

Iron at medium setting

Do not iron

Do not tumble dry

When substituting yarn, you will need to determine how much of the new yarn will be required. First, multiply the number of yards per skein in the pattern yarn by the number of skeins required. Divide this number by the number of yards per skein of the substitute yarn to determine the number of skeins needed in the new yarn.

For example, if the pattern requires 12 skeins of yarn with 110 yards per skein: 110 yards per skein × 12 skeins = 1,320 yards. Substitute yarn has 120 yards per skein. 1,320 yards divided by 120 yards = 11 skeins.

> **Note:** Many yarn labels give meters per skein instead of yards. To get an approximate number of yards per skein, simply multiply the meters by 10% and add to the number of meters per skein.

100 meters per skein x 10% = 10 meters. 100 + 10 = 110 yards. A skein with 100 meters has approximately 110 yards.

GAUGE AND TENSION

The terms "tension" and "gauge" may be used interchangeably. U.S. crochet terminology uses the word "gauge" in two different ways:

1. As a hook gauge when referring to the sizing of a crochet hook.

2. As a term to describe the number of stitches in a standard sized sample of work, usually a 4" (10 cm) swatch. UK terminology refers to this sample swatch as "tension."

Gauge is the number of stitches and rows (or rounds) to 1" (2.5 cm) of crochet work. The required gauge is specified in crochet patterns, and determines the finished size of the project. Gauge is determined by the size of the hook and by how tightly the yarn is held as the stitches are worked. Gauge is the most important factor in successful crocheting. Unless you obtain the gauge given for each design, you will not achieve satisfactory results.

Gauge swatch
Work a swatch of crochet in the appropriate stitch to determine how many stitches and rows per inch you get. Because all patterns are based on a certain number of stitches per inch, you must work a sample gauge for every project before you start. Crochet a square at least 4" by 4" (10 × 10 cm) in the pattern stitch you will be using. Place the sample on a flat surface and mark out the gauge

width of the pattern with pins. Count the number of stitches between pins.

If the gauge is correct, proceed with your project.

If you have *more* stitches per inch than specified, change to a *larger* hook.

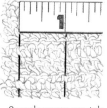

Sample gauge swatch

If you have *fewer* stitches per inch than specified, change to a *smaller* hook.

> **Note:** *Usually, if you obtain the correct gauge widthwise, you will also meet it lengthwise. Row gauge is not as crucial as stitch gauge, as most pieces are worked to a certain length, not a certain number of rows.*

HOW TO READ CROCHET INSTRUCTIONS

Crochet instructions may look like a foreign language, but they are merely a code of abbreviations and symbols. Instructions for working specific stitches should be included in the pattern on which you are working. Crochet abbreviations are typically specified at the beginning of a pattern, or in the front or back of a crochet pattern book.

The following is a chart of common abbreviations. But be aware that there are inconsistencies, especially when you compare vintage patterns to contemporary ones.

Abbreviations

beg	begin(ning)		**esc**	extended single crochet
bl	block		**fdc**	chainless foundation double crochet
BPdc	back post double crochet		**fhdc**	chainless foundation half double crochet
ch(s)	chain(s)		**FPdc**	front post double crochet
cl(s)	cluster(s)		**fsc**	chainless foundation single crochet
dc	double crochet		**hdc**	half double crochet
dec	decrease		**inc**	increase
dtr	double treble crochet		**lp(s)**	loop(s)
edc	extended double crochet		**p**	picot
ehdc	extended half double crochet		**pat(s)**	pattern(s)

rnd(s)	round(s)
sc	single crochet
sk	skip
sl st	slip stitch
sp(s)	space(s)
st(s)	stitch(es)
tog	together
tks	Tunisian knit stitch
tps	Tunisian purl stitch
tr	treble crochet
tr tr	triple treble crochet
tss	Tunisian simple stitch
yo	yarn over

HOW TO READ A CROCHET PATTERN

Crochet patterns usually begin with a foundation chain. Sometimes the foundation chain consists of many stitches, as for an afghan. Other times, it is short, for example when creating a motif that begins in a circle. The chainless foundation technique is discussed beginning on page 22.

Holding your project

Hold your project the way you feel most comfortable. Be sure you are able to complete the stitches correctly. You should regularly advance your grip on the project so that you are holding the stitches closest to the hook; this helps you maintain an even gauge.

Turning your work

When working in rows and the pattern instructs you to "turn the piece," turn it so you are working from the opposite end on the other side of the fabric. It is best to turn the piece as if you are turning the page of a book.

WRITTEN INSTRUCTIONS— TERMS AND SYMBOLS

* ASTERISK: Denotes that a group of stitches shown after this sign must be repeated.

[ ] BRACKETS: When enclosing a stitch combination within a parenthetical combination, the combination will be repeated in the order shown. For example, "(ch 5, [sc in next sc] 2 times, sc in next sc) 5 times" means to repeat the bracketed stitches two times within the larger combination, which will be repeated five times.

† DAGGER: Identifies a portion of instructions that will be repeated later in the same row or round.

FASTEN OFF: At the end of the last row, do not make any turning chains. Cut the yarn about 6" (15 cm) from the work. Draw the end through the last loop on the hook and pull tight.

GAUGE OR TENSION: The number of stitches and rows per inch required for a pattern.

" INCHES: Denotes inches (in U.S. only).

MULTIPLE OF STITCHES: Generally used at the beginning of directions to mean that a certain multiple of stitches is necessary to work one pattern. For example, a "multiple of four stitches" would mean any number divisible by four: four, eight, twelve, sixteen, twenty, etc.

MULTIPLE OF STITCHES PLUS: Used to specify the number of stitches for a foundation chain. For example, if the pattern states "multiple of five stitches plus two," it will take five, ten, fifteen, etc. stitches for the foundation chain, plus two stitches at the end of the foundation chain for the height of one stitch to make the five-stitch pattern.

( ) PARENTHESES: When used to designate various sizes, the figure preceding the brackets pertains to the smallest size, and instructions for any larger sizes are within the parentheses. When enclosing a stitch combination, that combination is repeated in the order shown. For example, "(ch 5, sc in next sc) 5 times" means to work the combination of stitches in parentheses five times.

WORK EVEN: Continue working in pattern, without increases or decreases.

WORK EVEN IN PATTERN: Continue working in the pattern stitch in which you are instructed, keeping continuity of design.

International stitch symbols and terms

	U.S. TERM	*BRITISH TERM*		U.S. TERM
○	chain (ch)	*chain*	ʒ	front post double crochet (FPdc)
●	slip stitch (sl st)	*slip stitch (ss) or tight stitch*	ʒ	back post double crochet (BPdc)
	skip (sk)	*miss*	⩓	sc2tog (single decrease)
+	single crochet (sc)	*double crochet (dc)*	⩓	sc3tog (double decrease)
T	half double crochet (hdc)	*half treble (htc)*	⊖	Dc2tog cluster worked in single st
Ŧ	double crochet (dc)	*treble (tr)*	⊕	Dc3tog cluster worked in single st
Ŧ	treble crochet (tr)	*double treble (dtr)*	Ⱥ	3 dc cluster worked in space or several sts
Ŧ	double treble crochet (dtc)	*triple treble (trtr)*	⌣	front loop only [e.g., ⟂ single crochet, front loop only]
℣	2 dc worked in a single st		⌢	back loop only [e.g., ⟂ single crochet, back loop only]
℣	3 dc worked in a single st		⊕	five loop popcorn
℣	4 dc worked in a single st		⊕	five loop puff stitch
℣	5 dc worked in a single st		⊕	five loop cluster
℣	6 dc worked in a single st		⊗	picot of chain three
	fasten off	*bind off*		
	gauge	*tension*		

SKILL LEVEL SYMBOLS

The skill level symbol is a horizontal bar divided into four sections. When one section of the bar is shaded, it indicates a beginner pattern; four shaded sections indicate a pattern for experienced crocheters.

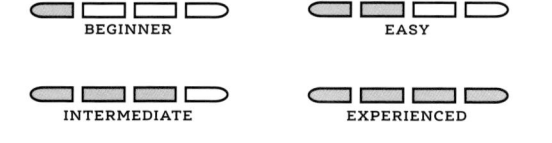

HOW TO READ A STITCH DIAGRAM

Stitch diagrams are especially useful for reading crochet patterns. When crochet instructions are very long, it is easier to find your place when viewing a chart that "duplicates" your work in symbols instead of written words. Most countries outside the United States use stitch diagrams to avoid language barriers, so you can use and enjoy books and patterns from all over the world, many of which are available via the Internet.

Even if you are adept at reading crochet patterns and have done so for years, a crochet pattern written in a diagram with symbols will help you visualize the project and perhaps simplify your work. Each stitch has its own symbol (see chart on page 17), so a pattern diagram is created to illustrate the order of the stitches and their relationship to other stitches. Stitch diagrams can represent patterns worked in rows or in rounds.

Stitch diagram working in rows

The right side row number is placed on the right-hand side of the stitch diagram, which means you work from the right side to the left side. On wrong side rows, the number is on the left-hand side, so you follow the diagram from left to right.

Stitch diagram working in rounds

When working in rounds and beginning at the center, you read the stitch diagram counterclockwise. Do no turn between rows unless instructed to do so.

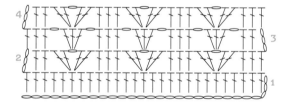

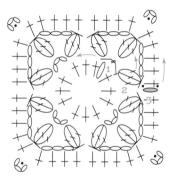

BASIC CROCHET STITCHES

FOUNDATION CHAIN

A chain of stitches known as the foundation chain is the basis for most crochet projects. Other stitches are worked off this foundation.

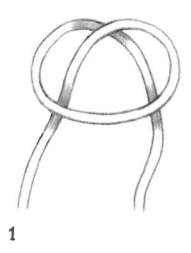

1

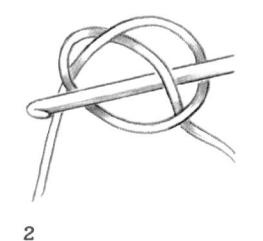

2

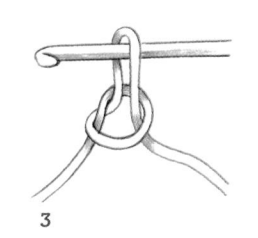

3

1. Make a slip knot on the hook *(fig. 1)*, about 6" (15 cm) from the end of the yarn *(fig. 2)*. Gently pull short end of yarn to tighten the knot, then gently pull the end attached to the ball to tighten the loop on the hook *(fig. 3)*.

Note: The slip knot becomes part of the first chain, so be careful not to pull too tightly or you will not be able to work into that chain.

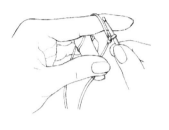
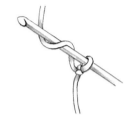

4   **5**   **6**

2. Place the hook between your right index finger and thumb. In your left hand, place the yarn over your ring finger, under your middle finger, and over your index finger, creating tension by holding the short end between the thumb and middle finger. If you want more tension, wrap the yarn around your little finger as well. Place the hook under then over the strand on your index finger *(fig. 4)*.

3. Catch the strand with the hook and draw a loop through the slip knot *(fig. 5)*.

4. Repeat, drawing a new loop through the loop on the hook, until the chain is the desired length *(fig. 6)*.

CHAINLESS FOUNDATIONS

A chainless foundation is an alternative to creating a foundation chain. This technique creates your stitch and chain at the same time. The foundation stitches replace the traditional foundation chain and create the first row of stitches. This method produces a foundation row that is sized more like a regular row. Because this method eliminates the chain altogether, it makes your foundation row and rest of the rows and stitches in your project more evenly aligned. This method helps to maintain an even tension and consistent measurement from the first row to the last.

Chainless foundation single crochet (fsc)

1. Make a slip knot on the hook.

2. Chain two *(fig. 1)* and then insert the hook into the second chain from the hook, under the two upper strands.

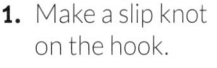

1

3. Draw a loop through *(fig. 2)*. There are now two loops on the hook.

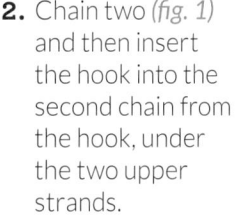

2

4. Yarn over hook *(fig. 3)*.

3

5. Draw a new loop through one loop on the hook. There are still two loops on the hook (fig. 4).

6. Yarn over hook.

7. Draw a new loop through both loops on the hook, completing the fsc (fig. 5).

To start the next fsc

1. Insert the hook under both loops of the previous stitch (fig. 1).

2. Yarn over hook.

3. Draw a new loop under both loops of the previous stitch. There are two loops on the hook (fig. 2).

4. Repeat Steps 4 through 7 of fsc.

5. Repeat instructions to start the next fsc until you have the desired number of fsc stitches (fig. 3).

Chainless foundation half double crochet (fhdc)

1. Make a slip knot on the hook and chain two *(fig. 1)*.

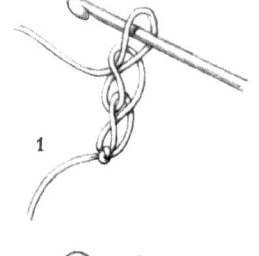

1

2. Yarn over hook *(fig. 2)*.

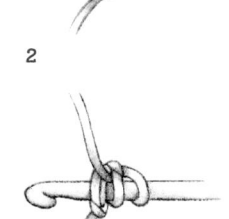

2

3. Insert the hook into the second chain from hook, under the two upper strands *(fig. 3)*.

3

4. Draw a loop through. There are now three loops on the hook (the foundation chain stitch) *(fig. 4)*.

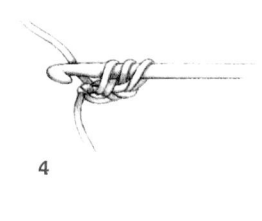

4

5. Yarn over hook *(fig. 5)*.

5

6. Draw a new loop through one loop. There are still three loops on the hook *(fig. 6)*.

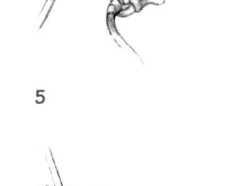

6

7. Yarn over hook (*fig. 7*).

7

8. Draw a new loop through three loops on the hook, completing the fhdc (*fig. 8*).

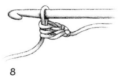

8

To start the next fhdc

1. Yarn over hook (*fig. 1*).

2. Insert the hook under both strands of the foundation chain stitch (*fig. 2*).

3. Yarn over hook.

4. Repeat Steps 4 through 8 of fhdc.

5. Repeat instructions to start the next fhdc until you have the desired number of fhdc stitches.

1

2

Chainless foundation double crochet (fdc)

1. Make a slip knot on the hook and chain three *(fig. 1)*.

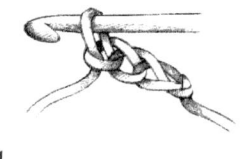

1

2. Yarn over hook *(fig. 2)*.

2

3. Insert the hook into the third chain from the hook, under the two upper strands *(fig. 3)*.

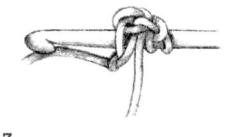

3

4. Draw a loop through. There are now three loops on the hook (the foundation chain stitch) *(fig. 4)*.

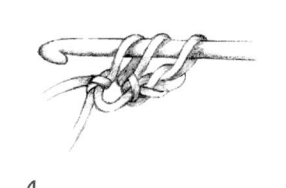

4

5. Yarn over hook *(fig. 5)*.

5

6. Draw a new loop through one loop on the hook. There are still three loops on the hook *(fig. 6)*.

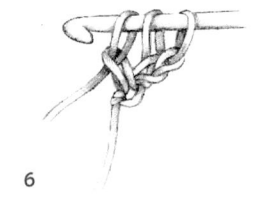

6

7. Yarn over hook *(fig. 7)*.

7

8. Draw a new loop through two loops on the hook. There are still two loops on the hook *(fig. 8)*.

9. Yarn over hook.

8

10. Draw a new loop through two loops on the hook, completing the fdc.

To start the next fdc

1. Yarn over hook *(fig. 1)*.

2. Insert the hook under both strands of the foundation chain stitch *(fig. 2)*.

3. Repeat Steps 4 through 10 of fdc.

4. Repeat instructions to start the next fdc until you have the desired number of fdc stitches.

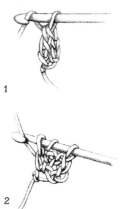

1

2

SINGLE CROCHET (sc)

Make a foundation chain the desired length. If you want a row of ten sc stitches, you need a chain of eleven stitches.

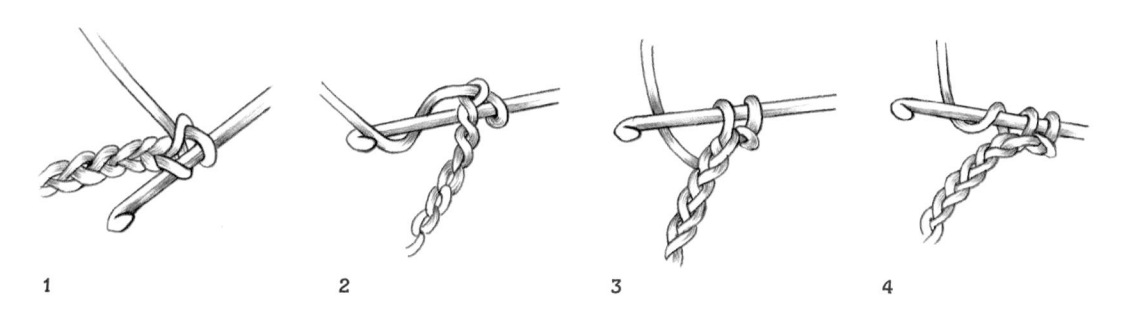

1   2   3   4

First row

1. Insert the hook into the second chain from hook, under the two upper strands *(fig. 1)*.

2. Draw a loop through *(fig. 2)*. There are now two loops on the hook *(fig. 3)*.

3. Yarn over hook *(fig. 4)*.

4. Draw a new loop through both loops on the hook, completing the sc (*fig. 5*).

5. Insert the hook into the next chain and repeat Steps 2 through 4. Continue until the row is complete (*fig. 6*).

5

6

2. Insert the hook under both top loops of the first sc and, following Steps 2 through 5 of first row, complete the stitch (*fig. 2*).

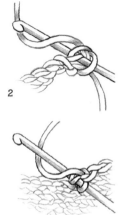

2

3. Continue working one sc into each stitch in the row. All succeeding rows of sc are the same as this row (*fig. 3*).

3

Succeeding rows

1. After completing the first row, chain one and turn to begin next row (*fig. 1*).

1

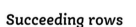

Note: Unless otherwise instructed, *always* pick up both loops of the stitch you're working in. When only one loop is picked up, it is "rib stitch."

EXTENDED SINGLE CROCHET (esc)

The extended single crochet stitch is similar to a single crochet stitch, but as the name implies, the stitch adds two steps and is extended to be slightly taller.

Make a foundation chain the desired length. If you want a row of ten esc stitches, you need a chain of eleven stitches.

First row

1. Insert the hook into the second chain from hook, under the two upper strands *(fig. 1)*.

1

2. Draw a loop through. There are now two loops on the hook *(fig. 2)*.

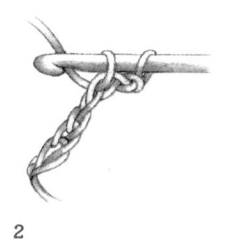

2

3. Yarn over hook *(fig. 3)*.

3

4. Draw a new loop through one loop on the hook. There are still two loops on the hook *(fig. 4)*.

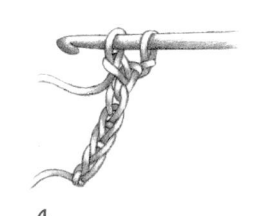

4

5. Yarn over hook (fig. 5).

5

6. Draw a new loop through remaining two loops on the hook, completing the esc (fig. 6).

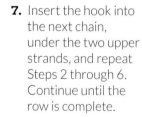

7. Insert the hook into the next chain, under the two upper strands, and repeat Steps 2 through 6. Continue until the row is complete.

6

Succeeding rows

1. After completing the first row, chain one and turn to begin next row (fig. 1).

1

2. Insert the hook under both top loops of the first esc and, following Steps 2 through 6 of first row, complete the stitch (fig. 2).

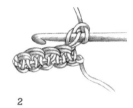

2

3. Continue working one esc into each stitch in the row. All succeeding rows of esc are the same as this second row.

HALF DOUBLE CROCHET (hdc)

Make a foundation chain the desired length. If you want a row of ten hdc stitches, you need a chain of eleven stitches.

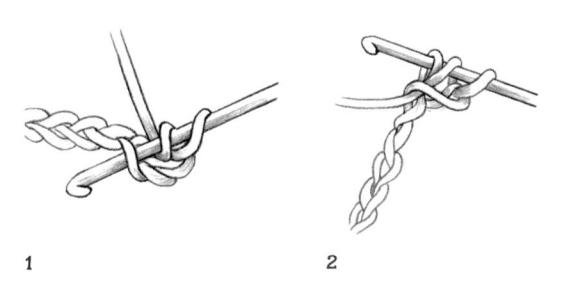

1

2

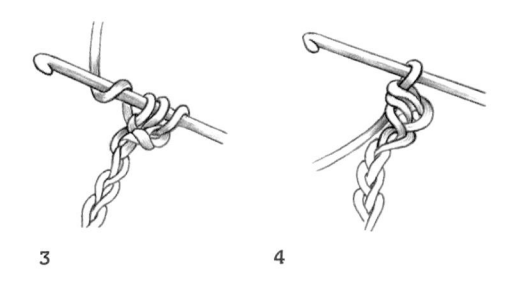

3

4

First row

1. Yarn over hook, then insert the hook into the third chain from hook, under the two upper strands *(fig. 1)*.

2. Draw a loop through *(fig. 2)*.

3. Yarn over hook *(fig. 3)*.

4. Draw a loop through the three loops on the hook, completing the hdc *(fig. 4)*.

5. Insert the hook into next chain and repeat Steps 2 through 4. Continue until the row is complete.

Succeeding rows

1. After completing the first row, chain two and turn to begin next row *(fig. 1)*.

2. Yarn over hook, skip the first stitch, and insert the hook under both loops of the top of next stitch *(fig. 2)*.

3. Following Steps 2 through 4 of first row, complete the stitch. Continue until the row is complete.

1

2

EXTENDED HALF DOUBLE CROCHET (ehdc)

Make a foundation chain the desired length. If you want a row of ten ehdc stitches, you need a chain of twelve stitches.

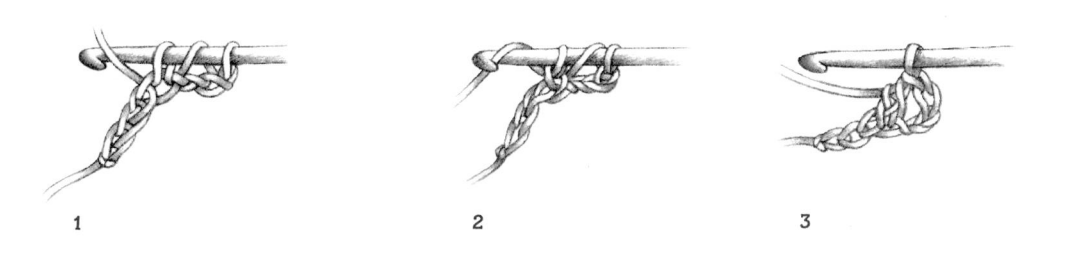

1　　　　　　　**2**　　　　　　　**3**

First row

1. Yarn over hook, then insert the hook into the fourth chain from hook, under the two upper strands.

2. Draw a loop through. There are three loops on the hook *(fig. 1)*.

3. Yarn over hook and draw through one loop. There are still three loops on the hook *(fig. 2)*.

4. Yarn over hook and draw through all three loops, completing the ehdc *(fig. 3)*.

5. Yarn over hook, insert the hook into next chain under the two upper strands and repeat Steps 2 through 4. Continue until the row is complete.

Succeeding rows

1. After completing the first row, chain three and turn to begin next row.

2. Yarn over hook, skip the first stitch, and insert the hook under both loops of the top of next stitch *(fig. 1)*.

3. Following Steps 2 through 4 of first row, complete the stitch. Continue until the row is complete. Continue until the last ehdc has been worked in the row below, and work last ehdc into the third chain of the beginning chain-three *(fig. 2)*.

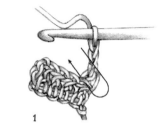

1

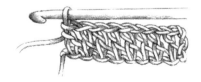

2

DOUBLE CROCHET (dc)

Make a foundation chain the desired length.
If you want a row of ten dc stitches, you need
a chain of twelve stitches.

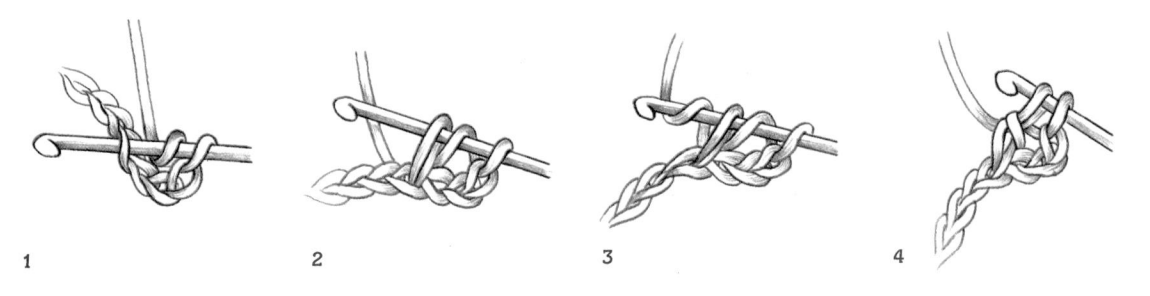

1   2   3   4

First row

1. Yarn over hook, then insert the hook into
fourth chain from hook, under the two
upper strands *(fig. 1)*.

2. Draw up a loop *(fig. 2)*.

3. Yarn over hook *(fig. 3)*.

4. Draw a loop through two of the loops
on the hook *(fig. 4)*.

5. Yarn over hook and draw a loop through the two remaining loops on the hook, completing the dc.

6. Yarn over hook, then insert the hook into the next chain, under the two upper strands *(fig. 5)* and repeat Steps 2 through 5. Continue until the row is complete.

5

Succeeding rows

1. After completing the first row, chain three and turn to begin next tow. This chain-three will *always* count as the first dc you are working on.

1

2. Yarn over hook, skip the first stitch and insert the hook under both loops of the top of next stitch *(fig. 1)*.

3. Following Steps 2 thorough 5 of first row, complete the stitch. Continue until the row is complete *(fig. 2)*.

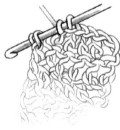

2

EXTENDED DOUBLE CROCHET (edc)

Make a foundation chain the desired length. If you want a row of ten edc stitches, you need a chain of twelve stitches.

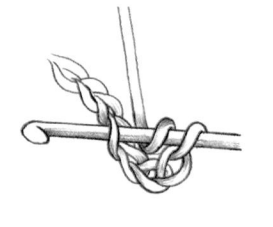

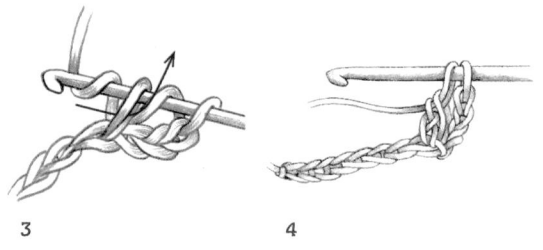

1   2   3   4

First row

1. Yarn over hook, then insert the hook into fourth chain from hook, under the two upper strands *(fig. 1)*.

2. Draw up a loop. There are three loops on the hook *(fig. 2)*.

3. Yarn over hook. Draw a loop through one of the loops on the hook. There are still three loops on the hook *(fig. 3)*.

4. Yarn over hook and draw a loop through two loops on the hook *(fig. 4)*.

5. Yarn over hook and draw a loop through the two remaining loops on the hook, completing the edc (*fig. 5*).

5

6. Yarn over hook, then insert the hook into the next chain, under the two upper strands, and repeat Steps 2 through 5. Continue until the row is complete (*fig. 6*).

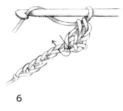

6

Succeeding rows

1. After completing the first row, chain three and turn to begin next row. This chain-three will *always* count as the first edc of the row you are working on.

2. Yarn over hook, skip the first stitch, and insert the hook under both loops of the top of next stitch (*fig. 1*).

1

3. Following Steps 2 through 5 of first row, complete the stitch. Continue until the row is complete. The last edc is worked in the third chain of the beginning chain-three (*fig. 2*).

2

TREBLE CROCHET (tr)

Make a foundation chain the desired length. If you want a row of ten tr stitches, you need a chain of thirteen stitches.

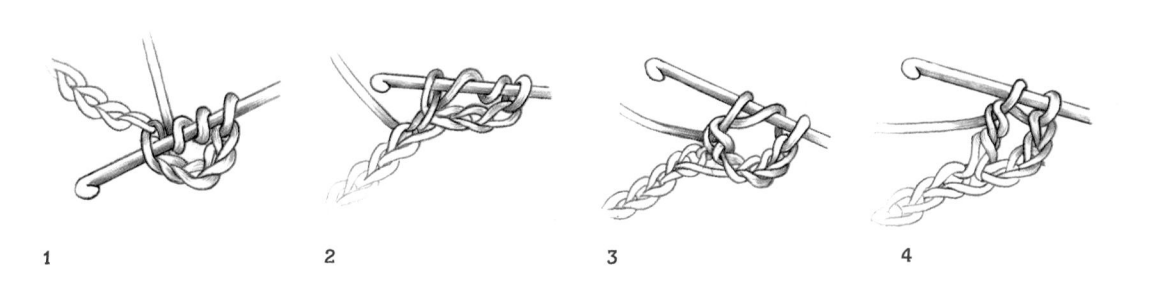

1   2   3   4

First row

1. Yarn over hook twice, then insert the hook into fifth chain from the hook, under the two upper strands *(fig. 1)*.

2. Draw a loop through *(fig. 2)*.

3. Yarn over hook and draw a loop through two of the loops on the hook *(fig. 3)*.

4. Yarn over hook and draw a loop through the next two loops on the hook *(fig. 4)*.

5. Yarn over hook and
draw a loop through
the last two loops on
the hook, completing
the tr *(fig. 5)*.

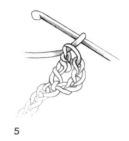

5

Succeeding rows

1. After completing the first row, chain four to
begin next row. This chain-four will *always*
count as the first tr of the row you are
working on.

2. With yarn over hook
twice, skip the first
stitch and insert the
hook under both
loops of the top of
next stitch *(fig. 1)*.

1

3. Following Steps 2
through 5 of first
row, complete the
stitch. Continue
until the row is
complete *(fig. 2)*.

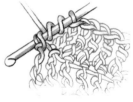

2

Variations of the treble crochet

More loops are created in these treble crochet stitches, making the stitches deeper. Make a foundation chain the desired length.

Double treble crochet (dtr)

1. Yarn over hook three times and insert the hook into the sixth chain from the hook, under the two upper strands.

2. Draw a loop through the chain—five loops on the hook. Yarn over and draw through two loops at a time four times, completing the dtr.

3. After completing the first row, chain five and turn to begin next row. This chain-five will *always* count as the first dtr of the row you are working on.

4. With yarn over hook three times, skip the first stitch and insert the hook under both loops of the top of next stitch.

5. Following Step 2 of first row, complete the stitch. Continue until the row is complete.

Triple treble crochet (tr tr)

1. Yarn over hook four times and insert the hook into the seventh chain from the hook, under the two upper strands.

2. Draw a loop through the chain—six loops on the hook. Yarn over and draw through two loops at a time five times, completing the tr tr.

3. After completing the first row, chain six and turn to begin next row. This chain-six will *always* count as the first tr tr of the row you are working on.

4. With yarn over hook four times, skip the first stitch and insert the hook under both loops of the top of next stitch.

5. Following Step 2 of first row, complete the stitch. Continue until the row is complete.

SLIP STITCH (sl st)

Slip stitch is not normally used exclusively to crochet fabric, but it makes a good cord when worked off a foundation chain or a neat edging when worked off the last row of a crocheted piece. It is also used to join one end of a round to the other.

1. Make a foundation chain the desired length.

2. Insert the hook into the second chain from hook, under the top strand. In one motion, draw a loop through the chain and the loop on the hook.

3. Insert the hook under the top strand of next chain and draw a loop through the chain and the loop on the hook. Repeat to end of chain.

WORKING IN THE FRONT LOOP ONLY AND THE BACK LOOP ONLY

Each crochet stitch creates a front and a back loop. Unless otherwise instructed, always pick up both loops of the stitch you are working in.

1. To work in the front loop of a stitch, insert your hook underneath the front loop only and complete the stitch as indicated *(fig. 1)*.

1

2. To work in the back loop of a stitch, insert your hook underneath the back loop only and complete the stitch as indicated *(fig. 2)*.

Note: When instructed to work in the back loop only, you are probably working in a rib stitch pattern. For instructions, see page 63.

2

BASIC CROCHET TECHNIQUES

WORKING IN ROWS

A row consists of a group of stitches crocheted from one end of the work to the other. With the exception of reverse single crochet (see page 103), rows are worked from right to left. Unless the pattern indicates otherwise, odd-numbered rows form the right side of the work and even-numbered, or return rows, form the wrong side.

When the work is turned at the end of a row, turning chains are worked, and these usually form the first stitch of a new row.

Key to turning rows

As stitches vary in height, each requires a different number of chain stitches for turning at the end of a row. The hook must be taken up to the correct level before the next stitch can be worked. The table below shows the number of chain stitches needed to make a turn for each stitch.

Single crochet (sc)	Chain 1 to turn
Half double crochet (hdc)	Chain 2 to turn
Double crochet (dc)	Chain 3 to turn
Treble crochet (tr)	Chain 4 to turn
Double treble (dtr)	Chain 5 to turn
Triple treble (tr tr)	Chain 6 to turn

WORKING IN ROUNDS

Many patterns start with a chain of a specified number of stitches, where the last chain is joined to the first chain with a slip stitch, forming a circle. When crocheting in rounds, you are always working from right to left, without turning the work, and you are always working on the right side.

Instructions may read, "Ch 8, join with sl st to form a ring."

The pattern will then commence the rounds. Instructions may read, "Sc 12 sts into ring."

When you come back to the starting place, a round has been completed. If you are working a spiral, the rounds simply continue. If you are working even rounds, you may be instructed to join with a slip stitch to the first stitch.

If you are making a circular flat piece, you must increase evenly around the work. Your pattern will instruct you where to make the increases. Different shapes can be created depending on where the increases are made.

When making a tubular shape (like a sock or a hat), increases or decreases are worked to make the tube wider or narrower, or to change the shape, such as for a heel.

Adjustable ring or magic loop

The adjustable ring, also known as the magic loop, is another way to begin working in the round. Using this method to begin your project, you are able to control the size of the hole in the center, making it as large or as small as you want (or no hole at all).

1. Leaving a yarn tail of about 6" (15 cm), make a loop by pulling the tail counterclockwise behind the yarn coming from the ball. The strand of yarn coming from the ball should be at the left *(fig. 1)*.

2. Insert the hook in the center of the loop.

3. Yarn over hook using the yarn from the ball *(fig. 2)*.

4. Draw loop through.

5. Chain one.

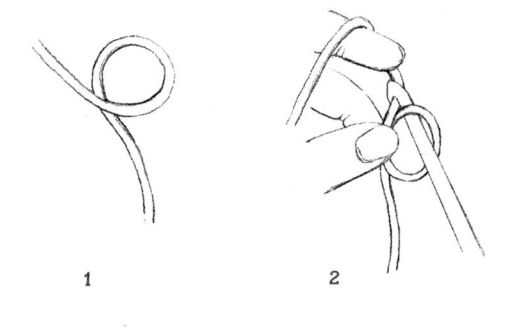

1

2

First round

Work in the desired stitch pattern. Example is worked in single crochet.

1. Insert the hook in the center of loop.

2. Yarn over hook *(fig. 1)*.

1

3. Draw yarn through. There are two loops on the hook.

4. Yarn over hook (fig. 2).

2

5. Draw yarn through both loops on the hook (fig. 3).

3

6. Repeat Steps 1 through 5 for desired number of stitches (fig. 4).

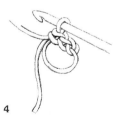

4

7. Pull tail to tighten ring to desired size (fig. 5).

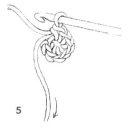

5

8. Slip stitch into the beginning stitch to complete the circle (fig. 6).

6

Succeeding rounds

After completing the first round, work in rounds in stitch pattern desired.

JOINING NEW YARN

Whenever possible, join new yarn at the beginning of a row.

1. Fasten off the old yarn.

2. With a slip knot on the hook, start the next row with a new yarn.

If you cannot join a new yarn at the beginning of a row, proceed as follows.

> **Note:** *Never make knots in your work—they will always work themselves to the outside.*

1. When the yarn you are using is coming to an end, place the new yarn along the top of the work and crochet a few stitches over the new with the old yarn.

2. Before the old yarn has completely run out, change to the new yarn and work stitches with the new yarn over the old yarn.

3. With a tapestry needle, weave the ends into the work on the wrong side (see page 111).

SHAPING

If you are going to make anything other than a straight piece, you must shape the piece as you crochet by adding or subtracting stitches. If you want to make your piece wider, *increase* stitches. If you want to make your piece narrower, *decrease* stitches.

Decreasing

To decrease is to eliminate one or more stitches. *Internal decreases* are worked within the row. *External decreases* are worked at the beginning or the end of a row, at a side edge.

Decrease instructions will be given in individual patterns to suit the particular stitch being worked.

Internal decreasing

METHOD ONE: Simply omit a stitch, working into the second, rather than the next, stitch.

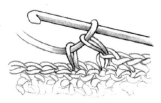

METHOD TWO: Work two stitches together, as illustrated on page 52 (internal decreasing method two in single crochet).

Note: If your pattern directs you to decrease one stitch at the beginning and at the end of the row, work a decrease in the first two stitches and in the last two stitches.

Internal decreasing method two in single crochet

Draw a loop through each of the next two stitches, yarn over and draw a loop through all three loops on the hook. One stitch has been made from two stitches.

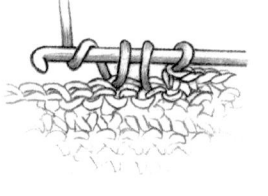
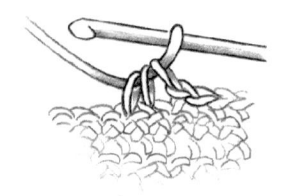

Internal decreasing method two in half double crochet

1. Yarn over hook, insert the hook into the first stitch, and draw a loop through.

2. Yarn over hook, insert the hook into the second stitch, and draw a loop through—five loops on the hook.

3. Yarn over and pull a loop through all five loops on the hook.

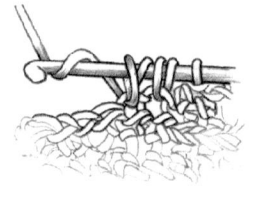

Internal decrease method two in double crochet

1. Yarn over hook, insert hook into the first stitch, draw a loop through, yarn over hook, draw a loop through two of the loops on the hook. Two loops remain on the hook.

3. Yarn over and draw a loop through all three loops. One loop remains on the hook.

2. Yarn over, insert the hook into the second stitch, draw a loop through, yarn over, draw a loop through two loops. Three loops remain on the hook.

External decreasing

To decrease at the beginning of a row, work slip stitches into the stitches to be decreased, work the turning chain stitches, and proceed as usual.

To decrease at the end of a row, leave the stitches to be decreased unworked, work the turning chain stitches, and begin the next row.

Increasing

To increase is to add one or more stitches. *Internal increases* are worked within the row. *External increases* are worked at the beginning or the end of a row, at a side edge.

Always count your stitches after you have completed an increase row, and after you have worked the next row, to make sure you are maintaining the number of stitches required.

Internal increasing

To increase one stitch, work two stitches into one stitch.

To make a double increase, work three stitches into one stitch.

External increasing

This method of increasing should be used to increase a large number of stitches at the beginning and end of a row; for example, at the armhole edge for a cap sleeve.

Increasing at the right edge of the work

1. At the end of the previous row, work one additional chain stitch for each stitch to be increased, then work the number of turning chains required by the stitch being used.

2. Work the chosen stitch into the extra chain stitches, then complete the row as usual.

Increasing at the left edge of the work

1. At the end of the row to be increased, drop the yarn you're working with.

2. With a slip stitch, attach a new strand of yarn to the last stitch of the previous row, and work one additional chain stitch for each stitch to be increased.

3. Fasten off the new yarn.

4. Pick up the dropped loop and work the chosen stitch into the extra chain stitches.

Binding off

If you are instructed to bind off stitches, you are to begin your next row several stitches in from the end of your work and end that row several stitches in from the other end of your work. Do this by working external decreases on each side of the row (see page 54).

FAMILIAR STITCHES and FAVORITES

There are many ways to use various pattern stitches, such as shells, popcorns, clusters, and ribbings. Here are some basic instructions.

AROUND THE POST

Working around the back or front of a post of the previous row gives an interesting raised ridge or ridges on the front of the crochet. While this is usually worked in double crochet, the same methods apply to single or treble crochet.

Around the post is worked either from the front or from the back, and abbreviations usually read "FPdc" or "BPdc." Around-the-post double crochet is worked by inserting the hook from the front (or from the back) and around the "post" of the double crochet of the previous row.

- When the hook is worked around the front of the post, it produces a raised stitch on the right side.

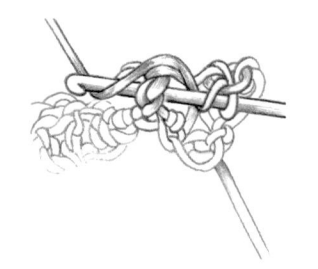

- When the hook is worked around the back of the post, it produces a raised stitch on the wrong side.

Around the post can be worked in many ways: every second stitch, every third stitch, or every fourth stitch, as described below. The pattern is up to you.

To begin this sample, chain 15.

FOUNDATION ROW: Dc in fourth ch from hook, dc in each ch across. Ch 3. Turn.

ROW 1: Dc in second st, work a FPdc around the post of next st. *Dc in each of next 3 sts, FPdc around the post of the next st. Repeat from *, ending with dc in last st and in turning ch. Ch 3. Turn.

ROW 2: Dc in second st. *BPdc around next st, dc in each of next 3 sts. Repeat from *, ending with BPdc in next st, dc in next st, dc in turning ch. Ch 3. Turn.

Repeat Rows 1 and 2 for pattern.

CLUSTER STITCH

A cluster stitch is a group of three or four stitches (dc, hdc, or tr) worked in the same place with the last loop of each stitch worked off together to form a petal-shaped stitch.

This lovely little bobble is created by working three or more double crochet stitches into the same stitch of the previous row. Cluster stitches may be placed in a pattern or at random. Here we skip two stitches between clusters.

Holding back last loop of each dc, work 3 dc in same st *(fig. 1)*, yo and pull lp through 4 lps on the hook, ch 1 to secure.

To begin this sample, chain a multiple of 3 plus 5 stitches.

ROW 1: Work cluster stitch in fifth ch from hook, *ch 2, sk next 2 ch, work a cluster stitch in next st. Repeat from *. Ch 2. Turn *(fig. 2)*.

ROW 2: *Work a cluster stitch in next ch-2 sp, ch 2. Repeat from *, ending with cluster stitch under turning ch *(fig. 3)*. Ch 2. Turn.

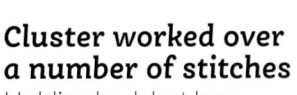

Repeat Row 2 for pattern, working a cluster stitch into each ch-2 space of the row below for desired length.

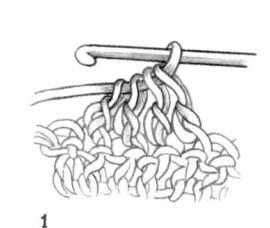

Cluster worked over a number of stitches

Holding back last loop of each st, work 1 dc into each of the next 4 sts, yarn over hook, and draw through all loops on the hook (a 4-dc cluster made) *(fig. 1)*.

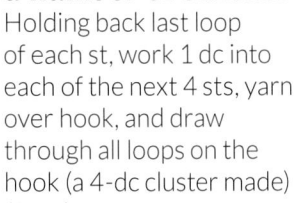

LOOP STITCH

The loop stitch, also called the fur stitch, is similar to creating a single crochet stitch, except a long strand of yarn is looped around a "tool" that is the desired length of the loop, and the yarn is then caught up in the back of the work.

An effective "tool" can be a piece of cardboard cut to the desired width and long enough to accommodate the stitches in the row.

For this sample, cut a piece of cardboard 1" × 4" (2.5 × 10 cm).

Chain 11 for the foundation chain.

ROW 1: Work 1 sc in second ch from hook and in each ch across *(fig. 1)*. Ch 1. Turn.

ROW 2: *Insert hook in next st, holding cardboard in back of work, wind yarn around it from back to front or toward you, pick up yarn and pull through st, yarn over and complete sc *(fig. 2)*. Repeat from *across. Slip cardboard out of loops. Ch 1. Turn.

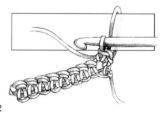

ROW 3: Work 1 sc in each st across. Ch 1. Turn.

Repeat Rows 2 and 3 for desired length.

PICOT

Use picot crochet for a decorative finish (see page 104) or as part of a pattern such as the mesh or netting base for Irish crochet (see page 77).

Single or slip stitch crochet picot

*At the point where a picot is required, chain 3 (or more according to height of picot desired), sc or sl st in third ch from hook (1st ch). Continue in single crochet to point where next picot is desired and repeat from *.

Picot variation #1

At the point where a picot is required, *work the desired number of chain stitches, then continue in single crochet to the point where next picot is desired and repeat from *.

Picot variation #2

At the point where a picot is required, *work the desired number of chain stitches, remove hook, place hook in the 1st (or beginning) ch and in the dropped ch, sl st firmly, then continue in single crochet to the point where the next picot is desired and repeat from *.

POPCORN STITCH

A popcorn stitch is a raised group of stitches used to add interest and texture.

1

2

3

1. Make a foundation chain the desired length.

2. Work 5 dc into 6th ch from hook (*fig. 1*).

3. Drop loop from hook, insert hook into the top of the 1st dc of this 5-dc group and into the dropped loop (*fig. 2*).

4. Pull this loop through the top of the 1st dc (popcorn stitch made).

5. Ch 1 to secure the popcorn. *Ch 1, sk 2 ch, popcorn in next ch. Repeat from * (*fig. 3*).

PUFF STITCH

This pretty little puff is created by drawing up three or more loops in the same stitch of the previous row.

1

2

For this sample, make a foundation chain of a multiple of 3 plus 6 stitches.

1. (Yarn over hook, insert hook into 6th chain from hook, yarn over and draw up a loop) 3 times. Yarn over hook and draw through all 7 loops on the hook *(fig. 1)*.

2. Chain 1 to close the puff. *Chain 1, sk 2 ch, work a puff stitch in next st. Repeat from * *(fig. 2)*.

Note: The number of loops required for the puff stitch may vary. For a puffier stitch, draw up more than three loops in the same stitch. Written directions may require that the loops be drawn up to a certain height, such as ¼" (0.6 cm) or ½" (1.3 cm).

RIBBINGS
Single crochet ribbing

When worked vertically and sewn onto jackets and sweaters, single crochet ribbing makes wonderful bands for cuffs, necklines, and hemlines.

- Working into the back loop only creates a ridge on the front side of the work.

- Working into the front loop only creates a ridge on the back of the work.

Make a foundation chain the desired length.

ROW 1: Work 1 sc in second ch from hook and in each ch to end. Ch 1. Turn (*fig. 1*).

ROW 2: Work 1 sc in back loop of each st. Ch 1. Turn (*fig. 2*).

Repeat row 2 for desired length.

1

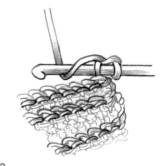

2

Half double crochet ribbing

This produces an effect similar to single crochet ribbing, but the ribs are wider and have more elasticity.

Make a foundation chain the desired length.

ROW 1: Work 1 hdc in third ch from hook and in each ch to end. Ch 2. Turn.

ROW 2: Sk 1st st, work 1 hdc in back loop of each st across, ending with hdc in turning ch. Ch 2. Turn.

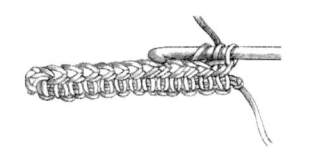

Repeat Row 2 for desired length.

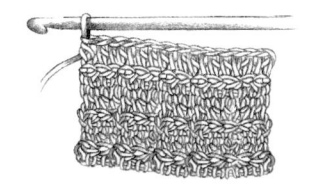

Post stitch ribbing

Also known as vertical ribbing, this is usually worked in the double crochet stitch around the posts of stitches in the row below.

For this sample, chain 16 for foundation chain.

ROW 1: Work a dc in the fourth ch from hook and in each chain across. Ch 3. Turn.

ROW 2: Sk first dc *work a FPdc (see page 56) around the post of the next dc *(fig. 1)*, work a BPdc *(fig. 2)* (see page 56) around the post of the next dc. Repeat from *, ending with dc in turning ch. Ch 3. Turn.

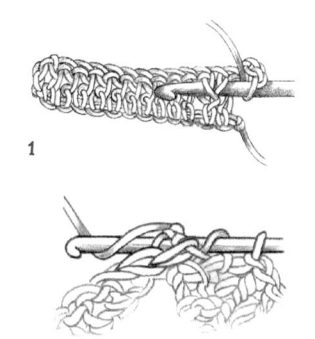

1

2

Repeat Row 2 for desired length *(fig. 3)*.

3

SEED STITCH

The seed stitch is produced by alternating single and double crochet stitches across a row. It makes a solid fabric and is a nice alternative to a solid fabric produced by single crochet.

For this sample, make a foundation chain a multiple of 2 stitches plus 1 *(fig. 1)*.

ROW 1: Sc in second ch from hook *(fig. 2)*, dc in next ch, *sc in next ch, dc in next ch. Repeat from * across. Ch 1. Turn.

ROW 2: Sc in next dc, dc in next sc. Repeat from * across. Ch 1. Turn.

Repeat Row 2 for desired length *(fig. 3)*.

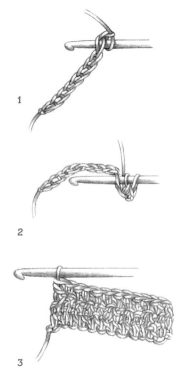

1

2

3

SHELL STITCH

Shell stitch patterns produce a lacy, open, and airy crocheted piece.

Shell stitch #1

For this sample, make a foundation chain a multiple of 6 plus 4 stitches.

ROW 1: Work 2 dc in fourth ch from hook (half shell), sk 2 ch, sc in next ch, *sk 2 ch, 5 dc in next ch (shell), sk 2 ch, sc in next ch. Repeat from *, ending with 3 dc in last ch (half shell). Ch 1. Turn *(fig. 1)*.

ROW 2: Sc in 1st dc, *sk 2 dc, shell (5 dc) in next sc, sk 2 dc, sc in center dc of next shell. Repeat from *, ending with sc in turning ch of half shell. Ch 3. Turn *(fig. 2)*.

ROW 3: Work 2 dc in 1st sc, *sc in center dc of next shell, shell in next sc. Repeat from * ending with 3 dc in last sc. Ch 1, turn *(fig. 3)*.

Repeat Rows 2 and 3 for desired length.

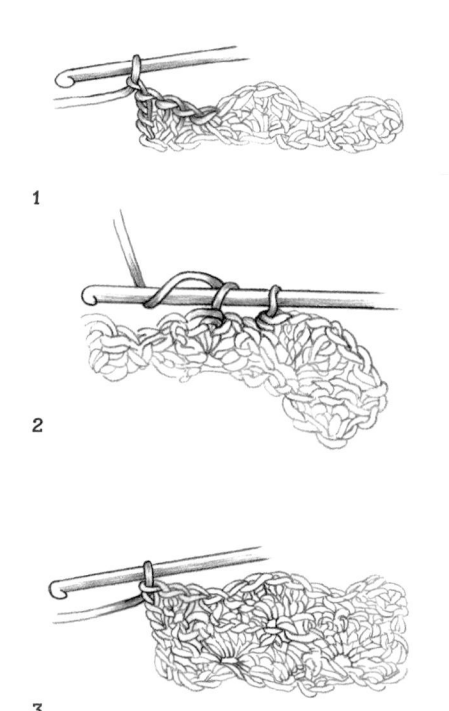

1

2

3

Shell stitch #2

Make a foundation chain the desired length.

ROW 1: Work 2 dc (half shell) in fourth ch from hook, *sk 2 ch, (2 dc, ch 2, 2 dc [shell made]) in next ch. Repeat from *, ending with sk 2 ch, 2 dc (half shell) in last ch. Ch 3. Turn *(fig. 1)*.

ROW 2: Work half shell in 1st dc, *shell in ch-2 sp of next shell, repeat from *, ending with half shell in last dc. Ch 3. Turn *(fig. 2)*.

Repeat Row 2 for desired length.

1

2

ADVANCED CROCHET TECHNIQUES

ARAN CROCHET

Aran crochet is a series of stitches that creates a variety of textured designs on fabric. The stitches are raised by crocheting around the post of the stitches, rather than in both loops of the stitch. This creates a pattern with raised stitches.

Aran crochet starts with a basic chain, usually followed by at least one row or round of single crochet stitches. Continue making single crochet stitches in the succeeding rows or rounds while substituting around the post stitches (see page 56) for some of the single crochet stitches, which create twists and cables. Popcorn stitches (see page 61) can be used for added interest.

BEAD CROCHET

Bead crochet often involves following a charted pattern. It is usually worked in single crochet into the back of the stitch, and the beads will appear on the reverse side; bead crochet is worked from the wrong side. Sequins may also be used for a beautiful and unique effect.

Choose beads that fit easily on your yarn. To begin, you'll need to string the beads onto the yarn. When following a chart, string the beads in the color sequence indicated, beginning with the last bead and ending with the first.

Stringing beads

If your yarn is close to the same size as the hole in the beads, it may be necessary to make a transfer loop of sewing thread. Use a sewing needle that will fit through the holes of the bead.

1. Thread a sewing needle with about 8"
   (20.5 cm) of sewing thread. Join ends by
   tying a knot.

2. Thread about 10" (25.5 cm) of the end of the
   yarn through the loop.

3. Place a bead on the sewing needle and slide it
   down over the thread loop and onto the yarn.
   Continue stringing all beads in this manner.

Bead crochet in rounds

Placing a bead in every stitch of every round
will produce a surface completely covered with
beads. When worked as a tube, this method
creates wonderful spirals and ropes for jewelry.

Bead crochet in rows

When working back and forth in rows, beads can
only be worked on every row and will not form a
continuous surface.

To form a continuous beaded surface, you must
work entirely from the same side, cutting the
yarn at the end of every row.

In the round, flat

In the round, tube

Back and forth
in rows

Cutting the yarn at the
end of every row

How to work bead single crochet (bsc)

String beads according to instructions on page 68, and work to the place where you want a bead.

1. Insert the hook into the back of the stitch, yarn over and draw the yarn through.

2. Move a bead up to the two loops, yarn over and draw the yarn through the loops. The bead is now fixed to the reverse side of the work.

When working where beads are not required, work in chosen pattern stitch and slip the beads down along the yarn, out of the way.

Sample bead single crochet

ROW 1: Ch 11. Work 1 row sc. Ch 1, turn.

ROW 2 (wrong side): *Work a bsc (see above) in next st, sc in next st. Repeat from * to end of row. Ch 1, turn.

ROW 3: Work 1 sc in each st.

Repeat Rows 2 and 3 for pattern.

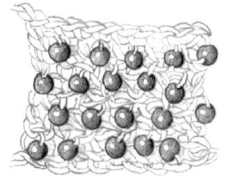

How to work bead double crochet (bdc)

String beads according to instructions above and work to the place where you want a bead.

1. Yarn over, insert hook, yarn over, and draw the yarn through.

2. Yarn over and draw through two loops.

3. Move a bead up to the two loops, yarn over and draw the yarn through the loops. The bead is now fixed to the reverse side of the work.

Sample bead double crochet

ROW 1: Ch 12. Dc in third ch from hook and in each ch to end of row. Ch 3, turn.

ROW 2 (wrong side): Sk 1st st, *bdc (see above) in next st, dc in next st. Repeat from * to end of row. Ch 3, turn.

ROW 3: Sk 1st st, work 1 dc in each st. Ch 3, turn.

Repeat Rows 2 and 3 for pattern.

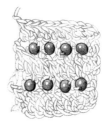

FILET CROCHET

This technique is based on forming designs from a series of filled-in and open squares called "blocks" and "spaces." Filet crochet is usually worked in straight rows of double crochet following a charted pattern such as a graph with a symbol diagram. Patterns are created by combining spaces and blocks, usually working the design in blocks and the background in spaces. One square on the chart will equal one "block" or one "space."

Row 1

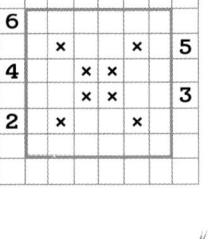

SPACE: On the chart, the blank square equals a space. To make a space, dc in next st, ch 2, sk 2 sts, dc in next st.

BLOCK: On the chart, the × equals a block. To make a block, dc in next st, 2 dc in ch-2 sp, dc in next st.

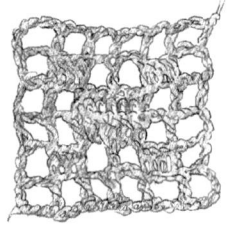

Sample filet crochet

ROW 1: Ch 23, dc in 8th ch from hook, *ch 2, sk 2 ch, dc in next ch. Repeat from * to end of chain. Ch 5, turn.

ROW 2: Sk 1st dc and next 2 chs, dc in next dc, 2 dc in next ch-2 sp, dc in next dc, (ch 2, dc in next dc) 2 times, 2 dc in next ch-2 sp, dc in next dc, ch 2, sk 2 chs, dc in next ch. Ch 5, turn.

ROWS 3–6: Follow chart, working spaces and blocks as indicated.

> **Note:** Some stitch keys will call a space a "mesh" and a block a "solid mesh." Some charts will use a different symbol, such as a circle or a filled-in block, instead of the × to equal the block.

Once you've mastered the technique, you can create your own original designs using graph paper. Try the sample below. Follow written instructions for the first two rows, then follow the chart.

Lacet stitch

The lacet stitch, sometimes called a fancy mesh, is one of the filet crochet stitches used in a 4-dc filet crochet pattern as described above. The lacet stitch is worked over two rows and over an area of two spaces, which is a total of seven stitches.

Sample lacet stitch

The first row, the last row, and the sides of the sample are worked in filet crochet with the center of the sample in the lacet stitch.

ROW 1: Ch 29, dc in 8th ch from hook,* ch 2, sk 2 ch, dc in next ch. Repeat from * to end of chain. Ch 5. Turn.

ROW 2: Sk 1st dc, dc in next dc, (ch 3, sc in next dc, ch 3, dc in next dc) 3 times, ch 2, dc in 6th ch of turning ch. Ch 5. Turn.

ROW 3: Sk 1st dc, dc in next dc, (ch 5, dc in next dc) 3 times, ch 2, dc in third ch of turning ch. Ch 5. Turn.

ROW 4: Sk 1st dc, dc in next dc, (ch 3, sc over next ch-5 lp, ch 3, dc in next dc) 3 times, ch 2, dc in third ch of turning ch. Ch 5. Turn.

Repeat Rows 3 and 4 for desired length.

LAST ROW: Sk 1st dc, dc in next dc, (ch 2, dc in next sc, ch 2, dc in next dc) 3 times, ch 2, dc in third ch of turning ch.

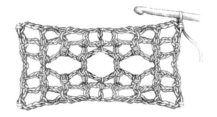

Many filet crochet patterns are worked in blocks and spaces only, with no lacets. Once you have mastered this technique, you can insert lacets within a design by substituting a lacet for two spaces or for two blocks on the chart from which you are working.

IRISH CROCHET

Irish crochet is traditionally worked with very fine white thread and is characterized by softly sculptured motifs such as roses, flowers, buds, leaves, stems, and berries, set into a background of crocheted mesh. Irish crochet is made in three distinct styles:

- Lace that is heavily padded, which historically has been considered the most valuable.
- Lace that is slightly padded.
- Lace that has no padding.

Irish crochet daisy (unpadded)

Chain 6. Join with sl st to form a ring.

RND 1: Work 15 sc into ring.

RND 2: (Sl st in next sc, chain 3, dc 2 tog over next 2 sc, ch 3) 5 times, ending with sl st in beg sl st. Fasten off.

Irish crochet rose (unpadded)

Chain 8. Join with sl st to form a ring.

RND 1: Work 18 sc into ring.

RND 2: Sc in first sc, (ch 3, sk 2 sc, sc in next sc) 5 times, ch 3, sl st in beg sc.

RND 3: (Sl st, ch 2, 5 dc, ch 2, sl st) in each ch-3 lp around.

RND 4: (Sl st between next 2 petals, ch 5) 6 times.

RND 5: (Sl st, ch 2, 7 dc, ch 2, sl st) in each ch-5 lp around. Join with sl st to beg sl st. Fasten off.

Irish crochet leaf (unpadded)

1. Chain 14.

2. Sc in second ch from hook, hdc in next ch, dc in each of next 3 ch, tr in each of next 4 ch, dc in each of next 3 ch, hdc in next ch, sc in last ch.

3. Ch 3, sl st in third ch from hook (picot made).

4. Working on opposite side of chain, sc in next ch, hdc in next ch, dc in each of next 3 ch, tr in each of next 4 ch, dc in each of next 3 ch, hdc in next ch, sc in last ch. Fasten off.

Irish crochet flower (padded)

Cut approximately one yard of thread from ball for padding. Wind padding thread three times around tip of index finger or a pencil to form foundation ring *(fig. 1)*.

RND 1: Work 12 sc in ring and over padding thread. Cut the padding thread close to the work *(fig. 2)*.

RND 2: *Sc in next st, ch 3, sk 1 st, sc in next st. Repeat from * 6 times, ending with sl st in beg sc. There are 6 ch-3 lps.

RND 3: Bring two strands of the padding thread in front of next ch-3 lp. Working over padding thread, work (sc, hdc, 3 dc, hdc, sc) in each ch-3 lp around *(fig. 3)*.

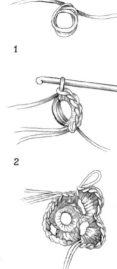

1

2

3

End with a sl st in 1st sc. There are 6 petals. Cut the padding thread close to the work. Fasten off and weave in ends. For highly padded motifs, use more strands of padding thread.

Assembling an Irish crochet piece

From sturdy fabric cut a pattern the size and shape of the finished piece, and arrange the motifs face down in desired pattern. With basting stitch, sew firmly in place.

Join motifs by crocheting a background mesh (see sample on page 77). Work mesh background to the place where motif will join background; join with a slip stitch. You will have to work in small areas between the motifs, ending the background and beginning again on the other side of the motif(s). Continue to join motifs to background with slip stitches where appropriate.

When the crocheted piece is complete, cut the basting thread from the wrong side of the fabric base and remove the fabric.

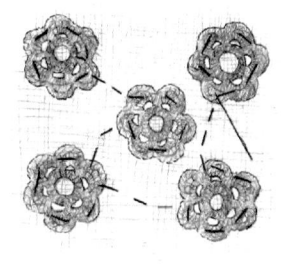

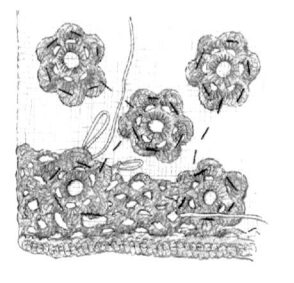

Note: If you're working a garment in Irish crochet, work an edging around all openings to stabilize the mesh background.

Sample Irish crochet mesh background

Chain 27.

ROW 1: Work 1 sc in 6th ch from hook, *ch 10, sk 6 ch, work (sc, ch 4, sc) in next ch. Repeat from *, working (sc, ch 2, dc) in last ch. Ch 11, turn.

ROW 2: *(Sc, ch 4, sc) in next ch-10 sp, ch 10. Repeat from *, ending with ch 5, 1 tr into third ch of beg ch-5. Ch 5, turn.

ROW 3: Sc in first lp. *Ch 10 (sc, ch 4, sc) in next ch-10 lp. Repeat from *, ending with ch 10 (sc, ch 2, dc) in last lp. Ch 11, turn.

Repeat Rows 2 and 3 for pattern.

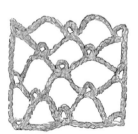

MULTICOLORED CROCHET

This is also known as jacquard crochet or mosaic crochet. Two or more colors are used to create a design or picture, and it is usually worked following a charted pattern.

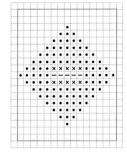

Stitches

Multicolored crochet is worked as a solid fabric and can be done in single crochet, half double crochet, or double crochet. Single crochet tends to give the best results when following a chart because the stitches are nearly square. Double crochet stitches are about twice as tall as they are wide.

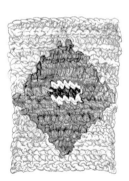

Changing colors

At the point where you are ready to change colors, work the last step of the last stitch of the old color in the new color (i.e., before the last loops are worked off, drop the old color and finish the stitch with the new color).

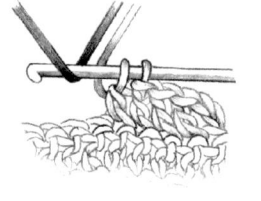 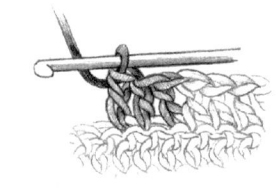

Allow the old color to hang at the back of the work and continue with the new color.

There are two methods for carrying yarn not in use.

METHOD ONE: Carry the color not in use loosely across the wrong side of the piece, then pick up again when needed.

METHOD TWO: Carry the color not in use across the top of the row just worked, and encase in the base of the new stitches of the second color.

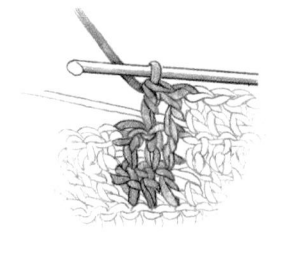

This second method will allow your piece to be reversible.

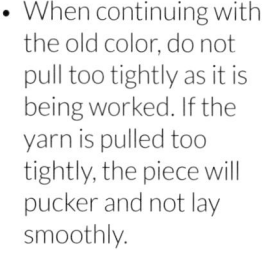

- When continuing with the old color, do not pull too tightly as it is being worked. If the yarn is pulled too tightly, the piece will pucker and not lay smoothly.

- To simplify your work when using several colors, use yarn bobbins to hold and release the yarns in smaller amounts.

RUFFLE CROCHET

Ruffle crochet is worked on a filet crochet or mesh background. Ruffles may be worked in single crochet, half double crochet, double crochet, or a combination of these stitches. Ruffles are worked on the right side and around the "bars" of the base crochet.

Sample ruffle

1. Work a filet crochet background of spaces only.

2. With right side facing, and starting at the upper right corner, work five double crochets around the top bar of the filet crochet space *(fig. 1)*.

3. Turn the piece and work five double crochets around the left vertical bar of the filet crochet *(fig. 2)*.

4. Continue, working across the top and bottom, and on the right or left side of the spaces *(fig. 3)*.

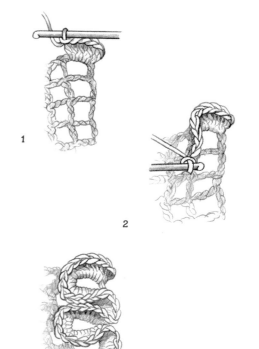

1

2

3

MOTIFS AND MEDALLIONS

The terms "motif" and "medallion" are used interchangeably in crochet work, and there are myriad patterns in all sizes and shapes, including squares, circles, hexagons, octagons, and diamonds. The ways in which the shapes can be joined to make a flat piece are limited only by your creative imagination. When joining circles and octagons, you will need an extra motif to fill in the gaps that result.

Different effects can be achieved depending on the yarn used. Simple, brightly colored motifs worked in wool produce an attractive patchwork suitable for afghans, rugs, or shawls, while more elaborate or lacy medallions worked in cotton, linen, or silk make elegant table accessories.

Most motifs and medallions are started in the center and worked in rounds rather than rows. The right side of the work is always facing you, and when you come back to the starting place, a round has been completed. Increases are placed evenly around, so the motif lies flat.

GRANNY SQUARES

One of the most popular and easy to crochet motifs is the granny square. Designed for the purpose of using leftover yarns, traditional granny squares change color on each round. The squares are assembled into afghans, skirts, or sweaters.

Sample granny square

With Color A, ch 5; join with sl st to form a ring.

RND 1: Ch 3, 2 dc in ring, (ch 2, 3 dc in ring) 3 times, end ch 2. Join with sl st to top of beg ch-3. There are four ch-2 sps (corners). Fasten off.

RND 2: Join Color B in any ch-2 sp, ch 3, (2 dc, ch 2, 3 dc) in same sp (1st corner made), * ch 1, (3 dc, ch 2, 3 dc) in next ch-2 sp, repeat from *

2 times, end ch 1. Join with sl st to top of beg ch-3. There are four ch-2 corners with one ch-1 sp between each corner. Fasten off.

RND 3: Join Color C in any ch-2 sp, ch 3, (2 dc, ch 2, 3 dc) in same sp (1st corner made), ch 1, 3 dc in next ch-1 sp, ch 1, *(3 dc, ch 2, 3 dc, ch 1) in next ch-2 sp, (3 dc, ch 1) in next ch-1 sp. Repeat from * 2 times, ending with sl st to top of beg ch-3. There are four ch-2 corners with 2 ch-1 sps between each corner. Fasten off.

ADDITIONAL RNDS:
Continue as above, working four corners on each rnd and working (ch 1, 3 dc, ch 1) into each ch-1 space.

Joining granny squares
You can sew all your squares together when you're finished with them, or you can join them as they are worked in a seamless joining as follows:

- Work one complete square as outlined above.

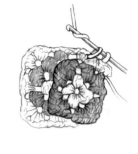

- Work Rounds 1 and 2 of next square.

RND 3 (joining rnd): Join Color C in any ch-2 sp, ch 3, 2 dc in same sp. With wrong sides of Square #1 and Square #2 facing you, ch 1, sc in opposite corner of Square #1, 3 dc in same sp on Square #2. Sc in next ch-1 sp of Square #1, 3 dc in next ch-1 sp

of Square #2, sc in next ch-1 sp of Square #1, (3 dc, ch 1) in next ch-2 space of Square #1, sc in next ch-2 sp of Square #1, 3 dc in same ch-2 sp of Square #2.

Complete as for Round 3 above.

WORKING HALF MOTIFS

A half motif may be used when a full motif would be too large. For example, to get the required width of a garment you may need a half, rather than a full, motif.

Half granny square

With Color A, ch 5, join with a sl st to form a ring.

ROW 1: Ch 5, (3 dc, ch 2 in ring) 3 times, dc in ring. Fasten off.

ROW 2: Join Color B in beg ch-5 sp, ch 3, 2 dc in same sp. *Ch 1, (3 dc, ch 2, 3 dc) in next ch-2 sp; repeat from * once; end ch 1, 3 dc in last ch-2 sp. Fasten off.

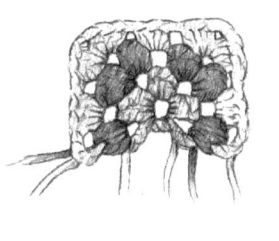

ROW 3: Join Color C in third ch of beg ch-3, ch 4. *3 dc in next ch-1 sp, ch 1, (3 dc, ch 2, 3 dc) in next ch-2 sp, ch 1. Repeat from * one time,

ending with 3 dc in next ch-1 sp, ch 1, dc in last dc. Fasten off.

Granny square triangle

Triangles may be used to shape a garment, such as at the neckline or armholes.

With Color A, ch 5, join with a sl st to form a ring.

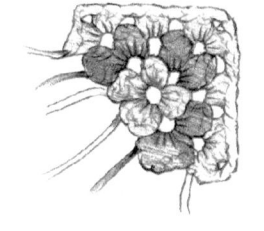

ROW 1: Ch 3, 2 dc in ring, (ch 2, 3 dc in ring) 3 times. Fasten off.

ROW 2: Join Color B in first ch-2 sp, ch 3, (2 dc, ch 2, 3 dc) in same sp. *Ch 1, (3 dc, ch 2, 3 dc) in next ch-2 sp. Repeat from * one time. Fasten off.

ROW 3: Join Color C in first ch-2 sp, ch 3, (2 dc, ch 2, 3 dc) in same sp. *Ch 1, 3 dc in next ch-1 sp, ch 1, (3 dc, ch 2, 3 dc) in next ch-2 sp. Repeat from * one time. Fasten off.

CIRCULAR MOTIFS

Many variations of circular motifs are possible, but the method is the same for all. Begin with a ring and increase on subsequent rounds so the piece will lie flat. Here is one example.

Chain 5, join with a sl st to form a ring.

RND 1: (Sc in ring, ch 1) 12 times. Join with a sl st to beg sc. There are 12 ch-1 spaces.

RND 2: Sl st in next ch-1 sp, ch 6, (dc in next ch-1 sp, ch 3) 11 times. Join to third ch of beg ch-6. There are 12 ch-3 lps.

RND 3: Sl st in each of next 2 chs; ch 3; holding back the last loop of each st, work 3 dc in same st, yarn over and draw through all 4 loops on the hook (beg cluster made); ch 4. *Holding back the last loop of each st, work 4 dc in second ch of next ch-3 loop, yarn over and draw through all 5 loops on the hook (cluster made), ch 4. Repeat from *, ending with sl st in top of beg cluster. There are 12 clusters.

RND 4: Ch 6, *sc in next ch-4 lp, ch 3, dc in top of next cluster, ch 3. Repeat from *, ending with sl st in third ch of beg ch-6. Fasten off.

HEXAGONS

As with other motifs, there are many possible variations of hexagons.

Here is one example.

Chain 6, join with a sl st to form a ring.

RND 1: Ch 3, work 17 dc in ring, join with a sl st to top of beg ch-3.

RND 2: Ch 6, dc in joining st. *Ch 2, sk 2 sts, (dc, ch 3, dc) in next st. Repeat from *, ending with ch 2, sk 2 sts, join with a sl st to third ch of first ch-6. There are 6 ch-3 sps.

RND 3: Sl st in next ch-3 sp, (ch 3, 6 dc) in same sp. *Ch 1, 7 dc in next ch-3 sp. Repeat from *, ending with ch 1, join with a sl st to top of first ch-3.

RND 4: Ch 4, dc in next dc, ch 1, dc in next dc. *Ch 1, (in next dc work dc, ch 3, dc [corner made]), (ch 1, dc in next dc) 6 times. Repeat from *, ending with ch 1, (dc, ch 3, dc) in next dc, (ch 1, dc in next dc) 3 times, ch 1, join with a sl st to third ch of beg ch-4. Fasten off.

TUNISIAN CROCHET

Tunisian crochet, also known as afghan crochet or tricot crochet, is a blend of knit and crochet. In its simplest stitch, Tunisian crochet resembles a woven fabric and has a potential for textured stitching. It also creates a dense fabric in a grid pattern with a definite front and back, which can be an ideal base for cross stitch.

TUNISIAN CROCHET HOOKS

Tunisian crochet uses a special hook called an Afghan hook. This is an elongated crochet hook with a stop on one end, like a knitting needle.

An Afghan hook differs from a regular crochet hook in that there is no finger grip depression, the shank does not taper (the thickness is the same for its entire length), and there is a knob at the end of the hook. Tunisian crochet requires a longer hook because all the stitches remain on the hook throughout the forward pass; on the reverse pass, the loops are all worked off.

Tunisian crochet hooks come in various sizes (see page 7), as do regular crochet hooks, but they are longer. Metal Afghan hooks usually have a knob on the end. Large Afghan hooks can be made of wood or plastic. Some hooks have a flexible cord attached to the end to accommodate a large number of stitches.

TUNISIAN CROCHET VERSUS CONVENTIONAL CROCHET

Tunisian crochet differs from conventional crochet in several ways.

- Loops for several stitches remain on the hook at one time, as opposed to conventional crochet, where the loop for only one stitch is on the hook at a time.

- The piece is not turned at the end of a row, so the right side is always facing.

- You start with a base row, and each row thereafter is a two-step process without turning your work.

FORWARD PASS AND REVERSE PASS

All Tunisian crochet stitches are worked with two steps to each row: the *Forward Pass* and the *Reverse Pass*.

1. The Forward Pass is worked from right to left, with the yarn in back and inserting the hook from right to left unless otherwise instructed. This is half a Tunisian stitch row.

2. The Reverse Pass is worked from left to right, completing each stitch as instructed. This is the other half of a Tunisian stitch row, and a row is complete.

> **Note:** As a general rule, the Reverse Pass of Tunisian crochet is worked exactly the same for any stitch. The Forward Pass defines the variations between the stitches.

TUNISIAN SIMPLE STITCH (tss)

The Tunisian simple stitch is commonly known as the Afghan stitch, but is sometimes called tricot stitch, tunis stitch, or basic Afghan stitch (bas).

The tss is a simple stitch that is usually learned first when mastering Tunisian crochet. As with most Tunisian crochet stitches, it is worked in two steps: the Forward Pass and the Reverse Pass. For this sample, use an Afghan hook to chain 10.

ROW 1: Base row: *Forward Pass:* Counting the loop on the hook as the first stitch, insert hook in top loop only of next chain, yarn over hook and draw up a loop. Keeping all loops on the hook, yarn over hook and draw up a loop in top loop only of each chain stitch. There are ten loops on the hook *(fig. 1)*.

1

ROW 2: *Reverse Pass:* Yarn over hook and draw a loop through the first loop on the hook. *Yarn over hook and draw a loop through next two loops *(fig. 2)*. Repeat from * until one loop remains on the hook. This loop counts as the first loop on the next row.

2

ROW 3: *Forward Pass:* Skipping the edge stitch, *insert hook under next vertical bar *(fig. 3)*, yarn over hook and draw up a loop. Repeat from * across. At end of pass, insert hook through double loop of last stitch *(fig. 4)*, yarn over hook and draw up a loop. This keeps the edge firm. There are ten loops on the hook.

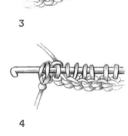

3

4

Repeat Rows 2 and 3 for desired length, ending with Row 2 or a Reverse Pass row.

> **Note:** **1.** Ordinarily the first bar, or edge stitch, is skipped. This gives an extra stitch at the right edge of your work. **2.** After the base row of the Tunisian crochet fabric is complete, any number of Tunisian crochet stitches can be worked.

Binding off in tss

Working a Forward Pass, *insert hook under next vertical strand, yarn over and draw loosely through the strand and the loop on the hook; repeat from * across. Fasten off (fig. 5).

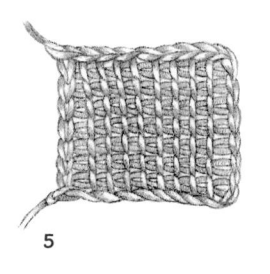

5

Increasing in tss

Patterns that require shaping, such as garments, will have increases and decreases within the Tunisian crochet stitch. The increases are always worked on the Forward Pass.

Increasing one stitch at the beginning and end of a row

To increase at the beginning of a row, pick up a loop in the first vertical bar, or the edge stitch (fig. 1).

1

Normally this first bar is skipped. This makes an extra stitch at the right side of the work.

In order to increase at the end of the row, pick up a loop between the last two upright bars, then pick up a loop in the last upright bar (fig. 2).

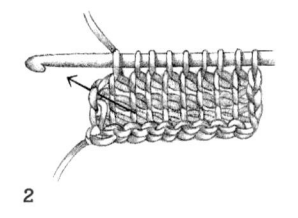

2

Note: When working the increased stitches at the end of the pass, do not place the hook in the entire space between the last two bars; this will create a large hole. Pick up the new stitch through the top part of the chain between the last two bars.

Note: Always count the number of loops on the hook to make sure you have the necessary number of stitches after each increase row.

Increasing several stitches at the beginning and end of a row

Before starting the Forward Pass, join a separate strand of yarn at the end of the last row and chain the desired number of stitches to be increased at the end (left side) of the row. Fasten off the new yarn. *(fig. 1)*.

Continuing with the old yarn, chain the desired number of stitches to be increased at the beginning (right side) of the row *(fig. 2)*.

2

Counting the loop on the hook as the first stitch, insert the hook into the top loop only of each chain and draw up a loop. Work a Forward Pass across established stitches, insert hook in the top loop only of each chain that has been added to the end of the new row and draw up a loop *(fig. 3)*.

1

3

The Reverse Pass is worked as usual.

Decreasing on the edge in tss

A decrease in tss is worked on both the Forward Pass and the Reverse Pass. To decrease at the right side of the work, the decrease is made on the Forward Pass by working the first and second stitches together as follows: Draw up a loop in the first bar (not the edge stitch) and in the second bar at the same time, bring the loop through both bars (*fig. 1*), and work as established to the end of the row.

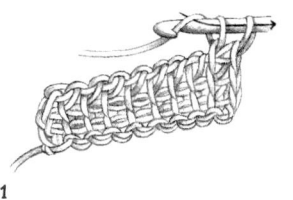

1

To decrease at the left edge of the work, the decrease is made on the Reverse Pass as follows: Yarn over and draw a loop through two loops (instead of the usual one loop for the first stitch) (*fig. 2*) and work as established to the end of the row.

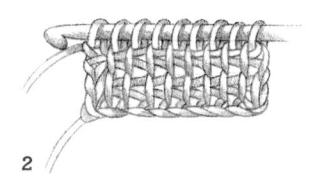

2

Note: *Count the number of stitches to make sure you have the necessary number of stitches after a decrease row.*

TUNISIAN KNIT STITCH (tks)

This is also known as the stocking stitch, stockinette stitch, or simple rib stitch.

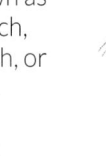

For this sample: Using an Afghan hook, chain 10.

ROW 1: BASE ROW: *Forward Pass:* Counting loop on the hook as first stitch, insert hook in top loop only of next chain, yarn over hook and draw up a loop. Keeping all loops on the hook, yarn over hook and draw up a loop in top loop only of each chain stitch. There are ten loops on the hook (*fig. 1*).

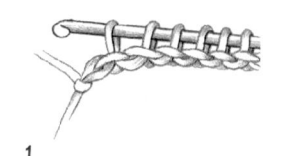

1

ROW 2: *Reverse Pass:* Yarn over hook and draw a loop through the first loop on the hook. *Yarn over hook and draw a loop

2

through next two loops *(fig. 2)*. Repeat from * until one loop remains on the hook. This loop counts as first loop on next row.

ROW 3: *Forward Pass:* Skipping the edge stitch, *insert the hook from front to back between the two vertical bars *(fig. 3)*, yarn over hook, and draw up a loop.

3

Repeat from * across. At end of row, insert hook through double loop of last stitch, yarn over hook and draw up a loop. This keeps the edge firm. There are ten loops on the hook *(fig. 4)*.

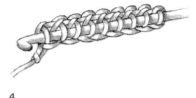

4

Repeat Rows 2 and 3 for desired length, ending with Row 2 or a Reverse Pass.

> **Note:** Increasing, decreasing, and bind-off can be worked the same as TSS.

TUNISIAN PURL STITCH (tps)

This produces a stitch that is similar in appearance to the purl stitch in knitting. As in knitting, the tps calls for the yarn to be held in front of the work for each stitch. It also produces a row of little bumps, but retains the characteristic vertical bars of tss. The fabric produced is much softer than that of the other Tunisian crochet stitches.

For this sample: Using an Afghan hook, chain 10.

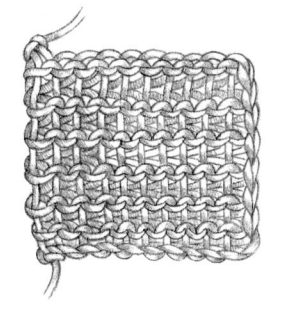

ROW 1: BASE ROW: *Forward Pass:* Counting loop on the hook as first stitch, insert hook in top loop only of next chain, yarn over hook and draw up a loop. Keeping all loops on the hook, yarn over hook and draw up a loop in top loop only of each chain stitch. There are ten loops on the hook *(fig. 1)*.

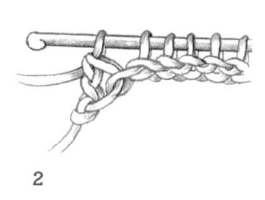

1

ROW 2: *Reverse Pass:* Yarn over hook and draw a loop through the first loop on the hook. *Yarn over hook and draw a loop through next two loops *(fig. 2)*. Repeat from * until one loop remains on the hook. This loop counts as first loop on next row.

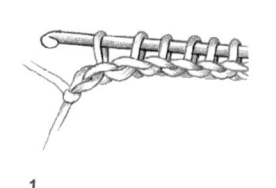

2

ROW 3: *Forward Pass:* Skipping the edge stitch, *bring the yarn to front of work, insert hook under next vertical bar *(fig. 3)*, bring yarn to back of work, pull up loop. Repeat from * across. At end of row, insert hook through double loop of last stitch, yarn over hook and draw up a loop *(fig. 4)*. This keeps the edge firm. There are ten loops on the hook.

3

4

Repeat Rows 2 and 3 for desired length, ending with Row 2 or a Reverse Pass.

> **Note:** Increasing, decreasing, and bind-off can be worked the same as TSS.

> **Note:** You can create a variety of stitches, depending on how and where you insert the hook and hold the working yarn. Tunisian stitches include variations on knit, purl, post stitch, and entrelac, to name a few.

DECORATIVE FINISHINGS

BUTTONS

Crocheted buttons can add a wonderful personal touch to your finished project. Buttons can be worked over plastic rings, round molds, ordinary buttons, or round beads. Use a smaller hook than suggested for the yarn used.

Ring buttons

Choose plastic rings slightly smaller than the required size for the finished button.

1. Beginning with a slip stitch on the hook, work a round of single crochet over the ring until it is completely covered.

2. Join with a slip stitch to the first stitch. If you're working on a large ring, it may be necessary to work another round of single crochet to fill the hole. Fasten off, leaving a 12" (30.5 cm) end.

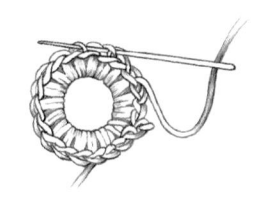

3. With a tapestry needle, sew a running stitch around the outside edge.

4. Turning the edge to the inside of the button, draw up tightly and fasten securely.

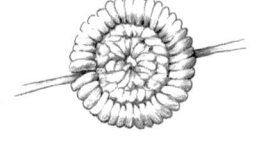

5. On the back of the ring, work strands of yarn diagonally across the button and sew the button to the garment through the center of these strands.

Covered buttons
Round buttons

These can be worked on round button molds or plain round buttons.

Chain 3 and join with a slip stitch to form a ring.

RND 1: 6 sc in ring, join with sl st to first st.

RND 2: 2 sc in each st of previous rnd, join with sl st to first st.

RND 3: *Sc in first st, 2 sc in next st; repeat from *. Join with sl st to first st.

Repeat Round 3 until the piece is slightly larger than the foundation button. Place button in cover and work last round.

LAST RND: *Sk 1 st, sc in next st; repeat from * around, joining with a sl st to first st.

With a tapestry needle, sew a running stitch around outside edge, draw up tightly, and fasten securely. Fasten off, leaving a 12" (30.5 cm) end of yarn for sewing the button on.

You can create variations by working only in the back or front loops of the stitches, or shifting between the back and the front loops.

Spherical buttons

These can be worked over a bead, or simply crocheted and stuffed with scraps of yarn used for crocheting.

Covered bead

Chain 2.

RND 1: 4 sc in beg ch. Do not join and do not turn.

RND 2: 2 sc in each st of previous rnd.

RND 3: *Sc in first st, 2 sc in next st; repeat from *.

Repeat Round 3 until piece covers half the bead. Slip bead into cover.

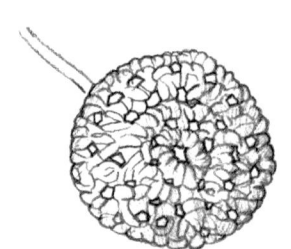

DECREASE RND: *Sc in next st, sc 2 sts tog; repeat from *.

Repeat the decrease round until the bead is completely covered. Take a few stitches with a tapestry needle to close the button. Fasten off, leaving a 12" (30.5 cm) tail for attaching.

Stuffed ball

Work as for a covered bead, without inserting the bead, until you've decreased to an opening just large enough to insert stuffing. Stuff and shape the button into a ball. Continue decrease rounds until button is almost closed. Close with a few stitches taken with a tapestry needle.

Attaching buttons to garment

- Whenever possible, sew buttons to a garment with matching yarn. Sewing thread has a different texture and the color will not match exactly. Split the yarn if it is too bulky for sewing.

- For most crocheted garments, buttons with shanks are recommended. You can also make a shank for a regular button or one with a short shank.

1. Sew the button to the garment, leaving a ¼" (0.6 cm) space between the button and the garment.

2. With the needle on the right side, wrap yarn around the threads between the garment and the button several times.

3. Bring the needle and yarn through to the wrong side and fasten off.

A small reinforcing button may be sewn with sewing thread on the wrong side of the garment, directly over the stitches where the button was attached. This gives the garment a more professional look and strengthens the attachment.

CORDS
Chain stitch cord

Crochet a chain the desired length and fasten off.

Slip stitch on a chain stitch cord #1

1. Crochet a chain to the desired length. Turn.

2. Beginning with second the chain from the hook, slip stitch in each chain. Fasten off.

Slip stitch on a chain stitch cord #2

1. Crochet a chain the desired length.

2. Beginning with the second chain from the hook, slip stitch in each chain by inserting the hook under the third strand (back strand) of the chain. Fasten off.

Two-color chain stitch cord

1. Make a slip knot with strands of yarn from two different-colored balls.

2. Make a chain the length desired by alternating stitches of each color. Be

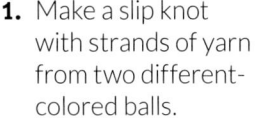

sure the working yarn is behind the yarn from the previous stitch.

If a thicker cord is desired, work with four strands of yarn, two strands of each color at a time.

Round cord

1. Chain 5, join with slip stitch to form a ring.

2. Work one slip stitch in each chain.

3. Continue working one slip stitch in each stitch (around and around) until the cord reaches the desired length.

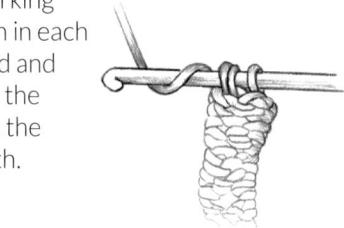

- The cord can be made thick or thin, depending on the size of the yarn.

- The cord can also be made thicker by working with more stitches.

Twisted cord

1. Cut yarn six times the length of the cord desired. (For a heavier cord, use several strands.)

2. Double the strand(s) of yarn and tie the yarn ends into a knot.

3. Secure the knotted end on a hook or a doorknob and place a pencil through the looped end.

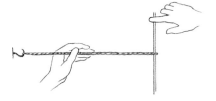

4. Spin the pencil around, twisting the cord until it is taut.

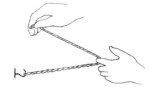

5. Holding the middle of the twisted yarn, bring the yarn ends together.

6. Let the yarn twist back on itself from the middle. Smooth the yarn with your fingers to even out any bumps.

Twisted cord fringe

1. Draw a double strand of yarn through the edge of the crocheted piece.

2. Twist the ends of each double strand until they are taut.

3. Twist the ends of the two strands together.

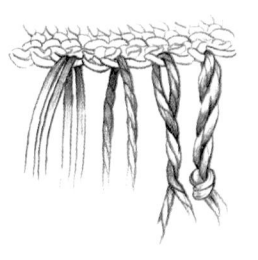

4. Knot the end at the bottom and clip off the excess.

Three-strand braided cord

1. Use three lengths of yarn about twice the desired length of the cord.

2. Knot the strands together at one end.

3. Fasten the knotted end to a firm surface with a pin.

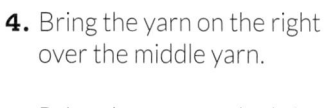

4. Bring the yarn on the right over the middle yarn.

5. Bring the yarn on the left over the middle yarn.

6. Continue to desired length.

When the cord is complete, knot the strands together at the other end.

Four-strand braided cord

1. Use four lengths of yarn about twice the desired length of the cord.

2. Knot the strands together at one end.

3. Fasten the knotted end to a firm surface with a pin.

4. Bring the yarn on the far right under the one next to it.

5. Bring the yarn on the far left over the one next to it and under the next one.

6. Continue to desired length.

When the cord is complete, knot the strands together at the other end.

BRAIDS AND INSERTIONS

Braids and insertions can be used to embellish, decorate, and enhance crocheted, knitted, and fabric items. The very nature of crochet lends itself to these wonderful little trims.

Braids

Braids are crocheted separately and appliquéd or sewn onto a finished item.

Sample braid #1
Chain 20.

ROW 1: Sl st in second ch from hook, *sk 2 ch, 5 dc in next ch, sk 2 ch, sl st in next ch. Repeat from * to end. Ch 1. *Do not turn.*

ROW 2: Working on opposite side of beg ch, sl st in first ch. *Sk 2 ch, 5 dc in next ch, sk 2 ch, sl st in next ch. Repeat from * to end. Fasten off.

Sample braid #2
Chain 17.

ROW 1: Sc in second ch from hook and in each ch to end. Ch 1. Turn.

ROW 2: Work 1 sc and 4 dc in first sc. *Sk 2 sc, work 1 sc and 4 dc in next sc. Repeat from * across, ending with sc in last sc. Fasten off.

ROW 3: Working on opposite side of beg ch, re-attach yarn in first ch. Work 1 sc in each ch. Ch 1. Turn.

ROW 4: Repeat Row 2.

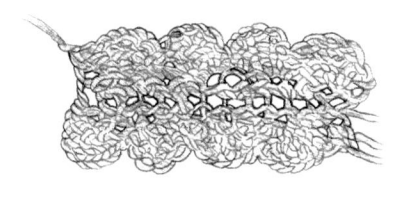

Insertions
Insertions are strips of crochet that are sewn between two pieces of fabric or inserted into a cut-out in a piece of fabric.

Sample insertion #1
Chain 8.

ROW 1: Work (dc, ch 3, dc) in 8th ch from hook. Ch 3. Turn.

ROW 2: Work 5 dc in next ch-3 sp, ch 2. In 6th ch of beg ch-8, work (dc, ch 3, dc). Ch 3. Turn.

ROW 3: Work 5 dc in next ch-3 sp, ch 2, sk next dc and next ch-2 sp. Work (dc, ch 3, dc) in next dc. Ch 3. Turn.

Repeat Row 3 for desired length. Fasten off.

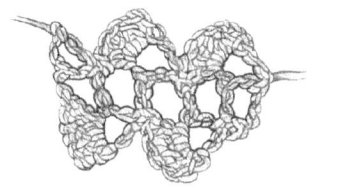

Sample insertion #2
Chain 16.

ROW 1: Sc in second ch from hook and each ch to end. Ch 1. *Do not turn.* Working on opposite side of beg ch, work 1 sc in each ch. Ch 2. *Do not turn.*

ROW 2: Sl st in first sc. **Ch 5, sc in third ch from hook, *sk 1 sc, hdc in next sc, ch 3, sc in third ch from hook. Repeat from *, ending with hdc in last sc of top of Row 1. Ch 3. Working on bottom of Row 1, sl st in first sc. Repeat from ** of Row 2. Fasten off.

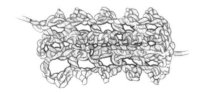

DECORATIVE EDGINGS
Decorative edgings are best worked on a foundation row of single crochet. If necessary, work a row of single crochet on the edge to be decorated.

When working an edging, *increase* at corners and on the outside of curves and *decrease* on the inside of curves.

Reverse single crochet edging (rsc)
This is also known as backward single crochet, crab stitch, and pie crust stitch. It produces a tailored edging suitable to almost any type of garment that requires a plain edging.

If necessary, work a
foundation row of single
crochet; do not fasten
off the yarn.

1. Ch 1, but *do not turn
the work*.

2. Work a row of
single crochet
from left to right.

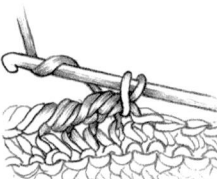

For a less pronounced
edge, work ch 1,
*sk 1, rsc in next st;
repeat from *.

Reverse half double crochet edging

For a deeper edging, work a row of reverse half
double crochet stitches. Proceed as for rsc,
working half double crochet stitches rather than
single crochet.

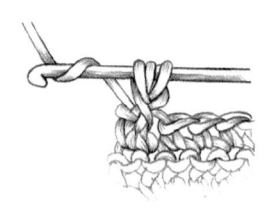

Picot edging

If necessary, work
a foundation row
of single crochet.

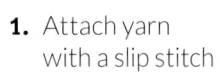

1. Attach yarn
with a slip stitch
at the beginning of the row.

2. *Ch 3, sl st into third ch from hook (picot
made), sk 1 st, sl st in next st. Repeat from *.

- For a variation, work in single crochet instead of slip stitch between picots.

- Make the picot larger or smaller by working more or fewer chains between stitches.

Shell edging

If necessary, work a foundation row of single crochet.

1. Attach yarn with a single crochet at the beginning of the row.

2. *Skip 2 sts, work 5 dc in next st, sk 2 sts, work 1 sc in next st. Repeat from *.

Shells with picot edging

If necessary, work a foundation row of single crochet.

1. Attach yarn with a single crochet at the beginning of the row.

2. The picot is worked as ch 3, sl st into third ch from hook.

3. *Sk 2 sts, work (2 dc, picot, 2 dc) in next stitch, sk 2 sts, work 1 sc in next st; repeat from *.

FRINGES

Fringes are made of strands of yarn knotted onto a crocheted edge, or they are crocheted as a separate piece and sewn on. Fringes provide a wonderful finish for crocheted shawls, bedspreads, and afghans. Also consider using them for the bottom of vests, jackets, and skirts.

Knotted fringes
Cutting the fringe

1. Cut a piece of cardboard the desired length of fringe plus ½" (1.3 cm) of trimming allowance.

2. Wind the yarn loosely and evenly around the entire length of the cardboard. Cut the yarn along one end and set aside. Repeat several times and begin the fringe, winding strands as needed.

Knotting the fringe

1. Hold together the number of strands needed for one piece of fringe. (This is determined by the thickness of the yarn and the desired fullness of the fringe.) Fold the strands in half.

2. Hold the piece to be fringed with wrong side facing you, and use a crochet hook to draw the folded end through the space or stitch from the right to the wrong side.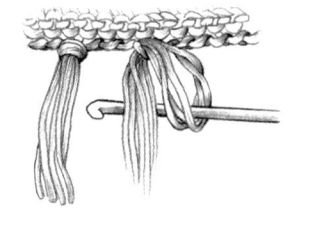

3. Pull loose ends through loop and draw up firmly.

To even the edges of the fringe, trim with a pair of sharp scissors.

Knotted lattice fringe

Follow the steps for Knotted Fringes (see page 106), but cut strands ½" (1.3 cm) longer than the desired length of the fringe.

1. When all the fringes have been knotted, take half the strands from one group and half the strands from the next group and knot them together a short distance down from the first knot.

2. Knot the remaining strands of the second group to half of the strands of the next group. Continue until complete.

Variations: *Work additional rows by alternating the knots and spaces left by the previous row. When cutting yarn for fringe, allow about an extra ½" (1.3 cm) per row of knots. If necessary, use a tapestry needle to move the knots so they all rest at the same height.*

Crocheted fringes
Chain fringe

Make a foundation chain the desired length of the finished fringe. Work rows of single crochet until fringe base is desired depth.

1. Sc in first st. (Sc, ch 25, sl st) in each stitch across. Fasten off.

2. Sew fringe to project. Adjust the number of chain stitches for a longer or shorter fringe.

Looped fringe

Make a foundation chain the desired length of the finished fringe. Work rows of single crochet until fringe base is desired depth.

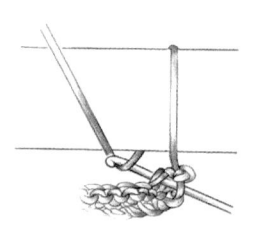

1. Cut a piece of strong cardboard the desired length of fringe.

2. Sc in first st. *Insert hook in next st and place the cardboard behind the work. Wrap the yarn from front to back and place back yarn on crochet hook. Draw up a loop, yarn over, draw through two loops on the hook. Repeat from *.

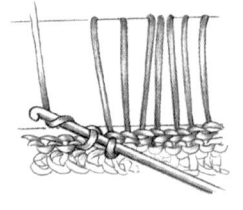

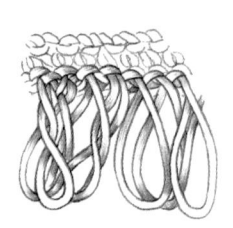

Free the fringe little by little, always keeping the last few loops on the cardboard until the end.

Corkscrew fringes
Thin corkscrew fringe

Make a foundation chain the desired length of the finished fringe. Work rows of single crochet until the fringe base is desired depth.

1. Sc in first st. *Sc in next st, ch 25, turn, work 1 sc in back loop only of each ch, sl st in same st as first sc. Sc in next st. Repeat from *.

2. Sew fringe to project. Adjust the number of chain stitches for a longer or shorter fringe.

Thick corkscrew fringe

Make a foundation chain the desired length of the finished fringe. Work rows of single crochet until fringe base is desired depth.

1. Sc in first st. *Sc in next st, ch 25, turn, 1 dc in back loop of third ch from hook, (work 3 dc in back loop of each ch) to last 5 sts. Hdc in next ch, sc in next ch, sl st in each of next 3 chs. Sc in next 4 sts of base. Repeat from *.

2. Sew fringe to project. Adjust the number of chain stitches for a longer or shorter fringe.

POMPONS

1. Cut two cardboard disks the size of the pompon desired. Cut a hole in the center and a small wedge from the side of both disks.

2. Hold the disks together, place a tie strand between the disks, and wind yarn around the disks as evenly as possible. When the disks are covered, cut the yarn along the outside edge, placing the scissors between the disks.

3. Knot the tie strand securely, leaving tails of about 8" (20.5 cm); use the tails for attaching the pompon to project. If longer ends are left, they can be used to crochet a chain, and long multiple ends can be twisted or braided.

4. Remove disks, fluff out pompon, and trim if necessary.

TASSELS

1. Cut a piece of cardboard the desired length of the tassel.

2. Wind yarn around the cardboard to the desired fullness *(fig. 1)*.

3. Insert a threaded tapestry needle under the wound yarn along the top edge.

4. Pull the threaded yarn ends together and tie a knot securely. Cut the yarn, leaving tails of about 8" (20.5 cm); use the tails to attach the tassel.

5. Cut the yarn along the opposite edge and remove cardboard.

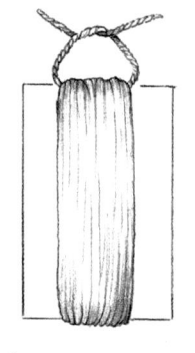

1

6. Wrap a second piece of yarn tightly around the tassel near the knotted end at the top several times and tie securely.

7. Cut off the wrapping yarn, leaving long ends, and work these ends down into tassel with a tapestry needle *(fig. 2)*.

8. Trim ends of the tassel evenly to desired length.

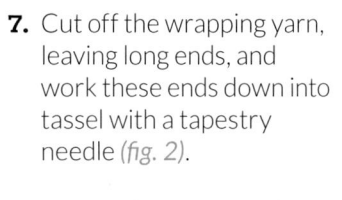

2

FINISHING TECHNIQUES

Many well-made crocheted projects are spoiled by careless finishing. Time spent on correct finishing will be rewarded with a neat, well-fitting, professional-looking garment.

FINISHING ENDS

When fastening off yarn ends, *always* leave at least a 6" (15 cm) end for weaving in. At the end of the last row, do not make any turning chains. Cut the yarn about 6" (15 cm) from the work. Draw the end through the last loop on the hook and pull tight.

- Weave in ends by running them through several stitches on the wrong side with a tapestry needle, then cutting the remaining tail.

- When working in *rows*, weave the yarn ends into seam allowances whenever possible.

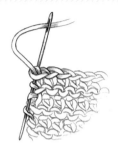

- When working in *rounds*, weave ends vertically back into the back of the work.

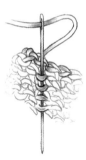

- Split the ends of bulky yarns and weave each half separately for a finer appearance on the right side.

SEAMING

> **Note:** If you have crocheted with a highly textured novelty yarn, use a smooth yarn with matching color for seaming.

- Crocheted pieces can be seamed with a tapestry needle or a crochet hook.

- Use the same yarn for seaming that you used in crocheting.

- Use a blunt-ended tapestry needle to avoid splitting the yarn.

- Use a piece of yarn no longer than 18" (45.5 cm) for seaming—longer strands will weaken before the finishing is completed.

- Do not use knots to start or end seams. Knots have a way of working through to the right side.

- Use a whip stitch (making several stitches in the same place) to start and end seams.

Sequence for assembling a garment

1. Sew the shoulder seams. Shoulder seams should match stitch for stitch.

2. Sew the body seams. Body seams should match row for row.

3. Sew the sleeve seams. Sleeve seams should match row for row.

4. Set in the sleeves. Mark the center top of each sleeve. Pin one of the marked tops to one of the shoulder seams. Pin the sleeve into position in the armhole. Sew the sleeve in place.

5. Add collar, pockets, and button and buttonhole bands.

6. Add crocheted trim.

> **Note:** If the garment has raglan sleeves, sew all raglan seams first, then complete Steps 2, 3, 5, and 6.

Seaming with a tapestry needle
Flat seams
Shoulder seams

1. Place back and front shoulder seams together with right sides up so the stitches match.

2. Working from the armhole toward the neck, take a small stitch through the center of the first stitch on one piece, then take a small stitch through the center of the first stitch of the other piece.

3. Continue, matching the seam stitch for stitch.

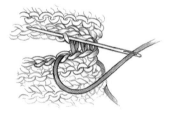

4. Fasten off and weave in ends.

Side seams

1. With right sides of the garment facing you, place the two pieces to be seamed together, side by side.

2. Secure the yarn at the beginning of the first row on one piece, then pass the needle through the post of this row.

3. Pass the needle through the corresponding post on the second piece.

4. Pass the needle through the post of the next row on the first piece.

5. Continue to the end of the seam.

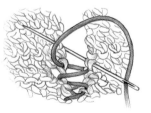

6. Fasten off and weave in ends.

Backstitch seam

A backstitch produces a very strong seam and should be used where there will be strain on the seam. It also works well for joining edges that are shaped or jagged, as it makes a straight line and, when done correctly, is invisible on the right side of the work.

1. Place the two pieces to be joined right sides together, making sure the ends meet perfectly; pin the seam together.

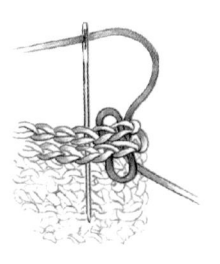

2. Starting from the right, insert the needle from front to back in the first stitch, and then from back to front in the next stitch to the left.

3. Pass the needle from front to back again at the point where you began, and bring it out from back to front two stitches to the left.

4. Make subsequent stitches from front to back at the end of the preceding stitch, and from back to front two stitches to the left. Work to end of seam, fasten off, and weave in ends.

Overcast or whip stitch seam

This seam is especially suitable for borders, textured stitches, and thick or bulky yarns. It is very strong and will not lose its shape.

1. Pin the two pieces to be joined with right sides together, making sure the stitches or rows match exactly.

2. Starting from the right, insert the needle from back to front in the first stitch.

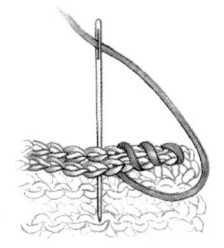

3. Make subsequent stitches by bringing the needle

over the top of the work and inserting it from back to front in the next stitch to the left.

Repeat to end, fasten off, and weave in ends.

Woven seam

A woven seam is particularly suitable for joining items crocheted in very fine yarns, such as baby clothes.

1. Lay the pieces to be joined side by side on a flat surface, wrong side up, matching stitches and rows where possible.

2. Keeping the thread fairly loose, insert the needle into the first stitch of both pieces from right to left.

3. Insert the needle into the next stitch of both pieces from left to right.

Repeat Steps 2 and 3 to end, fasten off, and weave in all ends.

Seaming with a crochet hook
Single crochet method

1. With right sides facing, pin the pieces together, matching stitches or rows.

2. *Joining stitches:* With a slip knot on the hook, insert the hook through the front loop of the first stitch of the first piece and the back loop of the first stitch of the second piece.

Joining rows: With a slip knot on the hook, insert the hook through the first

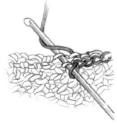

loop of the first piece and the first loop of the second piece.

3. Yarn over and draw a loop through both loops of crocheted piece.

4. Yarn over and draw a loop through the two loops on the hook (one single crochet made).

5. Insert the hook into the next two stitches or loops (see Step 2) and single crochet in these two loops.

6. Continue making single crochet stitches to the end of the seam. Fasten off and weave in ends.

> **Note:** For a decorative seam on the outside of the garment, work the single crochet on the pieces to be joined with wrong sides facing.

Slip stitch method

1. Work Steps 1 and 2 for Single Crochet Method (see page 115).

2. Yarn over hook and draw yarn through both stitches and through loop on the hook to complete slip stitch.

3. Continue to the end of the seam. Fasten off and weave in ends.

BUTTONHOLES

- Single crochet is recommended for button and buttonhole bands.

- For a cardigan, jacket, or vest, work the button band before the buttonhole band.

- Mark button locations with safety pins.

- Work the buttonhole band, making buttonholes opposite the safety pin markers.

Buttonholes worked horizontally

1. With the right side of the garment facing you, work a row of evenly spaced single crochet.

2. Work additional rows of single crochet until band is desired width for placement of buttonholes, or half the total width.

3. To make the buttonhole, skip a few stitches (a width to accommodate the  button) opposite the safety pin markers, and work a corresponding number of chain stitches over the skipped stitches.

4. Continue in single crochet, placing buttonholes opposite safety pin markers. For the next row, work one single crochet into every chain over the buttonhole(s).

5. Work additional rows of single crochet until band is desired width.

Note: Half double crochet stitches and double crochet stitches are not recommended because the height of the stitch produces a deeper, less stable buttonhole.

Buttonholes worked vertically

For this technique, button and buttonhole bands are worked vertically, in one piece, and sewn onto the garment. Crochet the button band vertically in single crochet to the width and length required. Mark button locations with safety pins.

1. Crochet the buttonhole band vertically in single crochet until you reach the position of the first button.

2. Work from the front edge to the location of the buttonhole (usually in the center of the band).

3. Turn at the point where a buttonhole will start, and work back and forth over those few stitches until you have a length the diameter of the button. Fasten off.

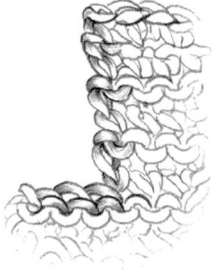

4. Re-attach the yarn. If the buttonhole is an odd number of rows, attach the new yarn at edge of buttonhole. If it is an even number of rows, attach the new yarn at edge of band. Continue on this piece until the same length as the other side of the buttonhole.

5. On the next row, work the entire width of the band and continue until you reach the next buttonhole location. Repeat Steps 2 through 4.

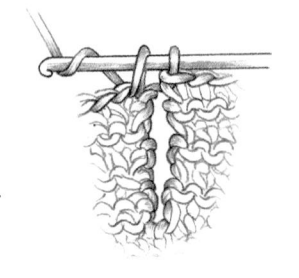

6. Continue until buttonhole band is completed.

7. Reinforce the buttonhole by sewing around it with the buttonhole stitch (see page 119).

Buttonhole stitch

Bring the needle from back to front and, keeping it above the yarn, insert it through next row and bring it up again through the buttonhole. Pull the needle through to finish the stitch. Continue around the entire buttonhole.

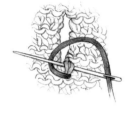 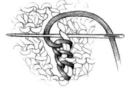

BUTTON LOOPS

Buttons and button loops are an attractive alternative to bands. They are particularly appealing when you have used a lacy pattern stitch.

1. Starting at the right side of the opening, work a row of single crochet, evenly spaced, to the bottom of the opening.

2. Mark button locations with safety pins.

3. Work single crochet up the left side of the opening. When you come to a point opposite a safety pin marker, crochet a chain long enough to accommodate a button. Continue in single crochet to the place for the next button loop and repeat.

Button loop tips

- Button loops can be reinforced by working slip stitches along the opening over the single crochets and chain-stitch loops.

- Button loops can also be covered with single crochet.

EDGINGS

Once a garment has been crocheted and seamed, you will need to "finish off" the edges. A garment is unfinished until an edging is completed.

Frequently the instructions will read, "Work a row/round of single crochet evenly spaced." *Sectioning* is the key to "working evenly spaced."

Sectioning

1. Divide the area (such as an armhole) into four sections and mark with safety pins. For a smaller area, such as a sleeve edge, divide into only two sections.

2. With right side facing, work single crochets evenly spaced in the first section. Count the number of stitches and work the same number in each of the other sections.

Edging a neckline

1. Place a marker at center front, center back, and each shoulder seam.

2. Join yarn at the left shoulder seam and, with right side of work facing you, work along the back neckline in single crochet, working the same number of stitches in each back section.

3. Continue along the front neckline, working the same number of stitches in each front section.

4. If another row of crochet or a fancy edge is required, work it in the single crochet stitches of the first row. You will have to decrease on the second and all subsequent rows to taper the neckline. Decrease at evenly spaced intervals and as necessary for the neckline to lie flat. For single crochet decrease, see page 52.

Edging armholes

Work armhole edgings as for a neckline.

Edging an entire jacket

If a jacket is to be worn open in the Chanel style, you'll need to work a continuous edging around the bottom, fronts, and neckline.

1. Divide each piece of the jacket into sections (see page 120). Section the bottom back edge, the bottom front edges, the fronts, and the neckline.

2. With right side facing you, join yarn at lower left side seam and, following the "sectioning" technique, work one row of single crochet evenly spaced around the entire edge of the jacket.

3. When you come to a corner, work three stitches into the same corner stitch or space.

4. On additional rows/rounds, work three stitches into the corner stitch on each row/round.

Hint: For a neater finish when adding an edging or border in a contrasting color, always work the first single crochet row in the main color and use the contrasting color on the second row.

BLOCKING

To give a garment a professional look, block it into shape. Always check the yarn label for any manufacturer's instructions. Projects may be blocked before or after seaming.

Blocking before seaming

Place thick towels on a flat surface. Gently tug matching pieces, such as sleeves and fronts, to identical shape and size and pin to the towels. Make sure corresponding edges are the same length.

METHOD ONE: Place a very wet cloth over each piece. When cloths and crocheted pieces are thoroughly dry, remove them and unpin the pieces.

METHOD TWO: Mist the pieces with water and allow to dry.

METHOD THREE: If yarn label indicates the fiber can be ironed, you may block with a steam iron. Cover pieces with a damp cloth. Hold the iron just above the surface and allow the steam to penetrate the fabric.

Blocking after seaming

Place thick towels on a flat surface. Gently tug the completed item to the desired finished measurements and pin to the towels. Place a very wet cloth over the article and allow to dry thoroughly.

CARING FOR CROCHETED ITEMS

Always read the manufacturer's suggestions for cleaning. (See chart of symbols on page 11.) Crocheted projects may be washed either by hand or by machine, or dry-cleaned.

General guidelines for cleaning

> **Note:** *Always support the weight of the garment with both hands while it is wet, or it will stretch out of shape.*

WOOL: Hand wash, as outlined on page 123, in cold water.

COTTON: Hand wash, as outlined on page 123, in lukewarm water.

SYNTHETICS: Nylon, polyester, and rayon may be hand washed in lukewarm water with a mild soap. Other synthetics should be dry-cleaned.

COLORFASTNESS: Check for colorfastness before washing. Immerse a piece of yarn in hot water, fold it in a piece of white cotton cloth, and squeeze. If any color stains the cloth, the article should be dry-cleaned or washed carefully in cold water.

Hand washing

Using a basin of water at the appropriate temperature, mix in mild liquid soap or soap flakes, then swish the garment around and gently squeeze the soap through.

Rinse thoroughly, at least three times, in clean basins of water. After the final rinse, gently squeeze the garment to remove excess water, and roll the garment in a clean dry towel. Without twisting the towel, gently squeeze out more water.

Place the garment on another clean dry towel and ease it back into the correct shape and size. Leave it to dry flat, away from direct sunlight or strong artificial light.

> **Note:** Even though some yarn labels suggest machine washing, fine crocheted items should be washed by hand.

Machine washing

Advances in technology have produced many easy-care yarns. Many cotton and synthetic blends are machine washable, as are some wools that have been specifically treated for this purpose. If machine washing is recommended, place the item to be washed in a cloth bag or pillowcase to prevent stretching and wash it in a gentle cycle with appropriate water temperature. Lay the item flat to dry away from direct sunlight or strong artificial light.

Storage

Crochet garments should always be stored flat to prevent stretching.

HELPFUL HINTS AND TROUBLESHOOTING

Beginning crocheters will find it easier to learn to crochet if they start with a large hook and a thick yarn.

Left-handed crocheters can use standard diagrams by following them in reverse. Prop the book open with the appropriate page facing a mirror.

FOUNDATION CHAINS

If on the first row you find you have too few foundation chains to finish the row, there is an alternative to starting all over—if you left a long tail of yarn at the beginning. When you come to the last chain, drop the loop you are working with and place the hook in the last chain. With the beginning yarn tail, yarn over, draw a loop through the last chain, and continue to chain the number of stitches needed to complete the first row. After making the second-to-last extra chain, draw the entire beginning end of yarn through the last loop on the hook (just as you do for fastening off) to create the final chain. Then pick up the dropped loop you were working with and continue on in pattern to the end of the first row.

> **Note:** There may be a slight difference in the appearance of the first stitch of the added chain.

- If written instructions call for a very long chain to begin with, as for an afghan, crochet several extra chain stitches. After the first row is completed, rip back any unused chain, being sure to fasten off the beginning tail of yarn at the last used chain stitch.

- Foundation chains tend to draw in the bottom of the work. To avoid this, work the base chain with a hook one size larger or with two strands of yarn.

TURNING CHAINS

- When the turning chain counts as the first stitch of a row, be sure to work the last stitch of the row into the top of the turning chain of the previous row. This method results in neater edges than the one below.

- When the turning chain does not count as a first stitch, remember to work the first stitch of the next row and do not work a stitch into the turning chain.

STITCH COUNT

Always count the stitches, either as you work or at the end of the row or round. This will ensure you do not lose or add stitches.

RIGHT/WRONG SIDE OF WORK

To establish if you are looking at the right or wrong side of the work, look for the end of the yarn at the beginning of the foundation chain. It will be at the left edge when the right side is facing you, provided the first row worked was a right side row.

JOINING NEW YARN MID-ROW

METHOD ONE: Put the hook into a stitch, yarn over with the new yarn, and pull a loop through. Continue with the new yarn.

METHOD TWO: Lay new yarn along the top of the current row being crocheted and work the next few stitches over the new yarn with the old yarn. Finish the last loop of the next stitch with the new yarn and continue.

MEASUREMENTS AND SIZING

- Always measure straight up and down, unless otherwise instructed.

- To increase or decrease the overall width of the crocheted piece, try changing to a larger or smaller hook.

> **Note:** The length of yarn required to complete a row is approximately two to four times the length of the row, depending on the stitch being worked.

- When working in pattern groups, add more chain stitches between the groups to increase the size of the piece.

Stretch

Crocheted garments worked in cotton in a close-textured stitch stretch less than those worked in wool in a loose, open-work stitch.

Lining

Most crocheted garments tend to lose their shape at the closest fitting points, so it is advisable to line crocheted skirt and pants. Cut a fabric lining slightly smaller than the garment being lined. The crocheted piece will drape nicely and retain its elasticity, and the lining won't show below the hemline. As a general rule, the lining for a crocheted skirt should be approximately 1½" (4 cm) shorter than the skirt itself.

FINISHING TECHNIQUES

- If the crochet yarn is suitable for seaming, leave long tails when fastening off; use these tails for seaming.

- Never work in ends until the project is complete. It is difficult to rip the work out to correct a mistake (particularly when working with motifs) if the ends are worked in correctly.

BIBLIOGRAPHY

Cosh, Sylvia and James Walters. *The Crochet Workbook*. London: B. T. Batsford Ltd, 1989.

Eaton, Jan. *A Creative Guide to Crochet*. New York: Sterling Publications, 1996.

Mathieson, Elizabeth L. *The Complete Book of Crochet*. New York: Crowell, 1979.

Mountford, Debra (ed). *The Harmony Guide to Crocheting*. New York: Harmony Books, 1992.

Nava, Marinella. *The Book of Crochet*. New York: St. Martin's Press, 1984.

Paludan, Lis. *Crochet: History & Technique*. Loveland, Colorado: Interweave, 1995.

Rankin, Chris. *The First Crochet Book*. New York: Sterling Publications, 1990.

Righetti, Maggie. *Crochet in Plain English*. New York: St. Martin's Press, 1988.

Taylor, Gertrude. *America's Crochet Book*. New York: Charles Scribner's Sons, 1972.

The Priscilla Publishing Co. *Irish Crochet Technique and Projects*. New York: Dover Publications, Inc., 1984.

Turner, Pauline. *The Technique of Crochet*. London: B. T. Batsford Ltd, 1987.

___. *How to Crochet*. New York: Sterling Publications, 2001.

ASSOCIATIONS AND WEBSITES

Association of Crafts & Creative Industries
1100 – H Brandywine Blvd.
PO Box 3388
Zanesville, OH 43702-3388
accishow@offinger.com

British Knitting & Crochet Guild
PO Box 287
Huntingdan PE29 7GU
www.knitting-and-crochet-guild.org.uk

Craft Yarn Council of America
PO Box 9
Gastonia, NC 28053
www.craftyarncouncil.com
www.learntocrochet.com

Crochet Guild of America (CGOA)
2502 Lowell Road
Gastonia, NC 28054
www.crochet.org

Hobby Industries Association
PO Box 348
Elmwood, NJ 07407
hia@hobby.org

The National Needlework Association
PO Box 3388
Zanesville, OH 43702-3388
www.tnna.org

Society of Craft Designers
PO Box 3388
Zanesville, OH 43702-3388
scd@offinger.com

For crochet books and patterns
www.cgoapresents.com

INDEX